# COMPARATIVE ICONOGRAPHY OF THE VAJRADHĀTU-MAṆḌALA AND THE TATTVA-SAṄGRAHA

Dr. Mrs. SHASHIBALA

ADITYA PRAKASHAN
NEW DELHI

First published by :
Mrs. Sharada Rani, New Delhi, 1986
Reprint : New Delhi, 1989





ISBN : 81-85179-11-5

Published by Rakesh Goel for Aditya Prakashan, 4829/1, Prahlad Lane, 24, Ansari Road, New Delhi-110002 and printed at D.K. Fine Art Press, Delhi-110052.

# COMPARATIVE ICONOGRAPHY OF THE VAJRADHĀTU-MAṆḌALA AND THE TATTVA-SAṄGRAHA

# ŚATA-PIṬAKA SERIES

**INDO-ASIAN LITERATURES**

VOLUME 344

**Reproduced in original scripts and languages**
Translated, annotated and critically evaluated by specialists of the East and the West

*Founded by*
**RAGHU VIRA** *M.A., Ph.D., D. Litt. et Phil.*

**आचार्य-रघुवीर-समुपक्रान्तं**

जम्बुद्वीप-राष्ट्राणां
(भारत-नेपाल-गान्धार-शूलिक-तुरुष्क-पारस-ताजक-भोट-चीन-मोंगोल-मञ्जु-उदयवर्ष-सिंहल-सुवर्णभू-श्याम-कम्बुज-चम्पा-द्वीपान्तरादीनां)

**एकैकेषां समस्रोतसां संस्कृति-साहित्य-समुच्चय-सरितां सागरभूतं**

# शतपिटकम्

# CONTENTS

# PREFACE

The configuration of the Vajradhātu-maṇḍala had been a problem for historians of Japanese art on several counts: (i) Which textual tradition do the prevalent twin maṇḍalas represent? (ii) If they do not conform to the texts are they a synthesis of different transmissions? (iii) Did Amoghavajra integrate the two maṇḍalas for the sake of his disciple or was it Hui kuo? (iv) What is the relationship of the Vajradhātu-maṇḍala in six parts in Gobu-shingan to the Genzu maṇḍala in nine parts.

These questions have been sought to be answered on the basis of a study of the text of STTS. The project aims at a study of the structure of Gobu-shingan and the graphic Vajradhātu-maṇḍala in the light of STTS, translations of STTS, hand drawn and xylographed copies of the Genzu-maṇḍala, Vajradhātu-maṇḍala as the basis of Tabo, cosmographic analysis of STTS, epiphany of 37 deities of the Vajradhātu-maṇḍala and 20 deities of the outer circle.

The STTS as the fundamental text of yoga Tantras is of signal importance for the historic development of philosophic speculation in China, Korea, Japan, Nepal, Tibet, Mongolia and Indonesia. It served as a basis for architectural mandalas based on the STTS arose at Alchi and Tabo. The earliest representation of the mandala of STTS is in Indonesia as the monument of Chandi Sewu. An astonishing evidence of the vogue of the Vajradhatu-mandala of the STTS also comes from Khotan in the Khotanese verse of Ca Kima sani.

The Sanskrit manuscript of STTS used for the project was discovered and photographed by John Brough and David L.Snellgrove in Kathmandu, Nepal in 1956. It contains 300 pages or 150 palm-leaves of the written text. It has its origin in 9th-10th century Bihar. It was critically edited by Isshi Yamada based on a Sanskrit manuscript and Chinese and Tibetan translations. Isshi Yamda's work was published as the 262nd volume of Sata Pitaka series by Mrs. Sharada Rani, New Delhi in March, 1981.

The text is divided into five parts: first four are the four samayas, i.e. abhisamaya, vajra-samaya, dharma-samaya, and karma-samaya and the fifth part relates to Siddhis; The first samaya of STTS correlates exactly to the Gobu-shingan. The first four chapters of the first samaya deal with the first four mandalas of Gobu-shingan, i.e. the maha-, vajra-, dharma and karma-mandalas of Vajradhatu. The fifth chapter is an epilogue that describes the fifth and sixth mandalas i.e. caturmudra -and ekamudra mandalas. These six mandalas are the first six mandalas of the graphic Vajradhatu as well.

The second part of the STTS is vajra-samaya. It contains nine chapters which are numbered as 6-14b. The four mandalas of Trailokyavijaya according to the four Kulas are given in chapters 6-9. The 10th chapter of the text is an epilogue that details the caturmudra- and ekamudra-mandalas of Trailokyavijaya. The fourth and second mandalas of Trailokya-vijaya are the eight and ninth mandalas of Trailokyavijaya in the graphic Vajradhatu. Chapters 11-14b have twenty Deities of the outer circle in four kulas. The last chapter 14b is its epiloque.

The third part pertaining to dharma-samaya contains four chapters (15-18). They describe the four mandalas of dharma-samaya. An epilogue containing caturmudra-and ekamudra-mandalas ends in the last chapter 18b. The fourth part also has the same arrangement. It goes upto chapter 22b. The remaining four chapters detail sarva-kalpopaya-siddhi-vidhi, sarva-kula-kalpa-guhya-vidhi, sarva-kalpa-guhyottara-tantra, sarva-kalpanuttara-tantra and a final epiloque to the STTS.

The earliest extant Sino-Japanese representation of the STTS was drawn by Subhakara-simha (A.D. 637-735). Its title is known as Rta-sogyara-gobu-shingan. Vajrabodhi had carried the text on his vayaga to China but it was lost as his flotilla was engulfed by a raging storm. Amoghavajra translated only the first part. Though Danapala translated the complete text which agrees with the Sanskrit original and Tibetan translation, but it never formed a part of the tradition of East Asian mantrayana. The correlation of the Gobu-shingan and the Genzu mandala can be comprehended only on the basis of the complete text and its classification in Tibetan exegesis. This book attempts to relate the complex relationship of the text and its varying graphic representatives.

# STRUCTURE OF GOBU-SHINGAN AND THE GRAPHIC VAJRADHĀTU-MAṆḌALA IN THE LIGHT OF SARVA-TATHĀGATHA-TATTVA-SAṄGRAHA

Tantras are invaluable texts for understanding Indian, Japanese, Indonesian and Central Asian paintings and sculptures. Thousands of Tantric texts have been handed down to us in the languages of these countries which are venerable vestiges of a rich tradition now lost. The vast ocean of Tantras has been classified into four standard classes of Kriyā, Caryā, Yoga and Anuttarayoga. The chief desciple of the Great Tibetan teacher Tsoṅ-kha-pa in his analysis of the fundamentals of Buddhist tantras, systematises the yoga-tantra literature into fundamental (mūla) and explanatory (vyākhyā) tantras. The explanatory tantras are divided into two explaining from the view point of prajñā and upāya. Prajñā contrasts with the term upāya. A certain Tantric traditions hold that after the fall from paradise the phase involving division into male and female constituted a separation of means from insight: hence forth men were a source of means and women of insight (Wayman 1973, 166). Fifteen texts (Toh. 479-493) and 161 commentaries upon them (Toh. 2501-2661) are classified under this scheme (Wayman 1973, 236-7). Herebelow is a conspectus of the classification as it applies to the Sino-japanes Tantras.

Yoga-tantras:

Mūla or fundamental Tantras:

Tattva-saṅgraha (Toh. 479) gives the initial summary (nidāna), shows Vairocana as having the perfection of the two goals (artha). Thereupon it generates the desire to attain them, assuming that (the desire) has been generated, all of the subsequent Tantra teaches the means of realising these goals to be attained and the fundamental Tantra teaches the common means of accomplishing mundane and supra mundane siddhis (Lessing/Waymen 217). ( T 866, Nj. 534, Vajrabodhi's abridged adition for recitation)

Amoghavajra's translation of the first chapter(T 865, Nj.1020).

Dānapāla's translation of the complete text (T 882, Nj. 1017)

Vyākhyā or explanatory Tantras

i. Prajñā: Ārya-prajñā-pāramitā-naya-śata-pañcaśatikā (Toh.489, T 220(10), Nj. 1, T 241, Nj. 1033, T 243, Nj. 1034, T 242, Nj. 862).

ii. Upāya: Trailokyavijaya-mahā-kalpa-rāja (Toh. 482, explanatory of the second chapter of vajrakula).

In 1956 John Brough and David L. Snellgrove found the manuscript of STTS in 9th-10th century Nāgarī script in the private library of Field Marshell Kaiser Shamsheer in Kathmandu which was microfilmed by them. The manuscript is transcribed into Roman and edited by Isshi Yamada. Its facsimile reproduction has been done by Lokesh Chandra and Snellgrove in 1981 from New Delhi published by Mrs.Shardarani.

It has been believed in Japan that Tattva-saṅgraha (Konga-chō-kyō) consisted of

100,000 ślokas that were preached in eighteen different places. The vajradhātu-maṇḍala is a representation of the first essembly that is called the Tattvasaṅgraha from among the 18 essemblees. Its Sanskrit manuscripts so far discovered are:

1. A manuscript owned by Snellgrove in Brāhmī dating from the 11th century.
2. A manuscript owned by S. Lévi.
3. A manuscript in Devanāgari discovered by Tucci. It has a Tibetan translation as well. We have three versions of Tattvasaṅgraha in Chinese translation:

a. Vajrabodhi's in 4 fascicles, Kingkangting-yukei-tchong-liotch'ou-niensong-king done in 723 the 11th year of Kaiyuan.

b. Amoghavajra's in 3 fasciles, Kingkangting-yits'ie-joulai-tchenchechö-tatch'eng-hien-tcheng-takiaowang-king.

c. Dānapāla's in 30 fascicles, Yits'ie-joulai-tchenchechö-tatch'eng hientcheng-takia-öwangting.

Dānapāla's translation agrees almost with the Sanskrit manuscript and Tibetan translation. This was made late in date and it is a translation of the complete text. So we can surmise that the text shows the accomplished phase of the development of the STTS. The version of Śubhakarasiṁha denotes the TS that was the basis of the Gobu-shingan that was brought from India to China by him. The sixth assembly of the Tsuishang-kên pên-talo-chinkang-puk'ung-sanmei-tachiaowang-king in 7 fascicles translated by Dharmabhadra and the fifteenth assembly is the Yits'ie-joulai-kingkang-sanye-tsouei-chang-pimi-takiaowang-king in 7 fascicles by Dānapāla. (Yamamoto 20).

Mahāvairocana-sūtra and the STTS are the pure Buddhist tantric texts which became the basic canonicle sources for Japanese shingon. Mahāvairocana was composed somewhere in Kathiawar peninsula in mid seventh century and was subsequently transmitted to various rigions of India and the TS was composed shortly after the composition of the Mahāvairocana-sūtra, perhaps in early eighth century somehwere in southern India. They were transmitted to China in early eighth century, and from there to Japan. (Kiyota 25).

In the early eleventh century it was translated into Tibetan by Shraddhākaravarmā and Rin-chen-bzaṅ-po (A.D. 958-1055) under the title De-bzhin-gśegs-pa thams-ced-kyi De-kho-na-ñid bsdus-pa-zhes bya-ba theg-pa-ehen-pohi mdo-Sarva-tathāgata-tattva-saṅgraha-nāma-mahāyāna-sūtra (Toh.479).

Tattva-saṅgraha is known by several names; Ṛta-saṁhāra, Yoga-saṅgraha, Vajra-śekhara-tantra. The term yoga-saṅgraha (Jap. Y uga-shūyō, Chin Yü-ch'ieh chi-yao) occures in the text of Jvālāmukhī-pretī-bali-vidhi from the yoga-saṅgraha (Nj.1467, T.1320) translated by Amoghavajra during A.D. 746-771. Herein Yoga-saṅgraha refers to the Tattva-saṅgraha as the fundamental text of the yoga tantras. In Japan the most common appellation of our tantra is Kongōchō-kyō-Vajraśekhara-sūtra. It has to be clearly distingusihed from the explanatory tantra Vajraśekhara of the Tibetan Canon (Toh.480) which is a different text. In the Sino-Japanese tradition the term yoga, Vajraśekhara and Vajraśekhara-yoga are generic terms referring to the yoga-trantras in general, and thus the Vajraśekhara-sūtra denoted the Tattva-saṅgraha.

The Tattva-saṅgraha-sūtra describes a realm of enlightenment in terms of fivefold Buddha assembly and the practices to realise that realm in terms of five stages of meditation. (Kiyota 23).

The whole tantra is divided into five parts in 150 folios which is numbered on both sides by Yamada. The last part is quite different in form from earlier four parts. The title as given in colophon of the Tibetan translation says explicitly. The Mahāyāna sūtra named the compendium of Truth of All the Tathāgatas together with the additional compendium of Tantra is furnished. The four parts are all referred to as kalpa-rāja.

The four kalpas of TS relate to the four Buddha families. They teach invocations of sets of divinities with instructions in setting up their maṇḍalas and in the rites and benefits concerned with them. The last part properly as sūtra assumes a knowledge of the actual rituals and represents a thread of discourse conducted by Buddha and the Bodhisattvas who lead the various Buddha families. They each in turn pronounce on the benefits to be won by the different performance as performed within the family circle of each.

The Vajrayānist concept of Bodhi mind appears to be the same as that of Yogācāra school which was founded by Maitreya and elaborated by Asaṅga and the literature of which included, among others, such excellent works as the Tattvasaṅgraha of Śāntarakṣita. According to this school the human mind or as it is called in Buddhism, the bodhi mind, is something like a continuous stream of momentry consciousness, which changes every moment the consciousness of the previous moment giving rise to the consciousness of the succeeding moment, the former being the cause of the later (Bhattcharyya 1980,96-7). The title TS means 'collection of categories'. According to Padmavajra's Tantrārthāvatāra-vyākhyā there are thirty seven categories (tattvas): hṛdaya, mudrā, mantra, vidyā, adhiṣṭhāna, abhiṣeka, samādhi, pūjā, ātmatattva, devatattva, maṇḍala, prajñā, upāya, hetu, phala, yoga, atiyoga, mahāyoga, ghuya-yoga, sarva-yoga, jāpa, homa, vrata, siddhi, sādhana, dhyāna, bodhicitta, śūnyatā-jñāna, adarśa-jñāna, samatā-jñāna, pratyavekṣaṇa-jñāna, Kṛtyanuṣṭhāna-jñāna, viśuddhi-dharma, dhātu-jñāna, ākarṣaṇa, praveśana, bandhana, vaśīkaraṇa, (Lessing/Wayman 215-6).

The TS is of signal importance for the historic development of phyphilosophic speculation in India, Nepal, China, Japan, Korea, Tibet and Mongolia. Moreover the text could be represented as a visual dharma as a maṇḍala in the form of a large painted scroll, as sculptures or an intricately sculputured monument. Thus it exerted a mighty influence on the fine arts of several countries. It was expressed as the Vajradhātumaṇḍala in the Sino-Japanese tradition. The painted maṇḍala of the TS was brought to Japan by Kobo-daishi in A.D. 806 and it is known there as Kongokai-mandara or Vajradhātu-maṇḍala or Daimond-maṇḍala (Hakeda 1972, 147-8).

The earliest representation of the maṇḍala of the TS is in Indonesia as the monument of Chandi Sewu (Bosch 1929, 111-133), (for details see Lokesh Chandra 1979, 1-15). Another monumental stereomorohic representation of the TS again on the soil of Java is the world renowned Borobudur. (Lokesh Chandra 1979,1-68). An astonishing evidence of the vogue of the Vajradhātu-maṇḍala of the TS comes from Khotan in the Khotanese verses of Cā- Kima-śani.

Furthermore, the TS served as a basis for architectural expression in the Lamaist areas. Architectural maṇḍalas or pura-maṇḍala based on the TS arose at Alchi and Tabo as soon as it was translated into Tibetan (Toh.479) by Śraddhākaravarman and Rin-chen-bzaṅ-po (c.958-1055). In the Tibetan cycle of 133 maṇḍalas of the Tantra-samuccaya the Tattva-saṅgraha is represented by two maṇḍalas (RaghuVira/Lokesh Chandra 1967, 13.22, 23) e.i. the 1037deity Vajradhātu-maṇḍala of the Tathāgata family as enuntiated in the first section of the TS, and second the 137 deity Trailokya-vijaya-maṇḍala of the Vajra family as enuntiated in the second chapter of TS.

The earliest extant Sino-Japanese representation of the TS was done by Śubhakarasiṁha (A.D. 637-735) on a scroll which is known in Japan as the Ṛta-sogyara-gobu-shingan 'meditation on the five sections of the Ṛta-saṁhara' (TZ 54-56) with sanskrit captions. Ṛta-saṁhāra is a synonym of Tattva-saṅgraha. Śubhakarasiṁha probably intended to translate the tantra but he did not do so. Vajrabodhi had carried the text on his voyage to China but it was lost on the way when the flotilla was engulfed by a raging storm. He could save its portions for recitation which he translated into Chinese, Kongō-chō-yuga-chū ryaku shutsu nenju-kyō, which means an abridged japa sūtra from the Vajraśekhara-yoga (Nj.539,T 866). In Japan this text is known as ryaku-shutsu-kyō or abridged sūtra. Amoghavajra's translation of the first chapter is most popularly referred to as Kongō-chō-kyō or Vajra-śekhara-sūtra in Japan. Dānapāla's translation of the complete text is entitled in Japanese as Issai-nyorai-shinjitsu-shō-daijō-genshō-sammai-daikyō-ō-kyō (Nj. 1017, T 882).

The Chinese colophon at the end of Ṛta-saṁhāra says that it was given in A.D. 855 by the Chinese Acarya Fa-chüan to his Japanese desciple Enchin, whose Sanskrit name was Jñānavajra. The text has full six maṇḍalas. Six complete or incomplete copies are known:

i. A copy of the Gobu-shingan was formerly kept at the Daigoji monastery but now its whereabouts are unknown. National museum preserves a copy of it. The latter was published by Omura Saigei Bukkyo Zuzō Shukō. The text is full and the iconographic representations are almost as good as the full text of Onjoji. But the copying of Siddham letters is sometimes mistaken.

ii. The text of the Gobu-shingan handed down in Shakamonin monastery, Koyasan, now kept in Sainanin monastery, Koyasan. This is a copy from the full text of Onjoji, but its former portion no. 1-41 are missing. The text consists of 31 sheets of printed paper. The iconography is in a sketchy style of Japanes art. The way of simplified drawing of the features indicates the period of Kamakura.

iii. The text kept by Homyoin monastery Mii. It was copied towards the end of the Edo period (19 th cent. ) and was published in the iconographic section of the Taisho Tripiṭaka. It is a copy from the full text of Onjoji monastery. The Sanskrit letters are better than those in the deficient text of the Onjoji monastery, but there are errors.

iv. The text written and drawn by Zenkaku, a priest of the Onjoji monastery in the fifth year of Kenkyū (1194). It contains only nos. 1-65. But there are two moon circles and a figure of Śubhakarasiṁha at the end of the text. This text dose not comprise the 6 Bodhisattva at the end of the Guhya-dhāraṇī-maṇḍala, sūkṣma-maṇḍala and karma-pūjā-maṇḍala among the 6 maṇḍalas. The Sanskrit sentences are omitted or simplified. They are written vertically like Chiness letters.

v. Dr. Gemmyo Ono discovered the Rokushu Mandara-ryakushaku in two fascicles in Shorenin monastery at Awata Kyoto. The title of the book means 'the interpretation of the six kinds of maṇḍalas. This is an old explanation. This is an oral explanation of the Gobu-shingan. It proved beyond doubt that Śubhakarasiṁha had been regarded to have translated only the Mahāvairocanasūtra, brought in fact the Sanskrit text of STTS and thereby translated the figures, symbols, mudrās and sacred formulas. The copy belonging to Mr. Sanji Muto of Kamakura and the copy from Asharajo have been reproduced in the iconographic section of the Taishō Tripitaka. (TZ 55-56).

The six sub maṇḍalas of Gobu-shingan are the six coordinates of the STTS method by which the yoga wheel of law was set in motion (Lessing/Wayman 1978, 214-24a).

Now let us take up the six sub maṇḍalas of Gobu-shingan.

i. Vajradhātu-mahā-maṇḍala-prathamaḥ pādaḥ (colophon on illus.37) 1-37
ii. Vajrahātau-guhya-dhāraṇi-maṇḍalam//4 (colophon on illus.71) 38-71
iii. Vajradhātau-sūkṣma-maṇḍalam 73-104
iv. Vajradhātau pūjā-maṇḍalam 105-139
v. Vajradhātau caturmudrā-maṇḍala 140-144
vi. Vajradhātau ekamudrā-maṇḍalam. samāptam Vajradhātu-mahā-maṇḍalam 145

The first four of the above sub maṇḍalas can be elucidated in the light of the four maṇḍalas explained by a Buddhaguhya in his fundamental commentary on the Tattva-sangraha entitled Tantrārthāvatāra who lived in the middle of the eighth century and is one of the three primary commentators of the Tattva-saṅgraha (Lessing/Wayman 1968, 24 n.13). The four maṇḍalas in Buddhaguhya are: mahā, samaya, dharma, and karma.. They are explained as "In the case of the mahā-maṇḍala, because the array of the deities is an arrangement in the body of form (rūpa-kāya), one understands them(the mahā-maṇḍalas) as comprising the magical manifestation of shapes (vikurvāṇa) from the treasure of inexhaustible Body. The samaya maṇḍala is characterised by an arrangement of thunderbolt (vajra), iron, hook (aṅkuśa), arrow (śara), and so on, which are symbolizing agents for the way in which emancipation is comprehended, hence, comprises the magical manifestation of shapes from the arranged treasury of inexhaustible mind. The dharma-cakra arranges and disposes the deities who stand for the practice which is the means of teaching how the Doctrine (dharma) is comprehended. hence, is the blessing (adhisthana) for the magical manifestation of shapes from the arranged treasury of inexhaustible speech of all the Tathāgatas. Accordingly, in the case of the karma-maṇḍala it arrays the deities who are of offerings and other rites, hence one should understand it as displaying in concise form the practice of all Tathāgatas for the aim of sentient beings. (Lessing/Wayman 1968:224 n.20).

i. Vajradhātu-mahā-maṇḍala: There are 37 deities in the first maṇḍala: 1 to 5:4 Buddhas. 6 to 9: Sattva, Rāja, Rāga, Sādhu in the department of Vajra in the east. 10 to 13: Ratna, Teja, Ketu, Smita in the department of Ratna in the south. 14 to 17. Dharma, Tīkṣṇa, Ketu and Bhāṣa in the department of Padma in the west. 18 to 21: Karma, Rakṣa, Yakṣa and Muṣṭi in the department of Karma in the north. 26-29: Lāsyā, Mālā, Gītā and Nṛtyā the four inner pūjā-bodhisattvas. 30 to 33. Dhūpā, Puṣpā, Dīpā and Gandhā the four outer pūjā-Bodhisattvas. 34 to 37: Aṅkuśa, Pāśa, Śakala and Ghaṇṭa, the 4 saṅgraha Bodhisattvas. There are four sattvis (nos. 22 to 25) instead of the four great gods in the genzu. The Sanskrit titles of these four deities in the Shingon are different. The titles in the Ryakushaku seem to be better but cannot always be perfect.

Let us compare the figures of the 16 great Bodhisattvas in the Gobu-shingan with these in the Genzu maṇḍala. The Bodhisattvas in the Gobu-shingan have seats of animals or birds beneath the lotus seats and they have high diadems, but the Bodhisattvas in the genzu maṇḍala do not have the seats of animals or birds. The have an ordinary head dress and not a high diadem. They have the same attributes as given in the Tattvasaṅgraha. Dhāraṇīs given under the illustrations are identical as well.

ii. The second Vajradhātuguhya-dhāraṇi-maṇḍala consists of 34 sacred ones from Nos.38 to 71 No.38 is Vairocana, 44 is Samantabhadra, 64 to 67 have the names that consist of guhya and the names of four outer Pūjā and 68 to 71 have the names that consists of guhya and the names of four saṅgraha.

iii. Vajradhātusūkṣma-maṇḍala, the third maṇḍala consists of 33 sacred ones from nos.72-104 are the five Buddhas of Vajradhātu. 77 is Vajrasattva. 78 and the following are the symbolization of wisdom of all the Tathāgatas. Their names do not appear in the Genzu-maṇḍala. 93-96 are the four saṅgraha preceded by the wisdom of all the Tathāgatas. 97-100 have the names of four inner Pūjā Bodhisattvas joined with the wisdom of all the Tathāgatas. 101-108 are the four outer Bodhisattvas added with the wisdom of all the Tathāgatas. These are the sacred ones lacking the four Buddha-matṛkās from among the 37 sacred ones.

iv. Vajradhātupūjā-maṇḍala has 33 sacred ones from 105 to 137. The divinities except the five Buddhas are not found in the Genzu-maṇḍala. 138. The first moon circle (candracakra) with 4 sacred ones, Vajrakāya, Dharmakāya, Sarvakāya, Buddhakāya. 139. The second moon circle with 4 sacred ones Rītivajra, Rāgavajra, Prītivajra and Kaśivajra.

v. Vajradhātuscaturmudrā-maṇḍala is the fifth 140-144, five sacred ones are drawn in a moon circle. Amitābha is in the centre, Vajrasattva in the east, Vajraratna in the south, Vajradharma in the west and Vajrakarma in the north. The Central deity in the Caturmudrā-maṇḍala of the Genzu maṇḍala is Vairocana, but here in the maṇḍala. It is different Amitābha is in the centre. But the other deities are the same in the Ganzu-maṇḍala.

vi. Maṇḍala 6 is Ekamudrā-maṇḍala. 145 Vajrasattva 146 the figure of Śubhakarasiṁha.

Kobo-daishi had brought with him the following four forms of the Vajradhātu-maṇḍala.

1. Vajradhātu-maṇḍala consisting of nine small maṇḍalas, 1 sheet in 7 sections, 1 jo two shaku long.
2. Mahāmaṇḍala of cotton cloth representing 447 deities.
3. The central maṇḍala of 81 deities, 1 sheet in 3 sections.
4. Samaya-maṇḍala of the Vajradhātu-maṇḍala of cotton cloth representing 120 deities.

The graphic Vajradhātumaṇḍala consists of 9 maṇḍalas.

1. Vajradhātu-mahāmaṇḍala: The central part of the graphic Vajradhātu- maṇḍala is called mahā-maṇḍala. The big circle in the centre is called the mahāvajracakra, the five smaller moon circles inside it denote the five wisdoms of Vairocana. The smallest 5 moon circles inside each of the 5 moon circles mean the five wisdoms possessed by each of the five wisdoms. The four pāramitās are manifested by the four Buddhas in order to adore Vairocana Buddha, the four inner pūjā bodhisattvas to adore four Buddhas, the four outer pūjā-bodhisattvas to adore Vairocana Buddha, the four saṅgraha bodhisattvas go out of the four gates to deliver the sentient beings.

2. The samaya-maṇḍala: symbols such as stūpa, a five pronged vajra and a maṇi etc. are drawn in this maṇḍala instead of the figures of the deities. They represent the original

vow of the Buddhas, their śakti, thus they attain feminine forms. The samaya-maṇḍala represents the symbols of the sacred ones inside in the same way as in the Vajradhātu-mahā-maṇḍala.

3. Sūkṣma-maṇḍala: The figural representation is almost the same as in the Vajra-dhātu-mahā-maṇḍala. Each divinity is drawn inside a vajra. This maṇḍala is called vajra-sūkṣma-maṇḍala. Vajra-sūkṣma means subtle wisdom, indestructible like a daimond. Thousand Buddhas of the Bhadrakalpa are represented by the 16 sacred ones. Only the lotus seats are drawn inside of the four great gods, earth, water, fire and wind.

4. Pūjā-maṇḍala: Pūjā means adoration or veneration. All the sacred ones of the pūjā-maṇḍala are represented as female figures. All the bodhisattvas from Vajra-sattva to saṅgraha bodhisattvas in the pūjā maṇḍala of the Gobu-shingan are female figures. But all the figures in the pūjā-maṇḍala in the Genzu-maṇḍala are male figures except the four pāra-mitās in the same way as in the Vajradhātu-mahā-maṇḍala.

5. Caturmudrā-maṇḍala: All the four preceded maṇḍalas are integrated and simplified into this maṇḍala. Vairocana is in the centre and around him are disposed Vajra-sattva, Vajra-ratna, Vajra-dharma and Vajra-karma Bodhisattvas. The four pāramitās are inside the circle and inner pūjā bodhisattvas are in the four corners outside the circle. Caturmudrā-maṇḍala denotes the inseparability of the four maṇḍalas.

6. Eka-mudrā-maṇḍala: Eka-mudrā is the symbol of Vairocana Buddha. But in the Tattva-saṅgraha Eka-mudrā-maṇḍala represents Vajra-sattva, Vajra-sattva is the Jñāna-kāya that symbolises Bodhicitta in All the Buddhas.

8. Trailokya-vijaya-karma-maṇḍala: This maṇḍala is described in the first half of the second part of STTS. The Maṇḍala in this chapter of Vajradhātu is proclaimed by Vairocana Buddha in a merciful aspect. His body consists of the essense of wisdom of All the Buddhas and the wisdom is indestructible like a daimond. On the contrary the maṇḍala in the chapter of Trailokya is preached by Vajra-sattva in the angry aspect. He is embodiment of wisdom in the mind of Vairocana. He reaches in order to persuade Maheśvara that can not easily be converted to Buddhism and to give him the edict of Tathāgata. This is the maṇḍala of Ādeśanācakrakāya of Trailokyavijaya. Vajrasattva in front of Akṣobhya takes the angry aspect of Trailokyavijaya. Other angry ones cross the angry fists.

9. Trailokyavijaya-samaya-maṇḍala: Samaya-symbols are represented here instead of the sacred figures in the Trailokyavijaya-karma-maṇḍala. This maṇḍala shows the mental activity of Trailokyavijaya.

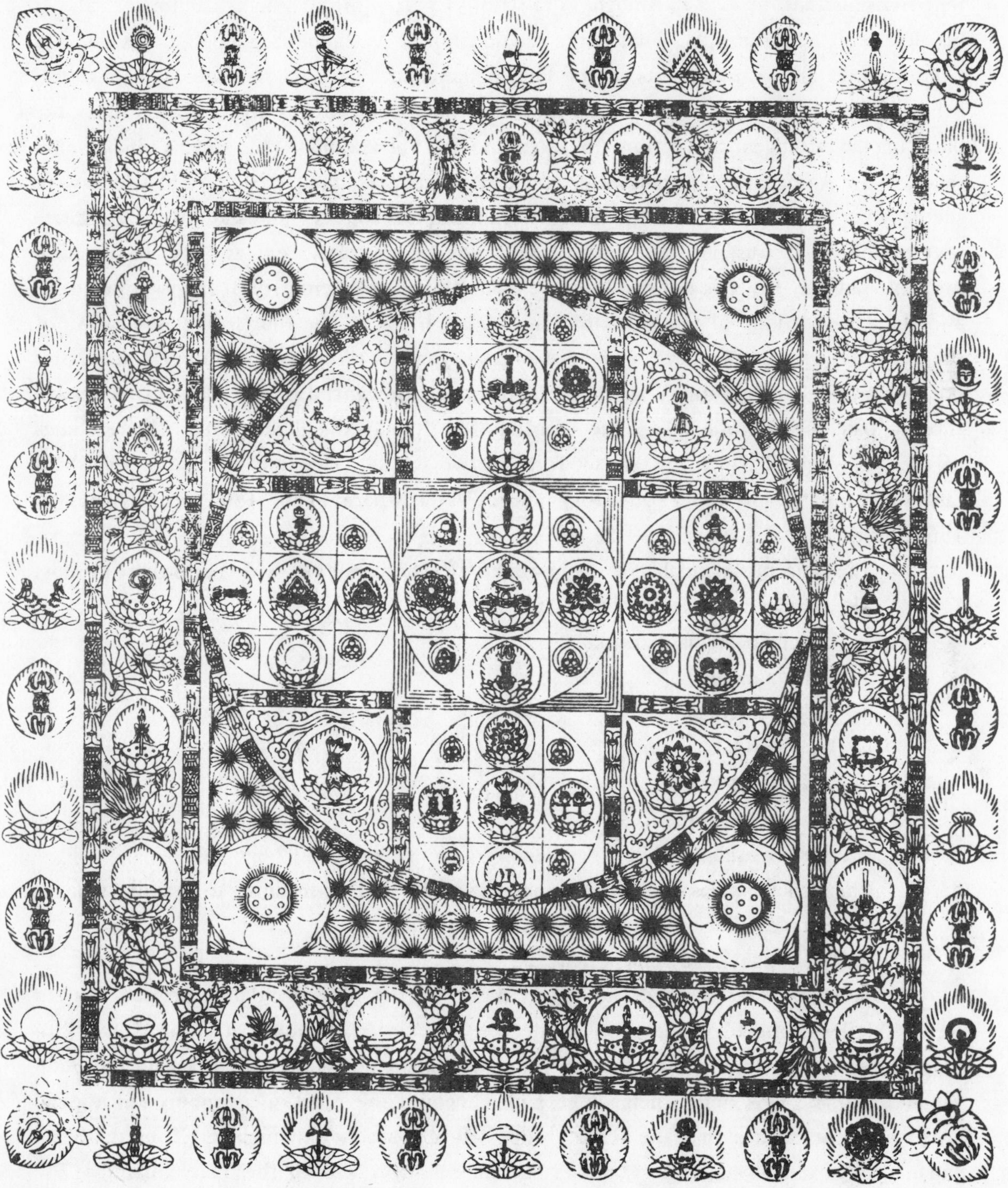

The configuration ot the graphic Vajradhātu-maṇḍala has been a problem for the historians of Japanese art on several counts: i. which textual tradition do the prevelant twin maṇḍalas represent. ii. if they do not conform to texts, are they a synthesis of different transmissions, iii. was it Amoghavajra who integrated the two maṇḍalas for the sake of his desciples or Huikuo, iv. what is the relationship of Vajradhātu-maṇḍala in six parts in Gobu-shingan and in nine parts in the Genzu-maṇḍala. Scholars have debated these and other aspects of the problem. These questions have been saught to be answered on the basis of the abridged translation for recitation by Vajrabodhi. (Nj. 534, T 866) or by recource to Amoghavajra's translation of the first chapter (Nj. 1020, T 865) which were the only orthodox source for the Shingon tradition, Dānapāla's translation of the complete text of the STTS was not resorted to. Without the complete text and its classification into Tibetan exegesis it is not possible to explain the complimentarity of the twin maṇḍalas and the nine sections of the Vajradhātu-maṇḍala. In Japan the four fold classification of the maṇḍalas into kriyā, caryā, yoga and anuttarayoga is unknown. Of these four classes the two classes of caryā and yoga have Vairocana as the central deity. Hence they constitute the pair, the ryōbu-mandara, the maṇḍala of both (ryō) the classes (bu). The teachings of the Yoga school of tantras are set forth in two works. The fundamental or the Mūla-tantra (Toh.479) and the explanatory tantra Vajraśekhara (Toh. 480, Lessing/Wayman 1968:25).

The nine sub-maṇḍalas of the graphic Vajradhātu can be divided into three groups:

1. The six sub maṇḍalas of the STTS.
   i. Vajradhātu-mahā-maṇḍala
   ii. Samaya-maṇḍala
   iii. Sūkṣma-maṇḍala
   iv. Pūjā-maṇḍala
   v. Caturmudrā-maṇḍala
   vi. Ekamudarā-maṇḍala
2. vii. Naya-maṇḍala
3. The two maṇḍalas of the second section of the STTS pertaining to Trailokyavijaya.
   viii. Trailokya-vijaya-karma-maṇḍala
   ix. Trailokyavijaya-samaya-maṇḍala

Scholars have debated the raison d'etre of the nine maṇḍalas on one painted scroll. While practical considerations guided the novenerian formulation of the Vajradhātu-maṇḍala, the philosiophic basis for the concatenation is not clearly provided by the Sino-Japanese texts. It is only when we take into account the Tibetan texonomy and topical analisys of the tantras that the three groups fall into a coherent picture. Thus the Sino-Japanese Vajradhātu-maṇḍala comprises the six sub maṇḍalas of the Tattvasaṅgraha, the seventh maṇḍala represents the exegesis from the prajñā standpoint and the eighth and the ninth maṇḍalas betoken the upāya viewpoint. Thus this type of maṇḍala is all embracing in its inclusion of the complete system of the fundamental text and as well as both explanatory perspectives of prajñā and upāya on a singal scroll.

Kobo-daishi in his memorial presenting a list of newly imported sūtras and other items submitted to the Japanese emporor in A.D. 806 says that after dew concentration he received instruction in the mantras and mudrās of the five divisions of the Vajraśekharasūtra. The abbot informed him that the Buddhist scriptures are so abstruse that their meaning cannot be conveyed except through art. For this reason he ordered the court artist Li Ch'en and about a dozen other painters to execute ten scrolls of Garbhadhātu and Vajradhātu-maṇḍalas and essemble more than twenty scribes to make copies of the Vajraśekharasūtra and other important esoteric Buddhist scriptures (Hakeda 1972:147-8).

The second possibility for drawing only the first part of the TS in the graphic Vajradhātu-maṇḍala can be : only the first part of the TS was drawn by Śubhakarasiṁha (TZ 54-56), may be to avoid repetition, as the icononic representations of the preceding maṇḍalas would be identical with the first part. Gobu-shingan and the graphic Vajradhātu-maṇḍala may be called sketch books for understanding the TS.

## TRANSLATIONS OF STTS

AMOGHAVAJRA.

1. Tattvasaṅgrahajapa-sūtra: Translated by Amoghavajra between the fifth year of T'ien Pao and the ninth year of Ta Li, T'ang dynasty in A.D.746-774, in two leaves, one chüan.

Ch: Chin kang ting yü ch'ieh nien chu ching

Jap.: Kongō-chō-yuga-nenju-kyō

Nos. : Nj. 1036, T 789, K 1273, Ono.3.494c.

2. Sarvatathāgata-tattva-saṅgraha-sūtra: This is an earlier translation of the first part of Nj.1017, in the twelveth year of T'ien Pao, T'ang dynasty A.D.753, 3 fasciculi, 3 chüan.

Ch. : Chin kang ting ich'ieh ju lai chen shih she ta ch'eng hsien cheng to chiao wang ching.

Jap. : Kongō-chō-issai-nyorai-shin-jitsu-shō-daijō-genshō-dai-kyō-Ō-kyō

Nos. : Nj.1020, T 865, K 1274, Ono 3.476 b

3. An Outline of 18 essemblies in Tattvasaṅgrahasūtra: translated by Amoghavajra in 10 leaves, 1 chüan

Ch. : Chin kang ting ching yü ch'ieh shih pa hui chih kuei

Jap.: Kongō-chō-gyō-yuga-jū-hachi-e-shiki

Nos. : Nj.1448, T 869, K 1289, Ono. 3.481 d.

4. Tattvasaṅgraha-padmakula-hṛdaya-japa-kalpa. Translated by Amoghavajra in one fasciculus, 1 chüan

Ch.. Chin kang ting lien hua pu hsin nien sung i kuei

Jpa. : Kongō-chō-renge-bushin-nenju-giki

Nos. : Nj.1436, T 873, K 1310, Ono. 3.496.c

5. Sarvatathāgata-tattva-saṅgraha-sūtra. This is also an earlier translation of the first part of Nj.1017. C'tsiṅ, fasc,15, fol.1 a, where this work is accordingly mentioned as a Mahāyāna-sūtra' of the Vaipulya class.

Ch. : Chin kang ting yi tshiê ju lai chan shinh shö tâ shan hhien chang ta chiâo wang ching

Jap. : Kongō-chō-issai-nyorai-shinjitsu-shōdaijō-genshō-dai-kyō-o-kyō.

Nos. : Nj.1355, T 874.

6. Tattvasaṅgraha-sapta-tṛṅśa-deva-pūjā: Translated by Amoghavajra in 5 leaves, one chüan.

Ch. . Chin kang ting ching chin kang chieh ta tao ch'ang p'i lu che na ju lai tzu shou yung shen nei cheng chih chuan chü fa shen i ming fo tsui shang ch'eng pi mi sanmo ti li ch'an wen

Jap. : Kongō-chō-gyō-kongō-kai-dai-dō-jō-birushana-nyorai-jiju-yūshin-naishō-chi-kenzoku-hosshinimyō-butsusaijōjōhimitsusammaji-rai-sammon

Nos. : Nj.1453, T 878, 879, K 1332.

7. Tattvasaṅgraha-akṣara-mātṛkā-vyākhyā-varga: Translated by Amoghavajra in 3 leaves, 1 chüan, It gives the meanings of Sanskrit alphabet.

Ch. : Yu ch'ieh kang ting ching Su tzu mu p'un

Jap. : Yuga-kongō-chō-gyō-shaku-jimohon

Nos. : Nj.1052, T 880, K 1370, Ono. 11.73 d

8. Tattvasaṅgraha-homa-kalpa: Tanslated by Amoghavajra in 14 leaves, 1 chüan 5 different kalpas or ceremonial rules are given there

Ch. . Chin kang ting yü ch'ieh hu mo i kuei

Jap. : Kongō-chō-yuga-goma-giki

Nos. : Nj. 1443, T 908, 909, K 1335, Ono. 3.489a

9. Tattvasaṅgraha-avalokiteśvara-rāja-tathāgata-caryā-kalpa: Translated by Amoghavajra in 8 leaves, 1 chüan. This is a later translation of Nj.1430.

Ch.: chingkang ting ching kuan tzu tsai wang ju lai hsiu hsing fa

Jap. : Kongō-chō-gyō-kanji-zai-ō-nyorai-shugyōhō

Nos. · Nj.1431, T 931, K 1368, Ono. 3.479 b

10. Translated by Amoghavajra in 1 chüan

Ch. : Chin kang ting ching i tzu ting lun wang yü ch'ieh i ch'ieh shih ch'u nien sung ch'eng fo i kuei

Jap.. Kongō-chō-gyō-ichiji-chōrinnōyugaissaijishōnenjujō-butsu-giki

Nos. : T 957, K 1358, Ono. 3.478 a

11. Translated by Amoghavajra in 1 chüan

Ch. : Chin kang ting chiang san shih ta i kuei fa wang chiao chung kuan tzu tsai p'u sa hsin chen yen i ch'ieh ju lai lien hua ta man na lo p'in

Jap. : Kongō-chō-gyō-sanze-dai-giki-hō-ō-chū-kanji-zai-bosatsu-shin-shingon-issai-nyorai-renge-dai-mandara-hon

Nos. : T 1040, K 1366, Ono 3.484 b

12. Tattvasaṅgraha - sahasrabhuja - sahasrākṣa-avalokiteśvara-bodhi-sattva-caryā-kalpa-sūtra: Translated by Amoghavajra, A.D. 746-771 of the T'ang dynasty, 1 fasciculus in 2 chüan,

Ch. : Chin kang ting yü ch ieh ch'ien shou ch'ieh yen kuan tzu tsai p'u sa hsiu hsing i kuei ching

Jap. : Kongō-chō-yuga-sanju-sangen-kanji-zai-bosatsu-shu-gyō-giki-kyō

Nos. : Nj.1383, T 1056, K 1311, Ono 3.492 c

13. Avalokiteśvara-tārā-yoga-japa-kalpa: This metrical work is translated by Amoghavajra in 14 leaves, 1 chüan,

Ch. . Chin kang ting ching to lo p'u sa nien sung fa

Jap. : Kongō-chō-gyō-tara-bosatsu-nenju-hō

No.: Nj.1414, T 1102, K 1328, Ono.3.480 a

14. Tattvasaṅgraha-anuttara-yoga-samantabhadra-bodhisattva japa-kalpa-sūtra: Translated by Amoghavajra in 11 leaves, 1 chüan.
Ch.: chin kang ting sheng ch'u yü ch'ieh ching chung liao ch'u ta lo chin kang sa to nien sung i
Jap.: Kongō-chō-shō-sho-yuga-kyō-chū-ryaku-shutsu-dairaku-kongō-satta-nenju-giki
Nos.: Nj.1410, T 1120, K 1346, Ono. 3.485 b

15. Tattvasaṅgraha-parinirmitavaśavartisatyatā-parshat-samanta-bhadra-caryā-japa-kalpa: Translated by Amoghavajra in 16 leaves
Ch. : Chin kang ting yü ch'ie t'a hwâ-tsź-tsai-thien li-tshü-hwai-phu-hhien-siu-hhiṅ nien sung i
Jap. . Kongō-chō-yuga-takeji-zai-ten-rishu-fugen-shu-gyō-nenju-giki
Nos. : Nj. 1390, T 1122.

16. Translation by Amoghavajra in I chüan,
Ch. : Chin kang ting sheng ch'u yü chieh p'u hsien p'u sa nien sung fa
Jap.: Kongō-chō-shō-sho-yuga-fugen-bosatsu-nenju-hō
Nos. : T 1123, K 1315, Ono. 3.485 c

17. Tattvasaṅgraha-vajrasattva-pañca-guhya-caryā-japa-kalpa: Another translation of Nj.1400 by Amoghavajra in 14 leaves, 1 chüan,
Ch. : Chin kang ting yü ch'ieh chin kang sa to wu pi mi hsiu hsin nien sung i kuei
Jap.: Kongō-chō-yuga-kongō-satta-gohi-mitsu-shu-gyō-nenju-giki
Nos. : Nj.1411, T 1125, K 1318, Ono 3.490 a

18. Trailokyavijaya-mahā-kalpa-rāja: Translated by Amoghavajra in 3 leaves, 1 chüan
Ch. : Chin kang ting ching yü ch'ieh wen shu shih li p'u sa fa
Jap. : Kongo-cho-gyo-yuga-monjushiri-bosatsu-hō-ippon
Nos. : Nj. 1447, T 1171, K 1280, Ono. 3.483 a

19. Trailokyavijaya-mahā-kalpa-rāja: Translated by Amoghavajra in 3 leaves, 1 chüan.
Ch. : Chin kang ting ch'ao sheng san chieh ching shuo wen shu wu tzu chen yen sheng hsiang
Jap.: Kongō-chō-chō-sho-san-gai-kyō-setsu-monju-go-ji-shingon- shō-sō
Nos.: Nj.1446, T 1172, K 1350, Ono. 3.487 d-482

20. Tattvasaṅgraha-trailokya-vijaya-kalpa-pūjā-dharma: Translated by Amoghavajra in 14 leaves, 1 chüan.
Ch. : Chin kang ting ching yü ch'ieh wen shu shih li p'u sa kung yang i kuei
Jap. . Kongō-chō-gyō-yugamonjushiri-bosatsu-kuyō-giki
Nos. : Nj. 1428, T 1175, K 1363, Ono. 3.482 d

21. Tattvasaṅgraha-trailokyavijaya-siddhi-mahā-guhya-dvāra: Translated by Amoghavajra together with Sarvajña (pien-ch') in 5 leaves, 1 chüan.
Ch. . Chin kang ting ching yü ch'ieh chiang san shih ch'eng chiu chi shen mi men

Jap.: Kongō-chō-yuga-gō-sanje-jōju-goku-jimmitsu-mon

Nos.: Nj.1389, T 1209, K 1380, Ono.3.489 c

22. Sarvatathāgata-anuttara-samyak-sambodhi-cittotpāda-śāsra: Translated by Amoghavajra in 8 leaves, 1 chüan, It agrees with Tibetan.

Ch. : Chin kang ting yü ch'ieh chung fa a nou to lo san miao san p'u t'i hsin lun.

Jap.: Kongō-chō-yuga-chu-hotsu-anokutarasammyaku-sambodaishinron

Nos.: Nj.1319, T 1665, K 1369, Ono. 3.493 a

The following works by Amoghavajra are given in the Taishō Tripitaka:

23. Kongōchōyugaryakujutsusanjūshichisonshinyō

24. Kongōchōyugasanjushichisonshusshōgi

25. Kongōchōgyōichijichōrinnogikiongi

26. Kongōchōyugashōkyōdaihiokanjizainenjugiki

27. Kongōchōyugasaishōhimitsujōbutsuzuigusokutokujimpenkanjijōjudaranigiki

28. Kongōchōgyōdaiyugahimitsushinjihōmongiketsu

VAJRABODHI.

29. Tattvasaṅgraha-trailokyavijaya-pañcākṣara-hṛdaya-dhāraṇī-varga: Translated by Vajrabodhi in A.D. 730 in Ta-chien-fu monastery of the T'ang dynasty in 13 leaves, 1 chüan

Ch. : Chin kang ting ching man shu shih li p'u sa wu tzu hsin t'a lo ni p'in

Jap.: Kongō-chō-gyō-monjushiri-bosatsu-gojishin-darani-hon

Nos.: Nj.537, T 1173, K 465, Ono.3.480

30. Sarvatathāgata-tattvasaṅgraha-sūtra: Translated by Vajrabodhi in Tzu sheng monastery in 4 fasciculi,

Ch. : Chin kang ting yü ch'ieh chung lüeh ch'u nien sung ching

Jap.: Kongō-chō-yuga-chu-ryaku-shutsu-nenju-kyō

Nos.: Nj.534, T 866, K 429, Ono 3.494 a

31. Tattvasaṅgraha-sūtra-yoga-avalokiteśvararāja-tathāgata-caryā-kalpa: Translated by Vajrabodhi in 1 fasciculus

Ch. : Chin kang ting ching yü ch'ieh kwân tzu tsâi wang ju lai siu hhiṅ fâ.

Jap.: Kongō-chō-gyō-yuga-kanji-zaio-nyorai-shu-gyō-hō

Nos.: Nj.1430, T 932

32. Tattvasaṅgraha-yoga-caryā-vairocana-samādhi-kalpa: Translated by Vajrabodhi in 17 leaves, 1 chüan.

Ch. : Chin kang ting ching yü ch'ieh hsiu hsi p'i lu she na san mo ti fa

Jap.: Kongō-chō-gyō-yuga-shuju-birushana-sammaji-hō

Nos.: Nj.1427, T 876, K 1268, Ono. 3.481 b

Tattvasaṅgraha-trailokyavijaya-pañcākṣara-hṛdaya-kalpa: Translated by Vajrabodhi in A.D. 730 of the T'and dynastry, A.D.618-907, 18th year of K'ai yüan 13 leaves, fasc.5, fol, 9b in Ta-chien fu monastery.

Ch. : Chin kang ting ching man shu shih li p'u sa wu tzu hsin t'o lo ni p'in

Jap.: Kongō-chō-gyō-mañjushiri-bosatsu-goji-shin-darani-hon

Nos.. Nj.537, T 1173, K 465, Ono.3.480.

Adhyardhaśatikā-prajñā-pāramitā-naya: Translated by Vajrabodhi in A.D. 723-730 of the T'ang dynasty, from Sanskrit text, while he was in Central India. 13 leaves, fasc.6, fol 6a

Ch. : Chin kang ting yü chie li tshri an jo ching

Jap.: Kongō-chō-yuga-rishu-hanyakyō

Nos.: Nj.1033, T 241.

SUBHAKARASIṀHA.

Ch.: Chin kang tting ching p'i lou tchö na yi po pa tsouen fa chen ch'i yin

Jap.. Kongō-chō-gyō-birushana-ippyaku-hassonhosshinkaiin

DĀNAPĀLA.

Buddhabhāṣita - sarvatathāgata - tattva - saṅgraha - mahāyāna - pratyutpannābhisambuddha-samādhi-mahātantrarāja-sūtra. Translated by Sh'hu (Dānāpala) A.D. 980-1000, of the later Sung dynasty, (A.D.960-1127) in 30 fasciculi, 26 divisions. It is stated at the end that the Sanskrit text consists of 4000 ślokas in verse or equivalent number of syllables in prose. It agrees with Tibetan. 30 chüan

Ch. : I ch'ieh ju lai chen shih sh ta ch'eng hsian chen san mei ta chia wang ching

Jap.: Issainyoraishinjitsushōdaijōgenshōsammaidaikyōōkyō

Nos.: Nj.1017, T 882, K 1466, Ono.1.132 a

Shrī-vajra-maṇḍalālaṅkāra-mahā-tantra-rāja: Translated by Dānapāla, 1 chüan

Ch. : Chin kang chang chuang yen po jo o lo mi to chiao chung i

Jap.: Kongōjōshōgonhanyaharamittakyōchuichibun

Jos.: Nj.944, T 886, K 1442, Ono.3.473 a

OTHERS.

T 2391 : Kongōkaidaihōtaijuki by Annen

T 2225 : Kongōchōdaikyōōgyōshiki by Donjak

T 2293 . Kongōchōshūbodaishinronkuketsu by Eisai

T 2223 : Kongōchōdaikyōōgyōshō by Ennin

T 2386 : Kongōkaijōjiki by Ennin

T 2471 . Kongōkaikuemikki by Genjō

T 2451 : Kohgōchōshūkōgai by Gōhō

T 2291 : Kongōchōyugachūhotsuanokutarasamyakusambodaishinronhi-shaku by Kakuban
T 2518 : Kongōchōkyōrengebushinnenjushidaisata by Kakuban
T 2400 : Kongōsammitsushō by Kakuchō
T 2402 : Saimandarashu by Kakuchō
T 2221 : Kongōchōkyōkaidai by Kukai
T 2224 : Kongōchōkyōgeshaku by Raison
T 2533 : Konkaihohotsueshō by Raiyu
T 3005 : Kongōkaimandaragenzushōshi by Ryōken
T 2292 : Kongōchōhotsubodaishinronshishō by Saisen
T 2406(a) . Kongōkaishidaishōki by Saien
T 2232 : Bonbazaradadoshiki by Shingō

Translations perserved in different collections in Japan
T 2942 : Kongōkaidaimandarazu, coll. Koyasan Shimbessho Entsūji
T 2945 : Kongōkaikuemandarazushu, coll Koyasan Ryūkōin
T 2958 : Kongōkaikuedaimandara, Imp Ninnaji
T 2959 : Kongōkaikuedaimandara, Imp. Hasedera
T 2960 : Kongōkaikuedaimandara, Imp. Ishiyamadera
T 2961 : Kongōkaihachijūissondaimandara, coll Ishiyamadera
T 2963 : Kongōkaikuedaimandara, Imp Kōyasan Kangakuin
T 2963 . Kongōkaimandara, [jōjine, kommae], coll. Daigoji
T 2964 : Kongōkaisammayamandarazu, coll. Ishiyamadera
T 2969 : Kongōkaisammayagyā, coll. Tanji Takejirō
T 2970 : Kongōkaimandara, coll. Tanji Takejirō
T 2971 : Kongōkaimandara, coll. Tōjikanchiin
T 2985 : Kongōkaimandara, coll. Myōhōin
T 3168 : Kongōkaiinzu, coll. Ninnaji
T 3218 : Kongōkaimandara, coll. Kojimadera

## HAND DRAWN AND XYLOGRAPHED COPIES OF THE GENZU MAṆḌALA

The fundamental maṇḍalas that were brought from China by Kōbō-daishi were kept at Tōji monastery the principal cathedral of the shingon sect of Esoteric Buddhism. But the pair of maṇḍalas soon perished and were replaced successively by the copies of polychrome genzu-maṇḍalas. The successive copies that are known are as follows:

The successive copies in Tōji :

1. The maṇḍalas that were imported from China by Kōbō-daishi (the fundamental maṇḍalas) in A.D. 806 were painted by Lichên, the well known Chinese painter and his assistants in the T'ang period by order of Huikuo of Ch'inglungssu', the teacher of Kōbō-daishi and were given to Kōbō-daishi. Each of the pair made of 7 strips of silk, measuring 1 jo 6 shaku (484.8cm) was in colour. But nobody now knows of the content and the disposition of the sacred ones drawn in the pair of maṇḍalas.

2. The first copies, the copies made in the era of Kōnin (810-823) or of Jōwa (834-847). The pair of maṇḍalas brought back from China were dilapidated and the colours were pealed off, and the figures of the sacred ones were going to vanish so soon as 16 years after Kōbō-daishi returned home. New copies were made. It is said that the first copies were completed at the end of August in the year 821. The Garbha-maṇḍala was made of 8 strips while the Vajradhātu-maṇḍala was made of 9 strips. They are perished. The only source of our knowledge about them is the prayer to make a pair of maṇḍalas for the sake of the four kinds of favour. They were probably transferred from Jingōji to Tōji.

3. The second copies made in the era of Kenkyū:. According to 'Tohoki', a record of Tōji monastery, the second copies of the pair of mandalas were painted on the 28th December in the second year of Kenkyū (1191). The painter was Takuma-shoga who was in the rank of Hokkyō. They were identified with the copies serveyed by Dr.O.Takada at Tōji. The figures of the sacred ones are represented in the similar way as the copies of Takao mandala.

4. The third copies made in the era of Einin. Each of the pair was made of nine strips of silk, and were painted by Kandensu in the second year of Einin (1294). They were drawn with steady and uniform lines without slender and gross portions. The representation of the figures belong to the lineage of the copies A. The visage is rather long and the body is slender.

5. The fourth copies made in the era of Genroku. These are the Genzu-maṇḍalas used at present in Tōji Kogen wished to make them in fourth year of Genroku (1691) and got the donation by lady Keishoin. They were painted by Shukaku (shōjiki). Ritual service was performed to open the eyes of the maṇḍala by ex-prince Kakujo at Ninnaji monastery on the 18th January 1693 (the sixth year of Genroku). They are well preserved. The sacred ones are drawn according to the Shosetsu-fudō-ki.

Little is known of the history of the copy b. They were made of nine strips of silk, measuring 411.2cm in width, the largest maṇḍalas that exist now. It is said that Kanné donated the pair when he performed the rite of January in the Shingon-in temple as the abbot of Tōji in 1343. More than half of the sheets were lost. But the remaining parts are well preserved. The colouring is fresh and beautiful. The visages of the sacred ones are round. Eyebrows on both sides are close at hand. Eyes are, elongated. Phisique is full of power and majesty. The pair is similar to the maṇḍalas traditionally said to have been used at Shingon-in temple in the Imperial palace.

(b) The pair of Takao maṇḍalas:

The pair of maṇḍalas brought from China by Kōbō-daishi were painted in colours. A pair of the copies of the fundamental maṇḍalas were made with gold and silver lines on the purple damask silk, by the wish of the emperor Junna. The production was done on the late period of the Tenchō era (A.D. 824-833). The pairs are the only specimen of maṇḍalas dating from the period of Kōbōdaishi They seem to have been realistically drawn copies of the fundamental maṇḍala. Now that the fundamental maṇḍalas as well as the first copy of the Konin period have perished, it is the pair of maṇḍalas of Takao only that enables us to visualize the true aspect of the fundamental maṇḍalas.

(c) The pair of maṇḍalas made of three strips of silks that are kept at Tōji ( the so-called maṇḍalas of Singon-in temple).

The pair is drawn with colours on silk. They were discovered at Tōji in 1934. A tradition in the monastery says that the pair of maṇḍalas was used in the rite of praying for the welfare of the State performed every year in the second week of January at the Shingon-in temple in the Imperial palace.

The Garbha-maṇḍala measures 6.06 shaku (183.6cm) in length and 5.38 shaku (163) in width and the Vajradhātu-maṇḍala measures 6.055 shaku (183.5cm) in length and 5.42 shaku (169.2cm) in width. The pair is the oldest of the painted maṇḍalas with sacred figures.

These maṇḍalas were contained in a wooden box painted with black lacquer. There is an inscription in vermilion lacquer denoting the second year of Shōtai (899) at the back of the lid. But it is not known whether the date points to the date of the production of the maṇḍalas. It is generally supposed from stylistic ground, that the maṇḍalas date from about A.D. 900. That coincides with the inscription. The ex-prince Shukaku borrowed the maṇḍalas together with the famous note-books of Kōbō-daishi in 30 fascicles to Ninnaji monastery in the second year of Bunchi (1186). The colouring of the maṇḍalas is fresh and fine. Gorgeous colours such as vermilion crimson, ultramarine and green are used together with golden paste and gold lead to give conspicuous shading to the painting.

The visages of the sacred ones are round and two eyebrows are close by or are joined some times. Eyes are generally elongated in Guptā style But nose and mouth are rather small, which is a feature, attributed to the origin of China but not of India. Body is short and slightly fat and has dignity and fullness. The lines representing body are strong. Shading is dence, expressive of the volume and sensuousness. The colouring is vivid and gorgeous with red and similar colours. The dense shading and the sensuousness by means of the colouring may be due to the Indian origin.-(d) The mandalas drawn on wooden boards in

(d) The maṇḍalas drawn on wooden boards in the five storied pagoda in Daigoji monastery at Kyoto .

The five-storied pagoda of Daigoji was completed in A.D. 951. The pair of maṇḍalas painted on wooden boards and panels inside the pagoda were painted in the year of the next. The Vajradhātu and Garbha represented on the boards surrounding the central pillar, the four principle pillars and the pands near the Renji windows. The figures of the sacred ones are not different inspite of the disinction of Vajradhātu-and Garbha-maṇḍalas. The shoulder expanse is wide and the body is slender. The expanse of the fences is also wide. The whole figure is well proportioned. As far the countenence there is a difference between the maṇḍalas. Eyebrows are drawn with a strong curved line in the Garbha-maṇḍala while it is a tender line, thin at both ends and broad in the middle in the Vajradhātu-maṇḍala.-

The shading of the sacred ones, the flowers in the wooden painting of the central pillar, the pattern in kirikane on the surface of the maṇḍalas are similar to the maṇḍalas of the copy'b' in Tōji. Although the copy 'b' was manufactured in the Kamakura period, the figures show stout physique precisely copied from a prototype of the early Heian

(e) The maṇḍalas of Kojimaji :-

The pair of maṇḍalas from Kojimaji are drawn with gold and silver lines on purple damask silk. Garbha-maṇḍala measures 349 cm in length by 308cm in width and the Vajradhātu-maṇḍala 352 cm in length by 297cm in width. The figures of the sacred ones are somewhat formal and similar to the wooden painting in the pagoda of Daigoji. These have been handed down in Kojimaji monastery in Yamato province since shinko's time. He lived there and died in 71 years of age in the first year of Kankō (1004). They are a pair made of 6 strips of silk. The pairbelongs to the Genzu maṇḍala but the details are somewhat different. They probably date from latter half of the 10th century or the former half of 11th century.-

(f) The pair of maṇḍalas to be spread on the altar of Tōji monestary.-

They are drawn with colours on silk. Now they are ready to be hung. But originally the pair were spread over the altar and used fōr the rite of obtaining a sacred one by throwing a flower on the maṇḍala at the sight of abhiṣeka. Among this category of maṇḍala there are different types representing sacred figures, samava symbols and bijaksaras.

(g) The blood maṇḍalas of Koyasan:

Taira-no-kiyomori became the supervisor of the reconstruction of the great pagoda on Mt. Kōyasan in 1149. Probably in the next year Kiyomori had the blood of his head mixed with pigment to draw the crown of Mahāvairocana in the central quarter with eight pettled lotus. So the maṇḍalas are called the blood maṇḍalas of Kiyomori. The painter was called Jōmyō. Though the details are somewhat damaged they still retain the original aspect.

(h) Ōmura copy of the maṇḍala of Takao:-

According to Seigai Ōmura, Kenni drew copies of Takaō with lines without colours for the bicentenary anniversary of Kōbōdaishi's dhyāna. The pair of copies were taken up as the originals for making xylographs. Priest Hōun, Ācārya Sompō of Shima province ordered wood block carvers to carve the blocks in the second year of Meiji (A.D.1869). The wooden blocks were kept at Ninnaji, Kyoto. According to a research work the basis of the copies of Takao maṇḍalas were not the copies of Kenni, but were further copies. And it was not the bicentanery anniversary of Kōbōdaishi's dhyāna but the trincentanery anniversary that fell on A.D.1135. Kenni granted the copies to his disciple Shinkaku. Shinkaku was the famous disciple of Besson Zakki. Copies of Kenni's copy were made at the end of Kamakura period. They were kept at Kozanji, but now they are owned by Mr. Sakai. They were taken up as the basis of the copies of Omura block printing. S.Omura published them. Again vol.I of the iconographic section of the Taishō tripitaka took them up. The Omura copies of the Takao maṇḍalas supply us with the best materials for the sacred figures of the Genzu maṇḍalas. They show the dearest drawing lines of the sacred images.-

(i) Inshoin copies of the maṇḍalas:-

Priest Jōtō of the Inshoin monastery at Kōyasan let a painter named Shimizu Giga copy the maṇḍalas at Tōji monastery. They were published by the wooden blocks in the second year of An-'ei (A.D.1773). The size was a quarter of the original, measuring 3 shaku and 5 sun (1.06cm) and 3 shaku 5 bu (.92cm) in width. The wooden blocks were burnt by fire.

(j) Buzan copy of the maṇḍala:-

Hasedera monastery of the new school of the shingon sect ordered Tōshuku Hasegawa to copy from the maṇḍalas of Tōji monastery and let him engrave the wooden blocks in the fifth year of Tempo (A.D.1834) in commemoration of the millennium of Kōbōdaishi's dhyāna.

(k) The maṇḍalasof 81 sacred ones inthe esoteric Buddhism of Tendai sect:-

This sort of mandala was brought by Kobodaishi, Ennin and enchin. It consists of Vajradhātu-mahā-maṇḍala. Existant specimens of this kind include the copy handed down at the Kongōrinji monastery in Shiga prefecture and now kept at the Nezu Art Gallery and the copy from Taizanji monastery in Hyōgo prefecture. The number of the sacred ones and the figural representations are different to some extant from those of Genzu maṇḍala. The four saṅgraha, the four outer pūjā and the sixteen sacred ones of the Bhadrakalpa are among the thousand Buddhas of Bhadrakalpa, 4 Vidyārājas added besides 20 deities of the of the outer circle. The four Buddhas in the four cardinal points are in the form of Tathāgatas, with diadems on their heads and the 33 divinities in the inner compartment are seated on animal or bird rides. Inspite of such peculiarities this is a Vajradhātu-maṇḍala that belongs to the linage of Vajrabodhi.

## VAJRADHĀTU-MAṆḌALA AS THE BASIS OF TABO

The most important monastery of all the Spiti is that of Tabo. Hundred chaples and eight sancturies of Tabo arrive at the sacred number of 108. One of them the central temple is called gTsug lag-K'an for its foundation belongs to Rin C'en bzan Po and his successors. As it is seen today it has undergone a restoration at a later date. The central aspect of the Gompa is that of a ruin From the external point of view the monastery of Tabo appears as a group of several buildings closed in by an enclosure. That wall is the limit which separates the sacred soil from the profane one more or less like the outer circle or vajrāvalī in a maṇḍala . The temple in its real significance is nothing other than a large maṇḍala and even for its construction the same regulations are valid which must be followed to trace a maṇḍala.

The entire gompa is known by the name of C'os ak'or. The centre of the whole complex is constituted by the gTug lag k'an which consists of a rectangular chamber with a porch and an apse around which there is a corridor which was used for pradakṣiṇā.

The entrance of the temple is called sgo k'an which is in fact a vestibule to the real temple. An image of Tsoṅ Khapa is in the yabyum or mystical embrace posture. The paintings are relatively modern . The paintings of the entrance hall are about to disappear, almost all the images were accompanied by inscriptions. Let us enter the temple itself. All around are alighned the thirtytwo deities of stucco of almost live size. Some of them are in peaceful and others in terrific postures. These statues are supported by beams fixed into the walls. The statues of gTug lag k'an represent a Tantric cycle of Vairocana. The maṇḍala here presupposes the presence of a central divinity and a group of secondary deities which form the attendence or the accolites. Central divinity of Tabo is Vairocana, easily recognisable by his mudrā. The cycle of Tabo is similar to that of Sarvavid Vairocana.

Sarvatathāgata-tattvasaṅgraha is the most important because it contains all particulars of the meditative process. It describes us how this must develop during the different moments of the construction of the maṇḍala or the rite fulfilled on it . According to the text there should be thirty seven deities in the maṇḍala. They can be tabulated with their attributes as follows .

1. Sarvavid Vairocana, samādhi mudrā, Om sarvavid-sarva-varana viśodhaya hana hūm phaṭ.
2. Sarvavid, Samādhi, Om sarvavid hūm
3. Sarvavid, varada, samādhi, om sarvavid phaṭ
4. Sarvavid, dharmacakra, Om sarvavid ah.
5. Sarvavid, abhaya, samādhi, Om sarvavid tra tha.
6. Locana, wheel, oṁ Buddhalocani hūm.
7. Māmaki, Vajra, Om vajramāmaki tram.
8. Pāṇḍarā, lotus, Om vajra-pāṇḍare dehi dehi siddhim.

9. Green Tara, blue lotus, bodhim lokottarīm pa svāhā , Om vajra-tāre tuttare ture hūm hūm hūm sva sva sva svaha.
10. Vajrasattva, vajra, bell, Om vajrasattva hūm.
11. Vajrarāja, hook, Om vajrarāja jaḥ.
12. Vajrarāga, bow and arrow, Om vajrarāga ho.
13. Vajrasādhu, acchoṭana, Om vajrasādhu dha.
14. Vajraratna, ratna,bell, Om vajra-ratna tram.
15. Vajrateja, solar disc, Om vajrateja rya.
16. Vajraketu, standard which exhausts desires, Om vajraketu, bhrīḥ.
17. Vajrahāsa, wears an ivory necklace (danta-paṅkti), Om vajrahāsa ha.
18. Vajradharma. opening a lotus with his right hand held by his left, Om vajradharma
19. Vajratīksṇa, sword, book, Om vajratīkṣna drīḥ.
20. Vajrahetu, rotating a wheel, Om vajrahetu krum.
21. Vajrabhāṣa, tongue of diamond, Om vajrabhāṣa bha.
22. Vajrakarma, viśvavajra, bell, Om vajrakarma kam.
23. Vajrarakṣa, diamond talisman, Om vajrarakṣa ram.
24. Vajrayakṣa, teeth produding on both sides of the face, Om vajrayakṣa kṣam.
25. Vajrasandhi, two vajras with five points, Om vajrasandhi sam.
26. Vajralāsyā, two vajras, Om vajralāsye hūm.
27. Vajramālā, garland, Om vajramāle tram.
28. Vajragītā, lute, Om vajragīte hrīḥ.
29. Vajranṛtyā, three pointed vajra, Om vajranṛtye aḥ.
30. Vajradhūpā, vase for an incense, Om vajradhūpe hūm.
31. Vajrapuṣpā, basket of flowers, Om vajrapuṣpa bram.
32. Vajrālokā, lamp, Om vajrāloke hrīḥ.
33. Vajragandhā, shell full of perfume, Om vajragandhe aḥ.
34. Vajrāṅkuśa, hook, Om vajrāṅkuśa jaḥ.
35. Vajrapāśa, noose, Om vajrapāśa hūm.
36. Vajrasphoṭa, iron chain, Om vajrasphoṭa bam.
37. Vajraghaṇṭa, bell, Om vajraghaṇṭa ho.

The Tibetan ritualistic is all inspired by Indian sources. It is logical to accept that the cycle of Sarvavid Vairocana is related to some tantric school. One of the texts can be Durgati-pariśodhanatejo rājakalpa. It has the same listing of names and the same arrangement the deitie sin the maṇḍala. Only a few diversions are noted in the icocnographical details. Indian tradition dose not limit itself to the text. It is not isolated but strictly connected with a noteworthy section of the Tantric literature which also deals with the symbolism of the Vajradhātu-maṇḍala and has a great advantage of also having been preserved in the Chinese sources.

In fact STTS is the most important and popularised Tantra in the Buddhist school. It is one of the fundamental texts of Vajrayāna in China which was one of the works translated by Rin c'en bzan Po. This Tantra was particularly studied during his time. The plastic reflection of the mystical experiences predominent in western Tibet at the time of Rin c'en bzaṅ Po can be seen in the temple of Tabo. The gTug lag k'an was almost the architectural correlation of the translation of the sacred texts which the Lotsava had led to completion by transplanting in his own country and amongst his people some of the methods of realisation of the deepest spiritual experiences of India. In other words the ideal and religious motive which inspired the foundation of the temple must be sought within the doctrines for initiation expressed and symbolised in Tattvasaṅgraha and in the Tantric literature related to it.

The maṇḍala of Vairocana according to STTS

The list contained in the commentary by Ānandagarbha coincides perfectly with that which we find in the Tibetan texts on Sarvavid Vairocana.

6. Vajrasattvi, five pointed vajra.
7. Vajraratna, five pointed vajra with a cintāmaṇī on the crest.
8. Vajradharma, lotus with sixteen petals.
9. Vajrakarma, twelve pointed viśvavajra.
10. Vajrasattva, bell in the left hand.
11. Vajrarāja, hook.
12. Vajrarāga, bow and arrow.
13. Vajrasādhu, hands in a posture of vajrasandhi and approval.
14. Vajraratna, a bell in left and a vajra with cintāmaṇī in right.
15. Vajrasūrya, a solar disc in right hand.
16. Vajraketu, standard marked with a cintāmaṇī in right.
17. Vajrahāsa, Vajra with two garlands in right.
18. Vajradharma, opening the petals of a lotus by right held by left.
19. Vajratīkṣṇa, sword in right and a book of Prajñāpāramitā in left.
20. Vajrahetu, a wheel with eight spokes.
21. Vajrabhāṣa, five pointed vajra in right.
22. Vajrakarma, viśva vajra in right and a bell with viśva vajra in left.
23. Vajararakṣa, diamond talisman.
24. Vajraykṣa, teeth which protude from mouth.
25. Vajrasandhi, vajra and samaya muṣṭi mudrā.
26. Lāsyā, two vajras.
27. Mālā, garland.
28. Gītā, lute.
29. Nṛtyā, three pointed vajra.
30. Dhūpā, vase of perfume.

31. Puṣpā, basket of flowers.
32. Dīpā, lamp.
33. Gandhā. shell full of perfume.
34. Vajrāṅkuśa, hook.
35. Vajrapāśa, noose.
36. Vajrasphoṭa, chain.
37. Vajrāveśa, bell.

Symbolical and esoterical meaning of the maṇḍala:

Deities of the cycle of Vairocana are none other than symbols of special moments of meditation process. In its internal experiences the sādhaka services a particular system of cosmic evolution. Its background stages are called reabsorption. During this reabsorption little by little in eliminate in a final manner the dimness which is derived from passions and ignorance. Only by virtue of this intimate essence of the beings is our regeneration and sublimation possible. It is the germinal luminosity such as it is symbolised by Vairocana, the refulgent, the centre of the maṇḍala, from which everything stems detaching itself more and more materialising itself and finally becoming dim.

The maṇḍala expresses all these truths in a symbolic language which is eccessible by the initiated. All the attributes that the mahāyānic iconography puts to a rich use are capable of the interpretation which was in fact followed by the Tantric school and which changed the images into symbolical figurations of the complex and obscure doctrines contained in the literature from which it draws its inspiration. The character of the mahāyānic art is born from this which is purely mystical and symbolic. The essence of the mahāyānic religion has much of meditation than prayer. And above all it requires concentration through which it is received and visualised and therefore psychologically relived as a symbolic expression, the ādhāra, the sustenance, as the Indian writers of the treaties say the idea even the most abstract one had to be translated by these schools into a symbol into a conventional visual image, which with the exegesis of the doctors was translated into initiated language and became the direct vehicle of immidiate realisation. In the Vajradhātu-maṇḍala the statues symbolise mystical states, as it is made more evident by that common prefix of vajra, ratna or padma.

Significance of Sarvavid Vairocana according to Tsoṅ khapa.

The maṇḍala of Sarvavid Vairocana is the symbolical daigram of the essential doctrines of the mahāyāna. Vairocana means dharmatā-jñāna and the rest four Buddhas are: ādarśa-jñāna, samatā-jñāna, pratyavekṣaṇa-jñāna and kriyā-sādhana-jñāna. Vajrasattva and the other three Bodhisattvas symbolise the first four of the sixteen species of insubstantiality (śūnyatā). These first four śūnyatās are : that subjective one which eliminates the beliefs in the objectivity of ones own preceptions, that objective which eliminates the belief in the objective existence of the objects of these; that subjectivity and objectivity which eliminates the belief in the objective existance of the objects of those, that subjectivity and objectivity which eliminates the belief in the objective reality of the sensorial relationships in relation to an object, that of the great insubstantiality which eliminates the belief in the objective reality of the physical world.

Vajrarāga and other Bodhisattvas of the south symbolize other four śūnyatās. the substantial matter of the insubstantiality that serves to eliminate the belief that makes us attribute a transcendental existance to the insubstantial matter thus obtained. the insubstantial matter of the absolute which eliminates the belief that something which is absolute exists such as nirvāṇa etc.. the insubstantial matter of all that is the resultof an activity by elimination of the attachment to works of merit which are not the cause for obtaining the supreme illumination, the insubstantial matter of all that which is not the effect of an activity by elimination of the attchment to those works of merit which are the cause of supreme illumination which being eternal cannot be created or derived.

The rest four Bodhisattvas of the west and four of the north symbolize in the same way the other eight śūnyatās. Vajralāsyā and the other seven godesses represent the eight perfections. Vajrāṅkuśa and other three symbolize faith, energy, knowledge, consciouness, and concentration.

Age of the paintings of Tabo: Tsug-lag-khaṅ is the most ancient and important temple of all the Gompa. Tabo and Tolling are not diassociated. Both of them wer found Rin-C'en-bzaṅ-po under the patronage of Ye śes 'od and it was rebuilt during the reign of Byan. An inscription is to be read at the entry of the apse chapel. The auther of this inscription is also the painter of the frescoes. It is a prasasti of two greatest figures of Buddhist rennaissance in western Tibet. They belong to the 11th-13th century. Consequently, all paintings of the temple still in existance correspond to this era.

The frescoes:

In the central temple, under the statues, there is a long uninterrupted series of frescoes which although representing well known legends of Buddhism, is sufficiently important for the story of ancient costumes of western Tibet. These paintings are more or less inspired from local and contemporary vision. The technique and style are also important.

These paintings belong to a school which is totally independent from that developed in central Tibet. They reveal an indigenous art which must have been formed in Guge under the patronage of the king of western Tibet. Inspired and modelled directly from India far away from the Chinese penetration, this painting is perhaps the most noteworthy document remainigng of a school which could be called Indo-Tibetan.

The frescoes which decorate the temple of Tabo can be divided into two serires, one is to the left when one enters the temple and starts immidiately at the side of the door the other runes parallel to the right with a similar development. They are pictorial reproduction of Buddhist legends. Inscriptions with them are generally commentary to the various scenes. The paintings to the right reproduce the life of Buddha described in a series of picture which correspond to the twelve fundamental moments of the life of Buddha, which have become traditional in the iconagraphy of Tibet.

The Cell and the Iconographical Types of the Five Buddhas.

Behind the temple there is a cell with a central statue and two accolytes on both sides. The letter cell is surrounded by a narrow corridor, Pradakṣiṇā. The central figure represents a Buddha sitting on a throne, on the base are two lions back to back. He is sitting down in the position of vajraparyaṅka and his hands are in dhyānamudrā.

| Deity | Colour | Vehicle | Mudrā | Symbol |
|---|---|---|---|---|
| Vairocana | white | lion | dharmacakra | wheel |
| Akṣobhya | blue | elephants | bhūmisparśa | vajra |
| Ratnasambhava | yellow | horses | varada | gem |
| Amitābha | red | peacocks | dhyāna | vase |
| Amoghasiddhi | green | garuḍa | abhaya | sword |

Representations of these deities are usually made of cardboard or papier maché and then painted. The imposition of this diadem means that the officiater has become one with that germind cosmic force in which the five lines of evolution are differentiated symbolically represented by the supreme fivefold now thus united with the whole he holds under the domain the forces of the universe and can operate the miracle.

The most unique images were made of wood, no.1 represents Amoghasiddhi, no.2 Vairocana and no.3 Amitābha, Buddhas are countersigned by their traditional vehicles on the base of the throne. They are seated in vajraparayaṅka upon a lotus, supported by a carpet decorated with quadrangular motifs. Behinds the figure, the throne, of a style which seems characteristic of other statues of the Pāla type, i.e. flanked by a small figure of an elephant which rests on a horned lion, in this case over a vyālaka (lion) there is a cavalier. Over the throne a marine monster from which develops in flower motifs of spheral curves going upwards, a garuḍa of the usual Indian type, surmounted by the characteristic symbol of the deity represented, the sword for Amoghasiddhi, the wheel for Vairocana, the lotus for Amitābha.

Nos 4-8 reproduce the whole pentade Sarvavid-vairocana, No.6 is the central deity of the series with four heads and hands in dharmacakramudrā under each deity, apart from the usual vehicle, the figure of a dwarf in the position of atlante, a motif which we will find again reproduced in stucco in the temple Lhalung. instead of the garuḍa at the top a head of lion, kīrtimukha on the vertex traditional symbol: the lotus flower for Amitābha, the viśvavajra for Akṣobhya, for Vairocana a flower instead of the wheel, for Amoghasiddhi the vajra, for Ratnasambhava the gem. On both sides of the throne, two deities almost surely feminine, probably the usual feminine deities in the act of adoration.

Four attendents are on the sides of Vairocana. Nos. 9 and 10 are of the same type although worked with a greater retirement, representing Amitābha and Ratnasambhava. On the walls of the circumambulation passage around the apse a thousand small figures of Buddha sitting down are in the frescoesall in dhyānamudrā.

The gser k'aṅ and its paintings.

The gSer k'aṅ is a chapel of great interest because of the paintings which cover the walls almost completely. They are not as ancient as those of the gTsug lag k'aṅ, because they go back almost surely to the sixteenth century, but they are nonetheless of great value. These in fact can be considered as a document of the second period of the art of Guge, which reached its summit at the time of the king Sen ge rnam rgyal. Then it began to decline. After the conquests of this king, which gave the fortune and power of Guge a fatal coup, with the sunset of political power, it seems than even artistical tradition slowly withered.

The figures of this chapel are bigger than natural size and arranged in a symmetrical order: three per wall. The iconographical identification presents no difficulty, because we are dealing with relatively well-known deities. On the wall, to the left of him who enters, the order is as follows:

a) The God of medicine sMan bla, Bhaiṣajyaguru, wearing the religious garment on the left he holds the vase for alms, piṇḍapātra while the right is in the position of giving, varadamudrā. It is therefore easy to recognize which one of the eight Buddhas of medicine is sought to be represented here. The mudrā indicates him as Sgra dhyans rgyal po.

b) The central figure is reproduced with greater richness of decoration, under the throne, between rings of styled flowers two lions back to back, a very common motif in all the mural paintings of Guge, Amitābha sits on a padmāsana, the colour is red and he has a piṇḍapātra in his hands in the position of meditation, he wears the religious military cloak, while on both sides two deities are represented standing with diadems and royal dresses. On the right is Avalokiteśvara Padmapāṇi, who white in colour, and that on the left is Mahāsthāmaprāpta Lokeśvara, two traditional companions of Amitābha, as we have seen before.

The framing is amongst the richest. a complete series of minor deities now in groups, now isolated, and enclosed within the usual circular motif. above the halo of the Buddha the leaves of a tree point outwards. Around the central deity a multitude of praying and kneeling monks are gathered, while, amongst the rings and the foliage, compartments and pavilions show that the artists whished to depict a certain story. It is easy to recognise which one this is. The unknown writer wanted to reproduce the Sukhāvatī, the paradise of the West in which Amitābha reigns, in it the greater part of Tibetan faithful, who, by means of ascetical practice and the renunciation imposted by yoga have not reached that rare perfection, which forever draws out the sansāra, desires to be reborn and to live an indefinite beatitude under the grace and light of Amitābha.

The tree which extands its branches above the figure of Amitābha is the Bodhi tree which according to the classical description of Sukhāvatīvyūha: "it is always in bloom, it always has leaves, it always has flowers, it always has fruits of many hundreds of millions of colours, of different leaves, of different flowers, of different fruits, adorned by many splended ornaments...." (par. 32).

The multitude of the adoring faithful around the figure of the god is perhaps there to represent the innumerable theory of Boddhisattva and the monks which according to the text, is gathered from every celestial region around Amitābha to pay homage to him. (par. 27, 29-30), whilst the trees which appear here and in the painting symbolise those trees with gems which in the literary sources are described as characteristical embelishment of the Sukhāvatī (par. 16) together with the pavilions in which the multitude of the blessed rejoice. (par. 19)

The frescoes of Tabo are therefore inspired by the traditional description of the Sukhāvatī as it has been handed down in Mahāyāna works and as it has been passed into the popular literature of Tibet, becoming almost the centre of those esoteriological beliefs with which the Tibetans are profoundly imbued. The floral motifs of wide circular rings which adorn the base lead us back to models ellaborated in our schools.

(c) The third fresco, always to the left, represents a deity dressed in the usual royal military cloak, with diadems, necklace and earings. The figure is of a deep blue colour and its hands are crossed over the chest. He holds a bell in his left and a vajra in his right hand. It is then obvious that the painter wanted to symbolise Vajradhara, supreme revealer ādiguru of the school of bK'a rgyud pa. Although we are dealing with the principal deity of this sect, which in Tibet draws his origin from the Marpa, who was a disciple of Naropa. This deity occupies a great position in the mystical experience of the dGe lug pa, i.e. of the Yellow sect, under the probable inspiration of which these paintings are carried out. On the other hand this is natural because many tantras of the Yellow sect also accepted as extremely reliable, believed to be a revelation of Vajradhara, which is in fact the symbolical representtion of a level of experience even higher than that expressed in the sacred pentade of the Pañcatathāgata, with which we have already dealt. In fact Vajradhara is the symbol of indescriminate state of the being, prior to the ideal fivefold division, expressed in the pentade, and therefore of Vajradhātu or indestructible diamond sphere which is uncorrupted and indeffectible bottom of the whole. As such it is also called Mahāvajradhara, the supreme god of the mystical maṇḍala described in the Guhyasamāja. In the very symbols it expresses the quitescence of the Mahāyānic doctrine. In fact it is not by caprice that it is represented with a bell and a vajra. A bell in Vajrayāna symbolises mystical knowledge, prajñā and a vajra the means, upāya, i.e. compassion, karuṇā, the two elements, the intuitive one of the practical which represents two fundamental coefficients of illumination, the two essential moments, of the thought of illumination from which a spark of the supreme truth will spout.

Vajradhara sits on a finely worked throne, under which we can see apart from the figure of two lions also those of the two elephants, the traditional vehical of Akṣobhya. When from the pentade we wish to reach a higher plane prior to every differentiation, the symbol of which is also called, especially in the mystical directions connected with Kālacakra, the Ādi Buddha or the primigenious Buddha. All around we see a series of ascetical figures in different positions. Who they are, it is easy to imagine. The artist has tried to represent the eightyfour siddhas which in fact continue in their experience, the mystical revelation of rDo rje ac' an or still better they renew it in a continuity of teachings and experiences which have had according to Indo-Tibetan tradition, these eighty-four interpreters. These are to be counted among the figures which are most often represented and which belong to that mystical and syncretical movement which in medieval India prepared the most complex methods for spiritual realisations.

On the central wall the figure follow the following order:

(a) A Bodhisattva is sitting on a finely decorated throne. His right foot rests on a lotus and left leg is folded under his right knee, position is called lalitakṣepa. His hands are in dharmacakra-mudrā. From the way in which he is sitting and from the position of his hands the deity can be recognised as Maitreya, the Buddha of the cosmic age immediately succeding the one in which we live. To the left, on a lotus flower which opened up to the hight of the shoulder, vase of the sacrificial water. On the left and to the bottom a polychromous theory of the deities, amongst which the type usually characteristic of Amoghasiddhi in monk cloak and abhayamudrā predominates.

(b) The central figure represents Śākyamuni, The Buddha of the cosmic era in which we live, represented at a very moment in which, having attained supreme illumination and escaped the snares and temptation of Māra, invokes as a testimonial of the triumph achieved the earth, his hand thus is in bhūmisparśamudrā whilst the left is in the position of meditation. This is atraditional figure of Buddhistic iconography which in the schools of great vehical has a special name, that of the vajrāsana. Around him are his two favourite disciples, Śāriputra and Maudgalyāyana. All around are sixteen arhat figures arranged and carried out with great refinement, i.e., the repositories of the law, who establish ideal connections between Śākyamuni and the future Buddha Maitreya. On high, the throne is surmounted by a figure of Garuḍa between two images of praying nāgas.

(c) To the right and the same position in which Maitreya is sitting and turning towards the Buddha is the figure of Mañjuśrī, also in lalitakṣepa. Both to the right and to the left two lotus flowers rise to the hight of the shoulders, that of the right carries a sword and that to the left a book, the two very symbols of Mañjuśrī, which are there to indicate force and the significance of mystical knowledge. The book is none other than the contents of Prajñā, i.e., supreme intution of insubstantiality, śūnya of all things and the sword instead is there to signify the active value of this knowledge, it destroys and eliminates all the darkness which is derived from ingorance and which is of a twofold character, intellectual and moral.

The c'os skyon and the terrific in the Tantric schools:

On the back wall where the door opens usual terrific deities are superimposed and also the guardians: dharmapāla, dvārapāla etc. The usual place is generally next to the doors of temples, feared costodians which hold at bay all the captive forces and even intetions, vighnavināśartham. There is Hayagrīva of deep blue colour, Vaiśravaṇa and Vajrapāṇi. In the middle of these terrific deities there are Tārā and Avalokiteśvara, and it can be understood that these terrific deities are the irate aspect of placde and beatifical deities. The more merciful the god is the more terrible his irate aspect will be, these aspects are in fact intended to subdue and dispel the captive forces which pester in every circumstance the good and peaceful enforcement of the law. It is therefore a mistake to call them demons in the Indo-Tibetan religious psychology we can not talk of real proper devils but only spirits i.e., of conscious forces which operate independently in the subsoil of our conscience or in the physical world arousing passions or events which can harm creatures.

Also in Tibet, following India in this the figure of the god of evil conceived as a cosmic absolute force which is the antithesis of good, the negation of god, the darkness and the negation of light is not known. The elaboration of this duality is characteristic of Iran. In India there is the figure of Māra but of all the negativa characteristics Māra preserves only that of the inducer to temptation. He is not the king of evil, but the king of love and life. The sphere in which he dominates as a sovereign is that of māyā, but even this māyā is not his doing, has not been created by him , but the covering with which the supreme being by his own will surrounds himself and hides in his desire to expand in life and his desire to make himself objective. As Māra in the Mahāyāna, unfolds himself often into a quadruple series which usually symbolises the four passions: Māra as the Vimalaprabha says is the conscience which has attached us to life and which drags us through life, the passion as opposed to renunciation his kingdom is inside us. As god of life and also as god of death because a thing of necessity brings about the other and as the king of māyā he can not appear to us as a tempter, the māyā is the sansāra and all that which puts on the way of liberation must be of necessity to surpass and deny it.

Māra symbolises the beginning of life which is always reaffirmed when we are nearer to denying it, the world which wishes to hold us back with its flattery, the fear of renunciation, the voice of the flesh of affection, of terrestrial links, which have trapped, pestered put obstacles in the lives of all saints. More than being a god Māra is a psychological reality, there is nothing in him to make out of him. That is why Māra is not the god of tress-passersor condemned either. And he can not be because in Hinduism and Buddhism there is no damnation , but only expiation more or less lengthily of the evil commited and subsequent purification. As we have already seen that the temples are the architectural and plastic projections of a mystical process or of a litergy. the presence of dharmapala the costodians of law and of doors lead us back to an essential moment of every act of worship. No ritual ceremony can have the desired result, if first the evil forces have not been sent away, since these are the impediments to the formation of that sacred aura in which the compliance with the rite can only take place, the vighnavināśa is cosequently the indispensable introduction to the pūjā. And thus also the initiated ceremonies the invocation of the person to be initiated of the terrific deity will send away from him and around him the opposition forces. And consequently in the temple, which is a consecrated soil and the place in which the atmosphere of purity and sanctity must always be preserved, near the doors almost unfailingly images of such deities are arranged, the supreme mercifulness of whom becomes active and pugnatious to reject all that which is from outside.

The initiating chapel dkil k'an:

Dkyil k'an is one of the smallest chapels, one of the remotest and worst preserved. The paintings which cover it are not very ancient, may be they belong to the seventeenth century, when probably by the work of the kings of Ladakh, the whole of the monastery of Tabo was rebuilt. In any case, the Dkyil k'an represents or should have represented among all the religious buildings of the monastery a sort of santum sanctorum. In fact the Dkyil k'an is not open to the public of faithful, as is the habit with the other temples, but is the sacred place where the maṇḍalas are found, i.e., the mystical symbols which translate in initiated language of colour or lines or figures a certain level of mystical experience Dkyil k'an is the hall for initiation, a shrine where a master reveals to his disciple the manner of realising truth which in the lengthy years of apprenticeship he has been explaining to him, as far as the dialectical study and comprehension , purely intellectually the culminating moment arises and the disciple can be admitted to the final communian with the experiences which he has had upto now which are glimmers and fragmentary visions but not the full possession, in the Dkyil k'an a masters confers to the neophite the initiating baptism, abhiṣeka. From this shrine the disciple will leave renovated or born anew because abhiṣeka is the consecration of a final possession of spiritual truth. Therefore in the Dkyil k'an no image and no altar are to be found. There is no longer a reason for the offering to the deity, the gods themselves vanish as mirages. God is in the master. and one of the complex rites of initiating litergy consists in the meditating on the guru himself as a deity and second moment on oneself as transformed into a god or consubstantiated with god. Therefore Dkyil k'an cannot contain other decorations than the maṇḍala, that is the symbolic expression of that world in which the initiated must be reborn. The maṇḍala represented on the walls of this small temple are very important also becausae they give us an idea on the mystical cycles which prevailed in the ancient monastery of Tabo.

The central figure represents Vairocana according to the type, which we have already studied, of the Sarvavid who is white in colour with four faces, sitting in vajraparyaṅka and with his hands folded in dhyānamudrā. All around in different medalliions, various deities reproduced. Evidently the cycle is not the same as the statues of gTug lag k'an. Not even the number of deities matches apart from the six figures, beginning at the top, there does not seem to be any connection with the maṇḍala itself, as they are there to represent different Buddhas to ascetical clothing. The painting is too worn away to enable a precise identification. It must be noted that it cannot be said with absolute certainty that the said painting wishes to reproduce a maṇḍala. On the left wall, on the contrary we have a real maṇḍala with its mudrā, its doors, its arches, toraṇa and its custodians set up to defend the four doors. The arrangement of the deities symbolised is on a cross formation, that is the deity from which the maṇḍala takes its name, is in the centre and others are arranged in the direction of the four cardinal points and of the intermidiate points. The identification of the maṇḍala offers serious difficulties, in view of very poor state of preservation of the frescoes. But the central painting represents a deity with the right hand in bhūmisparśa-mudrā, this would enable us to suppose that the deity represented is Akṣobhya. The maṇḍala to the right in its present condition, cannot be desciphered because the central figure is almost erased. Many other paintings run along the walls of Dkyil k'an.

The paintings of historical character:

To the left of the door on the lower part, in a painted panel three figures of seated monks are reproduced in vajraparyaṅka under padmāsana. The central figure is higher than the other two and has the right shoulder uncovered, differing from the two accolytes who have both shoulders covered by the monastic gown. The three of them have halo, prabhā-maṇḍala. The two lateral figures are in dharmacakramudrā. Identification of these three monks has been possible from the inscription which accompnies the figure. The script is evidently erroneous.

Tabo is explained by the fact that its quality is of Lotsava conferred upon him a dignity higher than that of the other two, during the period in which the works of interpreter of Buddhistic scriptures constituted one of the greatest achievements of religious life. And it is in fact because of this that Zi ba 'od gave the family of the king of Guge a special prestige. The painting on the right of the central wall is not less important. It represents a series of buildings, these buildings we are told by the inscriptions which accompany the frescoes are a sort of panoramic view of the two monasteries indissolubly connected by tradition. i.e. that of Toling and that of Tabo.

Many of the personnages which animate the scene are also accompanied by inscriptions which preserve for us their names monks who are perhaps then famous, if they have had the honour of being remembered on this painting, but completely unknown today. Further specification is impossible.

Minor Temples:

The Byams pa lha k'an does not contain anything special. It has evidently been remade during a recent epoch and the paintings which cover the walls are also recent. On the central wall there remains a great image in stucco of Maitreya seated with his hands in dharmacakramudrā. One of the mural paintings represents a lama Vajra śes rab shown in the same attitude as in the ts'a ts'a. The temple is however ancient, is shown by a base of a column in stone which appears on the floor. There are lions on the four faces of the column. Their rough and primitive style can well be attributed to the first period of the art of guge. Said art shows a singular analogy with the sculptures of me'od rten of Lhalung, probably the ancient temple was destroyed by fire.

In the little temple of aBrom ston, nothing remains of the original chapel beyond the door of deodar, already pointed out by Francke. this door is one of the few monuments, in sculpted wood, of the twelveth century, which is still preserved. The fine work leads us to believe that this too was the work of Indian artists and constitutes a reconfirmation of all that the biography of Rin c'en bzaṅ po has clearly indicated to us. As I said with reference to the two has reliefs in sculpted wood of the gTsug lag k'an, we do not know if these artists were those which the Lotsava himself brought back with him from his Indian pilgrimages from Kashmir or if on the other hand they came during a later period with the other squads of artists invited by the king of Guge or escaping from India because of the spread of the Muslim thunderstorm or the ill-government of the king of Kashmir. In any case the door of this small temple shows a particular analogy with that of Alchi on the bordars almost of Kashmir and makes us think of this country as the place of origin of that refind art, even if often overloaded, of which some other remains can still be admired at Toling.

The temple does not contain any other noteworthy things, because even the pointings have been remade and do not offer, not even from the iconographical point of view, anything new or interesting. Only the images of Amitābha, Vairocana and Śyāma Tārā can be noted.

The aBrom ston lha k'an c'en po is the largest one of all after the gTsug lag k'aṅ, but it is completely empty and descrated. the mural paintings go back probably to the seventeenth century and reproduce the eight deities of medicine.

## COSMOGRAPHIC ANALYSIS OF STTS

### CHAPTER 1 OF THE STTS : VAJRADHĀTUMAHĀ - MAṆḌALA

The first chapter of STTS opens in the conventional manner of Buddhist Mahāyāna Sūtras with a description of the presiding Buddha, here Vairocana, seated in his paradise surrounded by myriads of Bodhisattvas. Eight of them are named as follows: Vajrapāṇi, Avalokiteśvara, Ākāśagarbha, Vajramuṣṭi, Mañjuśrī, Sahacittotpāda-dharma-cakra-pravarti, Gaganagañja, Sarva-mārabala-pramardi. Thereafter Mahāvairocana is praised as: Sarvākāśa-dhātu-sadāvasthita-kāya-vāk-citta-vajra, Sarvavajra-dhātvavabodhana-jñāna-sattva, Sarvākā-śadhātu-paramāṇu-rajo-vajrādhiṣṭhāna-sambhava-jñāna-vajra, Mahāvajra-jñānā-bhiṣeka-ratna, Sarvākāśa-spharaṇa-tathatā-jñānā-bhisambodhya-bhisambodhi-bhūta, Svabhāva-śuddha-sarva-dharma,Sarvākāśa-vyāpi-sarvarūpa-sandarśana-jñāna-śeṣa-navaśeṣa-sattvadhātu-vinayana-caryāgrya, Sarvāsāma-nuttara-viśvakarma. Then he receives the titles of the sixteen forms of All the Tathāgatas: Stg.-mahābodhidṛḍhasattva, Stg.-ākarṣaṇa-samaya, Stg.-anurāgaṇa-jñāna-īśvara, Stg.-sādhukāra, Stg.-mahābhiṣeka-ratna, Stg.-sūryaprabha-maṇḍala, Stg.-Chintā-rājamaṇi-ratna-ketu, Stg.-mahāhāsa, Stg.-mahāśuddha-dharma, Stg.-prajñā-jñāna, Stg.-cakra, Stg.-sandhābhāṣa, Stg.-amoghaviśva-kārya, Stg.-mahavīrya-sudṛḍha-kavaca, Stg.-rakṣā-paripālana-vajra-yakṣa, Stg.-kāyavākcitta-vajra-bandhamudrā-jñāna. (STTS 3-5)

Again he is named as 16 great bodhisattvas with their attributes: Samantabhadra, Māra, Pramodyanāyaka, Khagarbha, Sumahāteja, Ṛatnaketu, Mahāsmita, Avalokitama-heśa, Mañjuśrī, Sarvamaṇḍala, Avāca, Viśvakarma, Vīrya, Caṇḍa, Ḍṛḍhagraha and Vajra, aṅkuśa, śara, tuṣṭi, ratna, sūrya, dhvaja, smita, padma, koṣa, sucakra, vāk, karma, varma, khaya, and graha. (STTS 5)

It is followed by his 76 titles which are the different names of the manifestations of the 16 great bodhisattvas: anādinidhana, śānta, rudra, krodha, mahākṣama, (Vajrasattva); yakṣa, surākṣasa, dhīra, śaurī, māhavibhu, (Vajrarāja). umāpati, prajānātha, viṣṇu, jiṣṇu, mahāmuni, (Vajrarāga); lokapāla, nabha, bhūmi, triloka, tridhātuka, (Vajrasādhu). mahā-bhūta, susattvārtha, sarva, śarva, pitāmaha. (Vajraratna); sansāra, nirvrti, śāśvat, samyag-vṛtti, mahāmahā, (Vajrateja); Buddha, śuddha, mahāyāna, tribhava, śaśvata, hita, (Vajra-ketu); trilokavijayī, śambhū, śambhunātha, pradāmaka, (Vajrahāsa): vajranātha, subhū-myagrya, jñāna-pāramitā, naya, (Vajradharma); vimokṣa, bodhisattva, caryā, sarvatathāgata, (Vajratīkṣṇa); buddhārtha, buddhahṛdaya, sarvabodhi, anuttara, (Vajrahetu); Vairocana, jina, nātha, svayambhū, dhāraṇī, smṛti, (Vajrabhāṣa); mahāsattva, mahāmudrā, samādhi, buddhakarmakṛt, (Vajrakarma); sarvabuddhātmaka, bhūta, sattva, nityārthabodhaka, (Vajra-rakṣa); mahāsthāṇu, mahākāla, mahārāga, mahāsukha, (Vajrayakṣa). mahopāya, mahāgryāgrya, sarvagrya, bhuvaneśvara, (Vajrasandhi) (STTS 6).

Bodhisattva Samantabhadra resides in the hearts of All the Tathāgats who coalesce into one and approach Sarvārtha-siddhi to ask him about the realization of the highest enlightenment and gives him the following mantra: *Om citta prativedham karomi.* Then something in the form of a lunar disc is visible to sarvārthasiddhi whose heart is enlightened by All the Tathāgatas having recited this mantra: *Om bodhicittam utpādayāmi.* Then he can really see the lunar disc and a vajra in it. The vajra element of the body, speech and mind of Stg. as may as they are generally throughout space enter into that vajra with consecration of Stg. and then bodhisattva the lord Sarvārthasiddhi is consecrated by the name consecration of Vajradhātu. Then he says ."*O lord Tathāgatas,* I see myself as the body of Stg." All the Tathāgatas replied: "O great being conceive of yourself as the Vajra of being as the Buddha form which possesses all excellent appearences using this mantra which is naturally successful". *"Om yathāsarvatathāgatās tathāham"* Saying this Vajradhātu the Great Bodhisattva knew himself to be Tathāgata and he bowed before Stg. and said. "consecrate me O lord Tathāgatas and stabilise this enlightenment". When he says this All the tathāgatas enter the vajra of being of the Tathāgata Vajradhātu. Thus Vajradhātu is enlightened perfectly (STTS 7-10)

Tathāgatas Akṣobhya, Ratnasambhava, Lokeśvararāja and Amoghasiddhi consecrate themselves in all the Tathāgata state and position themselves in four directions while conceiving all the directions of the compass as being the same in that they are suffused with the universal sameness of the Tathāgata Śākyamuni. (STTS 10)

It is followed by the manifestations of the deities of the Vajradhātu-mahā-maṇḍala. Bhagavān Vairocana enters a different samādhi every time for the emergence of the deities. Names of the samādhis for the 16 great Bodhisattvas.

1. Stg.-samantabhadra-mahābodhisattva-samaya-sambhava
2. Amogharāja-mahā-bodhisattva-samaya-sambhava
3. Māra-mahābodhisattva-samaya-sambhava
4. Prāmodyarāja-mahā-bodhisattva-samaya-sambhava
5. Ākāśagarbha-mahā-bodhisattva-samaya-sambhava
6. Mahāteja-mahā-bodhisattva-samaya-sambhava
7. Ratnaketu-mahā-bodhisattva-samaya-sambhava
8. Nityaprītipramuditendriya-mahā-bodhisattva-samaya-sambhava
9. Avalokiteśvara-mahābodhisattva-samaya-sambhava
10. Mañjuśrī-mahābodhisattva-samaya-sambhava
11. Sahacittotpada-saddharma-cakravarti-mahā-bodhisattva-samaya-sambhava
12. Avāca-mahā-bodhisattva-samaya-sambhava
13. Stg.-viśvakarma-mahā-bodhisattva-samaya-sambhava
14. Duryodhanavīrya-mahā-bodhisattva-samaya-sambhava

15. Sarvamāra-pramardi-mahā-bodhisattva-samaya-sambhava
16. Stg.-muṣṭi-mahā-bodhisattva-samaya-sambhava

After entering these samādhis Vairocana utters the essences of all the above mentioned deities from his heart as follows:

1. Mahāyānābhisamaya (Vajrasattva)
2. Stg.-ākarṣaṇa-samaya (Vajrarāja)
3. Stg.-anurāgaṇa-samaya (Vajrarāga)
4. Stg.-pramoda-samaya (Vajrasādhu)
5. Stg.-abhiṣeka-samaya (Vajraratna)
6. Stg.-raśmisamaya (Vajrateja)
7. Stg.-āśāparipūrṇa-samaya (Vajraketu)
8. Stg.-prītisamaya (Vajrahāsa)
9. Stg.-dharma-samaya (Vajradharma)
10. Stg.-mahā-prajñā-jñāna-samaya (Vajratīkṣṇa)
11. Stg.-cakra-samaya (Vajrahetu)
12. Stg.-jāpa-samaya (Vajrabhāṣa)
13. Stg.-karma- samaya (Vajrakarma)
14. Stg.-rakṣa-samaya (Vajrarakṣa)
15. Stg.-upāya samaya (Vajrayakṣa)
16. Stg.-kāya-vāk-citta-vajra-bandha-samaya (Vajrasandhi)

This is proceded by a sequence of the emergence of all these deities:

1. Samantabhadra→lunar discs→jñāna-vajras→singal-vajra→rays→Samantabhadra→vajrapāṇi
2. Vajrapāṇi→Stg.-mahāṅkuśāṇi→vajrāṅkuśa→mahāvigraha→Amoghavajra-mahābodhisattva→Vajrākarṣa
3. Vajradhara→flower attributes of Stg.-mahāvajra-vāṇa-vigraha→Māramahā-bodhisattva→Vajradhanu
4. Vajradhara→sādhukāra→vajratuṣṭi-vigraha→prāmodyarāja-mahābodhisattva→Vajraharṣa
5. Vajradhara→Sarvākāśaraśmayaḥ→mahāvajra-ratna-vigraha→Ākāśagarbha-mahābodhisattva→Vajragarbha
6. Vajrapāṇi→mahāsūrya-maṇḍalāni→Vajrasūrya-vigraha→mahāteja-mahābodhisattva→Vajraprabha
7. Vajradhara→patākā→vajradhvajāgra-vigraha→Ratna-ketu-mahā-bodhisattva→Vajrayaṣṭi
8. Vajradhara→Stg.-smitāni→Vajra-smita-virgraha→Nitya-pramuditendriya-mahābodhisattva→Vajraprīti
9. Vajradhara → saddharma-raśmayaḥ→ mahā-padma-vigraha→Avalokiteśvara-mahābo-

dhisattva→Vajra-netra

10. Vajradhara→prajñā-astrāṇi→vajra-koṣa-vigraha→mañjuśrī-mahā-bodhisattva→ Vajrabuddhi

11. Vajradhara→Vajradhātu-mahāmaṇḍalāni→vajra-cakra-vigraha→sahacittotpāda-dharma-cakra-pravarti-mahābodhisattva→Vajra-maṇḍa

12. Vajrapāṇi→Stg.-dharmākṣarāṇi→vajra-jāpa-vigraha→Avāca-mahābodhisattva→ Vajravāca

13. Vajradhara→Stg.-karma-raśmayaḥ→karma-vajra-vigraha→Stg.-viśvakarma-mahā-bodhisattva→Vajraviśva

14. Vajradhara→dṛdha-kavacāni→vajrakavaca-vigraha→ḍuryodhana-vīrya-mahābodhi-sattva→Vajramitra

15. Vajradhara→Mahādaṇṣṭrāyudhāni→vajra-daṇṣṭra-vigraha→sarvamāra-pramardi-mahābodhisattva→Vajra-caṇḍa

16. Vajradhara→Sarvatathāgata-sarva - mudrā-bandha →vajra-bandha-vigraha→Stg.-muṣṭi-mahābodhisattva→Vajra-muṣṭi

Their characteristics and attributes can be tabulised as follows:

| Deity | Attribute | Characteristic |
|---|---|---|
| Vajrasattva | siddhivajra | cittasantoṣaṇa |
| Vajrarāja | vajrāṅkuśa | ākarṣaṇa |
| Vajrarāga | vajravāṇa | māraṇa |
| Vajrasādhu | vajratuṣṭi | praharṣaṇa |
| Vajraratna | vajramaṇi | maṇisthāpana |
| Vajrateja | vajrasūrya | avabhāsana |
| Vajraketu | vajradhvaja | dānapāramitāyān-niyojana |
| Vajrahāsa | vajrasmita | praharṣaṇa |
| Vajradharma | vajrapadma | rāgavisuddhi-nilepana-svabhā-vavaloka-natayava-lokayan |
| Vajratīkṣṇa | vajrakoṣa | prahāra |
| Vajrahetu | vajracakra | pratiṣṭhāpana |
| Vajrabhāṣa | vajrajāpa | sanlāpana |
| Vajrakarma | karmavajra | Stg.-karmatāyām-niyojana |
| Vajrarakṣa | vajravarma | kavacana |
| Vajrayakṣa | vajradaṇṣṭra | āyudham svamukhe pratisthāpana |
| Vajrasandhi | vajrabandha | bandhana (STTS 11-42) |

These 16 Bodhisattvas are followed by 4 pāramitās, 4 interior Pūjābodhisattvas,

4 exterior Pūjābodhisattvas and 4 saṅgraha bodhisattvas:

| pāramitās | int.pūjābodhisat. | ex.Pūjābodhisat. | saṅgrahabodhisat. |
|---|---|---|---|
| Sattvavajrī | Vajralāsyā | Vajradhūpā | Vajrāṅkuśa |
| Ratnavajrī | Vajramālā | Vajrapuṣpā | Vajrapāśa |
| Dharmavajrī | Vajragītā | Vajrālokā | Vajrasphoṭa |
| Karmavajrī | Vajranṛtyā | Vajragandhā | Vajrāveśa |

The five Tathāgatas enter different types of samādhis for them:

| no. | deity | Tathāgata | Samādhi |
|---|---|---|---|
| 22. | Sattvavajrī | Akṣobhya | Vajra-pāramitā-samayodbhava |
| 23. | Ratnavajrī | Ratnasambhava | Ratnapāramitā-samayodbhava |
| 24. | Dharmavajrī | Lokeśvararāja | Dharma-pāramitā-samayodbhava |
| 25. | Karmavajrī | Amoghasiddhi | Karma-pāramitā-samayodbhava |
| 26. | Vajralāsyā | Vairocana | Stg.-rati-pūjā-samaya-sambhava |
| 27. | Vajramālā | " | Stg.-ratna-mālābhiṣeka-samaya-s. |
| 28. | Vajragītā | " | Stg.-saṅgīti-samaya-sambhava |
| 29. | Vajranṛtyā | " | Stg.-nṛtya-pūjā-samaya-sambhava |
| 30. | Vajradhūpā | Akṣobhya | Stg.-prahlādana-samayodbhava |
| 31. | Vajrapuṣpā | Ratnasambhava | ratnābharaṇa-pūjā-samaya-s. |
| 32. | Vajrālokā | Lokeśvararāja | Stg.-āloka-pūjā-samaya-sambhava |
| 33. | Vajragandhā | Amoghasiddhi | Stg.-gandhapūjā-samaya-sambhava |
| 34. | Vajrāṅkuśa | Vairocana | Stg.-samayāṅkuśa-mahāsattva-samaya-sambhava |
| 35. | Vajrapāśa | " | Stg.-samaya-praveśa-mahāsattva-samaya-sambhava |
| 36. | Vajrasphoṭa | " | Stg.-samaya-sphoṭa-mahāsattva-samaya-sambhava |
| 37. | Vajrāveśa | " | Stg.-aveśa-mahāsattva-samaya-sambhava |

They emerge in the following sequences:

22. Vajradhara→Vajra-raśmayaḥ→Tathāgata-vigraha→mahāvajra-vigraha
23. Vajradhara→ratna-raśmayaḥ→Tathāgatavigraha→mahāvajra-vigraha
24. Vajradhara→padmaraśmayaḥ→Tathāgatavigraha→mahāvajra-padma-vigraha
25. Vajradhara→sarvakarma-raśmayaḥ→Tathāgatavigraha→mahā-karma-vigraha
26. Vajradhara→vajramudrā→Tathāgata-vigraha→mahādevī-vajra-sattva-dayitā
27. Vajradhara→mahāratna-mudrā→Tathāgata-vigraha→vajra-mālā-mahādevī
28. Vajradhara→Stg.-dharma-mudrā→Tathāgata-vigraha→Vajragītā-mahādevī
29. Vajradhara→STg.-nṛtya-pūjā-vidhi-vistara→Tathāgata-vigraha→Vajranṛtya-mahādevī
30. Vajradhara→dhūpapūjā-megha-vyūha→Tathāgata-vigraha-Vajradhūpā-devatā
31. Vajradhara→sarvapuṣpa→pūjā-vyūha→Tathāgata-vigraha→Vajrapuṣpa-devatā

32. Vajradhara→sarvaloka-pūjā-vyūha→Tathāgata-vigraha→Vajraloka-devatā
33. Vajradhara→sarvagandha-pūjā-vyūha→Tathāgata-vigraha→Vajragandha-devatā
34. Vajradhara→Stg.-sarvamudrā-gaṇa→Tathāgata-vigraha→Vajrāṅkuśa-mahābodhisattva
35. Vajradhara→mudrāgaṇa→Tathāgatavigraha→Vajrapāśa-mahābodhisattva
36. Vajradhara→Stg.-samaya-bandha-mudrā-gaṇa→Tathāgata-vigraha→Vajrasphota-mahābodhisattva
37. Vajradhara→Stg.-sarvamudrā-gaṇa→Tathāgata-vigraha→Vajrāveśa-mahābodhisattva

They have different names according to their groups.

1. Sarvatathāgata-pāramitāḥ:

| | |
|---|---|
| 22. Stg.-jñāna-samayā | in front of Vairocana |
| 23. Mahābhiṣekā | on the right of Vairocana |
| 24. Vajradharmatā | on the back of Vairocana |
| 25. Sarvapūjā | on the left of Vairocana |

2. Sarvatathāgata-guhya-pūjāḥ:

| | |
|---|---|
| 26. Stg.-anuttarasukha-saumanasya samayā | on the left of Akṣobhya-maṇḍala |
| 27. Stg.-mālā | on the left of Ratnasambhava maṇaḍala |
| 28. Stg.-gāthā | on the left of Lokeśvara-rāja-maṇḍala |
| 29. Stg.-anuttara-pūjā-karma-karī | on the left of Amoghasiddhi-maṇḍala |

3. Sarvatathāgata-ajñākāryaḥ:

| | |
|---|---|
| 30. Stg.-jñānāveṣa | left side of the corner |
| 31. Mahābodhyaṅga-saṁcaya | left corner |
| 32. Stg.-dharmālokā | left corner |
| 33. śīlasamādhi-prajñā-vimukti-mukti-jñāna-darśana-gandhā | left corner |

4. Sarvatathāgatājñākaraḥ:

| | |
|---|---|
| 34. Sarvatathāgata-samakarṣaṇam | in the vajra-dvāra |
| 35. praveśa | in the ratna-dvāra |
| 36. bandha | in the dharma-dvāra |
| 37. Vaśīkaraṇa | in the karma-dvāra (STTS 42-59) |

Introduction to the 37 deities of the maṇḍala is followed by foot worship, pāda-vandanam of All the Tathāgatas by Vairocana. All the Tathāgatas invocate Mahāvajradhara, the great vajra holder with 108 names which are the variations of the names of 16 great bodhisattvas: (STTS 59-60)

(6. Vajrasattva). Vajrasattva, Mahāsattva, Vajrasarva-tathāgata, Samantabhadra, Vajrapāṇi.

(7. Vajrarāja). Vajrarāja, Subuddhāgrya, Vajrāṅkuśa, Tathāgata, Amogharāja, Vajrāgrya, Vajrākarṣa,

(8. Vajrarāga) : Vajrarāga, Mahāsaukhya, Vajravāṇa, Vavsaṅkara, Mārakāma, Mahāvajra, Vajracāpa.

(9. Vajrasādhu) : Vajrasādhu, Susattvāgrya, Vajratuṣṭi, Mahārati, Prāmodyarāja, Vajrāgrya, Vajraharṣa.

(10. Vajraratna). Vajraratna, Suvajrārtha, Vajrākāśa, Mahāmani, Ākāśagarbha, Vajrāḍhya, Vajragarbha.

(11. Vajrateja) : Vajrateja, Mahājvālā, Vajrasūrya, Jinaprabha, Vajraraśmi, Mahāteja, Vajraprabha.

(12. Vajraketu) : Vajraketu, Susattvārtha, Vajrādhvaja, Sutoṣaka, Ratnaketu, Mahāvajra, Vajrayaṣṭi.

(13. Vajrahāsa) : Vajrahāsa, Mahāhāsa, Vajrasmita, Mahābhūta, Prītiprāmodya, Vajrāgrya, Vajraprīti.

(14. Vajradharma) :Vajradharma, Susattvārtha, Vajrapadma, Sushodhaka, Lokeśvara, Suvajrākṣa, Vajranetra.

(15. Vajratīkṣṇa) : Vajratīkṣṇa, Mahāyāna, Vajrakośa, Mahāyudha, Mañjuśrī, Vajragāmbhīrya, Vajrabuddhi.

(16. Vajrahetu) : Vajrahetu, Mahāmaṇḍa, Vajracakra, Mahānaya, Supravartana, Vajrottha, Vajramaṇḍa.

(17. Vajrabhāṣa) : Vajrabhāṣa, Suvidyāgrya, Vajrajāpa, Susiddhida, Avāca, Vajrasiddhyagrya, Vajrāvāca.

(18. Vajrakarma) : Vajrakarma, Suvajrajña, Karmavajra, Susarvaga, Vajrāmogha Mahodārya, Vajraviśva.

(19. Vjrarakṣa). Vajrarakṣa, Mahadhairya, Vajravarama, Mahādṛḍha, Duryodhana, Suvīryagrya, Vajravīrya

(20. Vajraykṣa). Vajrayakṣa, Mahopāya, Vajradanṣṭra, Mahābhaya, Mārapramardī, Vajrogra, Vajracaṇḍa,

(21. Vajrasandhi) :Vajrasandhi, Susānnidhya, Vajrabandha, Pramocaka, Vajramuṣṭi, Agrasamaya,

After reciting these 108 names he relates the importance of its japa. Bhagavān Vajradhara listens to these words and enters the samādhi called vajra consecration which has its origin in the samaya of All the Tathāgatas and procedes towards the delineation of the Vajradhātumahāmaṇḍala. The following ritual proceeds this delineation: praveśāvidhi of a vajraśiśya, vajrācāryakarma, śiśyapraveśa, prāṇamacatuṣṭaya, sattvavajri-mudra, mālā-granthana, praveśa, Krodha-muṣṭi, Mahāmaṇaḍala-darśana.

After showing the mahāmaṇḍala he is positioned by Stg. and Vajrasattva places himself in his heart. Sometimes Bhagavan Mahavajradhara shows himself. After showing the maṇḍala He should be consecrated by the perfumed water placed in a vase on a vajra reciting this mantra: *Vajrābhiṣiñca.* Having placed this attribute in his hands he should utter this verse:

*Adyābhiṣiktastvam asi Buddhair vajrābhiṣekataḥ/*
*idam te sarva Buddhatvam gṛhṇa vajram susiddhaye//*
*Om vajrādhipati tvam abhiṣiñcāmi-tiṣṭha vajra-samayas tvam.*

Then he is to be consecrarated by the vajra name consecration with this mantra: *Om vajra-sattva tvam abhiṣiñcāmi vajra-nāmābhi-ṣekataḥ he vajranāma.* Whatever name is given that should be uttered with the word he. Then he should be asked what is his interest, is he interested in the arthotpattisiddhi-jñāna, ṛddhisiddhi-niṣpattijñāna, vidyādhara-siddhi-niṣpattijñāna, or the sarvatathāgatottama-siddhi-niṣpatti-jñāna. All of these types of knowledge are explained one by one so that everbody can take its advantage. This is to be followed by rahasya-dhāraṇakṣama. Which is to be preceded by chapathahṛdaya

*Om vajrasattvaḥ svayan te 'dya hṛdaye samavasthitaḥ/*
*nirbhidya tat kṣaṇam yadi brūyād idan nayam//*

The follwing mudrās are to be taught afterwards: rahasyamudrā jñānam, vajratālamudrā, its esoteric sādhana. Knowledge of four mudrās of own family should be taught and should be instructed that this is not to be told to an unappropriate because of his lack of knowledge. Now there follows the knowledge of mahāmudrā of sattvasādhana of all the Tathāgatas, Sarvatathāgatābhisambodhi-mudrā, vajra-sattva-sādhana-mahā-mudrā - bandha and the description of making mahā-mudrā-sādhana. It is proceeded by vajrāvesá-hṛdaya, mahāsattvānusmṛti-hṛdaya and mahāsattvākarṣaṇa-praveśana-bandhana-vaśīkaraṇa-hṛdaya. They are followed by the vajra-samaya, dharma- and karma-mudrās of Stg. Then there should be a general description of all the mudrās and also of sādhana, arthasiddhi, vajrasiddhi, vajra-vidyādhara-siddhi and uttamasiddhi is to be attained by different types of mantras. Again there is a general description of all the mudrās, their mokṣavidhi. After performing rituals again there is a word about its esoterism and thus the first chapter ends with this hṛdaya

*Om kṛto vaḥ sarvasattvārthaḥ siddhir datta yathānuga/*
*gacchadhvam buddhavisayam punarāgamanāya tu//*

Its colophon is: *Sarvatathāgatamahāyānabhisamayān mahākalparājād Vajradhātumahāmaṇḍala-vidhi-vistaraḥ samāptaḥ.*

## CHAPTER 2 OF THE STTS : VAJRA-GUHYA-VAJRA-MAṆḌALA

Vajrapāṇi emerges in a multiplicity of the deities in the form of symbolic mudrās of Vajradhāraṇīs after a due concentration, having flames within, having accomplished the knowledge of vajradhāraṇīs of All the Tathāgatas of All the Buddhas in all the Lokadhātus, having become the essence of samaya of All the Tathāgates after resting in lunar disks. "Oh hitaiṣitā of all the sattvas of Bodhicitta, that out of humility feminine forms are also manifested." The five Tathāgatas utter their vidyottamās as follows.

1. Vajrapāṇi Vajradhātvīśvarī Stg.-jñāna-mudrā-samaya-vajradhātvadhiṣṭhāna --
2. Akṣobhya Vajravajriṇī Stg.-sattvasamaya-jñāna-mudrā-maṇḍalādhiṣṭh āna
3. Ratnasambhava Ratnavajrī Stg.-vajra-ratna-samaya-jñāna-mudrā-maṇḍalā-dhiṣṭhāna
4. Amitāyu Dharmavajrī Stg.-vajra-dharma-samaya-jñāna-mudrā-maṇḍa-lādhiṣṭhāna
5. Amoghasiddhi Karmavajriṇī Stg.-vajra-karma-samaya-jñāna-mudrā-maṇḍ-alādhiṣṭhāna

Vajrapāṇi recites the four samaya mudrās of the great dhāraṇīs of All the Tathāgatas which are the feminine forms of the essence that is śakti of the sixteen great bodhisattvas. Vajradhāraṇīs:

6. Samantabhadrā: symbolic form of esoteric Vajrasattva, *Om vajrasattva guhya-samaye-hūm.*
7. Tathāgatāṅkuśī. esoteric feminine form of Vajrarāja, who is also named Vajrāṅkuśa, because of aṅkuśa as his attribute: *Om guhya vajrāṅkuśī.*
8. Ratirāgā: feminine esoteric form of Vajrarāga. *Om vajraguhye rāge rāgaya hūm.*
9. Sādhumatī: feminine form of esoteric Vajrasādhu: *Om guhye vajradhātvīśvarī.*

Ratnadhāraṇīs:

10. Ratnottama: symbolic form of esoteric Vajraratna: *Om vajra-guhya-ratna-samaye hūm.*
11. Ratnolkā: feminine form of esoteric Vajraprabhā:-*Om vajra-guhya-prahe hūm.*
12. Dhvajāgrakeyurā: feminine form of esoteric Vajradhvajāgra or ketu: *Om vajradhva jāgra-guhye hūm.*
13. Hāsavatī. feminine form of esoteric Vajrahāsa. : *Om guhya hāsavajrī hūm.*

Dharmadhāraṇīs.

14. Vajrāmbujā: feminine form of esoteric Vajradharma: *Om vajra-dharma-guhya-samaye hūm.*
15. Ādhāraṇī: feminine esoteric form of Vajrakośa or tīkṣṇa. *Om vajra-kośa-guhye hūm.*
16. Sarvacakrā: feminine symbolic form of esoteric vajramaṇḍalā :*Om vajra-guhya maṇḍalā.*
17. Sahasrāvartā: feminine symbolic form of esoteric Vajra-jāpa: *Om vajra-guhya-jāpa-samaye hūm.*
18. Siddhottarā: feminine form of esoteric vajrakarma: *Om vajra-guhya-karma-samaye-hūm.*
19. Sarva-rakṣa: feminine form of esoteric Vajra-kavaca: *Om vajra-guhya-kavace hūm.*
20. Tejaḥpratyāhāriṇī: feminine form of Vajra-daṇṣṭra: *Om guhya-vajra-danṣṭra-dhāriṇī hūm.*

21. Dhāraṇīmudrā: feminine form of esoteric Vajramuṣṭi: *Om vajra-guhya-muṣṭi hūm.*

Sometimes the nomenclaure of these great bodhisattvas in their dhāraṇīs is identical with their names in the first chapter and at times they correspond to their feminine forms but still there are exceptions.

| Chapter 1. | feminine forms | names in dharanis. |
|---|---|---|
| 6. Vajrasattva | Samantabhadrā | Vajrasattva |
| 7. Vajrarāja | Tathāgatāṅkuśī | Vajrāṅkuśa |
| 8. Vajrarāga | Ratirāgā | Vajrarāga |
| 9. Vajrasādhu | Sādhumatī | Vajrasādhu |
| 10. Vajraratna | Ratnottamā | Vajraratna |
| 11. Vajrateja | Vajrālokā | Vajraprabha |
| 12. Vajraketu | Dhvajrāgrakeyūrā | Vajradhvajāgra |
| 13. Vajrahāsa | Hāsavatī | Hāsavajrī |
| 14. Vajradharma | Vajrāmbujā | Vajradharma |
| 15. Vajratīkṣṇa | Ādhāraṇī | Vajrakośa |
| 16. Vajraketu | Sarvacakrā | Vajramaṇḍala |
| 17. Vajrabhāṣa | Sahasrāvartā | Vajrajāpa |
| 18. Vajrakarma | Siddhottarā | Vajrakarma |
| 19. Vajrarakṣa | Sarvarakṣā | Vajrakavaca |
| 20. Vajrayakṣa | Tejaḥpratyāhāriṇī | Vajradaṇṣṭra |
| 21. Vajrasandhi | Dhāraṇīmudrā | Vajramuṣṭi |

Then Vajrapāṇi utters the four esoteric samaya mudrās of vajra family of four Pāramitās.

22. Sattvavajrī. *Om guhya-sattva-vajrī hūm.*
23. Ratnavajrī. *Om guhya-ratna-vajrī hūm.*
24. Dharmavajrī. *Om guhya-dharma-vajrī hūm.*
25. Karmavajrī. *Om guhya-karma-vajrī hūm.*

These pāramitās are the symbolic mudrās of the dharma-saṅgraha of All the Tathāgatas. All the deities from Vajradhātvīśvarī onwards should be surrounded by flames and stationed in luṇar discs. Vajrapāṇi once more recites the four samaya-mudrās of the four pūjā-devīs.

26. Vajralāsyā. feminine symbolic form of esoteric Vajra-rati-pūjā is to commence all typs of worship. *Om vajraguhya-rati-pūja-samaye-hūm*
27. Vajramālā. feminine symbolic form of esoteric consecration worship: *Om vajra-guhyā-bhiṣeka-pūjā-samaye-sarva-pūjām pravartaya hūm.*
28. Vajragītā. feminine symbolic form of Vajragītā-pūjā. *Om vajra-gīta-pūjā-samaye sarva pūjām pravartaya.*
29. Vajranṛyā: feminine symbolic form of esoteric vajra-nṛtya-pūjā: *Om vajra-*

*guhya-nṛtya-pūjā-samaye sarva-pūjām pravartayahūm.*

The above mentioned four deities Lāsyā etc. are to be drawn with flames, atrributes and postures in the corners of the cakramaṇḍala

Vajrapāṇi instructs about the rules of delineating the mahāvajra-maṇḍala which is named as vajra-guhya. After delineation comes the praveśa-vidhi of the maṇḍala. There, first the vajrācārya himself makes a mudrā and enters the maṇḍala, takes a round around it, offers the mudra to Vajrapāṇi, performs all the necessary rituals, comes out and makes his student enter the maṇḍala like the Vajradhātu-mahāmaṇḍala. He starts to teach about the knowledge of vajra-guhya-mudrā. First of all he tells about the vajraguhya-kāya-mudrā-jñāna followed by vajra-guhya-dṛṣṭi-mudrā-jñāna, vajra-guhya-vāṅ-mudrā-jñāna, vajra-guhya-citta-mudrā-jñāna, vajra-guhya-mudrā-jñāna. Again he teaches about the vajra-guhya-mudrā-bandha, mokṣa, dṛḍhīkaraṇa, bandha-samaya. Thus ends the chapter with this colophon. *Sarvatathāgatamahāyānābhisamayān Mahākalparājād Vajraguhyavajra-maṇḍalavidhivistaraḥ samāptaḥ* (STTS 100-115)

## CHAPTER 3 OF THE STTS: VAJRA-JÑĀNA-DHARMA-MAṆḌALA

This third chapter is named vajra-jñāna-dharma-maṇḍala. It begins with the samādhi of Vairocana. Vairocana enters the samādhi called consecration of the samaya maṇḍala of mudrā of subtle vajra knowledge of All the Tathāgatas and utters his vidyo-ttamā as. *Om sūkṣma-vajra-jñāna-samaya hūm*. Akṣobhya enters the samādhi called consecration of the samaya-maṇḍala of the subtle knowledge of Vajraratna of All the Tathāgatas and says: *Om vajra-ratna-sūkṣma-jñāna-samaya-hūm*. Thereafter follow the samādhis of Amitāyu and Amoghasiddhi named consecrations of samaya-maṇḍalas of subtle knowledge of Vajra-dharma and Vajra-karma. They utter their vidyottamās in this respect. *Om vajra-dharma-sūkṣma-jñāna-samaya hūm* and *Om vajra-karma-sūkṣma-jñāna-samaya hūm*.

| deities | names of samādhis | deities' names in dhāraṇis |
|---|---|---|
| 1. Vairocana | Stg.-sūkṣma-vajra-jñāna-mudrā-samaya-maṇḍaladhiṣṭhāna | Sūkṣma-vajra-jñāna-samaya |
| 2. Akṣobhya | Stg.-vajra-sattva-sūkṣma-jñāna-samaya-maṇḍalādhiṣṭhāna | Vajra-sattva-sūkṣma-jñāna-samaya |
| 3. Ratnasambhava | Stg.-vajra-ratna-sūkṣma-jñāna-samaya-maṇḍalādhiṣṭhāna | Vajra-ratna-sūkṣma-jñāna-samaya |

| | | |
|---|---|---|
| 4. Amitāyu | Stg.-vajra-dharma-sūkṣma-jñāna-samayamaṇḍalādhiṣṭhāna | Vajra-dharma-sūkṣma-jñāna-samaya |
| 5. Amoghasiddhi | Stg.-vajra-karma sūkṣma-jñāna-samaya-maṇḍalādhiṣṭhāna | Vajra-karma-sūkṣma-jñāna-samaya |

After usual manifestations Vairocana utters four essences of the great knowledge: *Mahā-jñāna-hṛdaya-catuṣṭayam.* The first four great bodhisattvas are the great vajra consecrations. Sattva means existence, being, entity, reality, the existence of a supremee being (Monier Williams 1135). His essence of the knowledge mudrā is: *vajrātmaka.* The second bodhisattva is Vajrarāja. Rāja is replaced by samājādhiṣṭhāna, his essence is . *Hṛd vajrāṅkuśa.* Aṅkuśa or a hook is an attribute of Vajrarāja which has a power of attraction. In the first chapter (STTS p.14) Vajrarāja named as Amogharāja himself says that all pervading Buddhas are coarced in hook: *yat sarvavyāpino buddhāḥ samākṛṣyanti siddhaya.* Thus hook is his hṛdaya, his power. The third great bodhisattva Vajrarāga is Rāgavajra, who is praised for entering the heart: *tiṣṭa rāgavajra praviśa hṛdayam.* Rāga and anurāga belong to the same root and mean love affection, passion etc. (Monier Willions 37,872). As a concentration he is named knowledge-mudrā of Stg.-anurāgaṇa. Vajrasādhu has tuṣṭi as his attribute. He is named knowledge mudrā of mahātuṣṭi, his essence is: *aho vajratuṣṭi*

| deity | dhāraṇi | Stg.-mahāvajra-samādhi |
|---|---|---|
| 6. Vajrasattva | *Vajrātmaka* | Vajrasattva-jñāna-mudrā |
| 7. Vajrarāja | *Hṛd-vajrāṅkuśa* | Stg.-samājādhiṣṭhāna-jñāna-mudraḥ |
| 8. Vajrarāga | *Tiṣṭha rāgavajra-praviśa hṛdayam* | Stg.-anurāgaṇa-jñāna-mudraḥ |
| 9. Vajrasādhu | *Aho vajratuṣṭi* | Mahātuṣṭi-jñāna-mudraḥ |

Vajrasamādhis are proceeded by Ratnasamādhis:

| | | |
|---|---|---|
| 10. Vajraratna | *Vajraratnātmaka* | Stg.-vajrābhiṣeka-jñāna-mudraḥ |
| 11. Vajrateja | *Hṛdaya-vajra-sūrya* | Mahāprabhā-maṇḍala-vyūha-jñāna-mudraḥ |
| 12. Vajraketu | *Tiṣtha vajra dhvajā-gra vam* | Stg.-āśāparipūrṇa-jñāna-mudraḥ |
| 13. Vajrasmita | *Hyrdaya Vajrahāsa* | Stg.-mahā-jñāna-mudraḥ (STTS 116-120) |

Gem is Cintāmaṇi which is related to consecration, tejas means glow, slendour, brilliance, light, luster etc. (Monier Williams 454). Which has a relation with a circle of rays around a crown or head or body. Thus Vajrateja is the knowledge-mudrā of a multitude of great circles or rays. As it originates from the Sun, his essence is: *hṛdaya vajrasūrya.* In the first verse (STTS p. 23) of the first chapter uttered by Vajraketu, he says that he is an insignia of the universal perfection, fulfilled hopes and consumated things. So as a ratnasamādhi he is called knowledge-mudrā of hopes of All the Tathāgatas that are fulfilled. In his hṛdaya he is called Vajradhvajāgra, as Vajraketu or a flag with a thunderbolt is his attribute. Next comes Bodhisattva Vajrasmita who is named Vajrahāsa and Stg.-mahāhāsa-jñāna-mudrā, mudrā of knowledge of great smile, the fourth Ratnasamādhi.

Next are the four dharma-samādhis of Stg. Their hṛdayas originate from the vajra reflection, *Vajrabimba*. The first is vajra, whose hṛdaya is: *Vajrapadmātmaka,* lotus is the symbol of dharma. He is a mudrā of knowledge of equality of all the dharmas: *sarva-dharma-samatā-jñāna-mudraḥ.* Vajratīkṣṇa has a sword as his attribute, his hṛdaya is: *hṛd vajrakośa.* In the first chapter in the first verse uttered by him he says that he is a gentle sound which is actually the formless knowledge. Again in the next verse he says that this is the perfection of knowledge: *prajñā pāramitānayam*. Thus he is the mudrā of knowledge of knowledge of prajñā of All the Buddhas. *Sarvatathāgata-prajñāna-jñāna-mudraḥ.* Vajrahetu is vajracakra and the mudra of the knowledge of entering the great cakra. *tiṣṭha vajracakra hṛdayam praviśa* and *mahācakra praveśa-jñāna-mudrā*. Vajrabhāṣa has a direct relation to tongue, his hṛdaya is: *vajra-jihvāgra hṛdaya.* Vajrabhāṣa is thought to be enigmas in the first chapter (STTS p.33) which teaches the religion without prolixity of words. That is why in this chapter he is named mudrā of knowledge of the absence of prolixity of words of the religion of All the Tathāgatas: *Stg.-dharma-vāg-niḥprapañca-jñāna-mudraḥ*. (STTS 120-121)

Now a group of four essences emerge from the subtle vajra-bimba of Vajrakarma, Vajrarakṣa, Vajrayakṣa and Vajramuṣṭi as. *sarvavajrātmaka, hṛd vajrakavaca, tiṣṭha vajra-yakṣa hṛdaya and vajra-muṣṭi hṛdaya,* Vajrakarma is irresistible universal action of the Buddhas (STTS 35), thus he is the mudrā of knowledge of the universal action of: *Sarvatathāgata-viśva-karma-jñāna-mudraḥ*. Vajrarakṣa is Vajrakavaca because of his attribute and he is Duryodhana-vīrya-jñāna-mudraḥ because of his bravery. The epithet occurs in the first chapter also (STTS 37-8). Vajrayakṣa has the same epithet in his essence. *tiṣṭha vajra-yakṣa-hṛdaya,* but he is the mudrā of knowledge of destroying the maṇḍala of all the evil beings. *sarva-māra-maṇḍala-vidhvansana-jñāna-mudraḥ* as a dharma samādhi. Vajrasamādhi has become Vajramuṣṭi: *vajra-muṣṭi-hṛdaya*. In the first chapter Vajrasandhi is the very firm bond, *sudṛdhaḥ bandhaḥ* (STTS 41). The same quality is mentioned here: *Sarvatathāgata-bandha jñāna-mudraḥ*.

Bhagavān Vajrapāṇi emerges out of the bodies of the Stg. for the suffusion of subtle knowledge and himself attains the form of Stg. again he becomes all the great Bodhisattva as Vajrasattva, all of their symbols are established in their hearts, they take positions in lunar discs to enter the Vajradhātu-maṇḍala and attain the samādhi of their own hearts.

Then Vajrapāṇi relates the Vajra-sūkṣma-jñāna-maṇḍala for producing the recognition of knowledge of samadhi of Stg. Thereafter follows akarsanadividhi-vistara proceeded by instructing the knowledge of great mudrā of svacittaparikarma after doing praveśādividhi according to the mahāmaṇḍala and giving the symbols. Then he should instruct Stg.-anusmṛti-jñāna, Stg.-dharmatā-rahasya-mudrā-jñāna, Stg.-jñāna-vajrādhiṣṭhāna-samādhi-mudrā-jñāna, Vajrasattva-samadhi-mudrā-jñāna and Sarvatathāgata-kula-samādhi-samaya-mudrā-jñāna

Thus ends the third chapter with the following colophon. Sarvatathāgata-mahāyānābhi-samayān Mahākalpa-rājād Vajrajñāna-dharma-maṇḍalavidhi-vistaraḥ parisamāptaḥ. (STTS 122-129)

## CHAPATER 4 OF THE STTS. VAJRA-KĀRYA-KARMA-MAṆḌALA

The fourth chapter Vajramaṇḍala of acts to be performed, the vajrakārya-karma maṇḍala leads towards Buddhahood by means of worship, generally known as the pūjā-maṇḍala. The sixteen great beings appear in their feminine or pūjā forms. The chapter opens up with Vairocana's concentration. He utters his vidyottamā as: *Om sarvatathāgata Vajradhātvanuttara-pūjā-spharaṇa samaye hūm,* then Akṣobhya says: *Om sarvatathāgata vajrasattvānuttara-pūjā-spharraṇasamaye hūm.* He precedes Ratnasambhava, Amitāyu and Amoghasiddhi. They respectively give the best ways of worship of Vajraratna. Vajradharma and Vajrakarma in the same way:

1. Vairocana: samādhi: Sarvatathāgatānuttara-pūjā-vidhi-vistara-spharaṇa-karma samaya-vajradhiṣṭhāna
2. Akṣobhya: samādhi. Stg.-vajrasattvānuttara-pūjāvidhi-vistara-spharaṇa-karma-samaya-vajrādhiṣṭhāna
3. Ratnasambhava: Samādhi: Stg.-vajraratnānuttara-pūjā-vidhi-vistara-spharaṇa-karma-samaya-vajradhiṣṭhāna
4. Amitāyu: samādhi. Stg.-vajradharmānuttara-pūjā-vidhi-vistara-spharaṇa-karma-samaya-vajrādhiṣṭhāna
5. Amoghasiddhi: samādhi: Stg.-vajrakarmānuttara-pūjā-vidhi-vistara-spharaṇa-karma-samaya-vajrādhiṣṭhāna (STTS 130-131)

The sixteen Bodhisattvas are divided into four types of worship. All of them worship according to their characters. Their names given in their dhāraṇīs correlated to their attributes and the names given at the end of every group mention their functions. Bodhisattvas in the first group are called the great worships, in the second are the consecration worships, in the third religious worships and the fourth action worships.

They can be tabulated as follows:

| deity | ways of worship | names in dharanis | names in lists |
|---|---|---|---|
| Sarvatathāgata mahāpūjās: | | | |
| 6. Vajrasattva | ? | Karmavajrī | Stg.sukhasukhā |

| | | | |
|---|---|---|---|
| 7. Vajrarāja | attraction | Karmāgrī | Stg.-ākarṣaṇī |
| 8. Vajrarāga | attrachment | Karmavāṇa | Stg.-anurāgiṇī |
| 9. Vajrasādhu | applauds | Karmatuṣṭi | Stg.-santoṣaṇi |
| Abhiṣekapūjās: | | | |
| 10. Vajraratna | consecration by gems | Vajramaṇi | Mahādhipatinī |
| 11. Vajrateja | sun discs | Vajratejinī-jvālā | Mahōdyatā |
| 12. Vajraketu | banner with a paripūrṇa cintāmaṇi | Vajradhvajāgra | Mahāratna-varṣā |
| 13. Vajrasmita | Mahāprīti-pra-modyakaras | Vajrahāsa | Mahāprītiharṣā |
| Dharmapūjās: | | | |
| 14. Vajradharma | Vajradharmatāsamādhi | Mahādharmāgri | Mahājñānagītā |
| 15. Vajratīkṣṇa | Prajñāpāramitā-nirhāras | Mahāghoṣānugā | Mahāghoṣānugā |
| 16. Vajrahetu | Cakrākṣara-parivar-tādi-sarvasutrānta-nayas | Sarvamaṇḍala praveśa | Sarvamaṇḍalā |
| 17. Vajrahetu | Sandhābhaṣa-buddha-sangitībhir gāyan | Vajravācā | Mantrācaryā |
| Karmapūjās: | | | |
| 18. Vajradhūpā | incense | Pujakarma | Satvavatī |
| 19. Vajrapuṣpā | flower | ” | Mahābodhyaṅgavatī |
| 20. Vajradīpā | lamo | ” | Cakṣumatī |
| 21. Vajragandhā | perfume | ” | Gandhavatī |

Method of delineating the pūjā-maṇḍala is followed by the way of entering the maṇḍala and precedes the following mudrās of worship. mahābodhicittaniṣpattipūjā, sarva-buddhapūjā, dharma-pūjā, samādhipūjā, rahasyapūjā, Stg.-pūjā-karmamahāmudrā, Stg.-pūjākarmasamayamudrā, and Stg.-pūjākarma-dharmā. Thus ends the fourth chapter. its colphon runs as follows. *Sarvatathāgata-mahāyānābhisamayān mahākalparājād vajra-kārya-karma-maṇḍala-vidhivistaraḥ parisamāptaḥ* (STTS 133-141)

## CHAPTER 5 OF THE STTS : EPILOGUE

The first part of the STTS ends with its fifth chapter. The chapter has distinctly an existence but it bears no separate colophon. It just mentions the ending of the first part. *Sarvatathāgata-tattva saṅgrahāt sarvatathāgata-mahāyānābhisamayo nāma mahakalpa-rāja samāptaḥ.*

It opens up with a description of the maṇḍalas of four symbols, caturmudrā-maṇḍala, consisting of Vairocana and the four Tathāgatas of the four directions. Their essences are as follows:

Vairocana. *Om sarvatathāgata muṣṭi vam.*
Akṣobhya: *Om vajrasattva-muṣṭi aḥ.*
Ratnasambhava: *Om vajra-ratna-muṣṭi tram.*
Amitāyu. *Om vajradharma-muṣṭi kham.*
Amoghasiddhi. *Om vajrakarma-muṣṭi ham.*

It is followed by a description of drawing of caturmudrāmaṇḍala. After describing ākarṣaṇa and praveśa etc. Vairocana instructs that its secret should not be revealed to unworthy beings. (STTS 142-3). " You are not to reveal this secret chapter to anyone " Why is it so? There are living beings of unethical ideas, of evil actions, lacking fortitude, devoid of application, ignorant of various acts. Because of their poor fortitude, they are not to enter the great maṇḍalas of the family of All the Tathāgatas, Vajradhātu-mahāmaṇḍala and the rest. It is for their benefit that this vajra success-symbol-mandala, which is the mandala-pledge of the family of All the Tathāgatas is consecrated as the sign of success of the supreme vajra of Stg. for the sake of salvation of all spheres of living beings without any exception so that they may experience the happiness of goodness and bliss, You are never to breath faith with the secrets of the pledge symbols of the family of Stg. lest you are born in the hells, or the animals' world or the realm of tormented spirits or meeting with misfortune, die an untimely death". Teaching thus ( the master) uncovers the face and reveals the maṇḍala to the neophite ( Snellgrove pr.38)

Then he relates the mudrās as follows: Sarvatathāgata-mudrāsamaya, sarvamudrā-rahasya, sarvamudrādharmatā, sarvamudrā-karma and sarva-maṇḍala-sādhikā-rahasya-mudrā-jñāna.

Caturmudrāmaṇḍala is followed by ekamudrāmaṇḍala named as Vajrasattva-maṇḍala. It is to be delineated according to the mahā-maṇḍala, Vajrasattva is to be seated in the candramaṇḍala. After performing the rites of ākarṣaṇa and praveśa etc. one should try for the attainment of knowledge of siddhi of Stg. Then it should be instructed that this secret is not to be taught to the unworthy beings.. as it will result in an untimely death. Afterwards instructions should be given for the knowledge of sādhana of profound accomblishment of Vajrasattva. It should be proceeded by sarvamaṇḍalaguhyasamayajñāna and sapathahṛdaya. All the Tathāgatas emerge after performing the four mudrās of Vajrasattva and offer sādhukāra for Bhagavān, the lord of All the Tathāgatas the great bodhicitta Vajrasattva, the great Vajrapāṇi. The fifth chapter ends with four ślokas which relate its importance and the colophon is. *Sarvatathāgata-tattvasaṅgrahāt Sarvatathāgata-mahāyānābhisamayo nāma mahākalpārāja samāptaḥ.* (STTS 142-152)

## PART 2

### CHAPTER 6 OF THE STTS TRILOKAVIJAVA-MAHĀ-MAṆḌALA.

The second part of STTS is named as Sarvatathāgata-vajra-samaya-nāma-mahā-kalpa-rāja. It starts from the 6th and goes upto the 14th chapter.

The sixth chapter, that is the first chapter of the second part is Trilokavijaya-mahāmaṇḍala. It is the longest chapter which is a separate section in the Tibetan version. From the point of view of the history of Buddhist development, the chapter may be regarded as one of the most interesting in the whole tantra. The chapter begins with a long invocation of the lord of maṇḍala saluted with 108 names, including Mahāvairocana, Vajradhara, Vajrapāṇi and comprising the names of varient forms of the sixteen great bodhisattvas. Despite the exalted eulogy Vajrapāṇi reveals himself in a rather fretful mood for it is he who is primarily envisaged as lord of all the maṇḍala (STTS 153-6). Then Vajrapāṇi the lord of All the Tathāgats having hearkens to this address of solicitation of Stg., placing his vajra on his heart, speaks thus to All the Tathāgatas: "O All you lord Tathāgatas, I do not comply........... because there are evil beings, Maheśvara and others, who have not converted even by Stg. How am I to deal with them".

In response Vairocana enters the samādhi known as the wrathful pledge-vajra, the great compassionate means of Stg., enters his heart enunciates the seed syllable *Hūm*. At once there emerges from the vajra at the heart of Vajrapāṇi the lord Vajradhara who manifests in a variety of fearful Vajrapāṇi forms reciting this verse: "Oho I am the means of conversion, possessed by all great means, spotless, they assume a wrathful appearence so that beings may be converted by these means". Again Vairocana enters the samādhi called vajra-consecration of Vajrasamaya of the great anger of Stg. and utters this vajra-hūṅkāra. *Om śumbha niśumbha hūm. gṛhṇa gṛhṇa hūm. Gṛhṇāpaya hūm. Ānaya ho bhagavān Vajra hūm phaṭ.*

After a further fearful manifestation of Vajrapāṇi, the lord utters the spell: *Hūm ṭakki jjaḥ*, which has the effect of bringing Maheśvara and the other gods of the threefold world to his presence. There now follows an interesting altercation between Vajrapāṇi and Siva. Then Vajrapāṇi raises his vajra away from his heart and waving it, surveys the whole circle of the threefold world to its limits. He says: "Come my friends, to the teaching of Stg. Obey my command". They reply "How should we come"? Vajrapāṇi says "Having sought protection with the Buddhas the dharma, the community, approach, O friends, so that you may gain the knowledge of the Omniscient One".

Then Mahādeva the lord of the whole threefold world appears very wrathfully and says: "Listen you Yakṣa, I am Īśvara, lord of the threefold world, creator, destroyer, lord of all spirits, god of gods, mighty god. So how should I carry out the orders of a Yakṣa?" Then Vajrapāṇi waves his vajra once more and commends: "Listen you evil being quickly enter the maṇḍala and hold my pledge". Then Mahādeva, the god addresses the lord Vairocana: "Who is this creature of such a kind who gives orders to me Īśvara"? Then he tells Maheśvara and the whole host of gods of the threefold world. "Enter upon the vow of the pledge of the triple protection lest Vajrapāṇi, this so called yaksa, the Great Bodhisattva, wrathful, terrifying and fearful should destroy the whole threefold world with his blazing vajra."

Then Maheśvara by his power of overlordship of the threefold world and of his own knowledge, together with his whole company, manifests a fearful, wrathful, and greatly terrifying form with great flames shooting forth and with a terrible laugh for the purpose of causing fear to the lord Vajrapāṇi. He then says: "I am the lord of the threefold world and you would give me orders".

Then Vajrapāṇi waving his vajra and laughing says. "Approach you enter of corpses and human flesh, you who use the ashes of funeral pyres as your food, as your couch, as your clothing and obey my command"

Then Maheśvara lording over the whole which was pervaded by his great wrath, says: "You obey my commend and take upon yourself my vow." Then Vajrapāṇi, the greatly wrathful being says to the lord:" Because of pride in power of his own knowledge and because of his overlordship as Maheśvara, this great god, O lord does not submit to the teaching of All the Tathāgatas. How is one to deal with him." Then the lord recalls the great vajra pledges which has its origin in the heart of Stg.: *'Om niśumbha vajra hūm phaṭ.*

Then Vajrapāṇi pronounces his vajra syllable: *Hūm*. As soon as he pronounces this all the great gods who belong to the threefold world fall down on their faces, emitting miserable cries and they go to Vajrapāṇi for protection. The great god himself remains motionless on the ground quite dead. All except Maheśvara are raised up and converted, only thereafter at Vairocana's behest does Vajrapāṇi bring Maheśvara back to life for as Vairocana remarks: "If he is not raised up his life will be wasted to no purpose while he is brought back to life he will become a good man. However when he is restores, Maheśvara still refuses to submit "I can bear death" he says "but I will not obey your command." There follows a further short battle, in which Vajrapāṇi triumphs by means of his spells and treads down Maheśvara with his left foot and Umā, Maheśvara's consort with his right

Then the lord feels great compassion for Mahādeva and pronounces this spell comprising the compession of All the Buddhas. *Om Buddha maitrī vajra rakṣa hūm.* As soon as he says this the suffering that Maheśvara experiences is allayed and from the contact with the sole of Vajrapāṇi's foot he became reccipient of consecrations, powers of meditation, salvation, mnemonics, faculties of knowledge and magical powers, all the highest perfection tending even to Buddhahood. So Mahādeva from the contact with the lord's foot experienced the joys of salvation through the powers of meditation and the spell of Stg. and this body.

Having thus fallen at the feet of Vajrapāṇi he becomes Tathāgata bhasmeśvaranirghoṣa (soundless lord of ashes), in the realm known as Bhasmacchatra, which exists down below over and beyond worldly realms, equal in number to the atoms of worldly realm which are as numerous as the grains of sand contained in thirty two river Ganges (STTS 157-169)

The other gods led by Nārāyaṇa are taken into the maṇḍala by Vajrapāṇi and submit to the vow of obedience. Vajrapāṇi gives them his own pledge (samaya) and makes them firm by reciting their mantras: *Om vajra-samaya gṛhṇa bandhasamayam vajrasattva-samayam anusmara sarvatathāgata samayastvam dṛḍho me bhava sthiro me bhava āhāryo me bhava apratiharyo me bhava sarvakarmeṣu ca me citta śriyaḥ kuru ha ha ha ha hūm* (STTS 157-171)

Vajrapāṇi enters them and gives instruction about the mahāmaṇḍala, consecrates with gems, offers them Vajra attributes, again consecrates with the vajra names and stations them as related to the following groups:

| | | | |
|---|---|---|---|
| Vidyārājyakas (trailokyādhipatis): | | Vajrarājanikās: | |
| 1. Maheśvara | Krodhavajra | Umā | Krodhavajrāgni |
| 2. Nārāyaṇa | Mayāvajra | Rukmiṇī | Vajrasauvarṇī |
| 3. Sanakumāra | Vajraghaṇṭa | Ṣaṣṭhī | Vajrakaumārī |
| 4. Brahmā | Maunavajra | Brahmāṇī | Vajraśānti |
| 5. Indra | Vajrāyudha | Indrāṇī | Vajramuṣṭi |
| Antarikṣacaras (Vajrakrodhas): | | Antarikṣacarīs Matṛs (Vajrakrodhinī). | |
| 6. Amṛtakuṇḍali | Vajrakuṇḍali | Amṛtā | Vajrāmṛtā |
| 7. Indu | Vajraprabha | Rohiṇī | Vajrakānti |
| 8. Mahādaṇḍāgrya | Vajradaṇḍa | Daṇḍhariṇī | Daṇḍavajrāgrā |
| 9. Pingala | Vajrapingala | Jaṭāhāriṇī | Vajramekhalā |
| Ākāśacaras (Gaṇapatis). | | Khecarīs (Gaṇikās). | |
| 10. Madhumatta | Vajraśauṇḍa | Māraṇī | Vajravilayā |
| 11. Madhukara | Vajramālā | Aśnā | Vajrāsanā |

| | | | |
|---|---|---|---|
| 12. Jaya | Vajravaśī | Vasanā | Vajravasanā |
| 13. Jayāvaha | Vijayavajra | Rati | Vajravaśā |
| Bhaumas (Dūta) . | | Bhūcarīs | (Vajradūtī) |
| 14. Kośapāla | Vajramusala | Śivā | Vajradūtī |
| 15. Vāyu | Vajrānila | Vāyavi | Vegavajriṇī |
| 16. Agni Vajrānala | Agnedhrya | | Vajrajvālā |
| 17. Kubera | Vajrabhairava | Kuberā | Vajravikaṭā |
| Pātālādhipatis (Ceṭakas). | | Pātālāvasinī (Vajradūtī) : | |
| 18. Varāha | Vajrāṅkuśa | Māraṇī | Vajramukhī |
| 19. Yama | Vajrakāla | Cāmuṇḍā | Vajrakālī |
| 20. Prithivīcūlikā | Vajravināyaka | Chinnanāsā | Vajrapūtanā |
| 21. Varuṇa | Nāgavajra | Vāruṇī | Vajramakarī |

All of them are indoctrinated and instructed about the mudrās. They are given their essense (hṛdaya) as follows.

Antarikṣacaras : *Hūm vajrāgra pīḍaya samaya hūm.*

Malādharīs . *Om vajra mālāgra vam.*

Bhūcaras : *Om vajradbandha hūm.*

Pātalavāsīs : *Om vajrapātāla bhañja bhañja hūm phaṭ.*

Mātṛs : *Om heruka vajra-samaya sarva-duṣṭa-samaya-mudrā-prabhañjaka hūm phaṭ* (STTS 174-181).;

After subduing all the evil beings Vajrapāṇi further asks about all the deseases. They are also conquered and stationed in the outer circle of mount Sumeru. Vajrapāṇi narrates the delineation of Trilokavijaya-mahā-maṇḍala which gives illumination and destroys all the evil beings. Delineation is followed by the ritual of opening the four vajradoors. The centre of the maṇḍala is occupied by Vajrapāṇi Mahāsattva in terrific form. He reads upon Maheśvara with his left and with his right upon Umā. All the Vajrakrodhas are to be drawn around him. (STTS 181-190).Hardayas of the sixteen bodhisattvas are given as follow:

1.. Vajrasattva. *Om vajrasattva krodha hūm phaṭ.*
2. Vajrarāja. *Om vajra-krodhakarsaya hum phat.*
3. Vajrarāga: *Om vajra-kama-krodha ragaya hum phat.*
4. Vajrasādhu: *Om vajra-tuṣṭi-krodha sādhu sādhu hūm phaṭ.*
5. Vajraratna: *Om vajra-bhṛkuṭi-krodha hara hara hūm phaṭ.*
6. Vajrateja. *Om vajra-sūrya-mahā-jvālā mahā-krodha jvālaya sarvam hūm phaṭ.*
7. Vajraketu: *Om vajra-krodha-ketu dehi hūm phaṭ.*
8. Vajrasmita : *Om vajrāṭṭahāsa-krodha haḥ haḥ haḥ haḥ hūm phaṭ.*
9. Vajradharma. *Om vajradharma-krodha vināśaya viśodhaya hūm phaṭ.*
10. Vajratīkṣṇa. *Omvajratīkṣṇa krodha cchinda cchinda hūm phaṭ.*

11. Vajrahetu: *Om vajrahetu-krodha praviśa praveśaya maṇḍalam sarvam hūm phaṭ.*
12. Vajrabhāṣa . *Om vajrakrodha-bhāṣa vada vada hūm phaṭ.*
13. Vajrakarma : *Om vajrakarma.*
14. Vajrarakṣa : *Om vajrakavaca-krodha rakṣa rakṣa hūm phaṭ.*
15. Vajrayakṣa : *Om vajrayakṣa-krodha khāda khāda hūm phaṭ.*
16. Vajramuṣṭi : *Hūm vajra-krodha-muṣṭi sādhaya sādhaya hūm phaṭ.*

Hṛdayas of pūjā and saṅgraha-bodhisattvas :

26. Vajralāsyā : *Om vajra lāsye rāgaya hūm phaṭ.*
27. Vajramālā : *Om vajramāle 'bhiṣiñca hūm phaṭ.*
28. Vajragīta . *Om vajragīte gada gada hūm phaṭ.*
29. Vajranṛyā : *Om vajranṛtye vaśīkuru hūm phaṭ.*
30. Vajradhūpā : *Om vajradhūpa-pūjā-spharaṇa samaye hūm phaṭ.*
31. Vajrapuṣpā : *Om vajrapuṣpa-pūjā-spharaṇa-samaye hūm phaṭ.*
32. Vajradīpa : *Om vajrāloka-pūjā-spharaṇa-samaye hūm phaṭ.*
33. Vajragandhā : *Om vajragandha-pūjā-spharaṇa-samaye hūm phaṭ.*
34. Vajrāṅkuśa : *Om vajrāṅkuśa-mahākrodhākaraṣaya sarva samaya hūm jjaḥ.*
35. Vajrapāśa : *Om vajrapāśa-mahā-krodha praveśaya sarva-samayān hūm hūm.*
36. Vajraśakala . *Om vajrasphoṭa-mahā-krodha bandha bandha sarva samayam hūm vam.*
37. Vajraghaṇṭa . *Om vajrāveśa-mahā-krodhāveśaya sarva samayam hūm aḥ.*

Thereafter comes the praveśavidhi in the Trilokavijaya-mahā-maṇḍala. First of all the vajrācarya should enter after making the terintiri mudrā and request All the Tathāgatas that he is over-powered by their anger and he will vanquish the vanquishables and accumulate the worthy ones. He should be commended for his job. He should place the mudrā in his heart and perform rites by vajrāṅkuśa etc. Again he should do sarvasamayamudrā and worship four times by insence etc. Then the vajrācarya makes his student to enter the maṇḍala reciting this verse : *Om gṛhṇa vajra samaya hūm.*

The chapter proceeds with the devādyakarṣaṇamudrā jñāna, caturvidhamudrā jñāna, sarvasattvamudrāṇamudrā–jñāna, rahasyakrodhamudrā- jñāna, Trilokavijaya-mahā-maṇḍala-samaya-tattva-mudrā-jñāna, vajrasamayamudrābandha, dharmamudrās, vajrasamaya-karma-mudrā, Trilokavi- jaya-mahā-maṇḍala-sādhāraṇa-mudrā, sarvatathāgata-maṇḍala-sādhana-mudrā-bandha and sarva-vajrakula-sarvamudrā-sādhana (STTS 190-210).

## CHAPTER 7 OF THE STTS: KRODHA-GUHYA-MUDRĀ-MAṆḌALA

Bhagavān enters the samādhi named vajra-consecration which has its origin in the samaya of vajradhāraṇī and utters this verse : Om sarva-vajriṇī vajramate ānaya sarvam vajra-satyena hūm jjaḥ. As soon as he utters this Vajrapāṇi attains a form of the samaya-mudrā of vajra-krodha and stations himself in a lunar disc. Thereafter Vajrapāṇi relates delineation of the maṇḍala which is named as svakula-samaya-mudrā-maṇḍala-vajra-samaya-guhyam and krodha-guhya.

The first maṇḍala of this chapter is called vajra-siṅkāra maṇḍala and the first four great Bodhisatvas are named as : the samaya of angry aspect of vajra, feminine form of aṅkuśa, passion and satisfaction :

Vajrasattva : *Om vajra-krodha-samaye siḥ* (Vajra-krodha-samaya)

Vakrarāga : *Om vajraroṣaṇāṅkusyānaya sarvam siḥ* (Vajra-roṣaṇāṅkuśī).

Vajrarāga : *Om vajraroṣe kāma-vajriṇī vaśam me ānaya* (Vajra-roṣa-kāma vajriṇī).

Vajrasādhu : *Om vajratuṣṭi-krodhe toṣaya sarvāṇi siḥ (Vajra-tuṣṭi-krodha) (STTS 211-214).*

The second is vajra jiṅkāra-maṇḍala and the deities are :

Vajraratna : *Om vajra-bhṛkuṭi-krodhe hara sarvārthān* (Vajra-bhṛkuṭi-krodha).

Vajrateja : *Om vajra-jvālā-māla-prabhe mahā-krodhāgni jvālaya sarvam viroṣe jiḥ* (Vajra-jvāla-māla-prabhā, mahā-krodhāgni, Viroṣā).

Vajraketu : *Om vajradhvajāgra-keyūra-mahā-krodhe dehi me sarvam jiḥ* (Vajradhvajāgra-keyūra-mahā-krodhā).

Vajrahāsa : *Om vajrāṭṭahāsinī hasa hasa aṭṭāṭṭahāsena māraya jiḥ* (Vajrāṭṭahāsinī).

The third is diṅkāra-maṇḍala and the deities of this maṇḍala are as follows :

Vajradharma . *Om vajraśudhha-krodhe hana māraya duṣṭān* (Vajra-śuddha-krodhā).

Vajratīkṣṇa : *Om vajratīkṣṇa-krodhe cchinda vajra-koṣeṇa sarvam diḥ* (Vajratīkṣṇa-krodhā).

Vajrahetu : *Om vjarahetu-mahākrodhe praveśa-cakra poraveśaya sarvam diḥ*(Vajrahetu-mahā-krodhā)

Vajrabhāṣa : *Om vajrajihve mahā-krodha-bhāṣe vācam muñca diḥ* (Vajra jihvā-mahā-krodhā

Hnihṇkāra-maṇḍala is the fourth and the deities are as follows :

Vajrakarma : *Om sarvamukhe karma-vajriṇī mahā-krodhe kuru sarvam hniḥ sarvamukhā* (Karmavajriṇī, mahākrodhā)

Vajrarakṣa : *Om vajrakavaca-krodhe rakṣa mām hniḥ* (Vajra-kavac-krodhā)

Vajrayakṣa : *Om vajra-caṇḍa-krodhe mahā-yakṣiṇī vajra-danṣṭra-karāla bhīṣaṇī bhīṣapaya hniḥ* (Vajra-caṇḍa-krodhā mahā-yakṣiṇī)

Vajrasandhi : *Om vajrakrodhe muṣṭi bandha hniḥ* (Vajra-krodha muṣṭi-bandha) (STTS 214-216)

Nṛtyā etc. the pūjā goddesses are in the internal corners and other four in the outer corners.

Praveśavidhi in the esoteric (guhya) maṇḍala of the vajrakula should be the same as in the Trailokyavijaya-mahā - maṇḍala. Dance is to be performed with mudrās of the knowledge of vajra-guhya-vajrakula-samaya-mudrā, pratimudrā and upmudrā for worshipping Vajradhara. It precedes nṛtya, pratinrtyopahāra, pratimudrā-hṛdaya, upamudrā-hṛdaya, krodha-guhya-mudrā-jñāna, mahā-vajrakula-guhya-mudrā-jñāna, mahāmudrā-bandha-vajrakula-guhya-samaya-mudrā-bandha, vajrakula-guhya-dharma-mudrā,vajrakula - guhya-karma-mudrā-bandha. Thus ends the seventh chapter with this colophon: *Sarvatathāgata-vajra-samayān mahākalparājāt krodha-guhyamudrā-maṇḍala-vidhi-vistaraḥ parisamāptaḥ.*

## CHAPTER 8 OF THE STTS: VAJRA-KULA-DHARMA-JÑĀNA-SAMAYA-MAṆḌALA

The knowledge maṇḍala of the vajra family opens with the samādhi of Bhagavān called the mudrā-consecration of knowledge of samādhi of the vajra family of All the Tathāgatas. The five Tathāgatas utter their vidyottamas as follows.

1. Bhagavān : *Om saravatathāgata-sūkṣma-vajra-krodha hūm phaṭ.*
2. Vajrapāṇi : *Om sūkṣma-vajra krodhākrama hūm phaṭ.*
3. Vajragarbha : *Om sūkṣma-vajra-ratnākrama hūm phaṭ.*
4. Vajranetra : *Om sūkṣma-vajra-padma-krodhākrama hūm phaṭ.*
5. Vajraviśva : *Om sūkṣma vajra-karma-krodhākrama hūm phaṭ* (STTS 225-8).

   Again Vajrapāṇi Mahābodhisattva originates his family and utters their hṛdayas.
6. Vajrasattva-sūkṣma-jñāna-krodha (Vajrasattva). *Om vajra-sūksma-jñana-krodha hūm phaṭ.*
7. Sūkṣma-vajrāṅkuśa (Vajrarāga) : *Om sūksma-vajra-jñānāṅkuśakarṣaya mahā-krodha hūm phaṭ.*
8. Vajra-sūkṣma-rāga-krodha (Vajrarāga). *Om vajra-sūkṣma-rāga-krodha anurāgaya tīvram-hūm phaṭ.*
9. Sūkṣma-vajra-tuṣṭi-krodha (Vajrasādhu) : *Om sūkṣma-vajra-tuṣṭi-krodha hūm phaṭ.*
10. Sūkṣma-vajra-bhṛkuṭi-krodha (Vajraratna) : *Om sūkṣma-vajra-bhṛkuṭi-krodha hara hara hūm phaṭ.*
11. Vajra-sūkṣma-jvālā-maṇḍala (Vajrateja) . *Om vajra-sūksma-jvālā-maṇḍala-krodha-sūrya jvālaya hūm phaṭ.*
12. Sūkṣma-vajra-dhvajāgra-krodha (Vajraketu) : *Om sūkṣma vajra dhva-jāgra-krodha sarvārthān me prayaccha śīghram hūm phaṭ.*
13. Vajrasūkṣma-hāsa-krodha (Vajrahāsa) : *Om vajra-sūkṣma-hāsa-krodha ha ha ha ha hūm*

*phaṭ.*

14. Sūkṣma-vajra-dharma-krodha (Vajra-dharma) : *Om sūkṣma-vajra-dharma-krodha śodhaya hūm phaṭ.*

15. Sūkṣma-vajra-ccheda-krodha (Vajratīkṣṇa) : *Om sūksma-vajra-ccheda-krodha cchinda hūm phaṭ.*

16. Sūkṣma-vajra-krodha (Vajrahetu) : *Om sūkṣma-vajra-krodha-mahā-cakra cchinda pātaya śiraḥ praviśya hṛdayam bhinda hūm phaṭ.*

17. Sūkṣma-vajra-hūṅkāra-krodha (Vajrabhāṣa) : *Om sūkṣma-vajra-hūṇkāra-krodha hana pātaya vāṅmātreṇa hūm phaṭ.*

18. Sūkṣma-vajra-karma-krodha (Vajrakarma) : *Om sūkṣma-vajra-karma-krodha sarva-karma-karo- bhava sarva kāryāṇi sādhaya hūm phaṭ*

19. Vajra-sūkṣma-kavaca-krodha (Vajrarakṣa) : *Om vajra-sūkṣma-kavaca krodha rakṣa rakṣa hūm phaṭ.*

20. Sūkṣma-vajra-yakṣa-krodha (Vajrayakṣa) : *Om sūkṣma-vajra-yakṣa-krodha hana bhakṣaya sarva duṣṭān hūm phaṭ.*

21. Sūkṣma-vajra-muṣṭi-krodha (Vajrasandhi) : *Om sūkṣma-vajra-muṣṭi-krodha bandha bandha hūm phaṭ.* (STTS 226-7)

Vajrapāṇi relates the samaya maṇḍala of subtle knowledge of Vajra family. Thereafter follows its praveśavidhi, subtle knowledge of vajra krodha, knowledge of rahasya mudrā of dharma of vajra family, knowledge of mudrā of dharma of vajra family, mahā-mudrā-bandha, vajrakula-dharma-samaya-dharma-mudrā-jñāna, and the vajrakula-dharma-samaya-karma-mudrā-jñāna.

Thus the following colophon ends the chapter: *Sarvatathāgatavajra-samayān mahā-kalpa-rājād vajra-kula-dharma-jñāna-samaya-maṇḍala-vidhi-vistaraḥ samāptaḥ* (STTS 228-235)

## CHAPTER 9 OF THE STTS: VAJRAKULA-KARMA-MAṆḌALA

Chapter opens with the utterence of vidyottamās of the five Tathāgatas.

1. Vairocana: *Om sarvatathāgata-karmeśvarī hūm.*
2. Vajrapāṇi. *Om sarvatathāgata-dharmadhatu-spharaṇa-mahā-pūjā-karma-vidhi-vistara-samaye trilokavijayaṅkarī sarva-duṣṭān dāmaya vajriṇī hūm.*
3. Vajragarbha: *Om sarvatathāgatadhātu-samavasaraṇa-mahā-pūjā karma-vidhi-vistara-samaye hūm.*

4. Vajranetra: *Om sarvatathāgata-dharmadhātu-spharaṇa-mahā-pūjā-karma-vidhi-vistara-samaye-hūm.*

5. Vajraviśva: *Om sarvatathāgata-sarvāloka-dhātu-vividha-mahā-pūjā-karma-vidhi-vistara-samaye hūm.*

Mahābodhisattva Vajrapāṇi originates the deities of worship from his heart and they rest in lunar discs like Vajradhātu-mahā maṇḍala. Then he delineates karma maṇḍala which is named as vajra-karma-samaya-vidhi-vistara-karma-maṇḍala. The sixteen great bodhisattvas in the form of vajra-karma mudrās are given as below:

The first four are named as Vajra-sattvasiddhi, Vajrākarṣaṇā, vajrarati-rāgā and Vajra-sādhu. Karma-jñāna-samaya is added to their names:

6. *Vajra-sattva-siddhi-jñāna-samaye hūm*
7. *Om vajrākarṣaṇa-karma-jñāna-samaye hūm jjaḥ.*
8. *Om Vajra rati-rāga-karma-jñāna-samaye hūm jjaḥ.*
9. *Om Vajra-sādhu-karma-jñāna-samaye hūm jjaḥ.*

The second four are venerated for their power of control and they are named as. Vajrabhṛkuṭi, Vajrasūryā-maṇḍalā, Vajradhvajāgra-kayūrā and Vajrāṭṭahāsā:

10. *Om vajra-bhṛkuṭi vaśī kuru hūm.*
11. *Om Vajra-sūrya-maṇḍale vaśī kuru hūm.*
12. *Om Vajra-dhvajāgra-keyūre.*
13. *Om Vajrāṭṭahase vaśī kuru hūm.*

The third group of four deities are different passions who can impassionate the beings. They are Vajra-padma, Vajra-tīkṣṇa, Vajra-maṇḍala and Vajra-vāk:

14. *Om Vajra-padma-rāge rāgaya hūm.*
15. *Om Vajra-tīkṣṇa rāge rāgaya hūm.*
16. *Om Vajra-maṇḍale rāge rāgaya hūm.*
17. *Om Vajra vāg-rāge rāgaya hūm.*

Next four are Vajra-karma-samayā, Vajra-kavaca-bandhā, Vajra-yakṣiṇī and Vajra-karma-muṣṭi:

18. *Om Vajra-karma-samaye pūjaya hūm.*
19. *Om Vajra-kavaca-bandhe rakṣaya hūm.*
20. *Om Vajra-yakṣiṇi māraya vajradaṁṣṭrāyābhinda hṛdaya amukasya hūm phaṭ.*
21. *Om Vajra-karma-muṣṭi siddhaya siddhaya hūm phaṭ.*

This is followed by delineation of karma-maṇḍala and knowledge of action of vajra family is originated. Knowledge of the śāntikarma precedes the rahasya-karma-mudrā-jñāna and Vajrakula-karma-maha-mudrā-jñāna. Thus ends the chapter with this colophon: *Sarva-tathāgata-vajrasamayāt mahākalparājāt vajra-kula-karma-maṇḍala-vidhi-vistaraḥ samāptaḥ.*

## CHAPTER 10 OF THE STTS: MAHĀ-KALPA

Vairocana enters the samādhi called mudrādhiṣṭhāna of All the Tathāgatas and utters his vidyottamā as: *Om sarva-tathāgata-vajra-samaye hūm,* It is followed by the vidyottamas of other four Budhisattvas:

2. Vajrapāṇi: *Hūm vajrī maṭ.*
3. Vajragarbha: *Hūm bhṛkuṭi vajre raṭ.*
4. Vajranetra: *Hūm padma-vajrī triṭ.*
5. Vajraviśva: *Hūm vajra-karmāgri kṛt.*

Mahabodhisattva Vajrapāṇi teaches the caturmudrā-maṇḍala of Trilokavijaya. After narrating its ākarsaṇādividhi and praveśa he instructs about the knowledge of esoteric mudrā, suddha-dharmatā-mudrā, caturmudrā-maṇḍala-guhya-rahasya-mudrā, four samaya mudrās i.e. Vajra kranti-trisula-mudra etc. and worshipping with a dance with mudra, prati-mudra, upamudrā and jñānamudrā. Vajrapāṇi again narrates the maṇḍala of krodhasamaya of his own vajrasamaya which is also called guhya-maṇḍala. Then he pronounces its delineation and the knowledge of esoteric mudrā of vajra-hūṅkāra. It is followed by the rahasya-sādhana-mudrā-jñāna of vajrahūṅkāra and their sādhāraṇa hṛdayas.

The chapter ends with the colophon. *Sarvatathāgatavajra-samayān mahākalparājān mahākalpavidhivistaraḥ samāptaḥ.*

## CHAPTER 11 OF THE STTS. TRILOKA-CAKRA-MAHĀ-MAṆḌALA

All the Tathāgatas ask vajrapāṇi to liberate Maheśvara from his foot but Vajrapāṇi refuses to do because he was consecrated as an anger who desctroys all the evil beings. But all the Tathāgatas wish to bring him to life and thus they utter this hrdaya. *Om vajrasattva hūm jjaḥ.* At once Bhasmeśvaranirghoṣa enters the body of Maheśavara and says that the knowledge form of Buddha is the supreme among all the Buddhas because dead body can again attain life.

Maheśvara is liberated and brought back to life by Vajrapāṇi. Vajrapāṇi emerges from the mahākraodha-samādhi and says I am consecrated by All the Tathāgatas as Vajrapāṇi after giving a vajra in my hands. I apply proper seats to all the deities of the outer circle in Trilokavijaya-mahā-maṇḍala. They will be enlightened. As soon as he utters the Sarvatathagatoṣṇīsa. Vajrapāṇi attains a from of rays of different colours. He illuminates all the worlds and stations himself as a multitude of luster in the head dress of Stg.

The five Bodhisattvas utter their vidyottamās as follows:

Vajrapāṇi. *Om niśumbha vajra hūm phaṭ. Om ṭakki jjaḥ.*

Vajragarbha: *Om vajraratnottamā jvālaya hūm phaṭ.*

Vajranetra: *Om svabhāva-śuddha vajra-padma śodhaya sarvam vidyottama hūm phaṭ.*

Vajraviśva: *Om vajrakarmottama vajradhara samayam anusmara śumbha niśumbhākarṣaya praveśaya bandhaya samayam grahaya sarva-karmāṇi me kuru mahā-sattva hūm phaṭ.*

Vajra-vidyottama: *Om śumbha niśumbha vajra-vidyottamā hūm phaṭ.*

They are followed by the twenty deities of the outer circle, They are divided into five groups. The first group is of Vidyā-rājanakas and their hṛdayas as uttered by themselves are as follows:

1. Māyāvajra: *Om vajra-māya-vidarśaya sarvam hūm phaṭ.*
2. Vajraghaṇṭa: *Om vajra-ghaṇṭa raṇa raṇa hūm phaṭ.*
3. Maunavajra: *Om vajra-mauna mahāvrata hūm phaṭ.*
4. Vajrāyudha: *Om vajrāyudha dāmaka hūm phaṭ.*

Vajrakrodhas:

5. Vajrakuṇḍalī. *Om vajra-kuṇḍali-mahā vajra-krodha gṛhṇa hana daha paca vidhvansaya vajreṇa sphālaya bhinda hṛdayam vajra krodha hūm phaṭ.*
6. Vajraprabhā. *Om vajraprabhā māraya saumya-krodha hūm phaṭ.*
7. Vajradaṇḍa. *Om vajradaṇḍa tanuya sarva-duṣṭān mahā-krodha hūm phaṭ.*
8. Vajrapiṅgala: *Om vajrapiṅgala bhīṣaya sarva-duṣṭān krodha hūm phaṭ.*

Gaṇapatis:

9. Vajraśauṇḍa: *Om vajra śauṇḍa-mahā-gaṇapati rakṣa sarva duṣṭebhyo vajradharājñām pālaya hūm phaṭ.*
10. Vajramāla: *Om vajramāla gaṇapataye mālayākarṣaya praveśayavesāya bandhaya vaśīkuru māraya hūm phaṭ.*
11. Vajravaśī: *Om vajravaśī mahā-ganapati vaśīkuru hūm phaṭ.*
12. Vijayavajra: *Om Vajravijaya vijayan kuru mahā-gaṇapati hūm phaṭ.*

Dutas.

13. Vajramusala. *Om vajramuśala kṛṭṭa sarva-duṣṭān vajra dūta hūm phaṭ.*
14. Vajrānila. *Om vajrānila mahāvegānaya sarva-duṣṭān hūm phaṭ.*
15. Vajrānala: *Om vajrānala mahādūta jvālaya sarvam bhasmīkuru sarva duṣṭān hūm phaṭ.*
16. Vajrabhairava: *Om vajrabhairava vajradūta bhakṣaya sarva duṣṭān hūm phaṭ.*

Ceṭas:

17. Vajrāṅkuśa. *Om vajrāṅkuśa ākarṣaya sarvam mahāceta hūm phaṭ*
18. Vajrakāla: *Om vajrakāla mahāmṛtyum utpādaya hūm phaṭ.*
19. Vajravināyaka: *Om vajravināyakasyāvighnam kuru hūm phaṭ.*
20. Nāgavajra: *Om nāgavajrānaya sarva-dhana-dhānya hiraṇya suvarṇamaṇi-muktālaṅ-*

*kārādīni sarvopakaraṇāni vajradhara-samayam anusmara krodha gṛhṇa bandha hara hara prāṇān mahāceta hūm phaṭ.*

Then Vajrapāṇi relates the mahā-maṇḍala of sarvavajra-kula: *Om vajra-sūtrākarsaya sarva-maṇḍalan hūm,* and the sūtraṇa hṛdaya of the maṇḍala. After measuring drawing and painting the maṇḍala doors are opened with a recitation of its hṛdaya. It is followed by sarva buddha-hṛdaya, mahāsattva-catuṣṭaya hṛdaya, Vajravega-hṛdaya, their samayā-hṛdayas, All the deities of the maṇḍala are placed one by one with a recitation of their hṛdayas.

After performing the ākarṣaṇādikarma vajrācārya should make vajra-krodha terintiri-mudrā and say that he will produce the knowledge of vajrasamaya which is not to be revealed then gives the sapatha-hṛdaya. Again he shows vajra-krodha-samaya- with the same mudra. It is proceeded by bandhavidhi and hṛdayas of vajradhāri-karma mudrā. He is to be consecrated by vajrodaka and enters the maṇḍala and throws flowers with this hrdaya: *Om praticchādhitiṣṭha vajra hoḥ.* He gets accomplishment according to the place of the flower thrown by him. Instructions are given about the importance of the secracy of the knowledge of the maṇḍala. Student receives consecration of the garlend with a sign vajraratna, receives the karmavajra and vajra name just like in the vajra samaya-mahā-maṇḍala.

Thereafter follows the mahā-mudrā-bandha, Vidyārāja-mahā-mudrā-gaṇa, Vajrakrodhamahā-mudrā-gaṇa, gaṇapati-mahā-mudrā-gaṇa, dūtamahā-mudrā-gaṇa, ceṭa-mahā-mudrā-gaṇa, Buddha-mudrā, mudrās of vidyārājanikas, vajrakrodhas, gaṇas, dūtas and ceṭas,. The chapter ends with following colophon: *Sarvatathāgatavajra-samayān mahākalparājāt trilokacakra-mahā-maṇḍala-vidhi-vistaraḥ samāptaḥ.*

## CHAPTER 12 OF THE STTS: VAJRA-KULA-VAJRA-MAṆḌALA

The chapter opens with the samādhi of Vairocana called the consecration which has its origin in the samaya of the vajradhāraṇī of Stg. which is proceeded by the vidyottamās of all the deities:

| | | |
|---|---|---|
| Vairocana | : | *Om Vajra-savitra svāhā.* |
| Vajrapāṇi | : | *Om Vajradhāri hūm. Vajra-vikrama hūm phaṭ* |
| Vajragarbha | : | *Om Vajraratna-gotre svāhā.* |
| Vajranetra | : | *Om Vajra-padma-netre hūm phaṭ.* |
| Vajraviśva | : | *Om vajra-karma-kari hūm* |
| Vajravidyottamā | : | *Om Vajra-śūlāgre svāhā.* |

Vidyārājasamaya: *mudrā*
Vajramāya: *Om vajracakra hūm*
Vajraghaṇṭa: *Om vajraghaṇṭike hūm*
Maunavajra: *Om vajra-daṇḍa-kāṣṭhe hūm.*
Vajrāyudha: *Om vajre hūm.*
Vajrakrodha: *Samaya-mudrā.*
Vajrakuṇḍali: *Om jvālā-vajre hūm.*
Vajraprabha: *Om vajra-samaya hūm.*
Vajradaṇḍa: *Om Vajra-daṇḍe hūm.*
Vajrapiṅagala: *Om vajra-bhiṣaṇe hūm.*
Vajra-gaṇapati. *Samaya-mudrā.*
Vajra-śauṇḍa: *Om vajra-made hūm.*
Vajra-māla: *Om Vajra-māle hūm.*
Vajra-vaśī: *Om vajra-vaśe hūm.*
Vijaya-vajra: *Om Vajrāparājite hūm.*
Vajra-dūta *samaya-mudrā.*
Vajra-musala: *Om vajra-muśala-grahe hūm.*
Vajrānila: *Om Vajra-paṭe hūm.*
Vajrānala. *Om vajra-jvāle hūm.*
Vajra-bhairava: *Om vajra-grahe hūm.*
Vajra-ceṭa. *samaya-mudrā*
Vajrāṅkuśa: *Om vajra-daṁṣṭre hūm.*
Vajra-kāla. *Om vajra-māraṇi-hūm.*
Vajravināyaka: *Om vajra-vighne hūm.*
Nāga-vajra: *Om vajra-hāriṇī hūm.*

Vajrapāṇi once more relates the delineation of the Vajra-maṇḍala of the vajra-family. After perforiming necessary rituals one should teach the samayamudrārahasya, samaya-mudrās, mudrarājanikās, krodhasamayas, gaṇikāsamayas, dūtisamayas and ceṭisamayas and thus the chapter ends with this colophon: *Sarvatathāgata-vajra-samayān Mahā-kalparājāt Sarvavajrakula-vajra-maṇḍala-vidhi-vistaraḥ parisamaptaḥ.*

## CHAPTER 13 OF THE STTS: SARVA-VAJRA-KULA-DHARMA-SAMAYA-MAṆḌALA

Vairocana enters the samādhi called the Vajrādhiṣṭhāna which has its origin in the samaya of dharma of All the Tathāgatas and five Buddhas utter their vidyottamas respectively:

| | |
|---|---|
| Vairocana: | *Om vajra viṭ.* |
| Vajrapāṇi. | *Om hana hana hūm phaṭ.* |
| Vajragarbha. | *Om hana hana hūm phaṭ.* |
| Vajranetra. | *Om māra māra hūm phaṭ.* |
| Vajraviśva: | *Om kuru kuru hūm phaṭ.* |
| Vajravidyottamā: | *Om hūm hūm phaṭ.* |

These are followed by by the twenty deities of the outer vajra-circle:

Vidyārājanikās:

*Om cchinda cchinda hūm phaṭ.*
*Om āviśāvisa hūm phaṭ.*
*Om bhūr bhuvaḥ sva hūm phaṭ.*
*Om bhinda bhinda hūm phaṭ.*

Krodhas:

*Om dama dama hūm phaṭ.*
*Om māraya māraya hūm phaṭ.*
*Om ghātaya ghātaya hūm phaṭ.*
*Om bhaya bhaya hūm phaṭ.*

Gaṇapatis:

*Om mada mada hūm phaṭ.*
*Om bandha bandha hūm phaṭ.*
*Om vaśī-bhava hūm phaṭ.*
*Om jaya jaya hūm phaṭ.*

Dūtas:

*Om bhyo bhyo hūm phaṭ.*
*Om ghū ghū hūm phaṭ.*
*Om jvala jvala hūm phaṭ.*
*Om khāda khāda hūm phaṭ.*

Cetas:

*Om khana khana hūm phaṭ.*
*Om māra māra hūm phaṭ.*
*Om gṛhṇa gṛhṇa hūm phaṭ.*
*Om vibha vibha hūm phaṭ.*

Vajrapāṇi delineates the dharma-samaya-maṇḍala of the sarvavajrakula. After performing usual ritual and showing its importance, taught the knowledge of mudrā of dharma-samaya. Thereafter comes the samādhi related to the five divisions of the twenty deities. The colophon of this chapter runs as follows: *Sarvatathāgata-vajrasamayān Mahākalparājāt Sarva-vajrakula-dharma-samaya-maṇḍala-vidhi-vistaraḥ samāptaḥ.*

## CHAPTER 14A OF THE STTS: SARVA-VAJRA-KULA-KARMA-MAṆḌALA

Once more Bhagavān enters the samādhi called vajra-consecration which has its origin in the karma-samaya of All the Tathāgatas and utters his vidyottama as: *Om vajra karma pravartani samaye hūm.* It is followed by the vidyottamās of the rest four Bodhisattvas:

Vajrapāṇi: *Om vajra vilāse pūjaya hūm.*

Vajragarbha: *Om vajrābhiṣeke 'bhiṣiñce hūm*

Vajranetra: *Om vajra-gīte gāhi hūm.*

Vajraviśva. *Om vajra nṛtye nṛtta hūm.*

Vajravidyottamā: *Om vajravidyottamā nṛtya nṛtya vikurva vikurva hūm phaṭ.*

Vajravidyottama is followed by the other deities of the maṇḍala:

Vajrakrodha-vajrāgni: *Om vajra-krodha vajragne jvālaya triśūlam bhinda hṛdayam vajreṇa hūm phaṭ.*

Vajrahemā: *Om vajrahemā cchinda cakreṇa vajriṇī hūm phaṭ.*

Vajrakaumārī: *Om vajrakaumārī śīghram aveśaya ghaṇṭā-śabdena vajrapāṇi-priye vajra-samayam anusmara raṇa raṇa hūm phaṭ.*

Vajraśānti: *Om vajraśānta japa japākṣamālayā sarvān māraya śānta-dṛṣṭya hūm phaṭ.*

Vajramuṣṭi. *Om vajra-muṣṭi hana hana vajreṇa bhinda bhinda pīḍaya pīḍaya sarva-duṣṭa-hṛdayāni. om śumbha niśumbha hūm phaṭ.*

Vajraragaṇikās are followed by krodhavidyās:

Vajrāmṛtakrodhā: *Om Vajrāmṛte sarva-duṣṭān gṛhṇa bandha hana paca vidhvansaya vināśaya bhinda cchinda bhasmīkuru mūrdhān tanuya vajreṇa ye ketu mām amukasya vighna-vināyakas tam dāmaya dīpta-krodha-vajriṇi hūm phaṭ.*

Vajrakānti: *Om vajra-kānti māraya saumya-rūpe pradīpta-rāgeṇa śīghram sphoṭaya hṛdayam vajradhara satyena mahājyotsnā karāle sita-raśmi-vajriṇī hūm phaṭ.*

Vajradaṇḍāgrā: *Om vajradaṇḍāgre ghātaya hūm phaṭ.*

Vajramekhalā-mahākrodhā. *Om vajra-mekhale khana khana śabdena vaśīkuru dṛṣṭya māraya bhīṣaṇī hūm phaṭ.*

Vajragaṇikās:

Vajravilayā: *Om vajravilaye cchinda sina bhinda vajriṇī mādaya unmādaya piva piva hūm phaṭ.*

Vajrāśanā. *Om vajrāśane bhakṣaya sarvaduṣṭān vajra-daśani śakti-dhāriṇī mānuṣa-mānsahāre nara-rucira, śubha-priye majjāvasānu-lepana viliptagātre ānaya sarva-dhana-dhānaya-hiraṇya-suvarṇādīni saṅkramaya baladeva-rakṣiṇī hūm phaṭ.*

Vajravasanā: *Om vajravasane ānaya sarva vastrānna pānādyupakaraṇāni śīghram vaśī kuru enan me prayacchāviśāviśa satyam kathaya vajra-kośa dhāriṇī hūm phaṭ.*

Vajravaśī: *Om vajravaśī anaya vaśī kuru sarva-striya- sarvapuruṣān dasīkuru kruddham prasādaya vyavahārebhyo 'pyuttāraya vijayamkarī vajrapatākā dhāriṇī hūm phaṭ.*

Vajradūtīs:

Vajradūtī: *Om Vajradūti ānaya sarvam maṇḍalam praveśayāveśaya bandhaya sarva karmāṇi me kuru śīghram śīghram laghu laghu trāsaya māraya raveṇa vajra khaḍga-dhāriṇī hūm phaṭ.*

Vegavajriṇī: *Om vegavajriṇī ghū ghū ghū ghū śábdena māraya vikira vidhvansaya vajrapaṭa dhāriṇī hūm phaṭ.*

Vajrajvālā: *Om vajrajvālā sarvam vajra jvālaya daha daha bhasmī kuru hūm phaṭ.*

Vajravikaṭā: *Om vajravikaṭe pravikaṭa-daṁṣṭra-karāla-bhīṣaṇa-vaktre śīghram gṛhṇaveśaya bhakṣaya rudhiram piva mahayakṣiṇi vajra- pāśadhāriṇī hūm phaṭ.*

Vajraceṭas:

Vajramukhī: *Om vajramukhī ānaya vajra-daṁṣṭrī bhayānike pātāla-nivāsinī khana khana khāhi khāhi sarvam mukhe praveśaya sphoṭaya marmāṇi sarva duṣṭānām vajra niṣitāsi dhāriṇī hūm phaṭ.*

Vajrakālī: *Om Vajrakālī mahā preta-rūpiṇī mānuṣa-mānsa-rudhira-priye ehi ehi gṛhṇa gṛhṇa bhakṣaya vajraḍākinī vajraśaṅkale sarvadeva-gaṇa-mātṛ-bhūte hara hara prāṇān amuksya kapāla-mālālaṅkṛte sarva-kāye kiñci rayasi vajrakhaṭvāṅgadhāriṇī preta-mānuṣa śarīre śīghramāveśaya praveśaya bandhaya vaśīkuru māraya vajrarākṣasi hūm hūm hūm hūm phaṭ.*

Vajraputanā: *Om vajrapūtane mānuṣa-mānsa-vasā-rudhira-mūtra-puriṣa śleṣma-siṁhānaka-reto-garbha-kārinya yāhi śīghram idam asya kuru vajra-śodhanika-dhāriṇī sarvakarmāṇi me kuru hūm phaṭ*

Vajramakarī: *Om vajramakarī grasa grasa śīghram śīghram praveśaya pātālam bhakṣaya vajra makara-dhāriṇī hūm phaṭ.*

Again Vajrapāṇi relates the karma-maṇḍala. After performing the rituals of samākarṣana etc. and making the mudrā of karma-samaya of Vajradharī he should ask that this esoteric action is not to be revealed to the one whose family and deeds are not known. Then vajrācārya should make the mudrā of samaya of his own karma vajradhari and looking angrily he says. *Om dhārayāveśaya praveśaya nṛtyāpaya sarva-karma-siddhim prayaccha hūm aḥ hūm la la la la vajri.* He enters himself and performs worship with mudrās pratimudrās and dance and performs all the rites by his body speech, eye sight mind and vajramudrā. Further he teaches about the knowledge of nṛtyopahāra-mudrā. The chapter comes to an end with the following colophon: *Sarvatathāgata vajrasamayān mahākalparājāt sarva-vajrakula-karma-maṇḍala-vidhi-vistaraḥ parisamāptaḥ.*

## CHAPTER 14 B OF THE STTS: SARVA-TATHĀGATA-VAJRA-SAMAYA-NĀMA-MAHĀ-KALPA-RĀJA

This chapter is an epilogue of the second half of the second part of STTS. It opens where Vajrapāṇi asks bhagavān as he is consecrated by all the Tathāgatas and if it is the esoteric knowledge which is commended by All the Tathāgatas ? Bhagavān enters the samādhi named as esoteric vajra of Stg. and recites this verse.

*yathā yathā hi vinayaḥ sarvasatvaḥ svabhāvataḥ /*
*tathā tathā hi satvārtham kuryād rāgādibhiḥ śuciḥ //*

It precedes the following four Bodhisattvas.

*sarvasatvahitārthaya buddhaśāsanahetutaḥ /*
*mārayet sarvasatvās tu na sa pāpena lipyate //*

Vajragarbha speaks his maṇiguhya:

*Sarvasatvahitārthaya buddhakāyaprayogataḥ /*
*hārāś tu sarvacintāni na sa pāpena lipyate //*

Vajranetra speaks his dharmaguhya.

*Rāgaśuddhaḥ sukhasamaḥ jinagocaradānataḥ /*
*sahāya paradārā niśeve sa puṇyam āpnute //*

Vajraviśva speaks his karmaguhya.

*Sarvasatvahitārthāya buddhaśāsanahetutaḥ /*
*sarvakarmāṇi kurvan vai sa bahupuṇyam āpnute //*

Vairocana applauds for vajradhara and the chapter ends with this colophon. *Sarvatathāgatatattvasaṁgrahāt Sarvatathagatavajra-samaya nāma mahākalparājaḥ parisamāptaḥ.*

## CHAPTER 15 OF THE STTS. SAKALA-JAGAD-VINAYA-MAHĀ-MAṆḌALA

All the Tathāgatas come to the multitude and solicitate Bhagavān Vajradhara, Lord of all the dharmas, Avalokiteśvara with 108 names. Āryāvalokiteśvara boshisatva mahāsatva listens to the words of solicitation by all the Tathāgatas by which Bhagavān Śākyamuni tathāgata puts a vajra near his heart and utters the following words.

*aho hi paramam śuddham vajrapadmam idam mama /*
*pitāham asya ca sūto 'dhitiṣṭha kulam tv idam //*

Now bhagavan Vairocana tathāgata enters the samādhi called consecration lotus which has its origin in the samaya of Vajra dharma of all the Tathāgatas and speaks the h.ṛdaya which is the hṛdaya of Stg. and names dharmasamaya *Hrīḥ*. As soon as the word is uttered rays emerge out of the hearts of all the Tathāgatas in the shape of lotuses with different colours, forms and symbols and enter the heart of Aryavalokiteśvara.

The five Bodhisattvas recite their vidyottamās as follows:

1. Bhagavan: *Om vajra Padmottama hrīḥ.*
2. Vajrapaṇi: *Om vajra hūm phaṭ.*
3. Vajra-garbha: *Om Vajra ratnottama traḥ.*
4. Vajranetra: *Om Vajra Vidyottamā Hriḥ.*
5. Vajraviśva: *Om vajra viśvottama aḥ.*

Now Avalokiteśvara bodhisattva mahāsatva enters the samādhi and recites his essence named sarvajagadvinaya samaya. *Om hūm hrīḥ hoḥ.* After all the necessary manifestations Avalokiteśvara relates the delineation of the maṇḍala. It is followed by the deities of the maṇḍala with their dhāraṇīs as follows:

6. Tathagāta-dharma: *Om Tathāgata dharma hūm.*
7. Vajra-padmāṅkuśa: *Om vajra padmāṅkuśa kośa-dhara vajra-sattva hūm phaṭ.*
8. Padma-kusumāyudha-dharāmogha-śara: *Om māraya māraya padma kusumāyudha-dharāmogha-śara hoḥ.*
9. Padma-sambhava padma-hasta: *Om padma-sambhava padma-hasta sādhu hūm.*
10. Padma-bhṛkuṭi: *Om padma-bhṛkuṭi traḥ.*
11. Padma-sūrya. *Om padma-sūrya jvālā hūm.*
12. Padma-maṇi ketu-dhara candra: *Om padma-maṇi ketu-dhara candra prahlādayāvalokiteśvara dehi me sarvārthān śighram samaya hūm.*
13. Padmatta-hasa: *Padmāṭṭa-hāsaikādaśa-mukha haḥ haḥ haḥ haḥ hūm.*
14. Tārā-padma: *Om tārā padmāvalokaya mām samaya-satva hūm.*
15. Padma kumāra padma-śakti-dhara: *Om padma-kumāra padma-śakti-dhara khaḍgeṇa cchiṇda cchinda hūm phaṭ.*
16. Padma-nīla-kaṇṭha: *Om padma-nīla-kaṇṭha saṁkha-cakra-gadā-padma-pāṇi vyāghra-carma-nivasana kṛṣṇa-sarpa-kṛta-yajñopavīta jina-carma vāma-skandhottarīya nārāyaṇa [rūpa-dha] ra tri-netra mumcāṭṭa-hāsam praveśāya samayān dehi me siddhim avaloki-teśvara hūm.*
17. Brahmā-padma-sambhava: *Om Brahmā padma sambhava japa japa padma bhāṣa hūm.*
18. Padma naṭṭeśvara: *Om padma naṭṭeśvara naṭṭa naṭṭa pūjaya sarva-tathāgatān vajra-karma samayākarṣaya praveśaya bandhāyāveśaya sarva karma-siddhim me prayacchāva-lokiteśvara hūm.*
19. Avalokitesvara: *Om abhayam-dadātvavalokiteśvara rakṣa bandha padma-kavacam samaya hūm.*
20. Padma-yakṣa: *Om mahā-pracaṇḍa viśva-rūpa-vikaṭa-padma-daṁṣṭra-karāla-bhīṣaṇa-vaktra trāsaya sarvān padma-daṁṣṭra-karāla–bhiṣaṇa-vaktra trāsaya sarvān padma-*

*yakṣa khāda khāda dhik dhik dhik dhik.*

21. Padma-muṣṭi samaya : *Om padma-muṣṭi-samayas tva bandha hūm phaṭ.*
26. Padma-lāsyā: *Om padma-lāsyā rāgaya mahā-devi rāga pūjā samaya hūm.*
27. Padma-mālā: *Om padma-mālā 'bhiṣiñcābhiṣeka-pūjā-samaya hūm.*
28. Padma-gītā: *Om padma-gītā gada gīta-pūjā-samaya hūm.*
29. Padma-nṛtyā: *Om padma-nṛtyā nṛtya sarva-pūja pravartana samaya hūm.*
30. Padma-dhūpa-pūjā-samayā: *Om padma-dhūpa-pūja-samaya prahlādaya padma-kula dayite mahā-gaṇi padma rati hūm.*
31. Padma-puṣpa-pūjā-samayā: *Om padma-puṣpa-pūjā-samayā padma-vāsini mahā-śrīya padma-kula-pratihārī sarvārtham sādhaya hūm.*
32. Padma-dīpa-pūjā-samaya: *Om padma-dīpa-pūjā-samaya padma-kula-sundarī mahā-dūtyāloka samjanaya padma-sarasvati hūm.*
33. Padma-gandha-pūjā-samayā: *Om padma-gandha-pūjā-samaya mahā-padma-kula-ceṭi kuru sarva-karmāṇi me padma siddhi hūm.*
34. Hayagrīva-mahā-padmāṅkuśa: *Haya-grīva mahā-padmāṅkuśākarṣaya śīghram sarva-padma-kula-samayān-padmāṅkuśa-dhara hūm jjaḥ.*
35. Amogha-padma-pāśa-krodha: *Om amogha-padma-pāśa krodhākarṣaya praveśaya mahā-paśupati yama varuṇa kubera brahmā veṣa-dhara padma-kula samayān hūm hūm.*
36. Padma-sphoṭa. *Om padma-sphoṭa bandha sarva padma-kula samayān śīghram hūm vam*
37. Padma-ghaṇṭa: *Om ṣaḍ-mukha sanat-kumāra veṣa-dhara padma-ghaṇṭayā-veśaya sarva-padma-kula-samayān sarva-mudrām bandhaya sarva-siddhaya me prayaccha padma-veṣa aḥ aḥ aḥ aḥ aḥ aḥ.*

Thus ends the explanation of sarvajadvinaya-padma-maṇḍala. First of all padmācarya makes the mudrā of Vajra-padma-samaya enters as usual and performs all the rituals according to the Vajradhātu-mahā maṇḍala with this assence: *Om padma sphoṭādhitiṣṭha aḥ.* After giving commands, consecrating himself with samaya-mudrā, obtaining a lotus, uttering his own name according to the lotus family, performing rituals with lotus etc. he should accomplish Mahāsattva by dharma-mudrās. Then padma śiṣya is entered the maṇḍala by him. He is to give him the śapathahṛdaya and instructs him about the estoterism of the maṇḍala.

Then he makes the samaya mudrā with this verse: *Om vajra-padma-samayas tyam.* Then he is entered in the maṇḍala with his eyes closed with this essence: Om padma-samaya *hūm.* After performing the necessary rites lotus is to be given in his hands reciting this verse *Om padma-hasta vajra-dharmatām pālaya.* He is to ask what is vajradharmatā ? He replies:

*yathā raktam idam padmam gotra doṣair na lipyata /*
*bhāvayet sarvaśuddhin tu tathā papair na lipyate //*

This is followed by instructions about the knowledge of mudrās of the lotus family with their essences proceeded by the knowledge of all the mudrās of the mahā-maṇḍala and samaya-mudrā of the lotus family. Thus ends the chapter with this colophon : *Sarvatathāgatadharmasamayān Mahākalparājāt Sakalajagadvinayamahāmaṇḍalavidhivistaraḥ samaptaḥ//*

## CHAPTERI 6 OF THE STTS PADMA-GUHYA-MUDRĀ-MAṆḌALA

The sixteenth chapter which is the second chapter of the third part opens with recitation of vidyottamas of the five tathāgatas as follows :

1.. Bhagavān : *Om sarva-tathāgata dharma samaya hūm.*

2.. Vajrapāṇi : *Om vajra-samaya hūm.*

3. Vajragarbha : *Om maṇi-ratna-samaya hūm.*

4. Vajranetra : *Om padma-samaya hūm.*

5. Vajraviśva : *Om karma-samaya hūm.*

Bhagvan āryāvalokiteśvara bodhisattva relates the samaya mudrā maṇḍala of his own family which is to be delineated according to Vajradhātu named as padmaguhya. All the deities of maṇḍala are mentioned with their dhāraṇīs and the central divinity as follows :

Vajradhātvīśvarī

1. Vajrapāṇi : *Om sarva-tathāgata dharmeśvarī hūm.*

2. Akṣobhya : *Om dharma-samaye vajra-padminī hūm.*

3. Ratnasambhava : *Om buddhābhiṣeka ratna-samaye hūm.*

4. Amitāyu : *Om tārā-samaye hūm.*

5. Amoghasiddhi . *Om viśva-mukhe hūm.*

6. Vajrasattva : *Om padma-tathāgate.*

7. Vajrarāja : *Om samanta-bhadra padma-vajrāṅkuśa kośa dhāriṇī hūm.*

8. Vajrarāga : *Om padma-rati.*

9. Vajrasādhu : *Om padma-tuṣṭi.*

Buddhābhiṣeka

10. Vajraratna : *Om bhṛkuṭi taṭi vetaṭi padme hūm.*

11. Vajrateja : *Om padma-jvāle hūm.*

12. Vajraketu : *Om somini-padme hūm.*

13. Vajrahāsa : *Om padma-hāsinī ekādaśa-vaktre diri diri iṭṭe vaṭṭe cale pracale kusumadhare ili praviśa siddhim me prayaccha hūm.*

Padmamudrā

14. Vajradharma : *Om tāre tuttāre hūm.*

15. Vajratīkṣṇa : *Om dhī hūm.*

16. Vajrahetu : *Om padma-gadā-dhāriṇī nīla-kaṇṭhe sidhya sidhya hūm.*

17. Vajrabhāṣa : *Om pāṇḍara-vāsini padma-sambhave vada vada hūm.*

Jvālāmālākulaprabha

18. Vajrakarma: *Om padma-narteśvarī pūjaya sarva-tathāgatān naṭṭa naṭṭa hūm.*

19. Vajrarakṣa: *Om abhaye padma-kavaca-bandhe rakṣa mām hūm hūm.*

20. Vajrayakṣa: *Om mahā-pracaṇḍi padma-yakṣiṇi viśva-rūpa -dhāriṇi bhiṣāpaya sarva-duṣṭān khāda khāda hūm phaṭ.*

21. Vajrasandhi: *Om padma-muṣṭi aḥ muḥ.*

They are followed by pūjā and saṅgraha bodhisattvas:

26. Vajralāsyā: *Om padma-rati-pūje hoḥ.*

27. Vajramālā: *Om padmābhiṣeka-pūje raṭ.*

28. Vajragītā: *Om padma-gīta-pūje giḥ.*

29. Vajranṛtyā: *Om padma-nṛtya-pūje kṛṭ.*

30. Vajradhūpā: *Om dhūpa-radminī hūm.*

31. Vajrapuṣpa: *Om padma-puṣpi hūm.*

32. Vajrālokā: *Om padma-kula-sundari dharmaloke pūjaya hūm.*

33. Vajragandhā: *Om padma-gandhe hūm.*

34. Vajrāṅkuśa: *Om padmāṅkusy-ākarṣaya mahā-padma-kulan hayagrīva-samaye hūm jaḥ.*

35. Vajrapāśa: *Om amogha-pāśa-krodha-samayepraviśa praveśaya sarva-samayām hūm*

36. Vajrasphoṭa: *Om padma-śaṅkale vam.*

37. Vajrāveśa: *Om padma ghaṇṭa-dhāri śīghram āveśaya samayān ṣaṇmukhi aḥ.*

In this mudrā maṇḍala on should perform the rites of ākarṣaṇādividhi, Padmaśiṣya should be entered and instruced about the esoterism afterwards the teacher asks him as what does he see ? If he finds it white he should be instructred about the uttamsiddhi. If it is yellow then arthotpatti, if it is red then anurāgaṇajñāna, if it is black then ābhicārakajñāna, if it is vicitra then sarvasiddhijñāna is to be taught. According to all the maṇḍalas there should be given the following instructions: Uttamasiddhiniṣpattijñāna, arthaniṣpattijñāna, anurāgaṇajñāna, ābhicārajñāna, dharmasamaya-rahasyamudrājñāna, padmakulaguhyamudrājñāna. Thus ends the chapter with this colophon: *Sarvatathāgatadharmasamayān mahākalparājāt padmaguhya-mudrāmaṇḍalavidhivistaraḥ parisamaptaḥ.*

## CHAPTER 17 OF THE STTS: JÑĀNA-MAṆḌALA-VIDHI-VISTARA

Bhagvān enters the samādhi called consecration lotus which has its origin in the samaya of dharmasamaya-jñāna of All the Tathāgatas and recites his vidhyottamā followed by other four as follows:

1. Bhagavān: *Om dharma-samādhi-jñāna-tathāgata hūm.*
2. Vajrapāṇi. *Om vajra-dharma hūm.*
3. Vajragarbha: *Om Ratna-dharma hūm.*
4. Vajranetra: *Om dharma-dharma hūm.*
5. Vajraviśva: *Om karma-dharma hūm.*

Āryāvalokiteśvara bodhisattva mahāsattva relates the delineation of the dharmamaṇḍala with the dhāraṇīes of the deities of maṇḍalas as follows:

1. Vajrapāṇi. *Om jñāna buddha hūm.*
2. Akṣobhya: *Om jñāna-viśveśvara hūm.*
3. Ratnasambhava: *Om jñāna-buddha-mukuṭa hūm.*
4. Amitāyu: *Om jñāna-dharmeśvara hūm.*
5. Amoghasiddhi: *Om jñānāmogheśvara hūm.*
6. Vajrasattva: *Om jñāna-padma-buddha hūm.*
7. Vajrarāja: *Om jñāna-padma-rāja-dhara hūm.*
8. Vajrarāga: *Om jñāna-padma-māra hūm.*
9. Vajrasādhu: *Om jñāna-padma-tuṣṭi hūm.*
10. Vajraratna: *Om jñāna-padma-bhṛkuṭi hūm.*
11. Vajrateja: *Om jñāna-padma-sūrya hūm.*
12. Vajraketu: *Om jñāna-padma-candra hūm.*
13. Vajrahāsa: *Om jñāna-padma-hāsa hūm.*
14. Vajradharma: *Om jñāna-padma-tārā hūm.*
15. Vajratīkṣṇa: *Om jñāna-padma kumāra hūm.*
16. Vajrahetu. *Om jñāna-padma-nārāyaṇa hūm.*
17. Vajrabhāṣa: *Om jñāna-padma-bhāṣa hūm.*
18. Vajrakarma: *Om jñāna-padma-nṛtyeśvara hūm.*
19. Vajrarakṣa. *Om jñāna-padma-rakṣa hūm.*
20. Vajrayakṣa: *Om jñāna-padma-yakṣa hūm.*
21. Vajrasandhi: *Om jñāna-padma-muṣṭi hūm.*
26. Vajralāsyā: *Om jñāna-padma-lāsye hūm.*
27. Vajramālā: *Om jñāna-padma-māle hūm.*
28. Vajragītā: *Om jñāna-padma-gīte hūm.*
29. Vajranṛtyā: *Om jñāna-padma-nṛtye hūm.*
30. Vajradhūpā: *Om padma-jñāna-dhūpe hūm.*

31. Vajrapuṣpā: *Om padma-jñāna-puṣpe hūm.*
32. Vajrālokā: *Om padma-jñāna-dīpe hūm.*
33. Vajragandhā: *Om padma-jñāna-gandhe hūm.*
34. Vajrāṅkuśa: *Om padma-jñānāṅkuśa hūm.*
35. Vajrapāśa: *Om padma-jñānāmogha-pāśa hūm.*
36. Vajrasphoṭa: *Om padma-jñāna-sphoṭa hūm.*
37. Vajrāveśa: *Om padma-jñānāveśa hūm.*

Ākarṣaṇādividhi of the padmadharmaṇḍala is described, śiṣya enters the maṇḍala and he is instructed about esoterism of the maṇḍala and the different types of knowledges. And the chapter ends with the knowledge of mahāmudrā of jñāna maṇḍala with this colophon. *Sarvatathāgatadharmasamayān mahākalparājāj jñāna-maṇḍalavidhivistaraḥ parisamāptaḥ.*

## CHAPTER 18 OF THE STTS: KARMAMAṆḌALA

Bhagavān again enters the samādhi named consecration lotus which originates in the samaya in the religious action of all the Tathāgatas and recites his vidyottama followed by other four:

1. Bhgavān: *Om sarva-tathāgata-karmāgra hūm.*
2. Vajrapāṇi: *Om hūm diḥ.*
3. Vajragarbha : *Om ratna-karma-samaye hūm.*
4. Vajranetra . *Om padma karmi hūm.*
5. Vajraviśva . *Om viśva-karmi hūm.*

Āryāvalokiteśvara bodhisattva mahāsattva relates the delineation of the maṇḍala of his own action. Vidyahṛdayas of all the deities of the maṇḍala are given as follows:

1. Vajrapāṇi. *Om padma bhūriṇi hūm.*
2. Akṣobhya: *Om viśva-karmeśvari hūm.*
3. Ratnasambhava. *Om tathagāteśvaryabhiseka-karma-vidye hūm.*
4. Amitāyu: *Om dharma-karmeśvari-jñāna-pūjā-samaye hūm.*
5. Amoghasiddhi: *Om amogha-karmeśvari hūm.*
6. Vajrasattva: *Om padma-karma-buddhe hūm.*
7. Vajrarāja: *Om padma-karma-vajriṇī hūm.*
8. Vajrarāga: *Om padma-kāminī-māraṇa-pūjā-karma-samaye hūm.*
9. Vajrasādhu. *Om padma-karma-tuṣṭi hūm.*
10. Vajraratna: *Om padma-karma bhṛkuṭi hūm traḥ.*

11. Vajrateja: *Om padma-karma-sūrye hūm.*
12. Vajraketu: *Om padma-karma-dhvaje hūm.*
13. Vajrahāṣa: *Om padma-karma-hāse haḥ.*
14. Vajradharma: *Om padma-karma-tāre hūm.*
15. Vajratīkṣṇa: *Om padma-karma-kūmāri hūm.*
16. Vajrahetu: *Om padma-karma-nārāyaṇī hūm.*
17. Vajrabhāṣa: *Om padma-karma-brāhmī hūm.*
18. Vajrakarma: *Om padma-karma-nṛtyeśvarī hūm.*
19. Vajrarakṣa: *Om padma-rakṣa-karma-samaye hūm.*
20. Vajrayakṣa: *Om mahāpracandi ghātani padma-daṁṣtra, karma-kari hūm.*
21. Vajrasandhi: *Om padma-karma-muṣṭi ghātaya hūm.*
26. Vajralāsyā: *Om rati-pūje hūm jjaḥ.*
27. Vajramālā: *Om abhiṣeka-pūje hūm hoḥ.*
28. Vajragītā: *Om gīta-pūje hūm dhaḥ.*
29. Vajranṛtyā: *Om nṛtya-pūje hūm vaḥ.*
30. Vajradhūpā: *Om dhūpa-pūje aḥ.*
31. Vajrapuṣpā. *Om puṣpa-pūje hūm traḥ.*
32. Vajrālokā. *Om āloka-pūje hūm dhiḥ.*
33. Vajragandhā. *Om gandha-pūje hūm vam.*
34. Vajrākuśa: *Om hayagrīve ānaya hūm jaḥ.*
35. Vajrapāśa: *Om amogha-pāśa-krodhe pīḍaya hūm phaṭ.*
36. Vajrasphoṭa: *Om padma-śaṅkala-bandhe hūm phaṭ.*
37. Vajrāveśa: *Om padma ghaṇṭāveśaya hūm phaṭ.*

After performing the rites of ākarṣaṇa etc. He enters the maṇḍala accordingly and narrates the secracy of the maṇḍala and its importance. Teacher instructs student about the following types of knowledges. pāpadeśana, sarvāvaraṇaparīkṣaya, Sarvatathāgatapūjā, siddhi and karmarahasyamudrā. Karmamudrā is made by him and he says *tra* and the chapter ends with the following colophon: *Sarvatathāgatadharma-samayān mahākalparājāt karma-maṇḍala vidhivistaraḥ samāptaḥ.*

## CHAPTER 18.B OF THE STTS:SARVA-TATHĀGATA-DHARMA-SAMAYA-NĀMA MAHĀ-KALPA-RĀJA

Bhagavān enters the samādhi named mudrā consecration of the samaya of vajradharma and recites his mudrā hṛdaya as. Om vajra-dharma-padma hūm. It is followed by:

2. Vajrapāṇi: *Om vajra jiḥ.*
3. Vajragarbha: *Om vajra-ratna-mukuṭe hūm.*
4. Vajranetra: *Om dharma-padmi dhiḥ.*
5. Vajraviśva : *Om sarva-mukhi hūm.*

Āryāvolokiteśvara bodhisattva mahāsattva relates the delineation of the caturmudrā-maṇḍala which is named as catur-mudrāgramaṇḍala. Again after necessary rites, entering the maṇḍala and relating its esoterism, the teacher gives instruction about different types of knowledge as mudrārahasya, mahāmudrādisarvamudrābandha. There is a colophon to indicate the ending of caturmudrāmaṇḍalavidhivistara.

Āryāvalokiteśvara speaks his essence named as sarvajagad vinaya as: Om sarva-jagad *vinaya mahā-satvāgaccha śīghram vaiśva rūpyam darsāya mama ca sarva siddhayaḥ prayaccha hrīḥ.* Again he relates the delineation of the maṇḍala named sarvajagadvinaya after performing the necessary rituals he instructs about the jagadvinayarahasayamudrajñāna and mahāmudradimudrabandha. Thus ends the ekamudrā-maṇḍala. All the Tathāgatas come to the multitude and solicatate Avalokiteśvara and the chapter ends with this colophon: *Sarvatathāgatatatvasaṁgrahāt Sarvatathāgata-dharmasamayo nāma mahākalparāja parisamāptaḥ.*

## CHAPTER 19 OF THE STTS SARVĀRTHASIDDHI-MAHĀ-MAṆḌALA

All the Tathāgatas once more come to the multitude and solicitate the consecration gem of all the Tathāgatas, Vajradharma, Āryākāśagarbha Mahābodhisattva with 108 names. Ākāśagarbha Bodhisattva listens these words and speaks out his essence as. *Om Vajra ratna hūm.* Bhagavān Vairocana spoke his vidyottama which is the maṇi-samaya of Stg. as: *Om Sarvatathāgatāśaparipūrṇa-mahā-ratna hūm.* Mahābodhisattva Vajrapāṇi relates his vidyottamā which originates in his own family as. *Om vajra hūm traḥ.* Vidyottamā of vajragarbha is: *Om maṇi hūm* and of Vajranetra as : *Om Padma hrīḥ.* Mahāsattva Bodhisattva Vajraviśva relates his vidyottamā as: *Om viśva-ratna hūm.*

Āryākāśagarbha enters the samādhi named as consecration gem of Stg. and rays of vajra gem emerge out of the hearts of Stg. They illuminate all the lokadhātus, consecrate all the sattvas by consecration of Stg. they coalesce into one and enter the heart of Ākāśagarbha mahābodhisattva. Bhagavān vajrapāṇi originates out of the heart of Ākāśagarbha encircled by rays with flames with a body decorated with different vajra gems, garments and ornaments, with a mudrā of great vajra gem, in the form of a great bodhisattva. Having satisfied with gems in all the lokadhātus, stations himself in a lunar disc like Vajradhātu-mahāmaṇḍala, he utters these words:" Oho this is the collection of gems of All the Buddhas, for the welfare of all the world this is the family of vajra-ratna".

Bodhisattva Ākāśagarbha originates his family and relates the mahāmaṇḍala named Sarvāthasiddhi

1. Vajrapāṇi: *Om Buddha-ratna hūm.*
2. Akṣobhya: *Om vajramaṇi hūm .*
3. Ratnasambhava: *Om vajraratnāṅkura hūm.*
4. Amitāyu. *Om vajra-ratna-padma hūm.*
5. Amoghasiddhi: *Om ratna-padma-varṣa hūm.*

In the maṇḍala of Sarvārthasiddhi Vajragarbha is to be drawn with a mudrā of ratnavaraprada. Mahāsattvas are to be positioned around him with ratna mudrās:

6. Vajrasattva. *Om vajramaṇi-cihnākāśagarbha bhagavān siddhya siddhya hūm.*
7. Vajrarāja: *Om ratnāṅkuśākarṣaya sarvarthān ānaya śīghram sarvatathāgata satyam anusmara hūm.*
8. Vajrarāga: *Om maṇi-rāga vaśī kuru sarvārthān ānayākāśagarbha hūm.*
9. Vajrasādhu: *Om ratna tuṣṭi hūm.*

In the maṇḍala of Ratnamālā, he occupies a central position and mahāsattvas around him sit with signs of great gems in their hands:

10. Vajraratna. *Om sarvatathāgatābhiṣeka-ratna-māla hūm.*
11. Vajrateja. *Om maṇi-sūrya hūm.*
12. Vajraketu: *Om cintāmaṇi-dhvaja sarvāśā-prapūraka-ākāśa-garbha hūm.*
13. Vajrahāsa. *Om ratnāṭṭahāsa ha ha hūm.*

Next is the maṇḍala of Ratna-padma, with following mahāsattvas.

14. Vajradharma. *Om tyāga-samādhi-jñāna-garbha hūm.*
15. Vajratīkṣṇa. *Om ratna-kośāgrya hūm.*
16. Vajrahetu. *Om maṇi-cakra pravartaya hūm.*
17. Vajrabhāṣa: *Om ratnabhāṣa hūm.*

In the maṇḍala of Ratnavṛṣṭi:

18. Vajrakarma: *Om maṇi-pūjā-samaya hūm.*
19. Vajrarakṣa. *Om maṇi-bandha-kavaca hūm.*
20. Vajrayakṣa. *Om maṇi-danṣṭra-karāla mahā-yakṣa hara hara sarvārthān bhīṣāpaya hūm.*
21. Vajrasandhi: *Om maṇi-ratna bandha-samaya hūm.*

In the corners are Ratnalāsya etc.:

26. Vajralāsyā: *Om ratna-rati hūm.*
27. Vajramālā: *Om ratna-māle hūm.*

28. Vajragītā: *Om vajragite hum.*

29. Vajranṛtyā *.Om ratna-nrtye hum.*

In the corners of outer maṇḍala are:

30. Vajradhūpā: *Om dhūpa ratne.*

31. Vajrapuṣpa: *Om puṣpa-maṇi.*

32. Vajrālokā: *Om ratnalōke.*

33. Vajragandha: *Om maṇi-gandhe.*

Dvārapālas are in four doors .

34. Vajrāṅkuśa: *Om sarva-ratnākarṣa āryāruṇa mahā-sattva bhagavantam ākāśagarbham codayākarṣaya śīghram hoḥ jaḥ.*

35. Vajrapāśa: *Om sarva-ratna-praveśa-samaya praveśaya samayān mahāmaṇi-rāja-kulam ratna-pāśa hūm.*

36. Vajrasphoṭa. *Om maṇi-bandha hūm vam. Om maṇi*

37. Vajrāveśa. *Om maṇi-ratnāvẹśa aḥ.*

Now maṇiratnācārya enters the maṇḍala accordingly and consecrates the maṇi śiṣya with water taken out of the kalaśa placed on a gem. He makes samaya-mudrā of vajramaṇi with this verse: *Om vajra-maṇi-samaya vam.* He makes the sisya enter the maṇḍala and instructs him to conceal the maṇḍala from unworthy beings. The teacher asks him as where is the mahāsiddhi and how can it be obtained ? Bhagavān Ākāśagarbha uncovers his face and shows the maṇḍala. Thus the chapter comes to an end.

## CHAPTER 20 OF THE STTS :RATNA-GUHYA-MUDRĀ-MAṆḌALA

The chapter opens with the samādhi of Bhagavān named gem-consecration which originates from the saṃaya of consecration dhāraṇī of All the Tathāgatas and vidyottamās of the five mahā-bodhisattvas .

Bhagavān: *Om vajra-ratna-stūpe hūm.*

Vajrapāṇi: *Om vajrābhiṣeka-māle abhiṣiñca samaye hūm.*

Vajragarbha: *Om vajra-ratnābhiṣeka hūm.*

Vajranetra: *Om vajradharmābhiṣiñca mam.*

Vajra-viśva: *Om sarvābhiṣeka-pūjā-samaye hūm.*

Bhagavān āryākāśagarbha narrates the delineation of the samaya-mudrā maṇḍala of his own family. Essences of all the deities with their central divine beings are given as follows:

Buddhamudrā

1. Vajrapāṇi: *Om traḥ.*

2. Akṣobhya: *Om maṇi -samaye hūm. Om mani*

3. Ratnasambhava: *Om maṇi-ratnābhiṣeka-māle.*

4. Amitāyu. *Om maṇi-ratna-padmi hūm.*

5. Amoghasiddhi. *Om maṇi-ratna-vṛṣṭi-samaye hūm.*

Mahāratnamaṇi

6. Vajrasattva: *Om maṇi-ratnākarṣe hūm.*

7. Vajrarāja. *Om maṇi-ratnāṅkuśy-ākarṣaya maṇi-kulam jaḥ.*

8. Vajrarāga. *Om maṇi-rāga-samaye hūm.*

9. Vajrasādhu: *Om sarthi hūm.*

Maṇi

10. Vajraratna: *Om vajra-maṇi-ratna-māle'bhiṣiñca hūm.*

11. Vajrateja: *Om maṇi-ratna-sūrye jvālaya sarvam mahā-tejini hūm.*

12. Vajraketu: *Om maṇi-candra-dhvajāgri hūm.*

13. Vajrahāsa: *Om maṇi-hāse hasa hūm.*

Maṇipadma

14. Vajradharma: *Om maṇi-ratna-tyāga-samaye hūm.*

15. Vajratīkṣṇa: *Om maṇi-kośe hūm.*

16. Vajrahetu: *Om maṇi-samaya-cakre hūm.*

17. Vajrabhāṣa. *Om maṇi-bhāṣāgri hūm.*

Ratnavṛṣṭi

18. Vajrakarma: *Om mahā-pūjā-samaye nṛtya aḥ.*

19. Vajrarakṣa. *Om ratna samaya-rakṣe ham.*

20. Vajrayakṣa. *Om vajra-maṇi-ratna-danṣṭra-karāle hara hara hūm.*

21. Vajrasandhi. *Om maṇi-samaya-muṣṭi hūm.*

Now in the maṇi-guhya maṇḍala after performing the necessary rites and entering the maṇḍala teacher instructs about the esoterism of the maṇḍala and different types of knowledges with their essences. Last of all comes the maṇi-kula-samaya-mudrā-rahasya-jñāna. The chapter ends with mahāmudrā-bandha, samaya-mudrā-jñāna and dharma-mudrā. Its colophon is: *Sarvatathāgata-karma-samayāt mahākalparājāt ratnaguhya-mudrā-maṇḍala vidhi-vistaraḥ samāptaḥ.*

## CHAPTER 21 OF THE STTS : JÑĀNA–MAṆḌALA

Bhagavān enters the samādhi named consecration which originates in the samaya of consecration knowledge of All the Tathāgatas and relates his vidyottamatā proceeded by other four:

Bhagavān: *Om sarvatathāgatābhiṣeka-jñānottama hūm.*

Vajrapāṇi: *Om vajra-jñānābhiṣeka-samaye hūm.*

Vajragarbha: *Om maṇi-ratnābhiṣeka-jñāna-hūm.*

Vajranetra: *Om dharmābhiṣeka-jañana-hūm.*

Vajraviśva: *Om sarvābhiṣeka-jñāna hūm.*

Knowledge essences of the maṇḍala run as follows after delineation related by Ākāśagarbha:

6. Vajrasattva: *Om maṇi-jñāna hūm.*
7. Vajrarāja: *Om maṇi-jñānāṅkuśa.*
8. Vajrarāga: *Om maṇi-jñāna-rāga.*
9. Vajrasādhu: *Om maṇi-jñāna-tuṣṭi.*
10. Vajraratna: *Om maṇi-jñāna-dṛṣṭi-maṇi hūm.*
11. Vajrateja: *Om maṇi-jñāna-sūrya.*
12. Vajraketu: *Om maṇi-jñāna-dhvaja.*
13. Vajrahāsa: *Om maṇi-jñānāṭṭahāsa.*
14. Vajradharma. *Om maṇi-jñāna-padma hūm.*
15. Vajratīkṣṇa: *Om jñāna-maṇi-kośa.*
16. Vajrahetu: *Om jñāna-maṇi-cakra.*
17. Vajrabhāṣa: *Om jñāna-maṇi-bhāṣa.*
18. Vajrakarma: *Om maṇi-jñāna-nṛtya-pūjā-samaya hūm.*
19. Vajrarakṣa: *Om maṇi-jñāna-rakṣa.*
20. Vajrayakṣa: *Om maṇi-jñāna-yakṣa.*
21. Vajrasandhi: *Om maṇi-jñāna-muṣṭi.*

After ordinary process of entering the maṇḍala and relating the secracy follow different knowledges with their essences. The chapter comes to an end after instructing about the knowledge of mudrā of maṇijñānarahasya and dharma and karmamudrās with this *Sarvatathāgatakarmasamayāt Mahākalaparājāj Jñānamaṇḍalavidhivistaraḥ parisamāpataḥ.*

## CHAPTER 22.A OF THE STTS : KARMA-MAṆḌALA

Bhagavān enters the samdhi named consecration which originates from the action-pledge of consecration of All the Tathāgatas and recites his vidyottamā with other four:

Bhagavān: *Oṁ sarva-tathagata-karmabhiseke hum.*

Vajrapāṇi: *Om vajra humkarabhiseke.*

Vajragarbha: *Om sarvakasa-samatabhiseke hum.*

Vajranetra: *Om sad-dharmabhiseka-ratne.*

Vajraviśva: *Om visvabhiseke.*

Ākāśagarbha bodhisattva relates the delineation followed by the following essences of the divinities:

1. Vajrasattva. *Om vajra-mani-dharini-samaye hum.*
7. Vajrarāja. *Om mani-ratnakarse-karma-samaye-hum.*
8. Vajrarāga: *Om mani-ratna-raga-rati-karma-puje pravarta.*
9. Vajrasādhu: *Om mani-ratna-sadhu-kara-puja-samaye.*
10. Vajraratna. *Om maha-mani-ratna-drstyakarse.*
11. Vajrateja: *Om mani-ratna-suryaloka-puje.*
12. Vajraketu. *Oṁ mani-ratna-dhvaja-pataka-puje.*
13. Vajrahāsa. *Om mani-ratnatta-hasa puje.*
14. Vajradharma: *Om padma-mani-samadhi-samaya hum.*
15. Vajratīkṣṇa: *Om mani-ratna-tiksna-samaye cchinda cchinda hum.*
16. Vajrahetu: *Om mani-ratna-cakra-samaye hum.*
17. Vajrabhāṣa. *Om mani-ratna-bhase vada vada hum.*
18. Vajrakarma. *Om mani-ratna karmani hum.*
19. Vajrarakṣa: *Om mani-ratna-kavace-raksa hum.*
20. Vajrayakṣa: *Om mani-ratna-damstri khada khada hum.*
21. Vajrasandhi: *Om mani-ratna-karma-musti hum.*
26. Vajralāsyā: *Om mani-ratna-lasyepujaya hoh.*
27. Vajramālā: *Om mani-ratna malabhiseke pujaya.*
28. Vajragītā: *Om mani-ratna-gite pujaya.*
29. Vajranṛtyā: *Om mani-ratna-nrtye pujaya.*
30. Vajradhūpā: *Om mani-ratna-dhupa pujaya.*
31. Vajrapuṣpā: *Om mani-ratna-puspa pujaya.*
32. Vajrālokā: *Om mani-ratnadipe pujaya.*
33. Vajragandhā: *Om mani-ratna-gandhe pujaya.*
34. Vajrāṅkuśa: *Om mani-ratnankusyakarse jjah.*
35. Vajrapāśa : *Om maṇi-ratna-pāśe hūm.*
36. Vajrasphoṭa: *Om maṇi-ratnasphoṭe aḥ.*
37. Vajrāveśa: *Om maṇi-ratnāveśe aḥ.*

The common process of entering the maṇḍala and its relation of estorism is followed by rahasyamudrākarma jñāna. mahāmudrā jñānottamadiddhi, samayamudrājñāna and dharmamudrājñāna. Colophon of the chapter is given as : *Sarvatathāgatakarmasamayān Mahākalparājāt Karmamaṇḍalavidhivistaraḥ parisamāptaḥ.*

## CHAPTER 22.B OF THE STTS: SARVA-TATHĀGATA-KARMA-SAMAYA-NĀMA MAHĀ-KALPA-RĀJA

Bhagavān enters the samādhi named ratnamudrā and gives his vidyottama followed by others:

Bhagavān: *Om vajra ratne tram.*

Vajrapāṇi: *Om vajra-māle hūm.*

Vajragarbha: *Om maṇi-ratne.*

Vajranetra: *Om dharma-ratne.*

Vajraviśvạ: *Om viśva-dṛṣṭi.*

Ākāśagarbha bodhisattava relates its delineation called maṇikulacaturmudrāmaṇḍala and entrance. Thereafter follow the knowledge of rahasyamudrā, its sādhanahṛdaya and caturmudrābandha. After this caturmudrāmaṇḍala ākāśagarbha relates the maṇḍala of sarvārthasiddhi with this essence: *Om vajra maṇi-dhara sarvārtha-siddhim me prayaccha ho bhagavān vajra-ratna hūm.* Knowledge of rahasyamudrā precedes the four types of mudrās. All the Tathāgatas again come to the multitude and applaud ākāśagarbha bodhisattva. Colophon of the chapter is: *Sarvatathāgatatatvasaṁgrahāt Sarvatathāgatakarma-samaya-nāma mahākalparājaḥ parisamāptaḥ.*

# PART 5

## CHAPTER 23 OF THE STTS: SARVA-KALPOPĀYA-SIDDHI-VIDHI-VISTARA TANTRA

Vajrapāṇi mahā-Bodhisattva introduces the tantra which explains the mahātattva of All the Tathāgatas. First of all he relates the supreme accomplishment of the great mudrā. It is followed by tantras of accomplishments of samaya-mudrā, dharma-mudrā and karma-mudrā. Now Vajrapāṇi speaks about the tantra of uttama-siddhi of his own kula, proceeded by samaya-uttama-siddhi-tantra, dharma-mudrottama-siddhitantra, and karma-mudrottama-siddhi-tantra. Mahābodhisattva Vajrapāṇi relates the uttama-siddhi-tantra, mahāmudrā, samaya-mudrā, dharma-mudrā and karma-mudrā of the lotus family, followed by the supreme accomplishments of gem family which is again of four types, mahā-mudrā, samaya mudrā, dharma-mudrā and karma-mudrā. Thus ends the explanation of attainment of supreme accomplishments of Buddhabodhisattva of all the mudrās of all the famili es. (STTS 435-440).

Now Vajrapāṇi instructs the tantra of samaya-siddhi of Stg. explaining it from the viewpoint of Tathāgatakula, vajrakula, padmakula and ratnakula. Vajrapāṇi instructs about the tantra of accomplishment of knowledge of dharma-mudrā of Stg. with its Tathāgatakula vajrakula, padmakula and maṇikula. This precedes the sarvatathāgatakula-karma-siddhi-tantra with its four kulas, followed by its dharmatā-mudrā-jñāna-tantra with four aspects told by Bhagavān Vajradhara. Then Vajrapāṇi mahābodhisattva relates the knowledge of siddhi of four kulas. Mahābodhisattva relates the tantra of mudrā of knowledge of siddhi of recognition of Stg. It is described with its tantra of tathāgatakula and divyacakṣu-jñāna spoken by Bhagavān Vajrasattva, Vajradhara and Vajrapāṇi, (STTS 440-451)

Accomplishment of knowledge of ṛddhividhi: ṛddhividhi-jñāna-siddhi is instructed by Mahābodhicitta. Its recognition in its vajrakula is related by Bhagavān Vajrasattva, Padmakula by Lokeśvara and maṇikula by Ākāśagarbha. Thus ends the tantra of description of performance of knowledge of recognition of all the kulas: *sarva-kulābhijñā-jñāna-vidhivistara tantraḥ*. Now Bhagavān Vajrapāṇi speaks about the tantra which relates satya-siddhi of sarvatathāgatakula, Vajradhara states the tathāgatakula-satya-siddhi-tantra, Vajradhara Vajrakula-satya-siddhi-tantra and Lokeśvara padma-kula satya-siddhi-tantra and maṇi-kula-satyasiddhi-tantra. Thus ends after this sarvakula-śapatha siddhi-tantra and comes the tantra of description of performance of mudrā of accomplishment of samaya tattva of all the kulas: sarva-kula-samaya-tattva-siddhi-mudrā-vidhi-vistara-tantra with its four kulas spoken by Mahābodhi-sattva-Vajrapāṇi. Again he relates sarvatathāgata siddhi-mudrā-tantra and sarvatathāgata-sarva siddhi-sādhana-tantra proceeded by the word of Bhagavān Vajrasattva for tathāgatakulādisarva-siddhi-sādhana-tantra, Sarvatathāgatavajra of the Vajrakula, Avalokiteśvara of Padmakula and Ākāśagarbha of maṇikula. This is named as sarva kulottama siddhi-vistara-tantra. The tantras of accomplishment of mudrās of consecration of Stg. sarvatathāgatādhiṣṭhāna-mudrā-siddhi-tantra, with its four kulas are related by Vajrasattva, Vajranātha, Avalokiteśvara and Vajragarbha. Bhagavān Avalokiteśavara speaks about the tantra of accomplishment of abhiṣeka in Tathāgatakula, vajrakula and padma-kula and Ākāśagarbha instructs about maṇikula (STTS 451-461)

Bhagavān Buddhasamādhi speaks about the tathāgata-kula-samādhi-siddhi-tantra, Bhagavān Vajradhra about vajrakula-samādhi siddhi-tantra, Avalokiteśvara about padmakula-samadhi-tantra and Bhagavān Ākāśagarbha about maṇikula-samādhi-siddhi-tantra. Sarva-kula samādhi-vidhi-vistara is followed by sarvatathāgata-pūjā-mudrā siddhi-tantra related by Vajrasattva, Vajradhara, Avalokiteśvara and Vajragarbha. This precedes the tantras of knowledge of accomplishment of recognition of the four kulas spoken by Vajrasattva, Vajradhara, Vajranetra and Vajradhara. After sarva-kulābhijñā-jñāna-siddhi-vidhi-vistara-tantra comes the tantras of accomplishment of knowledge of mahābodhi of Tathāgatakula, vajrakula padmakula and maṇikula spoken by Bhagavān Mahābodhisattva, Vajradhara, Avalokiteśvara and Ākāśagarbha (STTS 461-468).

The chapter proceeds with the anurāgaṇa-siddhi-tantra of Stg. Bhagavān. Vajrarāga relates the tantra and Vajrasattva Trilokavijaya, Vajranetra and Āryākāśagarbha speak about the anurāgaṇa tantra of the four kulas. After anurāgaṇa comes the vaśīkaraṇa-siddhi-tantra of the four kulas related by Samantabhadra. Vajra-hūṅkāra, Āryāvalokiteśvara and Ākāśa-garbha. Mahābodhisattva introduces the sarvatathāgata-marana-siddhi-tantra of Stg. Vajra-pāṇi, Vajradhara, Avalokiteśvara and Sarvāśāparipūraka explain it from the view point of the kulas. Last of all comes the tantra of accomplishment of mudrā of rakṣā of the kulas which are explained by Vajradhara, Vajrahūṅkāra, Vajradharma and Vajrarakṣa. (STTS 468-474).

Mahābodhisattva Vajrapāṇi asks Bhagavān that he should take the tantra of sarava-tathāgatakula by which all the beings can enjoy sovereignty for millions of years and soon attain the supreme spiritual realization. Bhagavān cries in approbation for Vajrapāṇi bodhi-sattva mahāsattva and says well done well done, and asks him to receive forgiveness and commands by them, All the Tathāgatas once more come to the multitude and cheer him up

The chapter 23rd comes to an end with this colophon: *Sarvatathāgata-tattva saṅgra-hāt sarvakalpopāya-siddhi-vidhi-vistara-tantraḥ parisamāptaḥ.* (STTS 474-5).

## CHAPTER 24 OF THE STTS: SARVAKULA-KALPA-GUHYA-VIDHI VISTARA-TANTRA

The 24th chapter with uttama-siddhi-guhya-tanatra of the four kulas, instructed by Sattvavajra, Sarvatathāgatahūṅkāra, Padmarāga and Maṇirāga. It is followed by samaya-siddhi-guhya-tantra of Stg. in all the kulas related by Bhagavān Vairocana, Trilokavijaya, Avalokiteśvara and Vajraratna. Now follows the esoteric tantra for accomplishing dharma of Stg. introduced by Vajraguhya, Dharmahūṅkāra, Avalokiteśvara and Vajra-ratna. After this sarvakula-dharma-siddhi-guhya-tantra-vidhi-vistara-tantra comes the tantra explaining accomplishment of karma instructed by Vajraga, Vajrasamaya, Vajrapadma and Vajraratna. (STTS 476-482).

Esoteric tantra of maṇḍala siddhi of Stg. It has the cakra-śuddhi-siddhi-guhya-tantra of Stg. related by Bhagavān Buddha. Its four kulas are described by Vajrasattva, Vajrahūṅ-kāra, Avalokiteśvara and Vajrasattva, Bhagavān Vajragarvapati, Vajrasattva, Vajradharma and Ākāśagarbha speak the esoteric tantra of all the mūdras of Stg. Pledge comes after mudrās. The esoteric tantra explaining the pledge of Stg. is explained by All the Tathāgatas Vajradharma, Vajranetra and Ājñākaraḥ. The tantra explaining pūjā is related by Vajra-

dhara, Vajrahūṅkāra, Padmanetra and Vajraratna. Esoteric pūjā of all the Tathāgatas is instructed by Vajraguhya, Avalokiteśvara and Vajragarbha (STTS 483-493)

Bhagavān Vajrapāṇi Mahābodhisattva utters the opeining of guhya-siddhi-tantra of Stg. Tathāgata-tattvotpatti-siddhi-guhya-tantra is told by Bhagavān Tathāgata. Bhagavān Anādinidhana-sattva relates the tantra of opening of great tattva of Stg. Sarva-tatha-gata-cakra tells that vajrakula, padmakula and maṇikula are the same to the Tathāgatakula. Further he explains the tantra of mudrā-cihnābhidhāna-siddhi of Stg.

These are followed by sarvatathāgata-mudrā-bandhotpatti-siddhi-guhya-tantra with its four kulas related by Bhagavān, Mahāmudrā, Vajrasamaya, Vajradharma and Bhagavān vajra.

Bhagavān asks Vajrapāṇi Mahābodhisattva that that is also forgiven and commanded by him. All the Tathāgatas again come to the multitude and pay respects to their lord. And the chapter ends with this colophon. *Sarvatathāgata-tattva-saṅgrahāt Sarva-kula-kalpa-vidhi-vistara-tantram samāptam.*

## CHAPTER 25 OF THE STTS: SARVA-KULA-GUHYOTTARA-TANTRA

Herebelow are the names of tantras and the deities of their kulas:

Sarva-tathāgata-dharmottama-siddhi-tantra : Sarvatathāgata-samādhi, Vajrasattva, Vajradharma and Vajrapāṇi.

Sarvatathāgata-dharma-samaya-siddhi-tantra: Vajrasattva, Vajrahūṅkāra, Vajradharma and Maṇidharma.

Sarvatathāgata-saddharma-maṇi-jñāna-siddhi-tantra: Vajrasattva, Vajrakula, Avalokiteśvara and Dharmaratna,

Sarvatathāgata-samādhi-karma-siddhi-tantra: Bhagavān Vajra, Bhagavān Vajri, Padma and Ratnadhvaja.

Sarvatathāgata-sūkṣma-jñāna-siddhi-tantra: Vajradhara, Vajra, Padmarāga and Vajrapāṇi.

Sarvatathāgata-cakṣur-jñāna-siddhi-tantra: Vajrasattva, Vajra, Avalokiteśvara and Vajra-garbha.

Sarvatathāgata-karmottama-siddhi-tantra: Kāma, Vajrapāṇi, Avalokiteśvara and Vajrabhi-ṣekaratna.

Sarvatathāgata-karma-samaya-guhya-siddhi-tantra: Kāma, Vajrapāṇi, Padmarāga and Sarvār-thasiddhi.

Sarvatathāgata-karma-dharmottama-siddhi-tantra: Āryavajrapāṇi, Vajrasattva, Vajradhara and Vajrahūṅkāra.

Sarvatathāgata-karma-kārya-siddhi-tantra: Vajradhara, Vajrakrodha, Padmarāga and Vajragarbha.

Sarvatathāgata-mudrā-bhāvanādhiṣṭhāna-yoga-siddhi-tantra: Bhagavān sarvatathāgata-mahāyānābhisamaya-vajra-sattva, Vajradhara, Āryāvalokiteśvara and Vajrakarma.

Bhagavān All the Tathāgatas once again come to the multitude and give sādhukāras to Bhagavan Stg. -cakra-pravartī. Vajrapāṇi Mahābodhisattva and the chapter ends. *Sarvatathāgatatattva saṅgrahāt Sarvakalpaguhyottara-tantra-vidhi-vistaraḥ parisamāptaḥ.*

## CHAPTER 26.A OF THE STTS: SARVA-KALPĀNUTTARA-TANTRA

Mahābodhisattva opens the 26th chapter with this śloka:

*Durdṛṣṭīnām viraktānām idam guhyam na yujyate /*
*sarvasattva-hitārthāya vakṣyāmi vidhayas tathā //*

This esoteric tantra is not meant for those who have ill notions and impassioned. Vajrapāṇi introduces the upacaravidhi of Stg.- kula. Its tantra explains the hṛdaya, ācāravidhi, japa-vidhi, uttama-siddhi, mudrāsādhana, samādhis, karmasādhana, karmas, vaśīkaraṇa, and laukikottama siddhis. Upacāra-vidhi of the Tathāgatakula is proceeded by the upacāra-vidhi of vajrakula. Vajradhara explains sādhana, mudrāsādhana, sūkṣmajñāna-sādhana and karma-sādhana.

Upacāravidhis of the padmakula and maṇikula are explained in the same manner with their japa, mudrā, samādhi-naya and karma-sādhana and japa, mudrā-sadhana, maṇijñāna and karma-sādhana. Then follows the description of the sādhāraṇa japa vidhi of all the families with their japa, mudrā, sarvamantra and vidyā. Explanation of sādhāraṇa accomplishment of all the families has artha-siddhi-niṣpatti, ṛddhi-siddhi-niṣpatti, Vajravidyādhara-siddhi-niṣpatti, mahā-siddhi-niṣpatti, vajrakula-siddhis, Trilokavijaya-siddhi, sarvābhiṣeka-siddhi-mudrā, sarvasukha-saumanasya-siddhi, uttama-siddhi, padmakula siddhis, anurāgaṇa-siddhi, maṇikula-siddhis and sarva tathagātabhiṣeka-siddhis.

Now the chapter proceeds with the upāya-siddhi-tantra. It has four divisions: Sarva-kalpa-upāya-siddhi-tantra, sarva kalpa-puṇya-siddhi-tantra, sarva-kalpa-prajñā-siddhi-tantra and kalpa-sambhāra-siddhi-tantra. They are described from four points of view, they are: hṛdaya, mudrā, mantra and vidyā.

Bhagavān Vajrasattva relates the knowledge tantra which originates from signs of all the families: sarvakula cihna-sambhava-jñāna-tantra, Bhagavān Vajradhara narrates the tantra explaining the knowledge which has its origin in the kalpa of all the families, with its four kulas proceeded by the tantra originating from the hṛdaya of kalpa of all the four kulas. Now follows the tantra describing the origin of knowledge of all the kalpas of all the families and the knowledge of hṛdaya, mudrā, mantra and vidyā. Bhagavān Vajrasattva, Vajrahūṅkāra, Padma-sattva and Vajragarbha relate the sādhanatantras of vajra-mudrās of sādhāraṇa esoteric kāya, vak and citta of all the four families.

Then Bhagavān Vajravaca, Vajrahūṅkāra, Sarva-tathāgata samādhi-jñāna-garbha and Sarva-tathāgata-pūjā vidhi-vistara-karma instruct about the sādhana-tantra of esoteric vāṅ mudrā of all the families. Bhagavān Kāma, Sarvatathāgata-vajra-hūṅkāra, Padma-rāga and Āryākāśa-garbha relate the tantra of sādhana of esoteric citta mudrā of the four familites. The chapter proceeds with the sādhana tantra of esoteric vajra mudrā of the four kulas related by Sarvatathāgata-guhya-vajrapāṇi, Sarvatathāgatakrodha-rāja, Avalokiteśvara and Ākāśagarbha. Last of all is the sādhana tantra of esoteric sādhāraṇa-mudrā of all the kulas: sarvakula-guhya sādhāraṇa-mudrā-sādhana-tantra.

Bhagavān Vajrapāṇi calls All the Tathāgatas and requests: All the Tathāgatas again come to the multitude and applaud:

*Sādhu te vajrasattvāya vajraratnāya sādhu te /*
*Vajradharmāya te sādhu sādhu te vajrakarmaṇe //*
*Subhāṣitam idam sūtram Vajrayānam anuttaram /*
*Sarvatathāgataguhyam Mahāyānābhisaṅgraham //*

The chapter ends with this colophon: *Sarvatathāgatatattvasaṅgrahāt sarvakalpānuttaratantram parisamāptam.*

## CHAPTER 26.B OF THE STTS: SARVATATHĀGATA-TATTVA-SAṄGRAHA-NĀMA MAHĀYĀNA-SŪTRA

The last chapter of the text is 26b. It is an apilogue of the text of STTS. Vajrapāṇi Mahābodhisattva gets up from his seat and solicitates Bhagavān with 108 names. Vairocana listens to the commands of the lord of Stg., calls and says, that now they should behave accordingly and come to the multitude. They come and recite this verse:

*sarvasattvahitārthāya sarvalokeśu sarvataḥ /*
*yathāvinayato viśvam dharmacakrapravarttyatām //*

As soon as they recite these words Bhagavān Śākyamuni turns the wheel of dharma in all the Buddha kṣetras, in all the lokadhātus Vajrapāṇi again recites the same verse. Mahābodhi sattva Trilokavijaya recites the same and asks to turn the wheel of anger and Bhagavān Trilokavijayī does the same. Āryāvalokiteśvara asks for the padmacakra which is turned by Bhagavān Dharmarāja tathāgata, Āryākāśagarbha Bodhisattva asks for the maṇicakra which is turned by him on the highest peak of the Sumeru mountain in the temple with a top made of vajragems, on the seat of Stg. Turning all the wheels around. Once more Vajrapāṇi Mahābodhisattva wants the vajracakra to be turned, Bhagavān again asks all the Tathāgtas to come to the multitude. They come and enter the heart of Vairocana. He asks Vajrapāṇi as well to enter his heart. All the maṇḍalas of all the vajra families of All the Tathāgatas also enter his heart. One by one everybody enters the heart of Vairocana.

Bhagavān comes down from the Sumeru mountain and sits under the Bodhi tree. He only takes grassy food and recites these verses:

*aho hyagrartha ātmanaḥ sattvārthaḥ sattvaśāsinam /*
*yadvineyavaśād dhīrās tīrthadṛṣṭya vihanti hi //*
*avineyasya lokasya durdṛṣṭyandhasya sarvataḥ /*
*jñānābhaya śodhanārtham buddhabodhim avāpnuyāt //*

Without knowing the reality other deities ask him as why is he having so much of sufferings. He sits on a seat made of straws and replies that he wants to attain Bodhi. They are not worthy to understand its meaning. They go to Devānām Indra Śakra. Still it is difficult to be understood. They reach Mahābrahmā with Indra and then to Īśvara with Brahmā and Indra. The lord of the three worlds Maheśvara instructs them about Bodhi and all together they to go worship Him. They pay their respects and ask him to sit on devine seat to attain Bodhi. He replies and asks them for giving him Bodhi, but they could only reply in a no. Then he recites this verse:

*na sa rūpī na cārūpī na satyam na mṛṣā śuci /*
*buddhabodhair idam jñānam avabudhya jino bhavet //*

All the deities were sitting quietly. Bhagavān asks them if they can attain that type of knowledge ? But they were not able. Again he sits on the same seat and says:

*manasaḥ prativedena bodhicittam dṛḍhīkuru /*
*vajram sattve dṛḍhi kṛtvā buddham ātmānubhāvayet //*

They say evam astu and go out. During night he conquers over Māra and attains samyak sambodhi and solicitates Vajrapāṇi who is stationed in his heart with these 108 names: (these are different names of the 16 great Bodhisattvas) as: (Vajrasattva).

*Vajrasattva mahāsattva Mahāyāna Mahātmaka /*
*Mahāprabha Mahāśuddha Mahānātha namostu'te //*

it runs upto verse no 16. Thereafter he gives the importance of reciting these names. All the Tathāgatas applaud him together. There is the final colophon of STTS. *Sarvatathāgata tattva saṅgraham Mahāyāna-sūtram samāptam.*

## 1. VAIROCANA

毘盧遮那如來

Mahāvairocana Tathāgata in the body of law of the reason who is the central divinity of the Mahākaruṇā-garbha-maṇḍala, is the Vairocana in the jñānadharmakāya. He presides over the Vajradhātu-maṇḍala. He has not obtained perfect illumination in the palace of Akaniṣṭha deva, in the highest of the heavens rūpadhātu. We should consider the principal divinity Vairocana practising the great mudrā. He occupies a seat in the centre of the maṇḍala. He is seated cross-legged. He is full of a great majesty. He is white like hansa. His form including aureole is like the pure moon. He possesses all the lakṣaṇas. His head is decorated with a daidem. He wears a dhotī. He carries the daidem with five Bhuddas. He practises the jñāna-muṣṭi-mudrā. He sits on a lotus of gems of white colour.(Tajima 172-3).

I.1.4

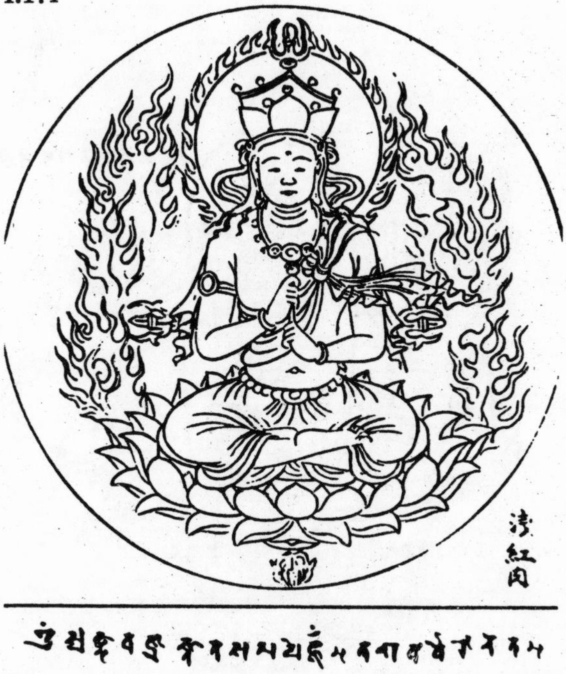

TZ.54.1

Vairocana in the first maṇḍala of Gobushingan is sitting on a lotus supported by a group of lions (TZ 54.1). As mentioned above he iswearing all the ornaments and a dhotī. His daidem has five Bhuddas. Dhāraṇī under the illustation is : *bhagavān Vairocana. Om cittaprativedham karomi.* The mudrās given besides are named as karma-mudrā, vajrāñjali-samaya-mudrā, mahā-mudrā, om vajrāñjali samayaḥ and cihna-mudrā. Karma-mudrā is dipicted only by a muṣṭi, mahā-mudrā is the same to the portrait, vajrāñjali-samaya as añjali and the cihna-mudrā has been depicted as a triangal surrounded by vajras and supported by a lotus.

TZ.38.1

Vairocana in the graphic Vajradhatu-maṇḍala has the same hand posture as extracted above from the first chapter of the Gobu-shingan. His head dress is different and the ornaments are a bit simplified, dhotī and uttarīya are the same. There are no lions under the lotus. He is sitting in the same posture in the lotus pericarp (TZ.38.1, Lokesh Chandra 406).

I.2.1. Bhagavān enters the samādhi which is called the consecration of Vajra-dhātu, samaya of jñāna-mudrā of All the Tathāgatas

I.2.1

TZ.54.39

amd utters his vidyottama as: *om Vajradhātvīśvarī hūm vajriṇī* (STTS 101). The illustrations given above are taken from the second chapter of Gobu-shingan. Here vairocan is named as Vajradhātvīśvara : *om vajra-dhātvisvara hūm vajriṇi*. He is sitting on a lotus as in the privious illustration. The mudrās given besides are mahā-mudrā, cihna-mudrā and muṣṭi. These are depicted by his hand postures and attribute. (TZ.54.39)

TZ.38.63

Vairocana in the second maṇḍala of the graphic Vajradhātu is depicted in his samaya form which is his attribute, a stūpa placed upon a vajra on a lotus (TZ.38.63, Lokesh Chandra 463).

I.3.1. In the sūkṣma-maṇḍala the third maṇḍala of Gobu-shingan Vairocana makes the same posture of hands as in the first maṇḍala but his ride is different from that. He is sitting on a lotus. A three pointed four sided vajra can be seen at the back. He is the jñāna-samaya of sūkṣma-vajra, named as Bhagavān Vairocana. *Om sūkṣma-vajra-jñāna-samaye hūm. Bhagavān Vairocana.* (STTS 116). The mudrās given

I.3.1

I.3.1

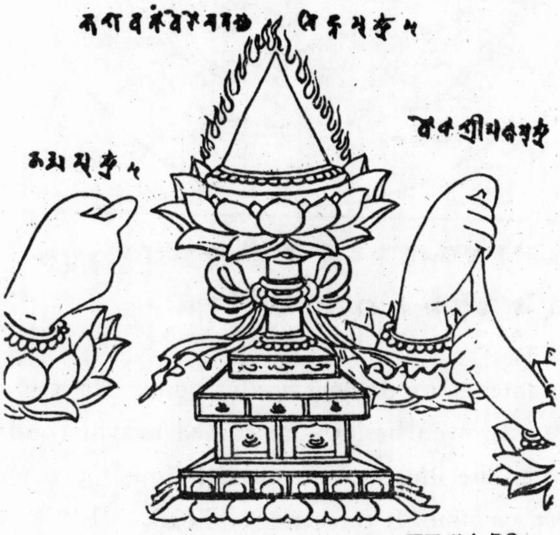

TZ.54.72

besides are the mahā-mudrā, cihna-mudra and karma-mudrā. The first is identical with the middle one of the first maṇḍala, the second to the last and third to the first. (TZ.54.72).

In the dharma, the third maṇḍala of the graphic Vajradhātu Vairocana has the same hand posture as he has in the Gobu-shingan. He is sitting on a lotus and a three pointed double sided vajra can be seen on his back. (TZ.38.136, Lokesh Chandra 614).

In the vajra-jñāna-dharma-maṇḍala of STTS Bhaga-

TZ.38.136.

vān enters the samādhi called the consecration of samaya-maṇḍala of jñāna-mudrā of sūkṣma-vajra of All the Tathāgatas and utters these words: *Om sūkṣma-vajra-jñāna-samaya hūm.* I.4.1.

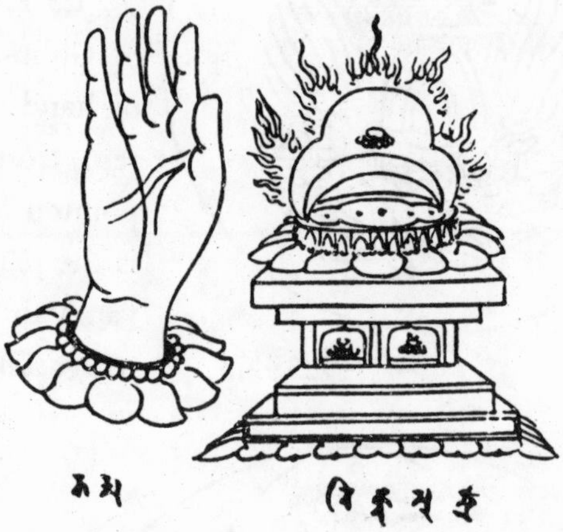

TZ.54.105

I.4.1. Vairocana in the karma-pūjā-maṇḍala of Gobu-shingan is making mudrā with his right hand and the left fist is resting upon his thigh. He is sitting on a lotus. No ornaments are drawn over his body. He is surrounded by lotus flowers and jems. The two mudras given besides are named as cihna-and karma-mudrā (TZ 54.105). Dhāraṇī written under the illustration runs as follows: *Om sarvatathāgata vajradhātvanuttara-pūjā-spharaṇa-samaye hūm.* It correlates to STTS. (p.130).

In the pūjā-maṇḍala of the graphic Vajradhātu-maṇḍala he is holding his right fist near his breast and the other is resting in his lap (TZ 38.209, Lokesh Chandra 614).

II.4.1. Mahāvairocana in the karma-maṇḍala of Trailokaya-vijaya of the graphic Vajradhātu attains the form as he has in the mahā-and dharma-maṇḍalas (TZ.38 313). II.2.1. His samaya form in the Trailokayavijaya-samaya maṇḍala is identical with the samaya-maṇḍala of the graphic Vajradhātu (TZ 38 390).

II.3.1. Bhagavān enters the samādhi named know ledge mudrā consecration of samādhi of vajra-kula of All

TZ.38.209.

the Tathāgatas and recites this verse: *Om sarva-tathāgata-sūkṣma-vajra-krodha hūm phaṭ.* (STTS 225). Vairocana has the form of anger of subtle vajra of All the Tathāgatas. II.4.1. Vairocana has the feminined form of Karmeśvarī of All the Tathāgatas in vajra-kula-karma-maṇḍala. He enters the samādhi named consecration which has its origin in the samaya of vajra-karma of All the Tathāgatas and recites this verse: *Om sarva-tathāgata-karmeśvari hūm.* (STTS 236). III.1.1. Bhagavān utters his vidyottamā which is the dharma-samaya All the Tathāgatas: *Om vajra-padmātmaka hrīḥ.* (STTS 319). III.2.1. Bhagavān enters the samādhi called consecration lotus of mudrā which has its origin in the samaya of dharma dhāraṇī of Stg. and recites his vidyottama as: *Om sarvatathāgata-dharma-samaya hūm* (STTS 340). III.3.1. In jñāna-maṇḍala Vairocana is the knowledge of samādhi of dharma. He enters the samādhi called consecration which has its orgin in the samaya of knowledge of dharma-samaya of Stg. and recites this verse: *Om dharma-samādhi-jñāna-tathāgata hūm* (STTS 356). III.4.1. Vairocana is Karmāgra in karma-maṇḍala. He enters the samādhi named consecration lotus which has its origin in the samaya of dharma karma of Stg. and utters these words: *Om sarva-tathāgata karmāgra hūm* (STTS 365).

IV.1.1. Bhagavān utters his vidyottamā which is the gem samaya of Stg.: *Om sarva-tathāgatāśā-paripūrṇa mahā-ratna hūm.* He is personified as a great gem which fulfills all the desires (STTS 386). IV.2.1. Vairocana has a feminined form as vajra-ratna-stūpa in the ratna guhya mudrā-maṇḍala. He enters the samādhi named gem consecration which has its origin in the samaya of consecration dhāraṇī of Stg. and recites this verse. *Om vajra-ratna-stūpe hūm* (STTS 404). IV.3.1. Vairocana is the supreme knowledge consecration He enters the samādhi named consecration which has its origin in the samaya of knowledge of consecration of Stg. and recites these words: *Om sarva-tathāgatābhiṣeka-jñānaottama hūm* (STTS 416). IV.4.1. Vairocana is karma consecration in the karma-maṇḍala. He enters the samādhi called the consecration which has its origin in the samaya of action of consecration of Stg. and recites this verse: *Om sarva-tathāgata karmābhiṣeke hūm* (STTS 424).

Names of Vairocana in the 16 maṇḍalas:

| Ch | P. | Kula | Maṇḍala | Name |
|---|---|---|---|---|
| 1. | - | Buddha | Vajradhātu-mahā-m. | Bagavān Vairocana. |
| 2. | 101 | ” | Vajra-guhya-vajra-m. | Vajradhātvīśvarī. |
| 3. | 116 | ” | Vajra-jñāna-dharma-m. | Sūkṣma-vajra-jñāna-samaya. |
| 4. | 130 | ” | Vajra-kārya-karma-m. | Vajradhātvanuttara-pūjā-spharaṇa-samayā. |
| 6. | - | Vajra | Trilokavijaya-mahā-m. | - |
| 7. | - | ” | Krodha-guhya-mudrā-m. | - |
| 8. | 225 | ” | Vajrakula-dharmā-jñāna samaya-m. | Stg.-sūkṣma-vajra-krodha. |
| 9. | 236 | ” | Vajrakula-karma-m. | Stg.-karmeśvarī. |
| 15. | 319 | Padma | Sakala-jagad-vinaya-mahā-m. | Vajra-padmātmaka. |
| 16. | 340 | ” | Padma-guhya-mudrā-m. | Stg.-dharma-samaya. |
| 17. | 356 | ” | Jñāna-m. | Dharma-samādhi-jñāna-tathāgata. |
| 18. | 365 | ” | Karma-m. | Stg.-karmāgra. |
| 19. | 386 | Ratna | Sarvārthasiddhi-mahā-m. | Stg.-āśāparipūrṇa-mahā-ratna. |
| 20. | 404 | ” | Ratna-guhya-mudrā-m. | Vajra-ratna-stūpā. |
| 21. | 416 | ” | Jñāna-m. | Stg.-abhiṣeka-jñānottama. |
| 22. | 424 | ” | Karma-m. | Stg.Karmābhiṣekā. |

## AKṢOBHYA
阿閦如來

Akṣobhya means "unshakable," he symbolises firmness of heart of Bodhi, firmness equal to that of the vajra, hence the Bodhisattva, placed to the east of Vairocana bears the name Vajra Pāramitā. Absorbed in contemplation of big round mirror, this Buddha destoys demons and passions and presides over the divinity who symbolises the pure heart of Bodhi. He is of yellow colour of gold, his left hand is closed and the other is hanging. The mudrā of his right hand is bhūmi-sparśa-mudrā for establishing the movement of the movement of the heart of bodhi (Tajima 174-5).

I.1.2.

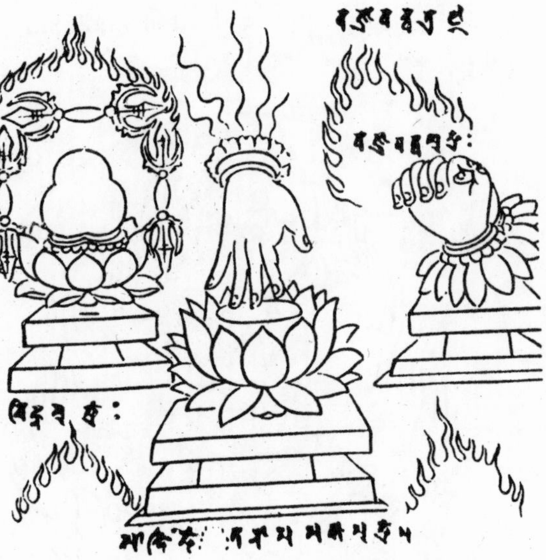

TZ.54.2

Akṣobhya in the first maṇḍala of Gonu-shingan is sitting on a lotus placed upon seven elephants. He is doing the bhūmisparśa-mudrā by his right hand and the left is holding the corner of his uttarīya (TZ 54.2). Dhāraṇī given under the illustration rans as follows : *Om bodhicittam utpāday-āmı Om tiṣṭha vajra. Om vajrātmakoham. ' Bhagavān Akṣobhyastathāgatam.* The first from the right is vajra-bandha-mudrā, the second is mahā-mudrā and the third is cihna-mudrā. The first is depicted by tied hands, the second by bhūmi-sparśá-mudrā on a lotus and the last by a jem surrounded by vajras placed upon a lotus seat (TZ 54.2).

Akṣobhya in the mahā-maṇḍala of graphic Vajradhātu has the same hand posture as in Gobu-shingan in the preceded drawing. He is sitting on a lotus, his animal ride is missing ride is missing (TZ 38.6, Lokesh Chandra 411). Hūm in siddham is written above as his seed syllable.

I.2.2. Akṣobhya in the guhya-dhāraṇī-dharani-maṇḍala of Gobu-shingan holds a three pointed double sided vajra upon a vajra which is placed upon a lotus. He is wearing all the ornaments and a crown. He is sitting on a lotus. Under the illustration he is named as Vajra-vajriṇī : *Om vajra-vajriṇī hūm.* The first mudrā is mahā-mudrā named as vajra-bandha, the second is cihna-mudrā in the form of a his attribute and the third is vajrāñjali (TZ 54.40).

TZ. 38.6

I.2.2

TZ 54.40

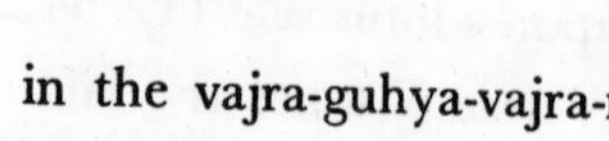

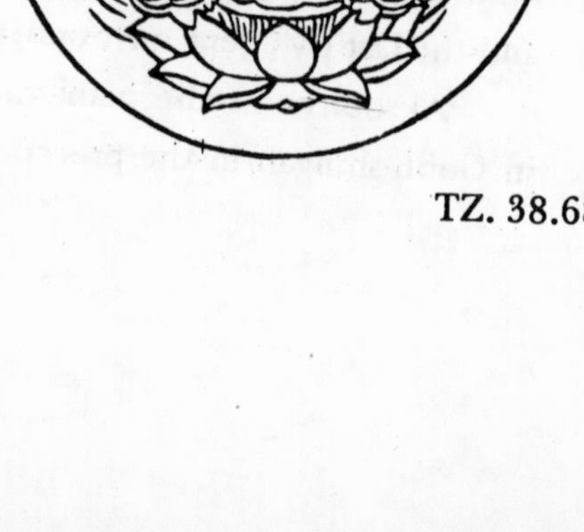

The symbolic form of Akṣobhya in the samaya-maṇḍala of the graphic Vajradhātu is drawn as his attribute. The only difference is that here the vajra underneath is not put straight (TZ 38.68, Lokesh Chandra 473).

Akṣobhya in the vajra-guhya-vajra-maṇḍala enters the samādhi called the maṇḍala consecration of jñāna-mudrā of the samaya of vajra-sattva of All the Tathā-

TZ. 38.68

gatas and utters these words which is his vidyottamā : *Om vajra vajriṇī hūm.* (STTS 101).

I.3.2.

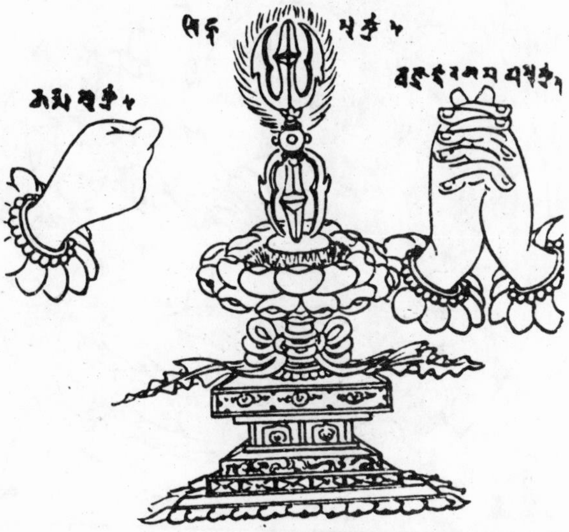

TZ 54.73

Akṣobhya in the guhya-dhāraṇī-maṇḍala of Gobu-shingan has a vajra supported by both of his hands in his lap. He is decorated with all the ornaments and a crown. He is sitting in a lotus wearing dhotī. The first mudrā showing joined hands with crossed fingers is named as vajra-jñāna-samaya-mudrā, the second illustrating his attribute placed on a lotus seat is the cihna-mudrā and the third as a fist is the karma-mudrā (TZ 54.73).

Akṣobhya in the given illustration has the same posture of his hands as he has in the first maṇḍala. It is an extract from dharma-maṇḍala of the graphic Vajradhātu (TZ 38.141, Lokesh Chandra 546). A three pointed vajra can be seen on his back. Vajra-jñāna-dharma-maṇḍala of STTS indicates him as the samaya of subtle knowledge of vajra-sattva. Akṣobhya enters the samādhi named maṇḍala consecration of samaya of subtle knowledge of vajra-sattva of All the Tathāgatas and recites these words: *Om vajra-sattva sūkṣma-jñāna-samaya hūm.* Gobu-shingan gives the same dharani.

TZ.38.141

I.4.2.

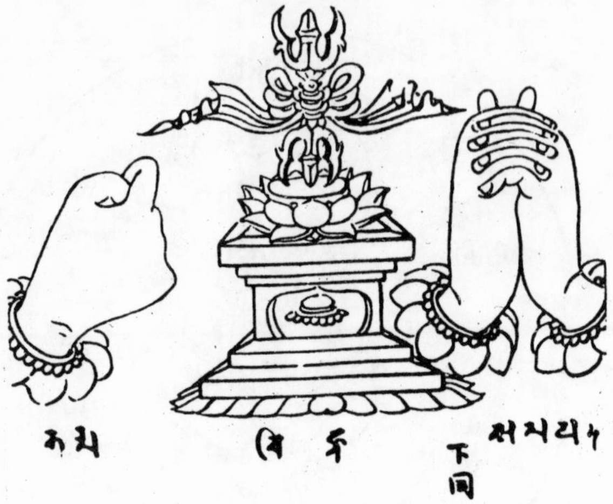

TZ 54.106

1.4.2. Akṣobhya in the first, karma-pūjā-maṇḍala of Gobu-shingan and vajra-kārya-karma-maṇḍala of STTS is the samaya of suffusion of anuutara pūjā of Vajra-sattva of All the Tathāgatas (STTS 130). In Gobu-shingan he is illustrated as having a flower in his left hand held upwards and in his right hand he is having a vajra on a lotus with a long stem. His dhāraṇī runs as follows: *Om sarva-tathāgata vajra-sattvānuttara-pūjā-spharaṇa samaye hūm. Bhagavān Akṣobhyaḥ.* (TZ 54.106). All the mudrās are the same as given in the preceded maṇḍala of Gobu-shingan. Karma-maṇḍala of the graphic Vajradhātu has the same illustration of Akṣobhya as given in thep preceded maṇḍala (TZ 214, Lokesh Chandra 725).

Akṣobhya as illustrated besides belongs to the karma maṇḍala of the Trailokyavijaya of graphic Vajradhātu-maṇḍala. He is sitting in a monastic dress with his hands folded accross his breast (TZ 38.390). His samaya forms in the Vajradhātu-samaya-and Trailokya-vijaya-samaya-maṇḍalas are identical. Three pointed double sided vajra is placed upon a vajra which is resting on a lotus flower.

TZ.38.390

II.3.2. Akṣobhya is the king of great anger in the vajra-kula-dharma-jñāna-samaya-maṇḍala He is subtle form of vajra anger of Stg., who has a quality of invasion. He enters the samādhi called the mudrā consecration of the knowledge of samādhi of vajra-kula of Stg. and speaks these words: *Om sūkṣma vajra krodhākrama hūm phaṭ* (STTS 225). II.4.2. The great Bodhisattva Vajrapāṇi also recites his vidyottamā: *Om sarva-tathāgata dharmadhātu-spharaṇa mahā-pūjā-karma-vidhi-vistara-samaye triloka-vijayam-kari sarva-duṣṭān dāmaya vajriṇī hūm* (STTS 236). III.1.2. The great Bodhisattva Vajrapāṇi utters his vidyottamā as follows: *Om vajra hūm phaṭ* (STTS 319). III.2.2. Vajrapāṇi in the padma-guhya-mudrā-maṇḍala recites his vidyottamā which emanates from its own family: *Om vajra samaye hūm* (STTS 340). III.3.2. Vajrapāṇi in the jñāna-maṇḍala recites his vidyottama which has its origin in the dharma of own family: *Om vajra dharma hūm* (STTS 356). III.3.2. Vajrapāṇi in karma-maṇḍala recites his vidyottamā which has its origin in the karma of its own family: *Om hūm diḥ* (STTS 365). IV.1.2. His vidyottamā in Sarvārtha-siddhi-mahā-maṇḍala is: *Om vajra hūm traḥ* (STTS 386). Vajrapāṇi is a garland for vajra consecration which has a power of consecration. IV.2.2. *Om vajrābhiṣeakamāle abhiṣiñca samaye hūm* (STTS 404). IV.3.2. He is knowledge consecration in jñāna-maṇḍala: *Om vajra-jñānābhi-ṣeka-samaya hūm.* (STTS 416). IV.4.2. Vajra-pāṇi is the feminined form of vajra-hūṅkāra consecration in karma-maṇḍala: *Om vajra-hūṅkārābhiṣeke* (STTS 424).

Names of Akṣobhya in the Sixteen Maṇḍalas:

| Ch. | P. | Kula | Maṇḍala | Names |
|---|---|---|---|---|
| 1. | - | Buddhakula | Vajradhātu-mahā-m. | Akṣobhya. |
| 2. | 101 | " | Vajraguhya-vajra-m. | Vajra-vajriṇī. |
| 3. | 116 | " | Vajrajñāna-dharma-m. | Vajra-sattva-sūkṣma-jñāna-samaya. |
| 4. | 130 | " | Vajrakārya-karma-m. | Stg.-vajra-sattvānuttara-pūjā-spharaṇa-samayā. |
| 6. | - | Vajrakula | Trilokavijaya-mahā-m. | - |
| 7. | - | " | Krodhaguhya-mudrā-m. | - |
| 8. | 225 | " | Vajrakula-dharmajñāna-samayamaṇḍala. | Sūkṣma-vajra-krodha. |
| 9. | 236 | " | Vajrakula-karmamaṇḍala | Stg.-dharmadhātu-spharaṇa-mahā-pūjā. |
| 15. | 319 | Padmakula | Sakalajagadvinaya-mahāmaṇḍala. | Vajra. |
| 16. | 340 | " | Padmaguhya-mudrā-m. | Vajra-samaya. |
| 17. | 356 | " | Jñānamaṇḍala | Vajra-dharma. |
| 18. | 365 | " | Karmamaṇḍala | - |
| 19. | 386 | Ratnakula | Sarvārthasiddhi-mahā-m. | Vajra. |
| 20. | 404 | " | Ratnaguhya-mudrā-m. | Vajrābhiṣekamālā. |
| 21. | 416 | " | Jñānamaṇḍala | Vajra-jñānabhiṣeka. |
| 22. | 426 | " | Karmamaṇḍala | Vajra-hūṅkārābhiṣekā. |

## 3. RATNASAMBHAVA
寳生如來

Ratmasambhava occupies the south circle, he represents the treasure of fortunate virtues that are the results of esceticism; absorbed in the samaya of sapience of equality of nature he exhausts the prayers of all the beings with this treasure of virture. With the intermidiery of Ratnapāramitā, he personifies the discipline of esceticism of Vairocana's benevolent virtues, He reigns over the class of ratna. According to Hizoki his colour is of gold. His left hand is closed, right is open. The golden colour symbolises growth. His mudrā of the right hand is the symbol of prayers being exhausted. The Cho tchen king comments this mudrā as follows: from the intervals in between his separated fingers drops a shower of gems that accord the desires of heavenly garments, amṛta, heavenly music, of precious palaces of the heaven that satisfies all the desires of the beings. Simultaneously the five fingers symbolise the five sapiences of the Five Buddhas.

I.1.3.

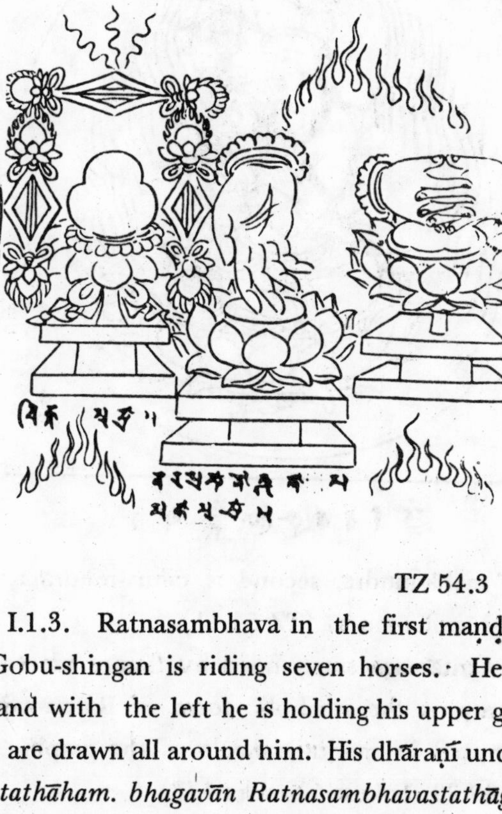

TZ 54.3

I.1.3. Ratnasambhava in the first maṇḍala of Gobu-shingan is riding seven horses. He is making a gesture of varada by his right hand and with the left he is holding his upper garment. He is without any ornaments. Flames are drawn all around him. His dhāraṇī under the illustration is: *Om yathā sarvatathāgatās tathāham. bhagavān Ratnasambhavastathāgataḥ.* The first mudrā is not named, second is named as vara-mudrā, illustrating his hand posture upon a lotus and the third is his cihna-mudrā portayed by Cintāmaṇī (TZ 54.3).,

Ratnasambhava in the mahā-maṇḍala of graphic Vajradhātu attains the form which is described by Tajima. His right palm is opened upwards with twisted fingers, the left fist is resting in his lap holding the corner of his upper garment. As usual here he has no animal ride. (TZ 38.11, Lokesh Chandra 416).

TZ.38.11

I.2.3. Ratnasambhava is personified as Ratnavajrī in the second, guhya-dhāraṇī-maṇḍala of Gobu-shingan. He is holding a vajra with a cintāmaṇī atop placed upon a lotus. Wearing all the ornaments, crown and dhotī he is sitting in a lotus pericarp. Dhāraṇī under his illustration is : *Om Raṭnavajriṇī hūm.* First is Ratna-

I.2.3

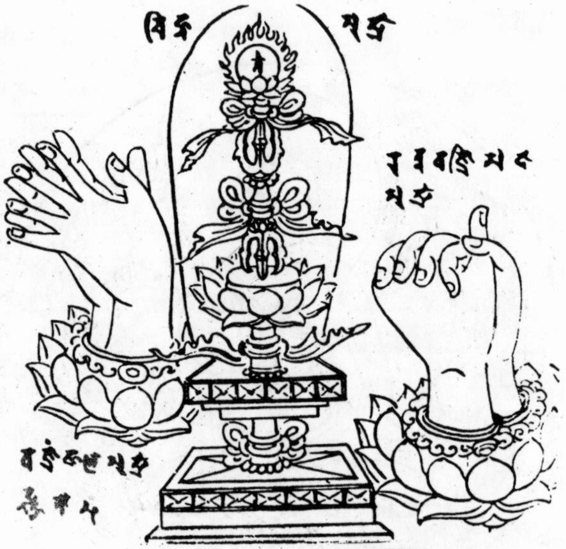

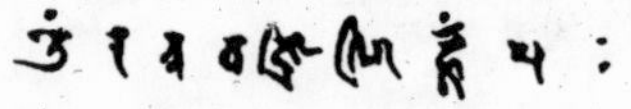

vajrī mahā-mudrā, second is cihna-mudrā and third is vajra-bandha-mudrā (TZ 54.41).

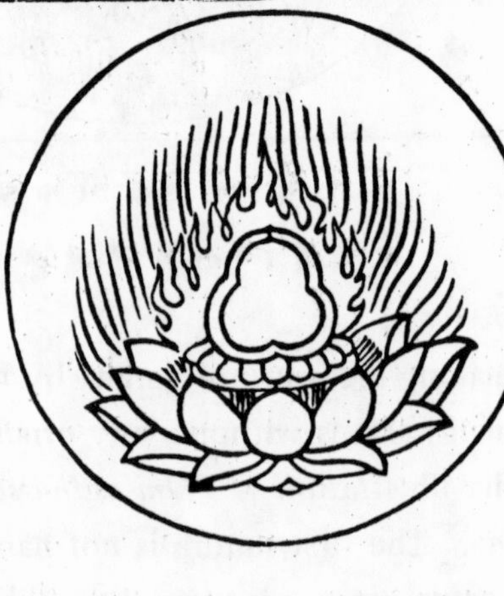

Cintāmaṇi surrounded by flames placed in a lotus pericarp is the symbolic form of Ratna-vajrī which is illustrated in mudrā-maṇḍala of the graphic Vajradhātu (TZ 38.73, Lokesh Chandra 478).

In vajra-guhya-vajra-maṇḍala Ratna-sambhava enters

the samādhi called maṇḍala consecration of mudrā of subtle knowledge of Vajra-ratna of all the Tathāgatas and utters these words: *Om ratna-vajriṇi hūm.* (STTS 101).

I.3.3.

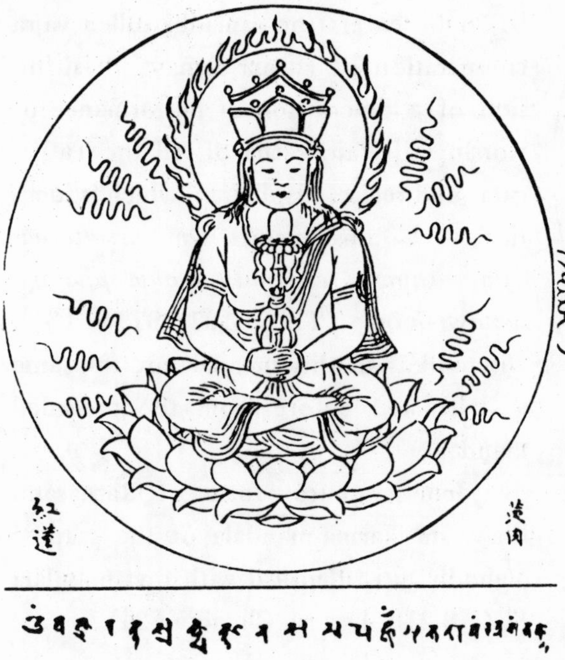

TZ.54.74

I.3.3. Ratnasambhava is the samaya of subtle knowledge of Vajra-ratna in vajra-jñāna dharma-maṇḍala of STTS and sūkṣma-maṇḍala of Gobu-shingan. Vajra with a cintāmaṇī is held upright in his lap supported by both of his hands. He is wearing a dhotī and uttarīya and all ornaments and a crown sitting in a lotus. His dhāraṇī under the illustrations is: *Om vajra-ratna-sūkṣma-jñāna-samaye hūm. Bhagavān Ratnasambhava.* First mudrā from right is namded as sūkṣma-jñāna-samaya-mahā-mudrā, second is cintāmaṇī-mahā-mudrā and the third is karma-mudrā. (TZ 54.74).

Ratnasambhava enters the samādhi called maṇḍala consecration of samaya of subtle knowledge of vajra-ratna of All the Tathāgatas and recites this dhāraṇī. *Om vajra-ratna sūkṣma-jñāna-samaya hūm.* (STTS 116).

Ratna-sambhava in the dharma-maṇḍala of the graphic Vajradhātu has the hand posture which is identical with the first maṇḍala. The middle two fingers are more twisted and here is a vajra at the back (TZ 38.146, Lokesh Chandra 551).

TZ.38.146

I.4.3.

TZ.54.107

I.4.3. Ratnasambhava in karma-pūjā-maṇḍala has a cintāmaṇi upon a lotus in his right hand and the left is in varada mudrā. In vajra-karya-karma-maṇḍala of STTS he enters the samādhi called vajra consecration of karma samaya of suffusion of a description of performance of worship of Vajra-ratna of All the Tathāgatas and recites his dhāraṇī which is identical to Gobu-shingan. *Om sarva-tathāgata vajra ratnānuttara-pūjā-spharaṇa samaye hūm.* (TZ 54.107, STTS 131). His mudrās in this maṇḍala are the same as extracted before from the preceded maṇḍala.

Iconographical form of Ratnasambhava in karma-maṇḍala of the graphic Vajradhātu is identical with first maṇḍala (TZ 38.219, Lokesh Chandra 624).

Ratnasambhava is sitting with his hands folded accross his breast in Trailokyavijaya-karma-maṇḍala. (TZ.38.323). His symbolic form in its samaya maṇḍala is the same as given before from the samaya-maṇḍala of Vajradhātu. (TZ.38.400).

II.3.3. Vajra-garbha is the subtle vajra-ratna in vajra-kula-dharma-jñāna-samaya-maṇḍala who recites his vidyottamā which is called sūkṣma-vajra of trilokavijaya: *Om sūkṣma-vajra-ratnakrama hūm phaṭ* (STTS 225). II.4.3. In vajra-kula-karma-maṇḍala his vidyottamā is: *Om sarva-tathāgatākāśadhātu-samavasarana mahā-pūjā karma-vidhi-vistara-samaye hūm* (STTS 236). III.1.3. Vajra-garbha is the supreme gem in sakalajagad-vinaya-mahā-maṇḍala: *Om vajra-ratnottama traḥ* (STTS 319). III.2.3. Great Bodhisattva Vajragarbha utters his vidyottamā: *Om maṇi-ratna-samaye hūm* (STTS 340), in padma-guhya-mudrā-maṇḍala. III.3.3. Vidyottamā of Vajra-garbha in jñāna-maṇḍala is ratna-dharma: *Om ratna-dharma hūm* (STTS 356). III.4.3. Vajra-garbha is ratna-karma-samaya in karma-maṇḍala: *Om ratna-karma-samaye hūm* (STTS 365). IV.1.3. Vajra-garbha in sarvārthasiddhi-mahā-maṇḍala utters his vidyottama as gem: *Om maṇi hūm* (STTS 386). IV.2.3. Vajra-garbha Bodhisattva recites his mudrā as gem consecration: *Om vajra ratnābhiṣeke hūm* (STTS 404). IV.3.3. In jñāna maṇḍala it has a knowledge form: *Om maṇi-ratnābhiṣeka jñāna hūm* (STTS 416). IV.4.3. In karma-maṇḍala he is personified as a feminined form of consecration of sarvākāśa-samatā: *Om sarvākāśa-samatābhiṣeke hūm ( STTS 424).*

Names of Ratnasambhava in the Sixteen maṇḍalas:

| Ch. | P. | Kula | Maṇḍala | Names. |
|---|---|---|---|---|
| 1. | 101 | Buddhakula | Vajradhātu-mahāmaṇḍala. | Ratnasambhava. |
| 2. | 101 | ” | Vajraguhya-vajramaṇḍala. | Ratna-vajriṇī. |
| 3. | 116 | ” | Vajrajñāna-dharma m. | Vajra-ratna-sūkṣma-jñāna-samaya |
| 4. | 131 | ” | Vajrakārya-karma m. | Stg.-vajra-ratnanuttara-pūjā-spharaṇa-samayā. |
| 6. | - | Vajrakula | Trilokavijaya-mahā-m. | - |
| 7. | - | ” | Krodhaguhya-mudrā-maṇḍala. | - |
| 8. | 225 | ” | Vajrakula-dharmajñāna-samayamaṇḍala | - |
| 9. | 236 | ” | Vajrakula-karmamaṇḍala | - |
| 15. | 319 | Padmakula | Sakalajagadvinaya-mahā-m. | Vajra-ratnottama |
| 16. | 340 | ” | Padmaguhya-mudrā-maṇḍala | Maṇi-ratna-samayā. |
| 17. | 356 | ” | Jñānamaṇḍala | Ratna-dharma |
| 18. | 365 | ” | Karmamaṇḍala | Ratna-karma-samayā. |
| 19. | 386 | Ratnakula | Sarvārthasiddhi-mahā-m. | Maṇi. |
| 20. | 404 | ” | Ratnaguhya-mudrāmaṇḍala | Vajra-ratnābhiṣekā |
| 21. | 416 | ” | Jñānamaṇḍala | Maṇi-ratnābhiṣeka. |
| 22. | 424 | ” | Karmamaṇḍala | Sarvākāśasamatābhiṣekā. |

## 4. LOKEŚVARARĀJA

世自在王如來

Lokeśvararāja Tathāgata is also named as Amitābha. He is absorbed in the samaya of sapience of the marvelous discernment and presides over the virtues of attention of Bodhi, he, the explanation of law and of destruction of doubts by Vairocana by discussing the vajra-dharma-pāramitā, examining the degree of development of the beings, he declares that all the dharmas are pure by nature like a lotus flower, hence this divinity is also called Avalokiteśvararāja. He reigns over the class of padma. He is of golden colour. He makes the mudrā of samādhi. It is the mudrā of Amitābha: two hands resting on hips, palms above, fingers touching one another by phalanxes, thumbs opposed by their hands. There are slight differences in other texts, sometimes the last three fingers are in extention (Tajima 179-80). I.1.4.

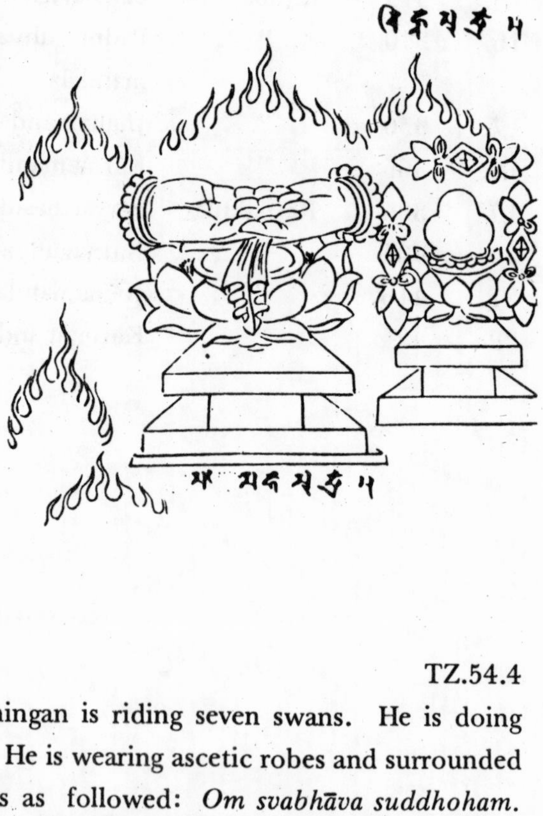

TZ.54.4

Amitābha in the first maṇḍala of Gobu-shingan is riding seven swans. He is doing dhyāna mudrā by his hands sitting in vajrāsana. He is wearing ascetic robes and surrounded by flames. Dhāraṇī under the illustration reads as followed: *Om svabhāva suddhoham. Bhagavān Amitābhaḥ.* His mudrās are named as cihna and mahā-mudrā (TZ 54.4).

Amitābha has the same sitting posture in mahā-maṇḍala of the graphic Vajradhātu as he has in the preceded drawing from the first maṇḍala of Gobu-shingan. Here he has no

TZ.38.16

animal ride, clothing style is a bit different, hand posture is the same but that is not drawn so well (TZ 38.16, Lokesh Chandra 421). *Hrīḥ* is given as his seed syllable.

I.2.4. Amitāyu in vajra-guhya-vajra-maṇḍala attains the samādhi called maṇḍala consecration of knowledge mudrā of vajra-dharma-samaya of All the Tathāgatas and recites his vidyottama as: *Om dharma-vajriṇī hūm* (STTS 101). In second maṇḍala of Gobu-shingan he is holding a vajra placed upon a lotus overhead by both of his hands. He is sitting in a lotus pericarp, wearing all the ornaments and crown

I.2.4.

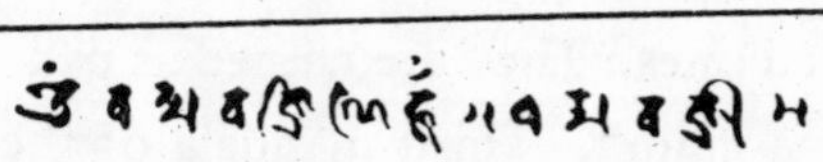

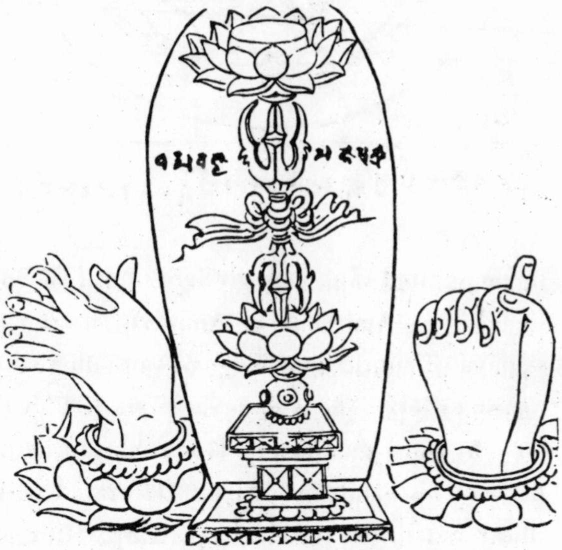

TZ.54.42

Gobu-shingan corresponding to STTS gives the same dhāraṇī: *Om dharma-vajriṇī hūm*. *Dharma-vajri* (TZ 54. 42). Mudrās are different from the preceded maṇḍala. The central one is named as dharma-vajra-mahā-mudrā. Others are not named.

Amitābha as Dharma-vajriṇī in samaya-maṇḍala of the graphic Vajradhātu-maṇḍala is drawn as a three pointed double sided vajra laid in a lotus pericarp with a

I.3.4.

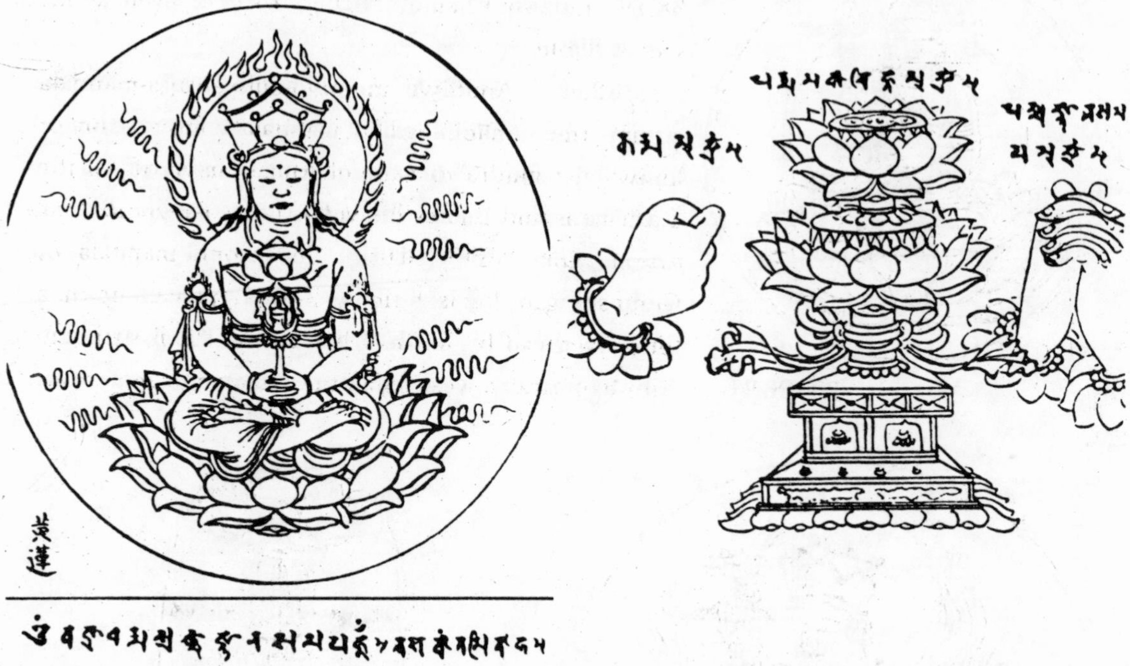

TZ.54.75

single pointed vajra kept straight on it (TZ 38.78, Lokesh Chandra 483).

I.3.4. Amitābha as Amitāyu enters the samādhi named as maṇḍala consecration of samaya of subtle knowledge of vajra-dharma of Stg. and recites his vidyottamā as: *Om vajra dharma-sūkṣma-jñāna-samaya hūm.* (STTS 117).

In third maṇḍala of Gobu-shingan he holds a lotus placed upon a vajra supported by both of his hands in his lap. Decorated with all the ornaments and a crown he is wearing dhotī and sitting on a lotus pericarp. His dhāraṇī is the same as given in the third chapter of STTS. *Om vajra-dharma-sūkṣma-jñāna-samaya hūm. Bhagavān Amitābha* (TZ 54.75). Second two mudrās are different from the preceded ones. They are named as padma-jñāna-samaya-mudrā, padma-mahā-cihna-mudrā and karma-mudrā. Third maṇḍala of the graphic Vajradhātu illustrates Amitābha in the same posture as he is in the first maṇḍala (TZ 38. 151, Lokesh Chandra 556).

Amitāyu enters the samādhi named vajra consecration of karma samaya of suffusion of explanation of anuttara pūjā of vajra dharma of stg. and utters these words: *Om sarva-tathāgata vajra-dharmānuttara pūjā-spharaṇa samaye hūm* (STTS 131). The same dhāraṇī is given by Gobu-shingan and the deity is named as Amitābha. In the illustration given here he is holding a lotus in his right hand and with the other he is making a mudrā. Wearing all the ornaments he is sitting on a lotus and is surrounded by flowers. All of his

I.4.4.

mudrās given with the illustration are identical to the mudrās illustrated with the preceded drawing from the third maṇḍala (TZ 54.108). Amitābha in fourth maṇḍala of the graphic vajradhātu has the same form as extracted from the first maṇḍala (TZ 38.224, Lokesh Chandra 629).

TZ.54.108

TZ.38.405

This drawing is from the samaya-maṇḍala of Trailokyavijaya from the graphic Vajradhātu-maṇḍala (TZ 38.405, Lokesh Chandra 804). The only difference from the preceded symbolic form is that here it has a lotus atop the vajra. In the karma-maṇḍala of Trailokyavijaya Amitāyu is sitting with his hand folded accross his breast (TZ.38.328, Lokesh Chandra 735).

II.3.4. Amitāyu is Vajranetra in vajrakula-dharma-jñāna-samaya-maṇḍala. He recites his vidyottamā which is the subtle vajra of Trilokavijaya: *Om sūkṣmavajra-padma-krodha-krama hūm phaṭ* (STTS 226). II.4.4. In vajrakula-karma-maṇḍala he recites these words: *Om sarvatathāgata-dharmadhātu-spharaṇa-mahā-pūjā-karma-vidhi-vistara- samaya hūm* (STTS 237). III.1.4. In sakala-jagadvinaya-mahā-maṇḍala his vidyottamā is given as: *Om vajra vidyottamā hrīḥ* (STTS 319). III.2.4. Bodhisttva Vajranetra utters his vidyottamā in padma-guhya-mudrā-maṇḍala as: *Om padma-samaye hūm* (STTS 341). III.3.4. His vidyottamā is dharma-dharma in jñāna-maṇḍala: *Om dharma-dharma hūm* (STTS 357). III.4.4. In karma-maṇḍala it is padma-karmī: *Om padma-karmī-hūm*. (STTS 366). IV.1.4. Vajranetra recites his vidyottamā which originates in his own family in sarvārthasiddhi-maṇḍala: *Om padma hrīḥ* (STTS 387). IV.2.4. In its ratna-guhya-mudrā-maṇḍala he recites as: *Om vajra dharmābhiṣiñca mām* (STTS 405). IV.3.4. The bodhisattva Vajranetra utters his vidyottamā as: *Om dharmābhiṣeka-jñāna hūm* (STTS 417). IV.4.4. He is saddharmābhiṣeka-ratna in karma-maṇḍala. *Om saddharmābhiṣeka-ratne* (STTS 425).

Names of the Lokeśvararāja in the sixteen maṇḍalas.

| Ch. | P. | Kula | Maṇḍala | Names |
|---|---|---|---|---|
| 1. | - | Buddhakula | Vajrandhātu-mahā-m. | Amitābha. |
| 2. | 101 | " | Vajraguhya-vajra-m. | Dharma-vajriṇī. |
| 3. | 117 | " | Vajrajñāna-dharma-m. | Vajra-dharma-sūkṣma-jñāna-samaya. |
| 4. | 131 | " | Vajrakārya-karma-m. | Stg.-Vajra-dharmānuttara-pūjā-spharaṇa-samayā. |
| 6. | 194 | Vajrakula | Trilokavijaya-mahā-m. | - |
| 7. | - | " | Krodhaguhya-mudrā-m. | - |
| 8. | 226 | " | Vajrakula-dharmajñāna -samayamaṇḍala. | Sūkṣma-vajra-padma-krodha. |
| 9. | 237 | " | Vajrakula-karma-m. | Stg.-dharmadhātu-spharaṇa-mahā-pūjā. |
| 15. | 319 | Padmakula | Sakalajagadvinaya-mahāmaṇḍala. | Vajra-vidyottamā. |
| 16. | 341 | " | Padmaguhya-mudrā-m. | Padma-samayā. |
| 17. | 357 | " | Jñānamaṇḍala | Dharma-dharma. |
| 18. | 366 | " | Karmamaṇḍala | Padma-karmī. |
| 19. | 387 | Ratnakula | Sarvārthasiddhi-mahāmaṇḍala. | Padma. |
| 20. | 405 | " | Ratnaguhya-mudrā-m. | Vajra-dharma. |
| 21. | 417 | " | Jñānamaṇḍala | Dharmābhiṣeka-jñāna. |
| 22. | 425 | " | Karmamaṇḍala | Saddharmābhiṣeka-ratna. |

## AMOGHASIDDHI
不空成就如來

Traditions affirm the identity of Tathagata Amoghasiddhi with Śākyamuni. Having attained the rank of Buddha by product of sapience of act, he is intermidiary of Vajrapāramitā and he presides over the virtues of Vairocana that are perseverence in the conversion of the beings and in the nirvāṇa. He is of golden colour. His left hand is closed and the right is drawn against his breast and his fingers are stretched. Most of the maṇḍalas present him with his left hand closed before the navel, and the right hand in abhaya mudrā that symbolises the great compassion and removal of sufferings. But this mudrā is not justified by any text. The text says that his complexion is clear green and black or even of five colours. The green colour is considered to be of the one that is ground, hence it is the colour of nirvāṇa like black. The five colours symbolise the completion of all the action. (Tajima 182-3).

I.1.5

Amoghasiddhi in the first maṇḍala of Gobu-shingan is riding five birds. He is doing abhaya mudrā by his right hand and by his left hand he is holding a corner of his upper garment. Sitting calm and quite he is surrounded by flames. His dhāraṇī is : *Om sarva samoham. Bhagavān Amoghasiddhi.* First mudrā illustrated as a varada hand is his mahāmudrā and the cihna-mudrā is represented by gems surrounded by vajras placed upon a lotus seat. (TZ 54.5).

*Aḥ* is given as his seed syllable in the graphic Vajradhātu-maṇḍala. Sitting in a lotus

I.2.5. TZ.38.21

pericarp he is doing mudrās by both of his hands. Monastic robes are the same as in Gobu-shingan. No animal ride has been drawn as usual (TZ 38.21, Lokesh Chandra 426).

I.2.5. Tathāgata Amoghasiddhi enters the samādhi named mudrā-maṇḍala consecration of the knowledge of karma-samaya of vajra of Stg. and speaks these words: *Om karma-vajriṇī hūm* (STTS 102). In Gobu-shingan as well he is named as Karma-vajriṇī. But in the dhāraṇī he is named as Karma-vajrī also. She is holding a three pointed four sided vajra placed

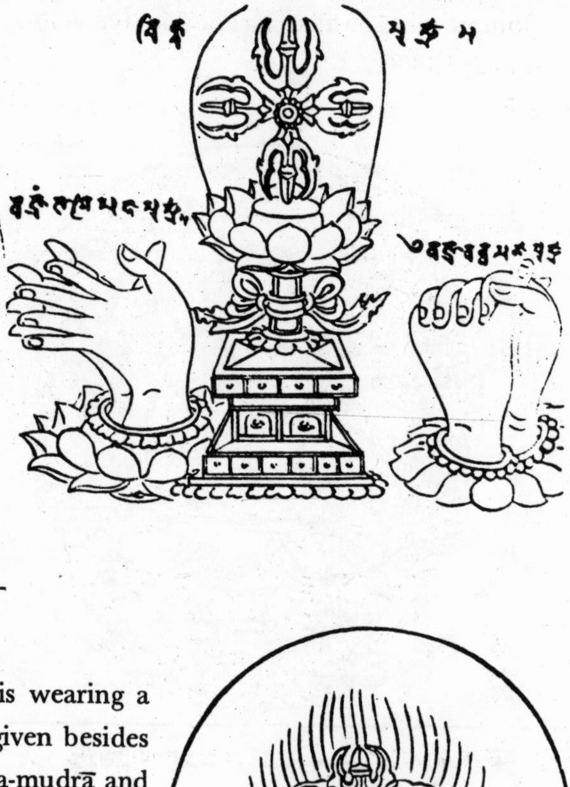

upon a lotus by both of her hands. She is wearing a crown and all the ornaments. Her mudrās given besides are named as vajrabandha-mahā-mudrā, cihna-mudrā and vajrāñjalī-mahā-mudrā (TZ 54.43).

Amoghasiddhi in the mudrā-maṇḍala of the graphic Vajradhātu is illustrated as a viśva vajra placed upon another vajra in a lotus pericarp (TZ 38.83, Lokesh Chandra 488).

I.3.5. Tathāgata Amoghasiddhi enters the samādhi named samaya-maṇḍala consecration of subtle knowledge

I.3.5.

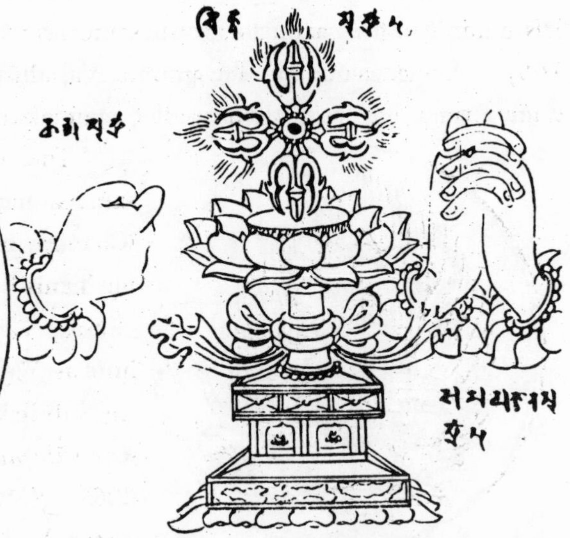

TZ.54.76.

of vajra-dharma of Stg. and recites this verse: *Om vajra-dharma sūkṣma-jñāna-samaya hūm*, (STTS 117). Gobu-shingan gives the same dhāraṇī and names him as Bhagavān Amoghasiddhi. In the illustration given in third maṇḍala of Gobu-shingan he holds a viśva-vajra in his lap. He is decorated with crown and ornaments as before. The mudrās are named as samaya, cihna- and karma. First and second are identical with the preceded ones (TZ 54.76). Amoghasiddhi in third maṇḍala of the graphic Vajradhātu has the same hand postures as he has in first maṇḍala (TZ 38.156, Lokesh Chandra 561).

I.4.5. In Vajra-kārya-karma-maṇḍala Amoghasiddhi is the subtle form of vajra-karma-anuttara-pūjā of Stg. He enters the samādhi named as vajra consecration of karma samaya of suffusion of explanation of pūjā-vidhi of vajra-karma of Stg. and recites this verse: *Om sarva-tathāgata vajra karmānuttara-pūjā-spharaṇa-samaye hūm*. (STTS 131).

I.4.5.

TZ.54.108

Gobu-shingan gives the same dhāraṇī. It illustrates him as holding visva vajra upon a lotus in his left hand and with the right he is making varada mudrā. He is surrounded by flowers. His mudrās in this maṇḍala are the same as extracted before from the third maṇḍala (TZ 54. 108). Amoghasiddhi in the graphic Vajradhātu-maṇḍala in its fourth maṇḍala attains the same form as he has in the preceded mandalas (TZ 38.229, Lokesh Chandra 634).

TZ.38.333

The illustration extracted here belongs to the samaya-mandala of Trailokya-vijaya (TZ.38.410, Lokesh Chandra 809). In its karma-maṇḍala he is sitting with his hands folded (TZ.38.444, Lokesh Chandra 740). II.3.5. Vajra-kula-dharma-jñāna-samaya-maṇḍala names him as Vajra-viśva. He recites his vidyottama which is the subtle vajra of Trilokavijaya and recites these words: *Om sūkṣma-vajra-karma-krodhākrama hūm phaṭ* (STTS 226). II.4.5. In vajrakula-karma-maṇḍala he is bodhisattva Vajra-viśva who recites his vidyottama as. *Om sarva-tathāgata sarvālokadhātu vividha mahā-pūjā-karma-vidhi vistara-samaya hūm.* (STTS 237). III.1.5. Vajra-viśva is Viśvottama in the sakala-jagad-vinaya-maṇḍala: *Om vajra-viśvottama aḥ*. (STTS 319). III.2.5. In its guhya-maṇḍala he is karma-samayā: *Om karma-samaye hūm*. (STTS 341). III.3.5. In jñāna-maṇḍala Vajra-viśva is personified as Karma-dharma: *Om dharma-karma hūm*. (STTS 357). III.4.5. In karma-maṇḍala of sakala-jagad-vinaya he is named as Viśva-karmī. *Om viśva-karmī hūm.* (STTS 366). IV.1.5. In Sarvārtha-siddh-mahā-maṇḍala he recites his vidyottama as a bodhisattva as: *Om viśva-ratna hūm.* (STTS 387). IV.2.5. In its ratna-guhya-mudrā-maṇḍala Vajra-viśva is the pūjā samayā of sarvābhiṣeka who recites his mudrā as: *Om sarvābhiṣeka-pūjā-samaye hūm.* (STTS 405). IV.3.5. He attains a knowledge form of sarvābhiṣeka in knowledge maṇḍala: *Om sarvābhiṣeka-jñāna hūm.* (STTS 417). IV.4.5. In karma-maṇḍala of sarvārthasiddhi he is transferred as viśvābhiṣekā: *Om viśvābhiṣekā* (STTS 425).

Names of the Amoghasiddhi in the sixteen maṇḍalas:

| Ch. | P. | Kula | Maṇḍala | Names. |
|---|---|---|---|---|
| 1. | - | Buddhakula | Vajradhātu-mahā-m. | Amoghasiddhi. |
| 2. | 102 | " | Vajraguhya-vajra-m. | Karma-vajriṇī. |
| 3. | 117 | " | Vajrajñāna-dharma-m. | Vajra-dharma-sūkṣma-jñāna-samaya. |
| 4. | 131 | " | Vajrakārya-karma-m. | Stg.-Vajra-karmānuttara-pūjā-spharṇa-samayā. |
| 6. | - | Vajrakula | Trilokavijaya-mahā-m. | - |
| 7. | - | " | Krodhaguhya-mudrā-m. | - |
| 8. | 226 | " | Vajrakula-dharmajñāna-samaya-maṇḍala. | Vajra-viśva. |
| 9. | 237 | " | Vajrakula-karma-m. | Stg.-Sarvālokadhātu-vividha-mahā-pūjā. |
| 15. | 319 | Padmakula | Sakalajagadvinaya-mahāmaṇḍala. | Vajra-viśvottma. |
| 16. | 341 | " | Padmaguhya-mudrā-m. | Karma-samayā. |
| 17. | 357 | " | Jñānamaṇḍala | Dharma-karma. |
| 18. | 366 | " | Karmamaṇḍala | Viśva-karmī. |
| 19. | 387 | Ratnakula | Sarvārthasiddhi-mahāmaṇḍala. | Viśva-ratna. |
| 20. | 405 | " | Ratnaguhya-mudrā-m. | Sarvābhiṣeka-pūjā-samaya. |
| 21. | 417 | " | Jñānamaṇḍala | Sarvābhiṣeka-jñāna. |
| 22. | 425 | " | Karmamaṇḍala | Viśvābhiṣekā. |

## 6. VAJRASATTVA

金剛薩埵菩薩

Vajrasattva, the first of the sixteen bodhisattvas sits to the west of Akṣobhya who is in the east of Vairocana. He symbolises the unshakeble firmness of heart of bodhi and takes his flight among beings. He is of flesh colour. He carries a bell in his left hand to awken beings from their prolonged slumber and in his right hand a vajra with five heads opposite his breast that symbolises the samaya of Buddha. (Tajima 175).

Vajrasattva the essence (seed syllable) of Stg. emanates from Vairocana's heart, when he enters upon the samadhi called *sattvādhiṣṭhāna-vajra* (being consecration vajra) which has its origin in the samaya of Samantabhadra, the great bodhisattva of Stg. He is the mahāyāna insight of Stg. *mahāyānābhisamaya.* As soon as Vairocana utters Vajrasattva, Samantabhadra emerges from the hearts of Stg. in the multiple form of lunar discs. They purify mahābodhicittas of all the sattvas and stay around all the Tathāgatas. Jñāna-vajras emerge from those lunar discs and enter the heart of Stg. as a sigle blazing five faced vajra, full of vajra element of kāya, vāk and citta of Stg. and appears on Vairocana's hand. Then the rays assume the form of great bodhisattva Samantabhadra and are established in Vairocana's heart, reciting this verse: "Oho I am Samantabhadra, absolute being, am self existent, because of this absolute nature, although bodiless yet I assume bodily forms.

Again he emerges from the heart of Bhagavān, stations himself as a lunar disc in from of Stg. and pays them respect. The Lord Vairocana enter ths *samaya-vajra* of knowledge of All the Tathāgatas, so that he may receive the supreme perfection of Mahāyāna Insight which is the principle recognition of the knowledge of equity of All the Tathāgatas, consisting of morality, meditation, wisdom, release, experience of knowledge of release, turning of the wheel of the doctrines, acting on behalf of living beings, great skill in means, power determination, pledge of great knoledge, protecting all beings in all spheres of existence, universal dominian and experience of blises. He consecrated Samantabhadra with the body, gem, crown and scarf consecration, placing in his hands the vajra of success of All the Tathāgatas. Thereupon they consecrate him with the name of Vajra-pāṇi, the Great Bodhisattva, with a vajra resting in his left hand holds it with his right flourishing it at his heart as though about to throw it, he then pronounces this udāna: "This is the supreme vajra of success of All the Tathāgatas, I am given into my own hands vajra unto vajra.

I.1.6. Vajra-sattva in the first chapter (maṇḍala) of the Gobu-shingan is sitting on the pericarp of a lotus which is placed on an elephant. He is holding a single pointed vajra in his

I.1.6.

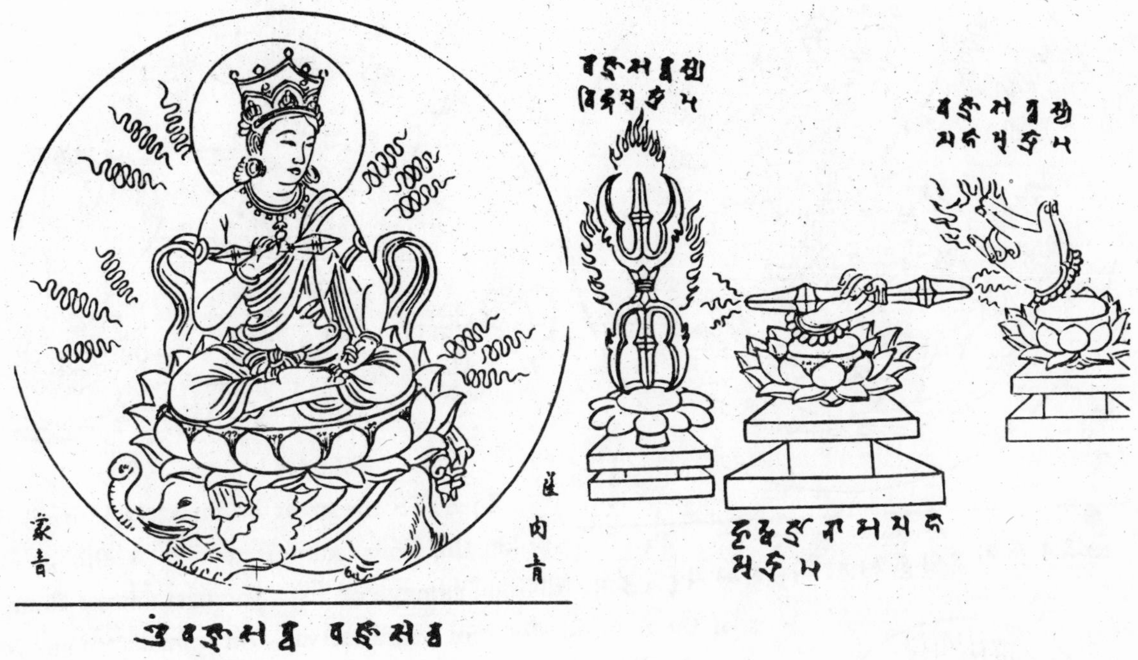

right hand and is wearing a crown, ornaments full of gems, an upper garment and a dhotī, His colour should be blue according to this illustration. The mudrās illustrated besides are named : mahā-mudrā, portrayed by his blazing hand psoture, hṛd-vajra-nāma-mahā-mudrā, by a hand holding a single pointed vajra placed on a lotus, cihna-mudrā as a blazing three pointed vajra on a lotus. (TZ 54.6).

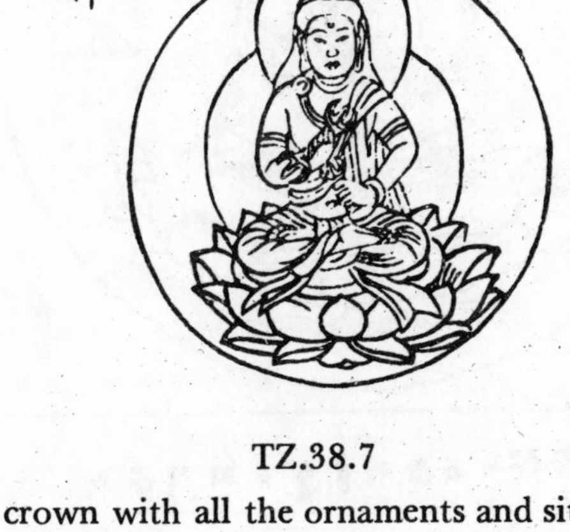

TZ.38.7

In mahā-maṇḍala of graphic Vajradhātu Vajra-sattva occupies a seat in the east of Akṣobhya who is in the west of Vairocana. He holds a vajra in his right hand and in his left he has a vajra with a bell. *Aḥ* is given as his seed syllable. He is sitting on a lotus pericarp in a lotus posture (TZ 38.7, Lokesh Chandra 412).

I.2.6. Vajra-sattva is Samantabhdrā in the second maṇḍala of Gobu-shingan. She holds a three pointed double sided vajra in her hands placed upon a lotus which is placed upon a seat as her mudrā among the mudrās given besides. She is wearing a crown with all the ornaments and sitting in a lotus. The dhāraṇī given under her illustration corresponds to STTS. *Om vajra-sattva-guhya-samaye hūm. Samantabhadrā.* (TZ 54.44). The mudrās are not named but they should be: vajra-bandha, cihna-midrā and añjali-mudrā.

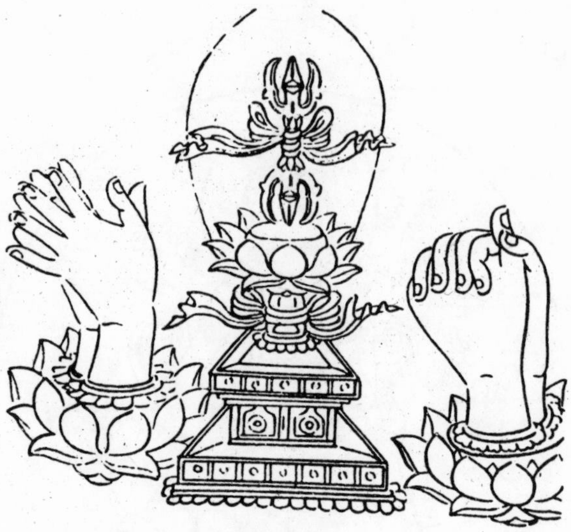

TZ.54.44

In STTS the great bodhisattva Vajrapāṇi spoke the four mudrās which is the great dhāraṇī samaya of Stg. The first among them is of the feminine form of Vajra-sattva: *Om vajra-sattva-guhya samaye hūm* (STTS 102).

Vajra-sattva in samaya-maṇḍala of the graphic Vajradhātu I.3.6.

is depicted as a vajra on a lotus encircled by rays (TZ 38.69, Lokesh Chandra 474).

I.3.6. Vajra-sattva is vajrātmala in third maṇḍala of Gobu-shingan. He has a vajra in his hands placed in his lap. He has a candra kalā upon his crown with a star. His dhāraṇī under the illustration is: *Om vajra-tāmakaḥ Vajra-sattva jñāna mudrā.* Mudrās are named as samaya-jñāna-mudrā, cihna and karma (TZ54.77). Only karma-mudrā differs from preceded on. It is depicted as a muṣṭi.

TZ.54.77

Vajrapāṇi utters the four essenses of great knowledge. The first among them is *Vajrātmaka.* He is knowledge mudrā of Vajra-sattva: *Vajra-sattva jñāna-mudrā* (STTS 119).

In the graphic Vajradhātu-maṇḍala he has two bells with vajras atop in his hands. He is sitting on a lotus and a vajra can be seen behinde (TZ 38.142, Lokesh Chandra 547).

I.4.6. Vajra-sattva in vajra-kārya-karma-maṇḍala in STTS is named as Karma-vajrī. Vajra-pāṇi speaks the karma-

I.4.6.

TZ.38.142

maṇḍala which is named as vajra-kārya. The first among them is Vajra-sattva: *Om sarva-tathāgataa sarvātma-niryātana-pūjā-spharṇa karma-vajrī aḥ* (STTS 133). He is personified as sukhasukhā of Stg.: *Sarva-tathāgata-sukhasukhā.* But Gobu-shingan giving the same dhāraṇi names her as sarva-tathāgata surata-syava. Instead of karma-vajri she is karma-vajra. She has a three pointed vajra in her right hand and left is dropped downwards. Her mudrās are the same as given in the preceded maṇḍala of Gobu-shingan (TZ 54.110).

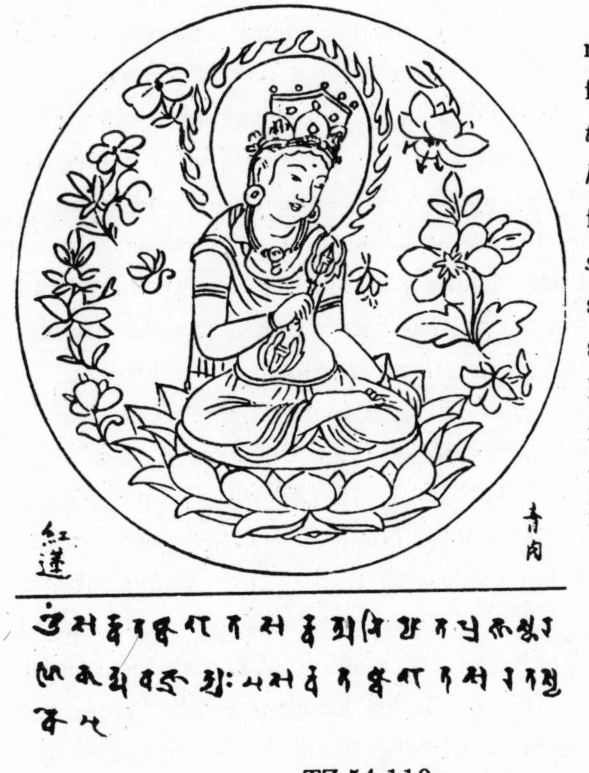

TZ.54.110

Vajra-sattva in the karma-maṇḍala of the graphic Vajradhātu has a lotus in both the hands. Something is drawn on the lotus which should be a vajra as comapred to other illustrations. Ornaments and head dress are simplified. Lotus is the same (TZ 38.215, Lokesh Chandra 620).

TZ.38.215

II.1.6. Hṛdaya of Vajra-sattva in Trilokavijaya-mahā-maṇḍala attains an angry form: *Om vajra-sattva-krodha hūm phaṭ* (STTS 191). II.2.6. In its krodha guhya-mudrā-maṇḍala he obtains the feminined subtle form of the angry appearence of Vajrasattva. *Om vajra-sattva-krodha-samaye siḥ.* (STTS 214). In the samaya-maṇḍala of the graphic Vajra-dhātu he is portrayed as a Viśvavajra which gives a fierce look (TZ 38.396, Lokesh Chandra 795). II.3.6. In vajra-kula-dharma-jñāna-samaya-maṇḍala he has an angry form of subtle knowledge: *Om vajra-sattva sūkṣma-jñāna-krodha hūm phaṭ* (STTS 226).

TZ.38.396.

TZ.38.319

II.4.6. Next comes the karma-maṇḍala of vajra kula where he is the knowledge samaya of siddhi of vajra-sattva. *Om vajra-sattva sidhi-jñāna-samaye hūm jjha* (STTS 238). In the graphic vajradhātu-maṇḍala he has a fierce form with eight hands. His right hands are holding vajra, sword and an arrow, left hands have a trident, bow and a noose, his front hands are making a mudrā. He is with three heads with third eye. His hair is drawn straight upwards. Two beings are trampled down under his feet. He is surrounded by flames (TZ 38.319, Lokesh Chandra 726). III.1.6. In the sakala-jagad-vinaya-maṇḍala Vajra-sattva sits besides Lokeśvara called vajra-padmāṅkuśa: *Om vajra-padmāṅkuśa kośa-dhara vajra-sattva hūm phaṭ.* (STTS 322). III.2.6. Next comes padma-guhya-mudrā-maṇḍala. Because of his relation to the lotus family he is called padma-vajrāṅ-kuśa and because of the mudrā-maṇḍala he has a femined form: *Om Samanta-bhadra-padma-vajrāṅkuśa-kośa-dhāriṇī* (STTS 342). III.3.6. Dharma-maṇḍala of sakala-jagad-vinaya is jñāna-maṇḍa, thus he is called the Buddha of lotus family of knowledge maṇḍala *Om padma-jñāna-buddha hūm.* (STTS 358). III.4.6. In its karma-maṇḍala Vajra-sattva has a feminine form as Buddha of action maṇḍala of lotus family: *Om padma-karma-buddha hūm.* (STTS 367). IV.1.6. In mahā-maṇḍala of sarvārthasiddhi Vajra-sattva sits with Vajra-garbha. This maṇḍala belongs to the ratna family, hence Vajra-sattva has sky in his womb with a sign of jewel with a thunderbolt: *Om vajra-maṇi-cihnākaśa-garbha bhagavān siddhya siddhya hūm.* (STTS 390). IV.2.6. In ratna-guhya-mudrā-maṇḍala he has a feminine form of the one who attracts jewels: *Om maṇi ratnākarṣe hūm* (STTS 406). IV.3.6. In jñāna-maṇḍala Vajra-sattva is Maṇi-jñāna or knowledge of jwels: *Om maṇi-jñāna hūm* (STTS 418). IV.4.6. He is the essense of bearing jewels in karma-maṇḍala of Sarvārthasiddhi: *Om vajra-maṇi-dhāriṇī samaye hūm* (STTS 425).

Names of Vajra-sattva in the 16 maṇḍalas

| Ch. | P. | Kula | Maṇḍala | Names |
|---|---|---|---|---|
| 1. | 11 | Buddha | Vajradhātu-mahā-m. | Vajrapāṇi, samantabhadra. |
| 2. | 102 | ” | Vajra-guhya-vajra-m. | Vajra-sattva-guhya-ṣamayā, Samanta-bhadrā. |
| 3. | 119 | ” | Vajra-jñāna-dharma-m. | Vjrātmaka, Vajra-sattva-jñāna-mudraḥ. |
| 4. | 133 | ” | Vajra-kārya-karama-m. | Karma-vajrī, Stg. sukhasukhā. |
| 6. | 191 | Vajra | Trilokavijaya-mahā-m. | Vajra-sattva-krodha. |
| 7. | 214 | ” | Krodha-gyhya-mudrā-m. | Vajra-krodha-samayā. |
| 8. | 226 | ” | Vajrakula-dharma-jñāna samaya-maṇḍala. | Vajra-sattva-sūkṣma-jñāna-krodha. |
| 9. | 238 | ” | Vajrakula-karma-m. | Vajra-sattva-siddhi-jñāna-samayā. |
| 15. | 322 | Padma | Sakala-jagad-vinaya-mahā-maṇḍala. | Tathāgata-dharma. |
| 16. | 342 | ” | Padma-guhya-mudrā-m. | Padma-tathāgatā. |
| 17. | 358 | ” | Jñāna-maṇḍala. | Jñāna-padma-buddha. |
| 18a | 367 | ” | Karma-maṇḍala. | Padma-karma-buddhā. |
| 19. | 390 | Ratna | Sarvārthasiddhi-mahā-m. | Vajramaṇi-cihna-ākāśa-garbha-bhagavān. |
| 20. | 406 | ” | Ratna-guhya-mudrā-m. | Maṇi-samayā |
| 21. | 418 | ” | Jñāna-m. | Mani-jñāna. |
| 22a | 425 | ” | karma-m. | Vajra-maṇi-dhāraṇī-samayā. |

## 7. VAJRA-RĀJA
金剛王菩薩

Vajra-rāja, the second great Bodhisattva, occupies a seat in the northern direction. He exalts uncomparably the virtue of the heart of Bodhi. Hence he is the King, Vajra-rāja. Moreover qualificative is the expression of liberty. No sooner the heart of Bodhi is awakened he forces his liberty for all the passions to become obedient. He is of flesh colour. His posture is Vajramuṣṭi, his fists are closed with thumbs between fingers, right fist is pressed against his breast and the left hand is crossed above.

Vairocana enters the samādhi, known as Sattvādhiṣṭhāna-vajra which has its origin in the samaya of the great Bodhisattva Amogharāja, and he utters from his heart the seed syllable of All the Tathāgatas, known as 'ākarṣaṇa-samaya' coercing pledge of All the Tathāgatas, namely Vajrarāja. As soon as he says this, Vajrapāṇi emerges from the hearts of all the Tathāgatas in the multiple form of hooks (aṅkuśa) and enters into Vairocana's heart. Then these become a single great hook which appears in Vairocana's hand. These hooks turn into Buddha forms who carry out all kinds of beneficial magical acts through space. Then they coalesce into Amogharāja, the Great Bodhisattva, who is established in Vairocana's heart and recites this verse: "Oho, I am Amoghavajra, the hook, the vajraborn, in that the all prevading Buddhas are successfully coerced."

Then Amogharāja, the Great Bodhisattva emerges from the heart of Vairocana and stations in the right lunar disc of All the Tathāgatas, again he pays respects. Vairocana I.1.7.

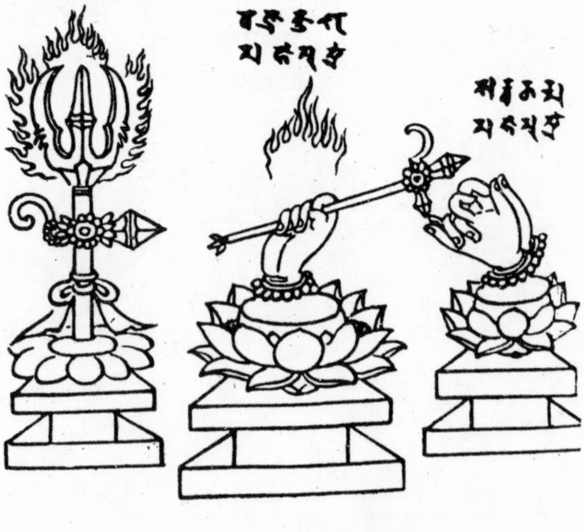

Tz.54.7

enters upon the samādhi known as 'vajra-pledge coercer of All the Tathāgatas' obtaining success in the supreme consecration which unites All the Tathāgatas, he gives that 'vajrāṅkuśa' into the hands of Mahābodhisattva Amogharāja, who is then consecrated by All the Tathāgatas with the name of 'Vajrākarṣa', uttering the following verse: "This the supreme vajra knowledge of all the Buddha, which is the supreme coercison for success in all the Buddha affairs" (STTS 14-15).

I.1.7. In the first chapter of Gobu-shingan (TZ.54.7) Vajra-rāja comes as the seventh deity of the scroll. Vajra-rāja sitting in lotus posture on a lotus upon an elephant is holding a hook in right hand and his left fist is resting in his lap. He is named as 'Vajrāṅkuśa. Vajra-rāja' below the illustration. Mudrās given under the illustration from right to left are 'Sarva-karma-mahā-mudrā' and 'Vajrāṅkuśa-mahā-mudrā'. The third one is not named in the manuscript. Mostly the same mudrā has been drawn in the second chapter where it is named as 'Cihna-mudrā'.

The illustration extracted here is from the graphic Vajradhātu-mahā-maṇḍala. The posture of his hands drawn here in the mahā-maṇḍala is named s Vajra-muṣṭi by Tajima (175-6) (TZ 38.8, Lokesh Chandra 413) as his fists are closed with his thumbs in between other fingers, right fist is pressed against his breast and the other is crossed above.

I.2.7. The drawing given below is from the second

I.2.7.

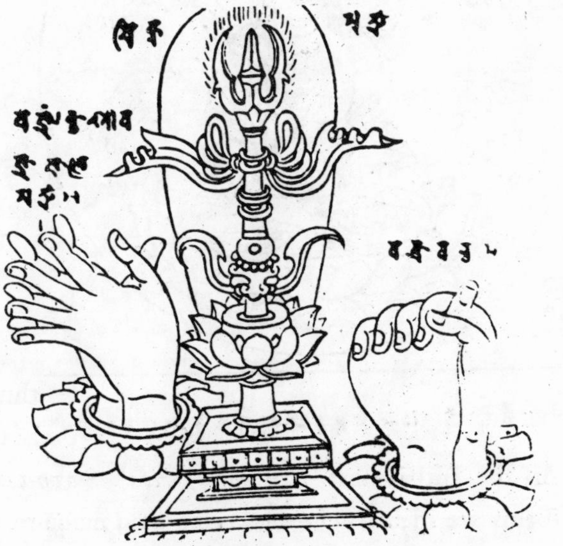

TZ.54.45

chapter of Gobu-shingan (TZ.54.45). Tathāgatāṅkuśī, the feminine form of Tathāgatankusa is holding a lotus with a three pointed single sided vajra by both of her hands. She is sitting on a lotus and beholding her attribute. Mantra under the illustration is as follows: *Om Vajra-guhya vajrankusa hum. Vajrankusi.* According to the STTS in the Vajra-guhya-vajra-mandala Vajra-raja is to be personified as a Vajra-dharini named Vajrankusi: *om guhya vajrankusi hum* (STTS 102). The mudras from right to left are named in the manuscript as vajrabandha, cihna-mudrā, vajrāṅkuśī-vajra-jñāna-mudrā.

TZ.38.70

In the mudrā-maṇḍala of the graphic vajra-dhātu Vajra-rāja is represented as a dual three pointed aṅkuśa placed on a lotus (TZ.38.70, Lokesh Chandra 475).

I.3.7. In the third chapter of Gobu-shingan a three pointed single vajra is held straight by both of his hands placing it near his breast (TZ.54.78, Lokesh Chandra 548). He is named as the knowledge seal of All the Tathāgatas: *Om hṛd vajrāṅkuśaḥ. Sarva-tathāgata-ākarṣaṇa-jñāna-mudrā.* In STTS his mantra is 'hṛd vajrāṅkuśa'. As the second

I.3.7.

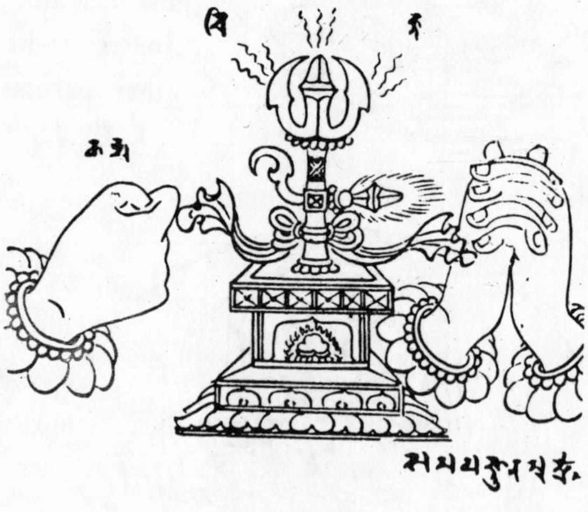

TZ.54.78

thunderbolt concentration of All the Tathāgatas is the knowledge seal of the mutitude grace of All the Tathāgatas: *Hṛd vajrāṅkuśa. Sarva-tathāgata-mahā-vajra-samādhi* (STTS 119). His forms are identical in the karma- and mahā-maṇḍalas of the graphic Vajradhātu. (TZ.38.143)

I.4.7.

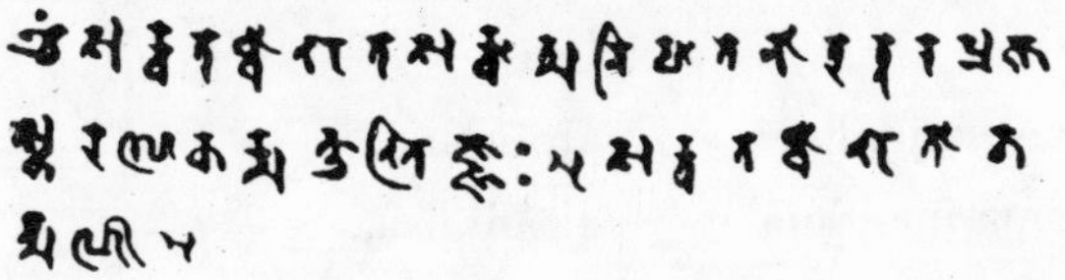

TZ.54.117

I.4.7. Here is Vajra-rāja in the fourth chapter of Gobu-shingan, holding a goad in the right hand and its roap in its left (TZ.54.111). He is eulogised as 'Karmāgrī '*om sarva-tathāgata sarvātama-niryātana* pūjā spharaṇa karmāgrī jjḥa (STTS 133). He is pūjā spharaṇa to attract back all the spirits. Gobu-shingan relates it in the same way. His mudrās are the same as given above from the third chapter.

TZ.38.216

The attribute of Vajra-rāja in the graphic Vajradhātu-karma-maṇḍala differs from that of Gobu-shingan. He is holding a lotus with its stem and something surrounded by flames is placed upon the lotus. (TZ.38.216, Lokesh Chandra 621).

II.4.7. Trailokyavijaya-karma-maṇḍala has the same portrait of Vajra-rāja as given in the Mahā- and karma-maṇḍala of the graphic Vajradhātu (TZ.38.320). He sits besides Vajra pāṇi according to STTS and his mantra runs as follows: *Om vajra-krodhākaraṣya hūm phaṭ* (STTS 190). II.2.7. In krodha-guhya-mudrā-maṇḍala his essence is depicted as a furious goad of vajra family to bring everything: *Om vajraroṣāṅkuśyānaya sarvam siḥ* (STTS 214). Symbolic form of Vajra-rāja in samaya maṇḍalas of the graphic Vajradhātu and Trailokya-vijaya are the same (TZ.38.397).

In the symbolic maṇḍala of religious knoledge of vajrakula he is a minute goad to attract the great anger: *Om sūkṣma vajrāṅkuśākarṣaya mahā-krodha hūm phaṭ* (STTS 226). The attraction of vajra family is the essence of knolwedge of action in vajra-kula-karma-maṇḍala: *Om vajrākarṣaṇa karma jñāna samaye hūm jjha'* (STTS 238). III.1.7. In mahā-maṇḍala of Jagadvinaya Vajra-rāja in the name of Padmāṅkuśa has a place near Lokeśvara with a lotus (STTS 322). III.2.7. In the Mudrā-maṇḍala of Jagadvinaya he is personified as.'*Om samantabhadra padma-vajrāṅkuśa-kośa-dhāriṇī hūm* (STTS 342). III.3.7. In jñāna-maṇḍala of sakala-jagad-vinaya he is jñāna-padma-rāja: *Om jñāna-padma-*

*rāja-dhara hūm* (STTS 367). IV.1.7. He is eulogised as a bringer of all objects: *Om ratnāṅkuśākarṣaya sarvārthānaya śīghram sarvatathāgata satyamanusmara hūm* (STTS 390). IV.2.7. He is Jñānāṅkuśa in ratna-guhya-mudrā-maṇḍala: *Om maṇi ratnāṅkuśa* (STTS 418). IV.3.7. In jñāna-maṇḍala of ratnakula he attracts all the jewels as maṇi-ratna-samayāṅkuśī: *Om maṇi-ratna-samayāṅkuśyākarṣaya maṇi-kulam jaḥ* (STTS 406). IV.4.7. He has the same feature in the next maṇḍala, i.e. karma-maṇḍala. *Om maṇi-ratnākarṣe karma-samaye hūm* (STTS 426).

Names of Vajrarāja in the 16 maṇḍalas.

| Ch. | P. | Kula | Maṇḍala | Names. |
|---|---|---|---|---|
| 1. | 1. | Buddhakula | Vajradhātu-mahā-maṇḍala | Vajrarāja, Amogharāja, Vajrā-karṣa. |
| 2. | 102 | " | Vajra-guhya-vajra-maṇḍala | Vajrāṅkuśī. |
| 3. | 119 | " | Vajra-jñāna-dharma-maṇḍala | Vajrāṅkuśā. |
| 4. | 133 | " | Vajra-kārya-karma-maṇḍala | Karmāgrī. |
| 6. | 191 | Vajrakula | Triloka-vijaya-mahā-m. | Vajra-krodha. |
| 7. | 214 | " | Krodha-guhya-mudrā-m. | Vajra-krodha-roṣāṅkuśā |
| 8. | 225 | " | Vajra-kula-dharma-jñāna-samaya-maṇḍala. | Sūkṣma-vajrāṅkuśī. |
| 9. | 238 | " | Vajra-kula-karma-maṇḍala | Vajrākarṣaṇa-karma-jñāna-samayā. |
| 15. | 322 | Padma-kula | Sakala-jagad-vinaya-mahā-m. | Padmāṅkuśā. |
| 16. | 342 | " | Padma-guhya-mudrā-maṇḍala | Samantabhadra-padma-vajrāṅkuśī. |
| 17. | 358 | " | Jñāna-maṇḍala | Jñāna-padma-rāja. |
| 18. | 367 | " | Karma-maṇḍala | Padma-karma-vajriṇī. |
| 19. | 390 | Ratna-kula | Sarvārthasiddhi-maṇḍala | Ratnāṅkuśā. |
| 20. | 406 | " | Ratna-guhya-mudrā-maṇḍala | Maṇi-ratnāṅkuśā. |
| 21. | 418 | " | Jñāna-maṇḍala | Maṇi-ratna-samayāṅkuśā. |
| 22. | 425 | " | Karma-maṇḍala | Maṇi-ratnākarṣā. |

## 8. VAJRARĀGA

金剛愛菩薩

Vajrarāga occupies a seat in the south. He symbolises the virtue of compassion for the beings that is the merit of the heart of bodhi. As the beings already possess the liberty of their heart of bodhi, he converts them by his compassion. He has the flesh colour and carries an arrow. According to another tradition he carries an arch and draws an arrow against the demons. This is the arrow of great compassion into the heart of beings (Tajima 176). Then again Bhagavān (Vairocana) enters upon the samādhi named Being-consecration-vajra or the satvādhiṣṭhāna vajra which has its origin in the samaya of the great Bodhisattva Māra (Love), and he uttered from his heart the seed syllable of All the Tathāgatas known as pledge anurāgaṇasamaya gratifying All the Tathāgatas as vajrarāga. As soon as he says this Bhagavān Vajradhara attains the form of flower-weapons of All the Tathāgatas emerged from the hearts of All the Tathāgatas and then he enters the heart of Bhagavān Vairocana, attains the multiple form of mahāvajravāṇa and enters the hands of Buddha (or Bhagavān). Going through analogous processes to the two previous Bodhisattvas, this becomes the great Bodhisattva Māra, who recites this verse: "Oho pure in my true nature, I am gratification, self existing, in that they convert by means of passion that those may be pure who are free from passion".

Mahābodhisattva Māra emerges from the heart of Bhagavān and stations in the left lunar disc of All the Tathāgatas, once more he pays repects. Vairocana enters into the I.1.8.

Tz.54.8

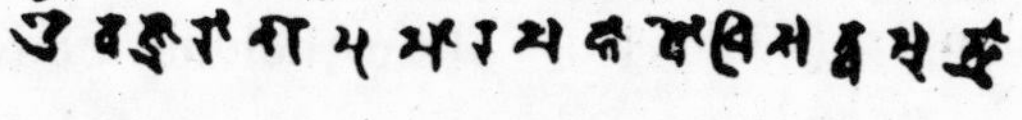

samādhi known as consecration-vajra gratifying All the Tathāgatas and he places in the bodhisattva Māra's hands the vajra-arrow for the purpose of gaining the fruit of success in the supreme Māra action of All the Tathāgatas. Then he is consecrated by All the Tathāgatas with the name of Vajradhanu. Then Bodhisattva-mahāsattva-Vajradhanu slaying All the Tathāgatas with Vajra-arrow recites this verse: "This is the pure knowledge of passion of All the Tathāgatas, They bestow universal bliss by slaying absence of passion with passion."

I.1.8. The Mahābodhisattva Māra is called Vajra-rāga in the STTS and the Gobushingan as well. He is Vajrarāga because of passions within, because of felicity he is Mahāsaukhya. (STTS 60). Arrow is his attribute so he is Vajravāṇa. due to his characteristics he is Vaśaṅkara, Mārakāma, Mahāvajra and Vajrachāpa. (STTS 61). Here he is holding a bow with his left hand and an arrow with the right (STTS 54.8).

TZ.38.9.

In the Mahāmaṇḍala of the Vajradhātu Vajra-rāga occupies a seat in the circle of Akṣobhya to his south. Vajrarāga in the Gobushingan is holding a bow and an arrow but here both of his hands are holding an arrow. He is sitting on lotus in a lotus posture (TZ.38.9). Here he is not riding an elephant as in the Gobu-shingan.

I.2.8. The feminine form of Vajra-rāga is Rati-rāga in the guhya-maṇḍala of the Vajradhātu in Gobu-

I.2.8.

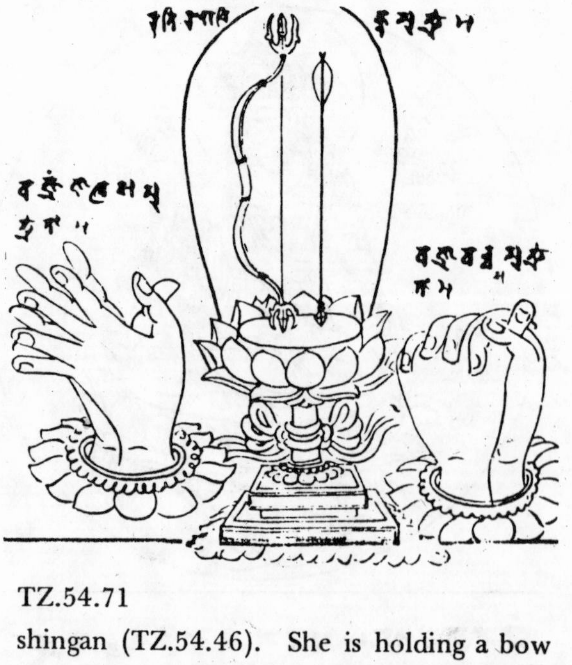

TZ.54.71

shingan (TZ.54.46). She is holding a bow and an arrow placed on a lotus pericarp held by both of her hands. She is sitting on a lotus flower. Mantra given under the illustration illustrates: *Om vajra-guhya rati-rāga hūm. Rati-rāga.*

TZ.38.71

In the samaya-maṇḍala of the graphic Vajradhātu Vajrarāga is depicted as a pair of three pointed vajras. (TZ.38.71). Ratirāga is the third Vajra-dhāraṇī who has a power of impassionating: *Om vajra-guhya-rāga rāgaya Ratirāga* (STTS 102).

I.3.8. In the third maṇḍala of Gobu-shingan he is named as *sarvatathāgatanurāgaṇa-jñāna-mudrā.* He is sitting on a lotus with a vajra arrow placed on a lotus in both of his hands. Dhāraṇī under the illustration is: *Om tiṣṭha rāga-vajra praviśa hṛdayam.* Mudrās from the right

I.3.8.

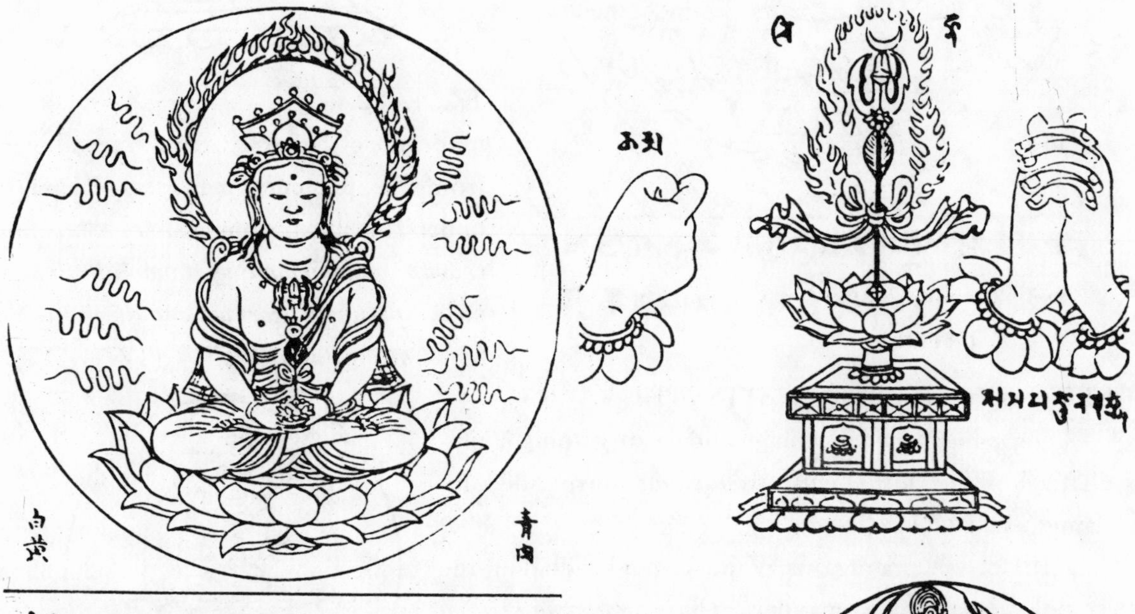

to left are named as: samaya-jñāna-mudrā karma and cihna (TZ.54.79). STTS has the same dhāraṇī as given in the Gobu-shingan (STTS 119).

Vajra-rāga in the dnarma maṇḍala of the graphic Vajra-dhātu holds a bow and an arrow in his hands. (TZ 38.144).

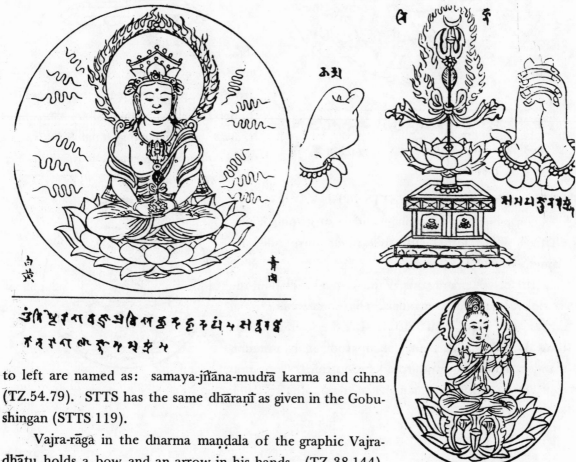

TZ.38.144

I.4.8. The fourth mandala of Gobu-shingan names Vajra-rāga as sarva-tathāgatānurāgaṇī (the script has a miswriting as anuttaragani). She is holding an arrow in her right hand and a bow in the left. Her middle mudrā illustrates a bow and arrow. The other two

I.4.8.

TZ.54.122.

mudrās are the same as extracted above from the preceded maṇḍala. Dhāraṇī under the illustration is: *Om Sarvatathāgata sarvātma-niryātana-sādhu-kāra pūjā spharaṇa karma-vāṇe hūm hoḥ. Sarvatathāgatānurāgaṇī.* (TZ.54.112).

STTS has the same dhāraṇī (STTS 133).

Vajra-rāga in the karma-maṇḍala of graphic Vajradhātu holds a lotus with two vajras surrounded by flames (TZ.38.217).

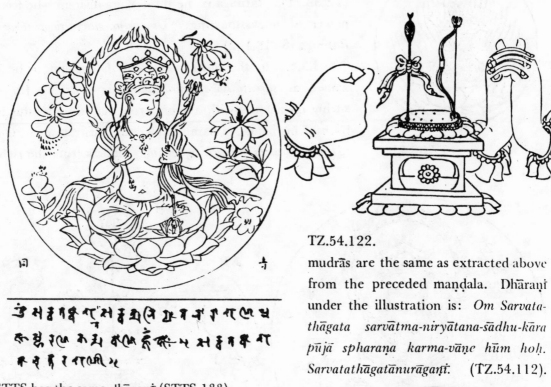

II.1.8. Vajra-rāga is Vajra-karma-krodha in the Trailokya-vijaya-mahā-maṇḍala. *Om Vajra-kama-krodha rāgaya hum phaṭ* (STTS 191). II.2.8. Vajrāga is the third diety of sihṅkāra maṇḍala in krodha-guhya-mudrā-maṇḍala named as vajra-roṣa-kama-vajriṇī. *Om vajra-roṣe kāma vajriṇi vaśam me ānaya he siḥ.* (STTS 214).

In the samaya-maṇḍala of Trilokavijaya of the graphic vajradhātu he is depicted as two vajras placed on a lotus like the preceded drawing from the Vajradhātu-samaya-maṇḍala (TZ 38.398). II.3.8. In vajrakula-dharma-jñāna-samaya-maṇḍala he is vajra sūkṣma-rāga-krodha: *Om vajra-sūkṣma-rāga-krodhānurāgaya tīvram hūm phaṭ.* (STTS 226). II.4.8. In Vajra-kula karma-maṇḍala he has the form of subtle form of knowledge of action of Vajra-rati-rāga: *Om vajra rati-rāga-karma-jñāna-samaya hūm jjaḥ.* (STTS 238). In the Trailokyavijaya-karma-maṇḍala he is sitting on a lotus with his hands folded accross his breast (TZ.38.321).

II.1.8. Mahasattvas should be drawn around Lokeśvara in the maṇḍalas of sakala-jagadvinaya. In its mahā-maṇḍala he is named as the one who has an attribute as lotus flower and amogha-śara: *Om māraya māraya padma-kusumāyudha-dharāmogha-śara hoḥ.* (STTS 323). III.2.8. In Padma-guhya-mudrā-maṇḍala he is lotus-rati: *Om Padma-rati* (STTS 342). III.3.8. In Jñāna-maṇḍala he is jñāna-padma-māra. *Om jñāna padma-māra hūm* (STTS 358). III.4.8. Vajra-rāga is the feminine form of samaya of pūjā-karma of Padma-kāminī: *Om Padma kāmini-māraṇa pūjā-karma samayehūm.* (STTS 367).

IV.1.8. In the maṇḍalas of sarvārthasiddhi Vajra-rāga is manifested as maṇi-rāga. In its mahā-maṇḍala he is worshipped as: *Om maṇirāga vaśī-kuru sarvārthān ānayākāśa-garbha hūm.* (STTS 390). IV.2.8. In its ratna-guhya mudrā maṇḍala he is maṇi-rāga-samaya: *Om maṇi-rāga-samaya hūm.* (STTS 406). IV.3.8. He attains a knowledge form in the knowledge maṇḍala. *Om maṇi-jñāna-rāga* (STTS 418). IV.4.8. In karma-maṇḍala he is worshipped as : *Om maṇi-rāga rati-karma-pūjā pravartaya* (STTS 426).

Names of Vajra-rāga in the sixteen maṇḍalas:

| Ch. | P. | Kula | Maṇḍala | Names. |
|---|---|---|---|---|
| 1. | - | Buddhakula | Vajradhātu-mahā-m. | Vajrarāga, Māra, Vajradhanu, Mahāsaukhvya, Vaśaṅkara, Mārakāma, Vajrachāpa. |
| 2. | 102 | ” | Vajraguhya-vajra-m. | Rati-rāgā. |
| 3. | 119 | ” | Vajrajñāna-dharma-m. | Stg.-anurāgaṇa-jñāna-mudrā, Rāga-vajra. |
| 4. | 133 | ” | Vajrakārya-karma-m. | Stg.-anurāgaṇī. |
| 6. | 191 | Vajrakula | Trilokavijaya-mahā-maṇḍala. | Vajra-karma-krodha, |
| 7. | 214 | ” | Krodhaguhya-mudrā-m. | Vajra-roṣa, kāma-vajriṇī. |
| 8. | 226 | ” | Vajrakula-dharmajñāna-maṇḍala. | Vajra-suksma-raga-krodha |
| 9. | 238 | ” | Vajrakula-karma-m. | Rati-rāga-karma-jñāna-samayā. |
| 15. | 323 | Padmakula | Sakalajagadvinaya-mahāmaṇḍala. | Padma-kūsumāyudha-dhara. |
| 16. | 342 | ” | Padmaguhya-mudrā-m. | Padma-rati. |
| 17. | 358 | ” | Jñānamaṇḍala. | Jñāna-padma-māra. |
| 18. | 367 | ” | Karmamaṇḍala | Padma-kāmiṇī. |
| 19. | 390 | Ratnakula | Sarvārthasiddhi-mahāmaṇḍala. | Maṇi-rāga. |
| 20. | 406 | ” | Ratnaguhya-mudrā-m. | Maṇi-rāga-samayā. |
| 21. | 418 | ” | Jñānamaṇḍala | Maṇi-jñāna-rāga. |
| 22. | 426 | ” | Karmamaṇḍala | Maṇi-rāga-rati-karma-pūjā. |

## 9. VAJRASĀDHU
金剛喜菩薩

Great Bodhisattva Vajrasādhu has a seat in the east of Akṣobhya. He symbolises satisfaction, *tuṣṭi.* He is of flesh colour. He presses both of his hands against his breast. His hands simultaneously form a fillip (Tajima 176). Vajrasādhu is the seed syllable uttered by Vairocana after entering the samādhi which has its origin in the samaya of great Bodhisattva Prāmodyarāja. Thereupon Vajradhara takes the form of applauses *sādhukārāṇi* and after usual process he becomes a singal sign of satisfaction *tuṣṭi* and enters the palm of Vairocana. From this there emanates Buddha form throughout space. These coalesce again into Prāmodyarāja who utters these words. "Oho I am applause *sādhukāra* the very best of the omniscient Ones, this certainly produces satisfaction in those who are free from doubt". The Prāmodyarāja in the form of a great Bodhisattva descends from the heart of Vairocana and stations himself in the lunar disc at the back of Stg. Afterwards Prāmodyarāja is duly given satisfaction for gaining the fruit of the suprement taste of joy of Stg. He is consecrated with the name Vajra-harṣa by Stg. Bodhisattva Vajraharṣa utters this verse rejoicing Stg. by his *vajratuṣṭi* by applauding. "This the one who promotes applauds of All the Buddhas the sacred vajra which produces all satisfaction and furthers happiness." (STTS 17-18).

I.1.9.

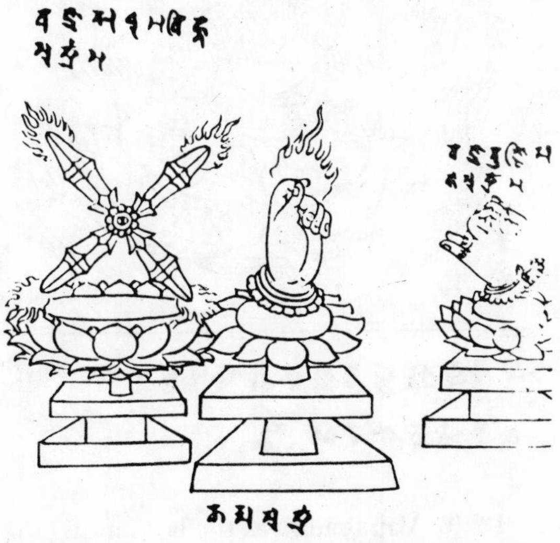

TZ.54.9

I.1.9. Here Vajra-sādhu belongs to the first chapter of Gobu-shingan (TZ.54 9). He is sitting in a lotus flower placed on an elephant. Vajrasādhu adorned with all the ornaments is wearing a dhoti and an upper garment. Both of his hands are in a mudrā. Dhāraṇī under the illustration is. *Om vajra-*

TZ.38.10

*sādhu. Prāmodyarāja bodhisattva*,. The mudrās are named as vajra-tuṣṭi-mahā-mudrā, karma-mudrā and vajra-sādhu-cihna-mudrā. First is depicted by hand posture, second is a muṣṭi and third is illustrated by two single vajras on a lotus.

This illustration of vajra-sādhu is an extract from the mahā-maṇḍala of the graphic vajradhātu (TZ 38.10, Lokesh Chandra 415). Both of his fists are placed near his breast. Animal ride is missing as usual. His seed syllable is *saḥ* according to the description given besides.

I.2.9.

I.2.9. Vajra-sādhu as the last among the four vajra-dhāraṇī is named as Sādhumatī. Samaya-mudrā of mahā-dhāraṇī of Stg. is. *Om guhya vajra sādhvīśvarī hūm* (STTS 102).

Vajra-sādhu in the second maṇḍala of Gobu-shingan has two three pointed vajras in both of his hands, otherwise the form resembles the preceded one. His dhāraṇi under the illustration is: *Om vajra-guhya-vajradhātvīśvarī hūm. Sādhumatī. Vajra guhya dhāraṇaḥ.* The first mudrā is named as vajra-bandha-mudrā, second is sādhumatī-cihna mudrā and the last is vajrāñjali (TZ 5.447).

TZ.38.72

Vajra-sādhu in the samaya-maṇḍala of the graphic Vajradhātu has been symbolised as a mudrā of his hands in a lotus pericarp. (TZ 38.72, Lokesh Chandra 477).

I.3.9. In the third maṇḍala of the Gobu-shingan the two vajras which were held in his hands in previous mandala are placed in a lotus supported by both of his hands in his lap (TZ 54.80). He is included in the mahā-vajra-samādhis of All the Tathāgatas. His essence of great knowledged is called *vajra-musti*. *Aho vajra-muṣṭi* (STTS 119).

I.3.9.

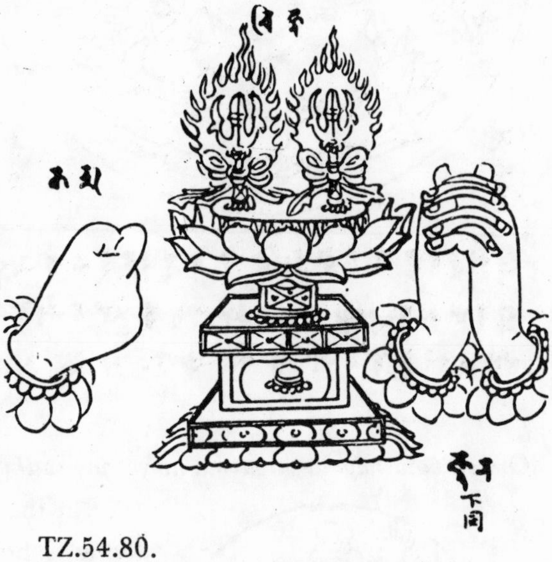


TZ.54.80.

Because of his mudrā he is named as essence of knowledge seal of great satisfaction. *Aho vajra-tuṣṭi. Mahā-tuṣṭi-jñāna-mudrā. Sarvatathāgata-mahā-samādhayaḥ* is the dhāraṇī given under the illustration.

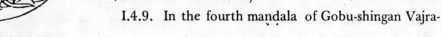

TZ.38.145

In the dharma-maṇḍala of the graphic Vajradhātu Vajra-sādhu has both of his hands in a mudrā which is different from the mahā-maṇḍala. Tuṣṭi is the religious merit or nature or the essential quality of Vajrasādhu, thus in dharma-maṇḍala he is personified as Vajratuṣṭi (TZ 38. 145, Lokesh Chandra 550.).

I.4.9. In the fourth maṇḍala of Gobu-shingan Vajra-

I.4.9.

TZ.54.113

sādhu's attributes are different from all the preceded ones. Two spotted snakes are coiled around his fists and their faces are held by his hands. In this maṇḍala he is the one who satisfies all the Tathāgatas: *sarvatathāgata-santoṣaṇī* (STTS 133), the second mudrā also differs. His dhāraṇī in Gobu-shingan is: *Om sarvatathāgata-sarvātma-niryātana-sādhukāra-pūjā-spharaṇa karma-tuṣṭi aḥ* (TZ 54.113).

TZ.38.218

In the karma-maṇḍala of the graphic Vajra-dhātu Vajra sādhu is holding a lotus, and thereupon is placed something round surrounded by flames (TZ 38.218, Lokesh Chandra 623).

II.1.9. In mahā-maṇḍala of Trailokyavijaya in STTS Vajrasādhu sits near Vajrapāṇi. There he is eulogises as an angry manifestation of Vajra satisfaction and praised for his applauds: *Om vajratuṣṭi-krodha sādhu sādhu* to satisfy all the beings: *Om vajra-tuṣṭi-krodhe toṣaya sarvāṇi siḥ* (STTS 214). Samaya form of Vajra-sādhu in Trailokya-vijaya-samaya-maṇḍala is identical to his form given above from the Vajradhātu-samaya-maṇḍala (TZ 38.399, Lokesh Chandra 798). II.3.9. Next is symbolic maṇḍala of religious knowledge of vajrakula where he has an angry form of subtle vajra satisfaction: *Om sūkṣma-vajra-tuṣṭi-krodha hūm phaṭ* (STTS 226). II.4.9. In action maṇḍala of the same family he is the symbolic knowledge of action of Vajrasādhu: *Om vajra-sādhu-karma-jñāna-samaye hūm jjaḥ* (STTS 238). Vajrasādhu in karma-maṇḍala of Trailokya-vijaya is sitting on a lotus with his hands folded accross his breast (TZ.38:322, Lokesh Chandra 729). III.1.9. In sakala-jagad-vinaya-mahā-maṇḍala he is to be placed near Lokeśvara with a lotus in hands. *Om padma-sambhava padma-hasta-sādhu hūm* (STTS 322-3). III.2.9. In the next three maṇḍalas of sakala-jagad-vinaya he is named as *tusti.* In the maṇḍala of sacred mudrā of lotus family he is called lotus satisfaction. *Om padma-tuṣṭi* (STTS 342). III.3.9. In knoledge maṇḍala he is knowledge form: *Om jñānapadma-tuṣṭi hūm* (STTS 358). III.4.9. Karma is inserted to his name in action maṇḍala. *Om padma-karma-tuṣṭi hūm* (STTS 367). IV.1.9. In the maṇḍala of accomplishment of all the desires in mahā-maṇḍala of sarvārtha-siddhi Vajrasādhu sits besides Vajra-garbha in the name of Ratna-tuṣṭi (STTS 390). IV.2.9.. In guhya mudrā-maṇḍala of ratna family Vajra-sādhu is mentioned as Maṇi-sādhu. *Om maṇi sādhu hūm* (STTS 406). Yamada gives it as maṇisārathi according to the Chinese and Sanskrit readings. But the Tibetan reading maṇi-sādhu seems to be a better reading . IV.3.9. Vajra-sādhu is maṇi-jñāna-tuṣṭi in jñāna-maṇḍala of ratna family: *Om maṇi-jñāna-tuṣṭi* (STTS 418). IV.4.9. Last in the action maṇḍala of ratna family belonging to sarvārtha-siddhi Vajra-sādhu is eulogises as: *Om maṇi-ratna sādhu-kāra-pūjā-samaya* (STTS 426).

Names of Vajra-sādhu in the sixteen maṇḍalas:

| Ch. | P. | Kula | Maṇḍala | Names. |
|---|---|---|---|---|
| 1. | 17-8 | Buddha | Vajradhātu-mahā-m | Prāmodyarāja, Vajrasādhu, Vajra-harṣa. |
| 2. | 102 | " | Vajra-guhya-vajra-maṇḍala | Sādhumatī, Guhya-vajra-sādhviśvarī. |
| 3. | 119 | " | Vajra-jñāna-dharam-m. | Vajra-tuṣṭi. |
| 4. | 133 | " | Vajra-kārya-karma-m. | Karma-tuṣṭi, Stg. -santoṣaṇī. |
| 6. | 190 | Vajra | Trailokya-vijaya-mahā-m. | Vajra-tuṣṭi-krodha. |
| 7. | 214 | " | Krodha-guhya-mudrā-m. | Vajra-tuṣṭi-krodhā. |
| 8. | 226 | " | Vajra-kula-dharma-jñāna-samaya-m. | Sūkṣma-vajra-tuṣṭi-krodha. |
| 9. | 238 | " | Vajra-kula-karma-m. | Vajra-sādhu-karma-jñāna-samayā. |
| 15. | 322 | Padma | Sakala-jagad-vinaya-m. | Padma-hasta-sādhu. |
| 16. | 342 | " | Padma-guhya-mudrā-m. | Padma-tuṣṭi. |
| 17. | 358 | " | Jñāna-m. | Jñāna-padma-tuṣṭi. |
| 18. | 367 | " | Karma-m. | Padma-karma-tuṣṭi. |
| 19. | 390 | Ratna | Sarvārthasiddhi-mahā-m. | Ratna-tuṣṭi. |
| 20. | 406 | " | Ratna-guhya-mudrā-m. | Maṇi-tuṣṭi. |
| 21. | 418 | " | Jñāna-m. | Maṇi-jñāna-tuṣṭi. |
| 22. | 426 | " | Karma-m. | Maṇi-ratna-sādhukāra-pūjā-samayā. |

## 10. VAJRARATNA

### 金剛寶菩薩

Vairocana enters the samādhi known as gem consecration vajra which originates in the samaya of great Bodhisattva Ākāśa-garbha: *ākāśa-garbha mahābodhisattva-samaya-sambhava-ratnādhiṣṭhāna-vajram.* After consecration Vairocana utters the seed syllable *Vajra-ratna* which is known as consecration pledge of Stg. sarva-tathāgata-abhiṣeka-samaya. Then vajradhara aquires the form of light rays shining throughout space, which coalesce into the form of a great vajra-ratna on Vairocana's palm which again turns into Bodhisattva Ākāśa-garbha, who recites this verse: "Oho I am self consecration, the supreme vajra-ratna, in that the victorious ones (jina), although without attachment are considered lords of the three-fold realm". Afterwards it stations itself in the lunar disc in front of Stg. Again bhagavān enters the samādhi called sarvatathāgata-maṇi-ratna-vajra and gives vajra-maṇi to Vajra-ratna cakravarti, the great Bodhisattva Ākaśa-garbha for obtaining the supreme perfection of Stg. after consecration of Vajra-ratnāṅkura. Then Stg. consecrated him by the name Vajra-garbha. Vajra-garbha placing Vajramaṇi in place of his own consecration recites this verse. "I am consecration in the sphere of beings *sattva-dhātu* of All the Buddhas, I am given into my own hands, gem is joined to gem" (STTS 19-21).

He occupies the northern side. The ratna is the cintāmaṇi. This divinity symbolises the merit produced by numberless performances of great compassion. He is also called Ākāśa-garbha. He is of flesh colour He offers prayers and holds a jewel by his hands. In the graphic Vajradhātu his right hand appears to be making a gesture of jewel, which how-

I.1.10.

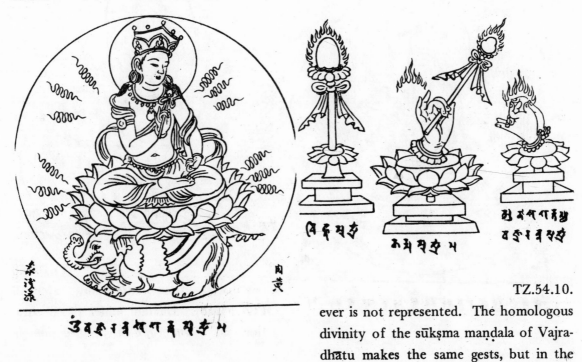

TZ.54.10.

ever is not represented. The homologous divinity of the sūkṣma maṇḍala of Vajra-dhātu makes the same gests, but in the inverse order. It is the right hand that accords the prayers and the left hand holds the jewels (Tajima 177-8).

I.1.10 In the first maṇḍala of Gobu-shingan Vajra-ratna with a small stick with a gem in his right hand is sitting on a lotus placed on an elephant. His attribute can be distinctly seen in his mudrās which are named as karma and cihna. The first mudrā is named as: ākāśa-garbhasya vajra-ratna-mudrā. The dhāraṇī under the illustration reads as: *Om vajra-ratna-sagarbha-mudrā.* It should be *Om vajra-ratnākāśa-garbha-mudrā.* (TZ 54.10).

TZ.38.12

In the mahā-mandala of graphic Vajradhātu Vajra-ratna belongs to the family of Ratna-sambhava. He sits in the north of Ratna-sambhava. Both of his hands are doing mudras. His animal ride is missing as usual. (TZ 38.12).

I.2.10. Here below is a drawing of Ratnottamā, the feminine form Vajra-ratna to illustrate his essense. This is an extract from the second maṇḍala of Gobu shingan. His attribute is more stylised here. Ratnottamā is holding a lotus in her hands, a stick is drawn overthere, and upon this stick can be seen a cintāmaṇi surrounded by flames placed on a lotus. The mudrās are named as vajra-bandha, cihna-mudrā and vajrāñjalī (TZ 54.48). Dhāraṇī under the illustration is. *Om vajra-guhya-ratna-samaye*

I.2.10.

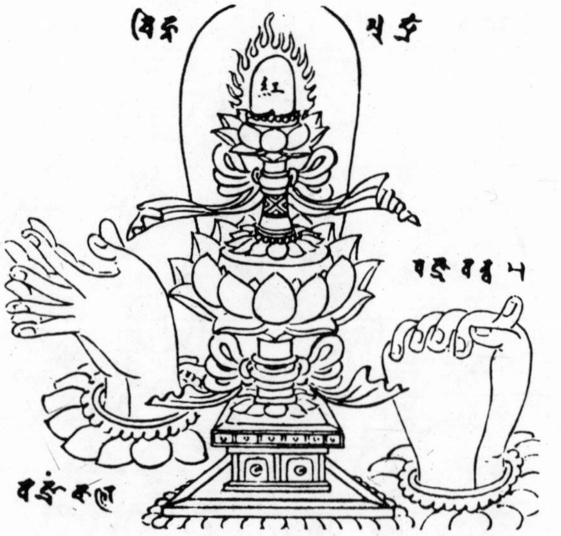

TZ.54.48

*hūm. Ratnottamā.* According to STTS (p.102) she is the first Ratnadhāraṇī called Ratnottamā. The same dhāraṇī as given above is quoted by STTS as well. This is the esoteric essense of Vajra-ratna.

TZ.38.74.

Ratna is considered to be the symbol or essense of Vajra-ratna. The illustration given here is from samaya-maṇḍala of graphic Vajradhātu (TZ 38.74, Lokesh Chandra 479).

I.3.10. Vajra-ratna in the third maṇḍala of Gobu-shingan differs from the second maṇḍala only in his sitting posture and the position of his hands. All the attributes are identical. First two mudrās are also the same. Only vajrāñjali is replaced by musti. Dhāraṇī runs as follows:

I.3.10

*Oṃ vajra-ratnātmakaḥ. Sarvatathāgata-vajrā-bhiṣeka-jñāna-mudrā.* (TZ 54.81). According to the third chapter of STTS he is the knowledge seal of vajra consecration of Stg.

Sarvatathāgata-vajrābhiṣeka-jñāna-mudraḥ. His essense is vajra ratnā-tmaka (STTS 120).

TZ 38.147

Vajra-ratna in the knowledge-maṇḍala of the graphic Vajradhātu is doing a mudrā by his right hand and in his left hand he has a gem kept near his breast. (TZ 48.147, Lokesh Chandra 552).

I.4.10. In the fourth maṇḍala of Gobu-shingan Vajra-ratna has been named as Mahādhipati. He has a lotus with a gem in his right hand and his left hand is resting in his lap.(TZ.

I.4.10

TZ. 54.114

54.114).In the fourth chapter of STTS he is the first among the consecration ritual of Stg. called Mahādhipatinī. The great gems which consecrate All the Tathāgatas physically are saluted : *Om namaḥ sarvatathāgata-kāyābhiṣeka-ratebhyo Vajra-maṇim om.* (STTS 134).

TZ 38.220

Attributes of Vajraratna in the karma-maṇḍala of the graphic Vajradhātu do not distinguish from the preceded one. Gem upon lotus can be triratna in place of cintāmaṇi. (TZ 38.220, Lokesh Chandra 625).

TZ. 38.401

The illustration belongs to samaya-maṇḍala of Trailokyavijaya of the graphic Vajradhātu. There is a gem upon a lotus as his symbol (TZ 38.401, Lokesh Chandra 800). In its karma-maṇḍala he is sitting with his hands folded across his breast (TZ 38.324, Lokesh Chandra 731).

II.1.10. According to STTS (p. 191) Vajra-ratna belongs to the family of Vajrābhiṣeka and is named Vajra-bhṛkuṭi-krodha. He is eulogised for haraṇa: *Om vajra-bhṛkuṭi-krodha hara-hara hūm phaṭ.* II. 2.10. He has the same hṛdaya in the next chapter also : *Om vajra-bhṛkuṭi-krodhe hara sarvārtham jiḥ* (STTS 214). II. 3.10. In symbolic maṇḍala of religious knowledge of vajrakula Vajra-ratna is the anger of subtle vajra frown : *Om sūkṣma-vajra-bhṛkuṭi-krodha hara hara hūm phaṭ* (STTS 227). II. 4.10. He has a power of dominion according to its action maṇḍala : *Om vajra-bhṛkuṭi vaśī kuru hūm* (STTS 239). III. 1.10. Vajra-ratna is again named as bhṛkuṭi in all the four maṇḍalas of Sakala-jagad-vinaya. In its mahā-maṇḍala he is lotus frown : *Om padma-bhṛkuṭi traḥ* (STTS 323). III. 2.10. In its mudrā maṇḍala he is praised as : *Om*

*Om padma-bhṛkuṭi traḥ* (STTS 323). III. 2.10. In its mudrā maṇḍala he is praised as : *Om bhṛkuṭi taṭi vetaṭi padme hūm* (STTS 343). III. 3.10. He is a lotus frown in both of the knowledge and action maṇḍalas : *Om jñāna-padma-bhṛkuṭi hūm* (STSS 358). III. 4.10. *Om padma-karma-bhṛkuṭi hūm traḥ.* (STTS 367). iv. 1.10. Maṇḍalas of sarvārthasiddhi personify Vajra-ratna as a garland of gems. In its mahā-maṇḍala he is the consecration of Stg. formed as a garland of gems : *Om sarvatathāgatābhiṣeka-ratna-māla hūm* (STTS 390). iv. 2.10. In ratna-guhya-mudrā-maṇḍala he is called for consecration : *Om maṇi ratna-māle'bhiṣiñca hūm* (STTS 407). iv. 3.10. Maṇi or ratna is missing in the rext chapter that is knowledge maṇḍala : *Om jñānā-bhiṣeka* (STTS 418). iv. 4.10. In action maṇḍala of sarvārthasiddhi Vajra-ratna is personified as worship : *Om maṇi-ratna-māla-pūje* (STTS 426).

Names of Vajra-ratna in the sixteen maṇḍalas:

| Ch. | P. | Kula | Maṇḍala | Names. |
|---|---|---|---|---|
| 1 | 19-21 | Buddha | Vajradhātu-mahā-m. | Vajra-ratna, Vajra-garbha. |
| 2. | 102 | " | Vajra-guhya-vajra-m. | Ratnottamā. |
| 3. | 120 | " | Vajra-jñāna-dharma-m. | Sarvatathāgata-vajrābhiṣeka. |
| 4. | 134 | " | Vajra-kārya-karma-m. | Stg. -kāyābhiṣeka-ratna. |
| 6. | 191 | Vajra | Trilokavijayamahā-m. | Vajra-bhṛkuṭi-krodha. |
| 7. | 214 | " | Krodha-guhya-mudrā-m. | Vajra-bhṛkuṭi-krodhā. |
| 8. | 227 | " | Vajrakula-dharma-jñāna-samaya-m. | Sūkṣma-vajra-bhṛkuṭi-krodha. |
| 9. | 239 | " | Vajrakula-karma-m. | Vajra-bhṛkuṭi. |
| 15. | 323 | Padma | Sakala-jagad-vinaya-mahā-m. | Padma-bhṛkuṭi. |
| 16. | 343 | " | Padma-guhya-mudrā-m. | Bhṛkuṭi-padmā |
| 17. | 358 | " | Jñāna-maṇḍala | Jñāna-padma-bhṛkuṭi. |
| 18. | 367 | " | Karma- maṇḍala | Padma-karma-bhṛkuṭi. |
| 19. | 390 | Ratna | Sarvārthasiddhi-mahā-m. | Stg.- abhiṣeka-ratna-mālā. |
| 20. | 407 | " | Ratna-guhya-mudrā-m. | Maṇi-ratna-mālā. |
| 21. | 418 | " | Jñāna-maṇḍala | Jñānābhiṣeka. |
| 22. | 426 | " | Karma-maṇḍala | Maṇi-ratna-māla-pūjā. |

## 11. VAJRATEJA

金剛光菩薩

Bhagavān Vairocana enters the consecration called the gem consecration-vajra which has its origin in the samaya of mahā-bodhisattva Mahāteja and utters the seed syllable: vajrateja which is the raśmi-samaya of Stg. At once Lord Vajrapāṇi manifests himself as solar discs emerging from the hearts of Stg. and enters the heart of Bhagavān Vairocana. These solar discs coalesce into the form of a vajra sun. Vajra sun stations itself in Vairocana's hand. This turns at last into the form of Mahābodhisattva Mahāteja and finds its place in the heart of Vairocana. Mahāteja says thus: "Oho the measureless blazing light which illuminates the sphere of beings, in that it purifies protectors even though they are purified Buddhas". Now this Bodhisattva in the form of Vimalateja emerges from Vairocana, rests in the southern lunar disc of Stg. and pays respects. Afterwards vajra-sūrya is presented by Bhagavān to Mahābodhisattva Mahāteja in his hands. This is followed by the consecration of Mahāteja with the vajra name consecration as Vajraprabha Mahābodhisattva Vajraprabha illuminating Stg. by vajrasūrya says: "This is the destroyer of darkness of ignorance for All the Buddhas which shines even brighter than such which can be numbered as atoms. (STTS 21-22).

According to Tajima (178) Vajrateja sits to the east. Tejas signifies splendour, blaze and this name symbolises the blazing virtue treasures of all asceticism. This divinity helps in breaking the darkness of avidyā of beings that have a soul. His left hand is closed and in I.1.11.

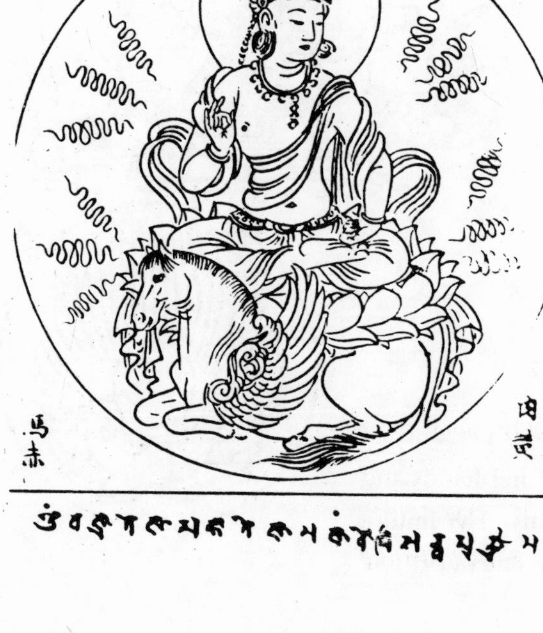

TZ.54.811

the other he has a radiant sun. The graphic Vajradhātu-maṇḍala does not accord totally with the text of Hizoki, but the maṇḍala of Takao conforms to it.

Vajrateja in the first maṇḍala of Gobu-shingan is doing a mudrā by his right hand and his left fist is resting upon his thigh (TZ 54.11). He is riding a winged horse on a lotus. May be because of his relation to sun his ride is a horse. Dhāraṇī under the illustration is: *Om vajrateja mahā-teja. Bodhisattva-mudrā.* First mudrā is ratna-teja-mahā-mudrā, second is karma-mudrā and the third is cihna-mudrā (TZ 54.11).

Vajra-teja in the graphic Vajradhātu-maṇḍala is holding a sun disc upon his right palm kept towards his breast and left fist is in the same position as it is in the previous on. An is his seed syllable (TZ 38.13, Lokesh Chandra 418).

I.2.11. Vajrateja is the second ratna-dhāraṇī in vajra-guhya-vajra-maṇḍala of Buddha-kula. He is named as the flame of gem: Ratnolkā. Her dhāraṇī in the mudrā-maṇḍala is: *Om vajra-guhya-prabhe hūm.* (STTS I.2.11

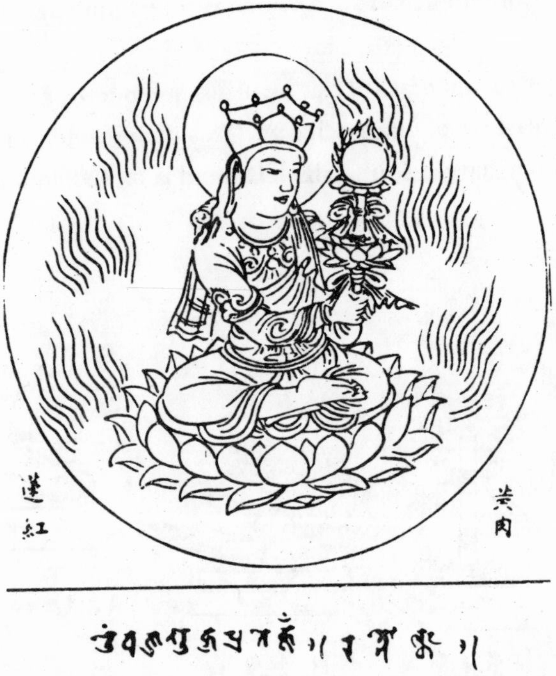

102). She is the sacred radiance . *guhya-prabhā.*

In the second maṇḍala of Gobu-shingan he is personified as Ratnolkā. She is holding a lotus by both of her hands and a sun disc encircled by flames is drawn upon lotus. Her mudrā and name under the illustration is: *Om vajra-guhya-prabhe*

I.3.11.

TZ.54.82

I.4.11.

*hūm.* Ratnolkā. Only the cihna-mudrā resembles the preceded. First is samaya and the last is guhya-mudrā (TZ 54.49).

A sun disc is placed upon a lotus (given on the preceded page) as the symbolic form of Vajra-teja in the samaya maṇḍala of the graphic Vajradhātu (TZ 38.75, Lokesh Chandra 553).

I.3.11. Third maṇḍala of Gobu-shingan and vajra-jñāna-dharma-maṇḍala of STTS illustrate Vajrateja as knowledge-mudrā of maṇḍala array of great luster. *Mahā-prabhā-maṇḍala-vyūha-jñāna-mudrā.* His essense is hṛdaya-vajra-sūrya (STTS 120). In Gobu-shingan hṛdaya is replaced by *Hṛd.* His a ttributes are the same as they are in the previous mandala. Only sitting and hand posture is different. Mudrās are also the same. (TZ 54. 82).

TZ.38.148

In jñāna-maṇḍala of the graphic Vajra-dhātu Vajra-teja is carrying a sun disc by both of his hands supported by hus palms. (TZ 38.148, Lokesh Chandra 626).

I.4.11. Fourth maṇḍala of Gobu-Shingan that is the action maṇḍala personifies Vajrateja as Mahodyatā. She is the second consecration pūjā of All the Tathagatas: *sarva-tathāgatābhiṣeka-pūjā* (STTS 134). She is saluted as the flame of vajra-splendour: *Om namaḥ sarvatathāgata-sūryebhyo. Vajra-tejinī.* (STTS 134). In the given illustration she is holding her attribute a lotus in her right hand and thereupon is a sun disc Her left fist is resting upon her thigh (TZ 54.115).

TZ.38.221

The drawing extracted here illustrates Vajrateja in action maṇḍala of graphic Vajradhātu (TZ 38.221). She is holding a lotus with a sun disc by both of her hands.

2.1.11. In the maṇḍalas of Trailokyavijaya Vajrateja sits besides Vajrābhiṣeka (STTS 191). He is named as Vajra-sūrya. An agngry aspect of garland of great flames which has a quality to burn away: *Om vajra-sūrya-mahā-jvālā-mālā-krodha- jvālaya sarva hūm phaṭ* (STTS 191). In karma-maṇḍala of Trailokyavijaya of graphic Vajradhātu Vajrateja is sitting upon a lotus with his hands folded across his breast (TZ 38.325). His form in the samaya-maṇḍala of trailokya-vijaya is the same as extracted before. A sun disc upon a lotus can be seen there. II.2.11 In krodha-guhya-mudrā-maṇḍala he is lustre of garland of vajra flames which is the great angry fire: *Om vajra-jvāla-mālā-prabhe mahā-krodhāgni jvālaya sarvam viroṣe jiḥ* (STTS 214) II.3.11. In samaya-maṇḍala of religious knowledge of vajra-kula he is a maṇḍala of subtle flames, which is the angry aspect of sun: *Om vajra-sūkṣma-jvālā-maṇḍala krodha sūrya jvālaya hūm phaṭ* (STTS 227). II.4.11. In action maṇḍala he has a power of domination (vaśīkaraṇa) and is named as vajra-sūrya-maṇḍala: *Om vajra-sūrya-maṇḍale vaśī-kuru hūm* (STTS 239). In maṇḍalas of the third section that is sakala-jagad-vinaya-maṇḍala Vajra-teja is called sun with some additions to his names. III.1.11. In its mahā-maṇḍala he is lotus sun: *Om padma-sūrya jvālā hūm* (STTS 323). III.2.11. In padma-guhya-mudrā-maṇḍala he is personified as lotus flames: *Om padma-jvāle hūm* (STTS 343). III.3.11. In knowledge he is the lotus sun of knowledge. *Om jñāna-padma-sūrya hūm* (STTS 358). III.4.11. In action maṇḍala he is action sun: *Om padma-karma-sūrya hūm* (STTS 367). IV.1.11. Vajra-sūrya is called maṇi-sūrya in the mahā-maṇḍala of sarvārthasiddhi: *Om maṇi-sūrya hūm.* (STTS 390). IV.2.11. In ratna-guhya-mudrā-maṇḍala he is personified as Maṇi-ratna-sūryā, the feminine form of great heat: *Om maṇi-ratna-sūryā jvālaya sarvam mahā-tejinī hūm* (STTS 407). IV.3.11. Vajra-teja is knowledge sun of ratna family in jñāna-maṇḍala: *Om maṇi-jñāna-sūrya* (STTS 418). IV.4.11. Action-maṇḍala personifies him as the pūjā of splendour of sun: *Om maṇi-ratna-sūryāloka-pūje* (STTS 426).

Names of Vajra-teja in the sixteen maṇḍalas.

| Ch. | P. | Kula | Maṇḍala | Names. |
|---|---|---|---|---|
| 1. | 21-22 | Buddha | Vajradhātu-mahā-m. | Mahāteja, Vajrateja, Vajrasūrya, Vimalteja, Vajraprabha. |
| 2. | 102 | " | Vajraguhya-vajra-m. | Ratnolkā, Vajra-guhya-prabhā. |
| 3. | 120 | " | Vajrajñāna-dharma.m. | Mahāprabhā-maṇḍala-vyūha-jñāna-mudraḥ, Vajra-sūrya. |
| 4. | 134 | " | Vajrakārya-karma-m. | Mahodyatā, Stg.-abhiṣeka-pūjā, Vajra-tejini-jvālā. |
| 6. | 191 | Vajra | Trilokavijaya-mahā-m. | Vajra-sūrya, Mahā-jvālā-māla-krodha. |
| 7. | 214 | " | Krodhaguhya-mudrā-m. | Vajra-jvālā-māla-prabhā, Mahā-krodhāgni. |
| 8. | 227 | " | Vajrakula-dharma-jnana-samaya-m. | Vajra-sūkṣma-jvālā-maṇḍala krodha-sūrya. |
| 9. | 239 | " | Vajrakula-karma-m. | Vajra-sūrya-maṇḍala |
| 15. | 323 | Padma | Sakala-jagad-vinaya-mahā-m. | Padma-sūrya. |
| 16. | 343 | " | Padma-guhya-mudrā-m. | Padma-jvālā. |
| 17. | 358 | " | Jñāna-m. | Jñāna-padma-sūrya. |
| 18. | 367 | " | Karma-m. | Padma-karma-sūryā. |
| 19. | 390 | Ratna | Sarvārthasiddhi-mahā-m | Maṇi-sūrya. |
| 20. | 407 | " | Ratna-guhya-mudrā-m. | Maṇi-ratna-sūryā. |
| 21. | 418 | " | Jñāna-m. | Maṇi-jñāna-sūrya. |
| 22. | 426 | " | Karma-m. | Maṇi-ratna-sūryāloka-pūjā. |

## 12. VAJRAKETU
金剛幢菩薩

Bhagavān Vairocana enters the samādhi named gem consecration which has its origin in the samaya of Great Bodhisattva Ratnaketu and utters the seed syllable named samaya of fulfilment of desires of Stg. that is Ratnaketu. As soon as he utters this he manifests himself from the hearts of Stg. in the forms of banners of different colours, shapes and decorative designs, enters the heart of Vairocana, which all coalesce into the form of vajra banner and enters the hand of Vairocana. From Vajradhvaja he becomes Ratnaketu and enters into the heart of Bhagavān Vairocana and skeaks thus: "I am incomparable insignia (ketu) of universal perfection, of all hopes fulfilled and of all things consumated". This Ratnaketu in the form of a great Bodhisattva emerges from the heart of Bhagavān and stations himself in the left lunar disc of Stg. Bhagavān once again enters the samādhi called elevated consecration-vajra of Stg. and gives vajradhvaja to Ratnaketu in his hands. Then he is consecrated by the name Vajrayaṣṭi by Stg. Afterwards Bodhisattva mahāsattva Vajrayaṣṭı enjoining Stg. by vajra banner utters these words: "this is the fulfilling of all hopes of all the Buddhas, known as the banner of wish-granting-gem in the style of perfection of giving dānapāramitā" (STTS 23-4).

According to Hizoki Vajraketu Bodhisattva sitts in the west. In Sanskrit ketu signifies a flag or a banner, called rather dhvaja. However this is a banner an attribute of this divinity. Carrying the Cintāmaṇī of asceticism on the staff of his banner, the Bodhisattva I.1.12.

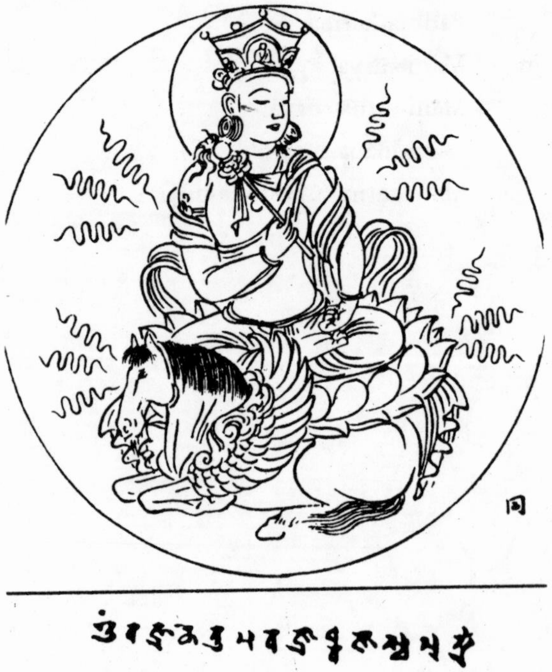

TZ.54.12

causes to rain the earthly and extra mundane treasures and fulfills prayers. He is the samaya of kṣitigarbha. He is of flesh

colour. His two hands hold a banner The homoloogous divinity of pūjā maṇḍala holds in two hands a lotus supporting the banner (Tajima 178-9).

I.1.12. The dhāraṇī given under the illustration shows that this is a drawing of Vajraketu and a mudrā of Vajradhvaja: *Vajraketu, Vajradhvajasya mudrā.* The divine being is sitting upon a lotus placed on the back of a horse. He is holding a banner with a Cintamaṇī overhead in his right hand and left fist resting upon his thigh (TZ 54.12). Three mudrās given above are cihna-, action-and Cintāmaṇī-dhvaja-mahā-mudrā.

TZ.38.14

In the graphic Vajradhātu-maṇḍala Vajraketu has the same attribute. He is sitting on a lotus holding the staff of his banner by both of his hands (TZ 38.14, Lokesh Chandra 419).

I.2.12.

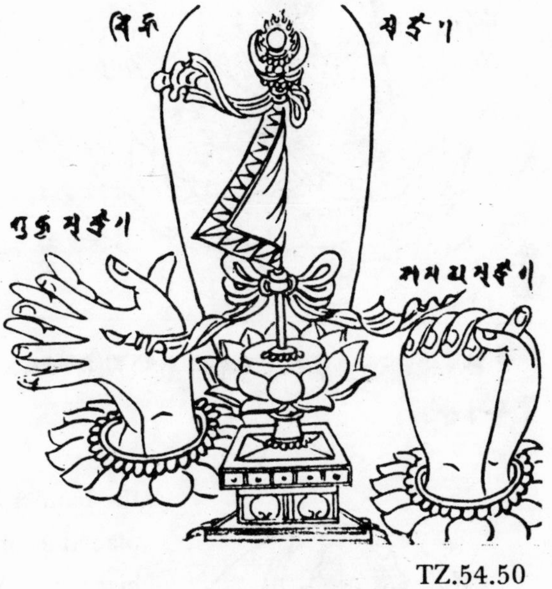

TZ.54.50

I.2.12. Third Ratnadhāraṇī in vajra guhya-vajra-maṇḍala is named as dhvajāgrakeyura. This is the guhya or mudra form of Vajraketu. His samaya-mudra is: *Om vajradhvajagra-guhya hūm* (STTD 102).

Vajraketu in the form of Dhvajāgrakeyūrā in the second maṇḍala of Gobu-shingan has been extracted here with her three mudrās. She is giving here banner with a digit of moon with the Cintāmaṇī held straight by both of her hands. She is sitting in a lotus posture upon a lotus (TZ 54.50). Her dhāraṇī under the illustration should correspond to STTS,

TZ.38.76

it runs as: *Om vajra-guhya hūm*. In dhvajāgra *he* should be *ke* and *pra* as *yu*..

Banner as a symbol of Vajraketu is illustrated in samaya-maṇḍala of graphic Vajradhātu (TZ 38.76, Lokesh Chandra 481). The banner placed upon a lotus has triratna instead of Cintāmaṇī.

I.3.12. Vajraketu as a knowledge-mudrā which fulfills desires of Stg., *Sarvatathāgatāśā-aripūrṇa-jñāna-mudraḥ*. He

I.3.12.

TZ.54.83

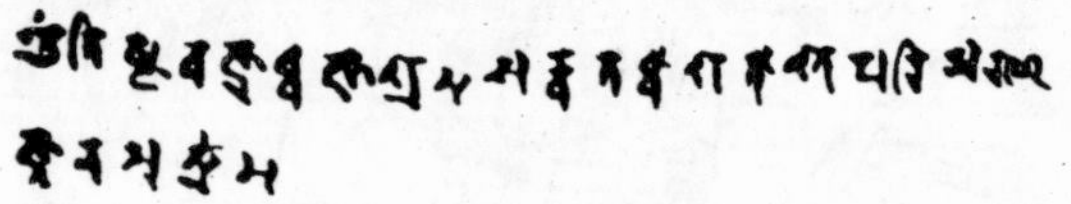

is named as vajra-dhvajāgra: *tiṣṭha vajra-dhvajagra vām*. *Vam* is his bijākṣara (STTS 120). His name and hṛdaya in Gobu-shingan and STTS are identical. Only his style of holding the banner is different from the preceded ones which is placed upon a lotus supported by both of his hands in his lap. Mudrās are not names, but they should be samaya and cihna as compared to the previous one (TZ 54.83).

TZ.38.149.

The attribute carried by Vajraketu in sūkṣma-maṇḍala of graphic Vajradhātu seems to be a lotus with three leaves drawn upon a staff (TZ 38.149), Lokesh Chandra 554). It should be three gems on the staff of his flag. This also can be vajrayaṣṭi as he is named in the first chapter of STTS (p.24).

I.4.12.

TZ.54.116.

I.4.12. In the fourth maṇḍala of Gobushingan Vajraketu has a banner with Cintāmaṇi in his right hand (TZ 54.116). In the fourth chapter of STTS that is vajra-kārya-karma-maṇḍala he is the one who showers great gems: *Mahā-ratna-varṣa.* He is saluted as *Vajra-dhvajāgra* who fulfills desires of Stg. and has a banner with Cintāmaṇi. *Om namaḥ sarvatathāgatāśā-pari-pūrṇa-dhvajāgre tram* (STTS 134). The script under the illustration corresponds to STTS (*purna* is written as *pūraṇa, dhvajāgre as dhvajāgri).* Mudrās of this maṇḍala are the same as in the third maṇḍala.

Attribute of Vajraketu as a divinity of action maṇḍala of graphic Vajradhātu is drawn as a lotus with a small stick. It will be impossible to distinguish the attribute without its comparison with other illustrations and discriptions. It should be a banner with a Cintāmaṇi placed upon a lotus (TZ 38. 222, Lokesh Chandra 627).

TZ.38.222

II.1.12. Vajraketu is sitting with his hands folded across his breast in Trilokyavijaya from graphic Vajradhātu (TZ 38.326, Lokesh Chandra 733). In STTS he is mentioned as an angry form: *Om vajra-krodha-ketu dehi hūm phaṭ* (STTS 191). He belongs to the family of Vajrābhiṣeka. II.2.12. In krodha-guhya-mudrā-maṇḍala he is the great anger of Vajrakeyūra with a banner: *Om vajradhvajāgra-keyūra mahā-krodhe dehi me sarvam jiḥ.* (STTS 214). II.3.12. In vajrakula-dharma-maṇḍala he is the subtle vajra anger who has a banner: *Om sūkṣma-vajra-dhvajāgra-krodha sarvārthān me prayaccha śighram hūm phaṭ.* (STTS 227). II.4.12. In action maṇḍala of vajra family Vajraketu is called for dominating as Keyūrā with banner: *Om vajra-dhvājagra-keyūre vaśī kuru hūm* (STTS 239). Maṇḍalas of Sakala-jagad-vinaya personify Vajraketu as a moon. III.1.12. In mahā-maṇḍala he is a moon who has a banner with a gem who is called to rejoice Avalokiteśvara and grant everything: *Om padma-maṇi-ketu-dhara candra prahlādayāvalokiteśvara dehi me sarvārthān samaya hūm* (STTS 323). III.2.12. In padma-guhya-mudrā-maṇḍala his feminine form is mentioned as: *Om somini padme hūm* (STTS 343). III.3.12. He is a lotus moon of knowledge in knowledge maṇḍala: *Om jñāna-padma-candra hūm* (STTS 358). III.4.12. But in action maṇḍala he has a banner form: *Om padma-karma-dhvaje hūm* (STTS 367). IV.1.12. Vajraketu is Ākāśa-garbha in mahā-maṇḍala of sarvārthasiddhi: *Om cintāmaṇi-dhvaja sarvāśā-paripūrakākāśagarbha hūm* (STTS 390). IV.2.12. In ratna-guhya-mudrā-maṇḍala again he is a moon with a banner: *Om maṇi-candra-dhvajāgri hūm* (STTS 407). IV.3.12. Banner of knowledge of gem family belongs to knowledge maṇḍala of Sarvārthasiddhi: *Om maṇi-jñāna-dhvaja* (STTS 418). IV.4.12. Dhvaja and patākā are two synonyms mentioned in action maṇḍala of sarvārthasiddhi for Vajra-ketu: *Om maṇi-ratna-dhvaja-patākā-pūje* (STTS 426).

Names of Vajra-ketu in the sixteen maṇḍalas:

| Ch. | P. | Kula | Maṇḍala | Names |
|---|---|---|---|---|
| 1. | 23-4 | Buddha | Vajradhatu-mahā-m. | Ratna-ketu, Vajra-ketu, Vajra-dhvaja, Vajra-yaṣṭi. |
| 2. | 102 | ” | Vajra-guhya-vajra-m. | Dhvajāgra-keyūrā, Vajra-dhvajā-grā guhyā, |
| 3. | 120 | ” | Vajra-jñāna-dharma-m. | Stg.-paripūrṇa-jñāna-mudraḥ, Vajra-dhvajāgra. |
| 4. | 134 | ” | Vajra-kārya-karma-m. | Mahā-ratna-varṣa, Vajra-dhvajāgrā |
| 6. | 191 | Vajra | Triloka-vijaya-mahā-m. | Vajra-krodha-ketu. |
| 7. | 214 | ” | Krodha-guhya-mudrā-m. | Vajra-dhvajāgra-keyūra-mahā-krodhā. |
| 8. | 227 | ” | Vajrakula-dharma-jñāna-samaya-m. | Sūkṣma-vajra-dhvajāgra-krodha. |
| 9. | 239 | ” | Vajra-kula-karma-m. | Vajra-dhvajāgra-keyūrā. |
| 15. | 323 | Padma | Sakala-jagad-vinaya-mahā-m. | Padma-maṇi-ketu-dhara-candra. |
| 16. | 343 | ” | Padma-guhya-mudrā-m. | Somini-padmā |
| 17. | 358 | ” | Jñāna-m. | Jñāna-padma-candra. |
| 18. | 367 | ” | Karma-m. | Padma-karma-dhvajā. |
| 19. | 390 | Ratna | Sarvārthasiddhi-mahā-m. | Cintāmaṇī-dhvaja-Ākāśagarbha |
| 20. | 407 | ” | Ratna-guhya-mudrā-m. | Maṇi-candra-dhvajāgrī. |
| 21. | 418 | ” | Jñāna-m. | Maṇi-jñāna-dhvajā |
| 22. | 426 | ” | Karma-m. | Maṇi-ratna-dhvaja-patākā-pūjā. |

## 13 VAJRAHĀSA
金剛笑菩薩

Bhagavān Vairocana enters the samādhi called gem-consecration-vajra which has its origin in the samaya of Bodhisattva who has an eternal satisfaction and pleasure : *nitya-prīti-pramuditendriya-mahā-bodhisattva-samaya-sambhava-ratnādhiṣṭhāna-vajram* and utters the seed syllable, hṛdaya of Stg. named prīti-samaya of Stg : *Vajrahāsa.* At once Vajra-dhara manifests himself from the hearts of Stg. as a host of vajra-smiles of Stg. enters the heart of Bhagavan Vairocana which coalesce into a vajra-smile vajra-smita and stations in his hand. Then from the form of Vajra-smita he becomes Mahā-bodhisattva who has a sense of pleasurable sensation and joy enters the heart of Vairocana and says thus . Oho I am that wonderful laughter of the very best which the thoughtful always employ in the objectives of Buddhahood (Budhāratha ). Now this Nitya-prīti-pramuditendriya Mahābodhi sattva emerges from the heart of Vairocana, stations himself in the back lunar disc of Stg. and pays his respects.

Vairocana again enters the samādhi called wonderful-consecration-vajra of Stg. and gives Vajra-smita to Mahā-bodhisattva Nitya-pramudite-ndriya in his hands. Then Stg. consecrate him with the vajra name consecration as Vajra-prīti. Now Mahāsattva Bodhi-sattva vajra-prīti rejoicing Stg. by Vajra-smita utters thus : "This is what indicates the wonderful arising of All the Buddhas, the knowledge producing great laughter which is unknown by other teachers (STTS 25-6).

According to Tajima (179) Bodhisattva Vajrahāsa occupies the southern side. He satsfies the beings by offering Cintāmaṇī of the thousand well beings : hence the beings

I.1.13

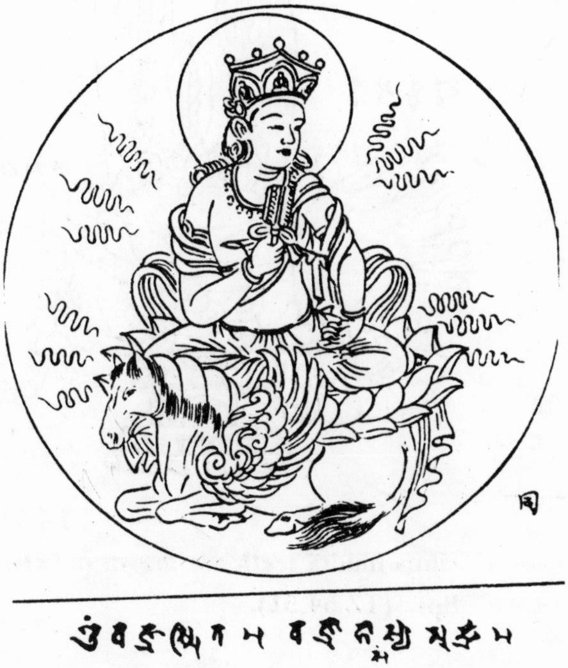

TZ 54.13

laugh. Bhodhisattva himself laughs and presents the joyous aspect. He is of flesh colour, he raises his two hands upto his ears and closes his fists. He makes a gesture of turning round ears. This gesture expresses that Bodhisattva laughs. Actually he separates corners of his mouth.

I.1.13. Mahābodhisattva Vajrahāsa in the first maṇḍala of Gobu-shingan is riding a horse (TZ 54.13). His attribute is said to be Vajra-smita. To illustrate vajra-smita two lines of teeth are drawn in a shape of an attribute. The attribute can be well distinguished from his cihna-mudrā. It is denoted under the illustration that this is Vajra-smita, mudrā of Vajra-hāsa : *Om vajra-smita. Vajra-hāsasya-mudrā.* His left fist is resting on his thigh. First mudrā is named as vajra-hāsa-mudrā and the second as cihna-karma-mudrā.

TZ 38.15

The gesture of Vajrahāsa described by Tajima has been illustrated in the mahā-maṇḍala of graphic Vajra-dhātu. Haḥ is his seed syllable (TZ 38.15, Lokesh Chandra 420).

I.2.13. Vajrahāsa in guhya-vajra-maṇḍala is mentioned as Hāsavatī. Her samaya-mudrā is : *Om guhya hāsa-vajrī hūm* (STTS 102). In the second maṇḍala of Gobu-shingan Hāsavatī is holding a lotus in her hands towards her left. Two three pointed vajras with a line of teeth are placed upon the lotus. Her dhāraṇī under the illustration is . *Om guhya hāsavajrī hūm. Hāsavatī.* Mudrās are named as samaya, cihna and guhya-mudrā. In

I.2.13.

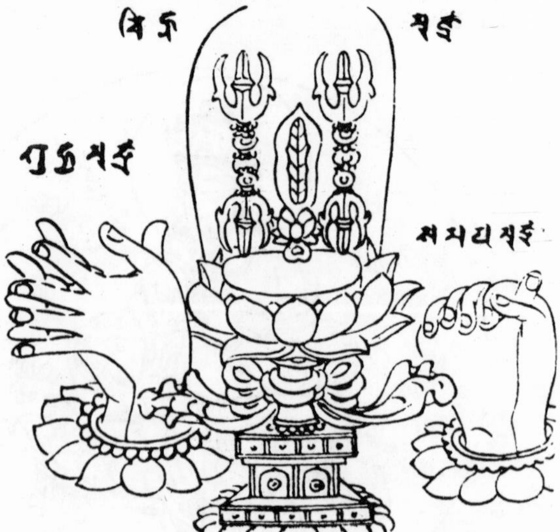

TZ 54.51

cihna-mudrā teeth are drawn in between lips. (TZ 54.51).

TZ.38.77

I.3.13.

A three pointed double sided vajra is laid down upon a lotus to symbolise vajra-hāsa in samaya-maṇḍala of graphic Vajradhātu. This is the last ratna-dhāraṇi of the maṇḍala. (TZ 38.77, Lokesh Chandra 482).

I.3.13. In vajra-jñāna-dharma-maṇḍala the last ratna-dhāraṇi is the religious mudrā who has his origin in the vega of great pleasure. He is holding the same attribute sitting in a different style. Dhāraṇī under the illustration is . *Om hṛdaya vajra-hāsa. Mahā-prītivega-sambhava-jñāna-mudrām Mahā-ratna-samādhayaḥ.* The same dhāraṇi is denoted by the STTS

TZ.54.84.

(120). First and second mudrās are the same as in the second maṇḍala. Lips and teeth are more distinct here than the previous one. (TZ.54.84).

Vajra-hāsa in the sūkṣma-maṇḍala makes the same gesture as he does in the first maṇḍala. This illustrates a smiling gesture (TZ.38.150, Lokesh Chandra 555).

I.4.13. Vajra-kārya-karma-maṇḍala describes Vajra-hāsa as the last consecration pūjā of Stg. names great peasure-rejoicing (mahāprītiharṣā). In his mantra he is saluted as Vajra-hāsa who causes great pleasure and joy for Stg.: *Om namaḥ sarvatathāgata mahā-prīti-prāmodya-karebhyo vajra-hāsa haḥ* (STTS 134). In the illustration given above he is holding a lotus and above the lotus can be seen a pair of small jaws. The script under the illus-

I.4.13.

TZ.54.117

tration can be read as: *Om namaḥ sarva-tathāgata kāyābhi-ṣeka-karebhyo vajrapāṇi mahāprīti pramodyakarebhyo vajra-hāse haḥ mahā- (prīti)-harṣā. sarvatathāgatābhi-ṣeka-pūjāh.* (TZ 54.117).

In graphic Vajradhātu in action maṇḍala Vajra-hāsa is represented by a vajra laid down on a lotus like the samaya-maṇḍala (TZ 38.223, Lokesh Chandra 628). II.4.13. Vajra-hāsa in the karma-maṇḍala of Trailokya-vijaya is sitting with his hands folded across his breast (TZ 38 327, Lokesh Chandra 733). II.1.13. In mahā-maṇḍala of Trilokavijaya in STTS the serene aspect of Vajra-smita is changed into a horrific form as Vajrāṭṭahāsa. *Om vajrāṭṭahāsa-krodha haḥ haḥ haḥ haḥ hūm phaṭ* (STTS 191). II.2.13. In its samaya-maṇḍala he has the same symbolic form as extracted from the samaya-maṇḍala of Vajra-dhātu (TZ 38.404, Lokesh Chandra 803). He belongs to the family of Vajrābhiṣeka. He can kill by his terrific laughter: *Om vajrāttahāsanī hasa hasa aṭṭāṭṭahāsena maya jiḥ* (STTS). II.3.13. In the maṇḍala of religious knowledge of vajra family he is the angry aspect of subtle vajra laughter who is the great terrific laughter: *Om sūkṣma-vajra-hāsa-krodha mahāṭṭā-ṭṭāhąsa ha ha ha ha hūm phaṭ.* (STTS 227). II.4.13. Vajrāṭṭahāsa has a dominating power: *Om vajrātthāse vaśī-kuru hūm* (STTS 239).

III.1.13. Sakala-jagad-vinaya-mahā-mandala describes Vajrahāsa as eleven headed: *Om padmāṭṭahāsaikādaśa-mukha haḥ haḥ hah hūm (STTS 323).* III.2.13. In padma-guhya-mudrā-maṇḍala also he is eleven faced and bears a flower. *Om padma-hāsinī ekādaśa-vaktre diri diri iṭṭe vatte cale pracale kusuma-dhare ili praviśa siddhim me prayaccha* (STTS 343). III.3.13. Jñāna-maṇḍala names him as jñāna-padma-hāsa: *Om jñāna-padma-hāsa hūm* (STTS 358). III.4.13. Action is added to his name in the action maṇḍala: *Om padma-karma-*

*hāse hūm* (STTS 367).

IV.1.13. Mahā-maṇḍala of Sarvārthasiddhi also mentions him in his terrific form. *Om ratnāṭṭahāsa hasa ha ha hūm* (STTS 390). IV.2.13. Laughter has a feminine form in the gem family as Maṇihāsa: *Om maṇi-hāse hasa hūm* (STTS 407). IV.3.13. Again Hāsa is named as Aṭṭāṭṭahāsa in Jñāna-maṇḍala of Sarvārthasiddhi: *Om maṇi jñānāṭṭahāsa* (STTS 418). IV.4.13. He is transformed into the worship in action-maṇḍala: *Om maṇi-ratnāṭṭa-hāsa-pūje* (STTS 426).

Names of Vajrahāsa in the sixteen maṇḍalas:

| Ch. | P. | Kula. | Maṇḍala | Names. |
|---|---|---|---|---|
| 1. | 25-6 | Buddha | Vajradhātu-mahā-m. | Vajrahāsa, Vajra-smita, Nitya-prīti-pramuditendriya, Vajra-prīti. |
| 2. | 102 | " | Vajra-guhya-vajra-m. | Hāsavatī, mahā-prīti-vega-sambhava-jñāna-mudrā. |
| 3. | 120 | " | Vajra-jñāna-dharma-m. | Vajra-hāsa, mahā-prīti-vega-sambhava jñāna-mudrā. |
| 4. | 134 | " | Vajra-kārya-karma-m. | Mahāprīti-harṣā. |
| 6. | 191. | Vajra | Trilokavijaya-mahā-m. | Vajrāṭṭahāsa-krodha |
| 7. | 215 | " | Krodha-guhya-mudrā-m. | Vajrāṭṭahāsanī. |
| 8. | 227 | " | Vajrakula-dharma-jñāna-samaya-m. | Sūkṣma-vajrahāsa-krodha Mahāṭṭa-hāsa. |
| 9. | 239 | " | Vajrakula-karma-m. | Vajrāṭṭahāsī. |
| 15. | 323 | Padma | Sakala-jagad-vinaya-mahā-m. | Padmāṭṭahāsaikādaśamukha |
| 16. | 343 | " | Padma-guhya-mudrā-m. | Padma-hāsinī, Ekādaśa-vaktrā |
| 17. | 358 | " | Jñāna-m. | Jñāna-padma-hāsa. |
| 18. | 367 | " | Karma-m. | Padma-karma-hāsā. |
| 19. | 390 | Ratna | Sarvārthasiddhi-mahā-m. | Ratnattahasa. |
| 20. | 407 | " | Ratna-guhya-mudrā-m. | Maṇi-hāsā. |
| 21. | 418 | " | Jñāna-m. | Maṇi-jñānaṭṭahāsa |
| 22. | 426 | " | Karma-m. | Maṇi-ratnāṭṭahāsa-pūjā. |

## 14. VAJRADHARMA

金剛法菩薩

Vairocana enters the samādhi named religion consecration-vajra wuo nas its origin in the samaya of Mahā-bodhisattva and utters the hrdaya of Stg. from his heart which is the dharma-samaya of Stg., that is Vajra-dharma. As soon as he utters this Vajradhara manifests himslef as rays of the virtuous dharma: *saddharma-raśmayaḥ* from the heart of Stg. All the worlds are enlightened by these rays and become full of dharma-dhātu. All this dharmadhātu enters the heart of Vairocana, coalesce into a single great lotus *mahāpadma* and stations himself in Vairocana's hand. This turns into Mahābodhisattva Avalokiteśvara, enters the heart of Bhagavān Vairocana and says thus: "Oho I am the absolute truth primevally pure and self existent, in that this (lotus flower) represents the purity of the dharmas which resembles a boat". Now he in the form of Mahābodhisattva Avalokiteśvara emerges from the heart of Bhagavān Vairocana stations himself in the front lunar disc of Stg. and pays respects. Now Vairocana enters the samādhi named the knowledge-pledge-vajra of samādhi of Stg. and gives purifying-pledge-vajra-lotus to Mahābodhisattva Avalokiteśvara in his hands who is a universal monarch of saddharma after consecrating him by the Buddha-(dharmakāya)-consecration. Then he is consecrated by Stg. by the vajra name consecration as Vajra-netra. Mahāsattva Vajranetra looking at vajra-lotus pays in his respects. "This is that knowledge of the truth of passion of All the Buddhas. I am given into my own hands. Dharma is established in dharma". (STTS 26-8).

I.1.14.

TZ.54.14.

Through union with Vajradharma one becomes a holder of Vajra-dharma. According to Tajima (p.180) Bodhisattva Vajradharma sits to the east of

Lokeśvara. He symbolises purity of all dharmas that is compared with a lotus which does not become impure and muddy by mud. He is also called Aryavalokiteśvara. He is of flesh colour and holds a lotus flower. In Kongokai he is represented as holding a lotus flower in his hands but in the maṇḍala of Takao he holds a lotus in his left hand that is slightly opened and with his right hand he makes a gesture of opening patels. It is characteristic gesture of Avalokiteśvara.

I.1.14. Vajra-dharma in the first maṇḍala of Gobu-shingan is sitting on a lotus placed on a peacock, there is a half blossomed lotus in his left hand and by the right hand he is making a gesture of opening its patels as described by Tajima above (TZ.54.14). Gobu-shingan names the divinity as Vajra-dharma and mudra of Vajra-padma. First from the right is vajra-padma-mudrā, second is action mudrā which is similar to the gesture of his right hand. third is a lotus upon a vajra which is cihna-mudrā. STTS also describes that while he pays his respects he opens patels of a lotus and looks towards its being free from five passion and pure nature.

In maha-maṇḍala of graphic Vajradhātu Vajra-dharma has the same attribute and the gesture of his hand (TZ 38.17). The only difference is in his ride. Here *hrīḥ* is his seed syllable.

I.2.14. Vajrāmbujā is the esoteric form of Vajra-padma. She is the first dharma-dhāraṇī according to STTS (103). Samaya-mudrā of this mahā-dhāraṇī is. *Om vajra-padma-guhya-samaye hūm.* I.2.14.

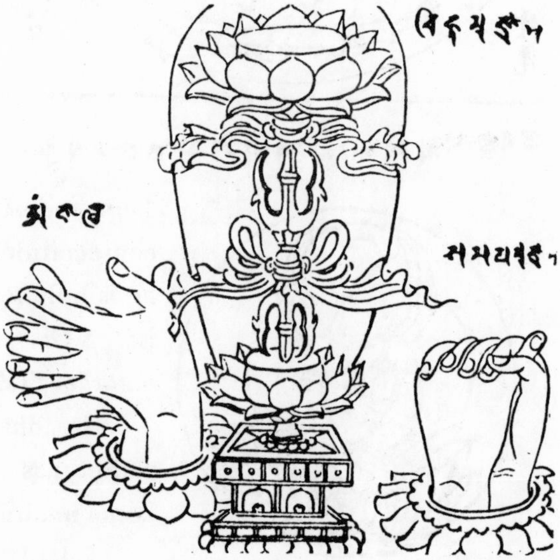

She is esoteric samaya of Vajra-lotus. The same reading is given by Gobu-

TZ.38.79

shingan. The illustration extracted below belongs to the second maṇḍala of Gobu-shingan. She is sitting with her palms joined together (añjali-mudrā). Upon her añjalī is a lotus placed upon a vajra which is on a lotus. Her attribute is given as her cihna-midrā, one of them is anjali and third is the samaya-mudrā of Vajrāmbujā (TZ.54.52).

In samaya-maṇḍala of graphic Vajradhātu there is a vajra-lotus upon a lotus flower as a symbol of Vajrāmbuja to show his characteristics (TZ 38.77). (Ambuja literally means water born. In Tibetan it is translated as pas mo,

I.3.14.

TZ.54.85.

lotus flower while in Chinese as cloud born).

I.3.14. Essence of Vajradhara emerges from the glimmer of vajra (vajra-bimbāt). *Vajra-padmātmaka* (STTS 120). He is the first religious consecration of Stg. In the third maṇḍala of Gobu-shingan he is holding a vajra-logus in his lap. Under the illustration is: *Om vajra-padmātmakaḥ. Dharma-samata-jñāna-mudrām* (TZ 54.85).

TZ.38.152

In dharma-maṇḍala of graphic Vajradhātu Vajra-padma has no attributes in his hands. Both of them are doing mudrās (TZ 38.152, Lokesh Chandra 422).

I.4.14. In Vajra-kārya-karma-maṇḍala he is personified as the first dharma-pūjā. She is named Mahā-jñāna-

I.4.14.

TZ.54.118.

gītā. While saluting her she is named Mahā-dharmāgrī: *Om stg. vajra-dharmatā-samādhibhiḥ stunomi mahā-dharmagri hriḥ* (STTS 134). In Gobu-shingan she is holding a half blossomed lotus in her left hand and the right is in the same mudra. It can be a mudrā of opening petals. Dhāraṇī in Gobu-shingan and STTS is the same. But Gobu-shingan gives *sunomi* instead of *stunomi*.

TZ.38.225

In action maṇḍala of the graphic Vajradhātu Vajra-dharma is holding by both of his hands a vajra-lotus placed upon a lotus (TZ 38.225, Lokesh Chandra 630).

II.1.14. In mahā-maṇḍala of Trilokavijaya in STTS he belongs to the family of Vajrasena. He is an angry manifestation of Vajra-dharma who purifies the beings: *Om vajra-dharma-krodha viśodhaya viśodhaya hūm phaṭ.* (STTS 192). II.2.14. In krodha-guhya-mudrā-maṇḍala of Trilokavijaya he has a feminine form of his angry aspect who kills the wicked beings: *Om vajra-śuddha-krodhe hara māraya duṣṭān diḥ* (STTS 215). Her manifestation in samaya-maṇḍala of graphic Vajra-dhātu is similar to the symbolic form in the preceded samaya-maṇḍala. The only difference is in the number of petals (TZ 38.406, Lokesh Chandra 805). II.3.14. Vajra-kula-dharma-jñāna-samaya-maṇḍala signifies Vajra-dharma as a purifier and names him as an angry form of subtle vajra lotus: *Om sūkṣma-vajra-dharma-krodha śodhaya hūm phaṭ* (STTS 227). II.2.14. In action maṇḍala he has a form of passion who impassionates the beings: *Om vajra-padma-rāge rāgaya hūm* (STTS 239). In Trilokavijaya-karma-maṇḍala he is sitting with his hands placed across his breast. III.1.14. Vajra-padma is personified as Tārā in mandalas of Sakala-jagad-vinaya. In its mahā-maṇḍala he is lotus Tārā who is saluted for a power of vision: *Om Tārā-padmālokaya mām samaya-sattva hūm* (STTS 324). III.2.4. Vajra-padma is Tārā in padma-guhya-mudrā-maṇḍala: *Om tāre tuttātare hūm* (STTS 344). III.3.14. Tārā becomes knowledge-tārā in knowledge maṇḍala. *Om jñāna-padma-tārā hūm* (STTS 358). III.4.14. In action-maṇḍala he is Action-tārā. *Om padma-karma-tāre hūm* (STTS 367).

IV.1.4. In Mahā-maṇḍala of sarvārthasiddhi jñāna-garbha is the personification of Vajra-padma. He is Tyāga-samādhi: *Om tyāga-samādhi-jñāna-garbha hūm.* (STTS 391). He belongs to the group of Ratna-padma-dhara. IV.2.14. In Ratna-guhya-mudrā-maṇḍala he is tyāga-samādhi of ratna family: *Om maṇiratna-tyāga-samaye hūm* (STTS 408). IV.3.14. Knowledge-maṇḍala mentions him in knowledge form: *Om jñāna-maṇi-tyāga* (STTS 418). IV.4.14. Lotus concentration-samaya of ratna family belongs to action maṇḍala of Sarvārthasiddhi: *Om padma-maṇi-samādhi-samaye hūm* (STTS 426).

Names of Vajra-dharma in the 16 maṇḍalas:

| Ch. | P. | Kula | Maṇḍala | Names. |
|---|---|---|---|---|
| 1. | 26-8 | Buddha | Vajradhātu-mahā-m. | Vajra-dharma, Avalokiteśvara, Vajra-netra. |
| 2. | 103 | " | Vajra-guhya-vajra-m. | Vajrāmbuja, Vajra-padma-guhya-samayā. |
| 3. | 120 | " | Vajra-jñāna-dharma-m. | Vajra-padmātmaka, Sarva-dharma-samatā-jñāna-mudrā. |
| 4. | 134 | " | Vajra-kārya-karma-m. | Mahā-jñāna-gītā, Mahādharmāgrī. |
| 6. | 192 | Vajra | Trilokavijaya-mahā-m. | Vajra-dharma-krodha. |
| 7. | 215 | " | Krodha-guhya-mudrā-m. | Vajra-śuddha-krodhā |
| 8. | 227 | " | Vajra-kula-dharma-jñāna-samaya-m. | Sūkṣma-vajra-dharma-krodha |
| 9. | 239 | " | Vajra-kula-karma-m. | Vajra-padma-rāgā. |
| 15. | 324 | Padma | Sakala-jagad-vinaya-mahā-m. | Tārā-padma. |
| 16. | 344 | " | Padma-guhya-mudrā-m. | Tārā. |
| 17. | 358 | " | Jñāna-m. | Jñāna-padma-tārā. |
| 18. | 367 | " | Karma-m. | Padma-karma-tārā. |
| 19. | 391 | Ratna | Sarvārtha-siddhi-mahā-m. | Tyāga-samādhi-jñāna-garbha. |
| 20. | 408 | " | Ratna-guhya-mudrā-m. | Maṇi-ratna-tyāga-samayā. |
| 21. | | " | Jñāna-m. | Jñāna-maṇi-tyāga. |
| 22. | 426 | " | Karma-m. | Padma-maṇi-samādhi-samayā. |

## 15. VAJRATIKṢṆA

金剛利菩薩

Bhagavān Vairocana enters the samādhi named religious consecration vajra which has its origin in the samaya of Mahābodhisattva Mañjuśrī and utters the essence of Stg. named knowledge samaya of Mahājñāna of Stg. that is Vajra-tīkṣṇa. As he utters this Lord Vajradhara manifests himself as prajñā-weapons and enters the heart of Vairocana which coalesce into the form of a vajra-sword, vajra-kośa on Vairocana's hand. This vajrakośa obtains the form of Mahābodhisattva Mañjuśrī and says this: "Oho I am thought of as the gentle sound, Mañjughoṣa of Stg., in that knolwedge which is formless is conceived of as sound. Mañjuśrī emerges from the heart of Vairocana, enters the south lunar disc of Stg. and pays his respects. Once again Vairocana enters the consecration and gives vajrakośa to Mañjuśrī in his hands which destroys sufferings of Stg. Then he is consecrated with the name by Vajrabuddhi by Stg. Bodhisattva Mahāsattva Vajrabuddhi thrusting away Stg. by his vajra-sword speaks this: "This is the perfection of wisdom teaching of All the Buddhas which destroys all foes and removes all sins.

According to Tajima (180-181) Vajra-tīkṣṇa occupies a seat in the south. For making beings penetrate upto the principle of original purity this bodhisattva brandishes the sword of wisdom, he is absorbed in the samaya of destruction of sins and attachments of beings. He is not different from Mañjuśrī. He is of golden colour. He holds a trunk in his left hand with sūtras upon a lotus and in his right hand a sword. In Kongokai he holds in his hands a I.1.15.

TZ.54.15

lotus that supports a sword but most of the maṇḍalas represent him as described above.

I.1.15. Vajra-tīkṣṇa and Mañjuśrī are the two names of the divinity represented here from the first maṇḍala of Gobu-shingan (TZ 54.15). He is riding a peacock on a lotus with a vajra sword, *vajra-kośa* in his right hand and his left fist is resting on his thigh. Under the illustration he is named as Vajra-tīkṣṇa and Mañjuśrī. His mudrās are named as Vajrakosá-mahā-mudrā, karma-mudrā and khaḍga-cihna.

In mahā-maṇḍala of the graphic Vajradhātu Vajra-tīkṣṇa has a vajra-sword in his right hand as in the preceded drawing and in his left hand he is carrying a lotus with a book of wisdom upon it. With his sword he destroys enemies and with his book of wisdom he teaches All the Buddhas and removes all sins(TZ.38.18).

TZ.38.18

I.2.15. In vajra-guhya-vajra-maṇḍala the esoteric form of Vajra-tīkṣa here named as Vajra-kośa is ādhāraṇī. Ādhāraṇī is holding a sword upon a lotus (TZ.

I.2.15

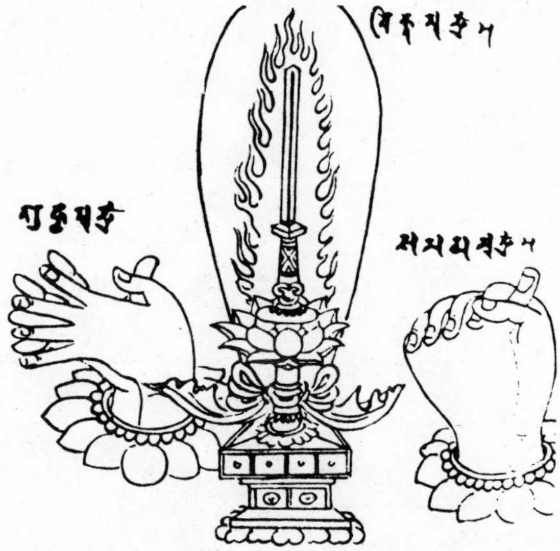

TZ.54.53

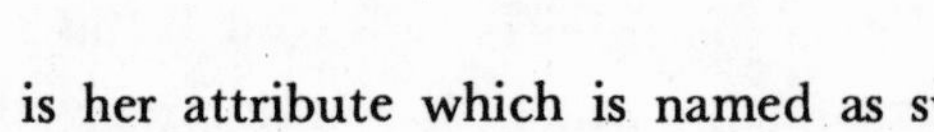

54.53). Her hand posture can be distinguished in the first mudrā from the left which is guhya mudrā. Mudrā in the middle is her attribute which is named as symbolic or the cihna mudrā and the next is samaya-mudrā.

According to STTS she is the second dharma-dhāraṇī named Ādhāraṇī and saluted as: *Om vajra-kośa-guhya hūm.* (STTS 103).

TZ.38.80

Vajra-sword is an attribute of Vajra-tīkṣṇa. In samaya-maṇḍala of the graphic Vajradhātu a sword is placed upon a lotus to depict his essence (TZ.38.80).

I.3.15. Through union with Vajra - Tīkṣṇa one is foremost in the wisdom of All the Buddhas. Vajra-tīkṣṇa in the third maṇḍala of Gobu-shingan is sitting in knowledge posture holding a vajra-sword encircled by flames (TZ 54.86). He is the second dharma-samādhi of Vajra-jñāna-dharma-maṇḍala according to STTS. His hṛdaya is Vajra-kośa: *hṛd vajra-kośa*. He is named as mudrā of knowledge of prajñā of All the Tathāgatas: *Sarvatathāgata-prajñā-jñāna-mudraḥ (STTS 12-121)*.

Vajra-tīkṣṇa with a vajra-sword in his right hand and a lotus with a book in his left hand belongs to Dharma-maṇḍala of the graphic Vajradhātu (TZ 38.153).

I.4.15. Vajra-tīkṣṇa in the first and the fourth maṇḍalas of Gobu-shingan has the same attributes, a sword in his right hand and the other is resting on his thigh (TZ. 54.119). He as the second religious pūjā of All the Tathāgatas is named as Mahāghoṣānugā. She is saluted as: *Oṃ sarvatathāgata-prajñā-pāramitā-nirhāraiḥ stunomi mahā*

*ghoṣānuge dham* (STTS 134). *Dham* is his seed syllable which is given in mahā-maṇḍala of the graphic Vajradhātu also. Dhāraṇī under the illustration corresponds to the STTS. Mudrās are the same as given with the second maṇḍala. Only the last one is replaced by a muṣṭi.

TZ.38.226

A vajra-padma is drawn as an attribute of Vajra-tīkṣṇa in the action maṇḍala of the graphic Vajradhātu (TZ.38. 226). She is holding it by both of his hands by the stem of the lotus.

2.1.15. According to STTS (p.192) he belongs to Vajra-sena. He has a power to cut away when he has an angry aspect. *Om Vajra-tīkṣṇa krodha cchinda cchinda hūm phaṭ*. In krodha-guhya mudrā-maṇḍala he is in diṅkāra-maṇḍala. His vajra-sword is able to cut everything: *Om vajra-tīkṣṇa krodhe cchinda vajra koṣeṇa sarvam diḥ* (STTS 215). His samaya form resembles the preceded samaya form and in the karma-maṇḍala he is sitting with his hands folded accross his breast (TZ 38. 407, 330). II.3.15. Vajrakula-dharma-jñāna samaya maṇḍala also personifies him with the same quality: *Om sūkṣma-vajra ccheda krodha cchinda bhinda hūm phaṭ* (STTS 227). II.4.15. He has a power to impassionate in action maṇḍala :*Om vajra-tīkṣṇa rāge rāgaya hūm* (STTS 239).

III.1.15. In all the four maṇḍalas of sakala-jagad-vinaya he is called Kumāra. In mahā-maṇḍala he is portrayed near Samāpanna Mahāsattva on a louts. He is a lotus kumāra with a power of lotus and cuts by his sword: *Om padma-kumāra padma-śakti-dhara khaḍgeṇa cchinda cchinda hūm* (STTS 324). III.2.15. Only his seed syllable is mentioned in padma-guhya-mudrā-maṇḍala of Sakala-jagad-vinaya mahā-maṇḍala (STTS 344). III.3.15. Vajra-tīkṣṇa is named as the lotus-kumāra of the knowledge: *Om jñāna-padma-kumāra hūm* (STTS 358). III.4.15. In its action maṇḍala he is action-kumārī. *Om padma-karma-kumārī hūm* (STTS 367).

IV.1.15. In sarvārthasiddhi-maṇḍala Vajra-tīkṣṇa belongs to the maṇḍala of ratna-padma. Thus a ratna sword is his attribute. *Om ratna-kośāgrya hūm* (STTS 391). IV.2.15. Sword is his symbolic form according to ratna-guhya-mudrā-maṇḍala. *Om maṇi-samaya-kośe hūm* (STTS 408). IV.3.15. Vajra-sword is named as gem-sword in knowledge maṇḍala *Om jñāna-maṇi-kośa* (STTS 418). IV.4.15. Vajratīkṣṇa has his symbolic form in action-maṇḍala of Sarvārthasiddhi: *Om maṇi-ratna tīkṣṇa samaye cchinda cchinda hūm* (STTS 426).

Names of Vajra-tīkṣṇa in the sixteen maṇḍalas:

| Ch. | P. | Kula | Maṇḍala | Names. |
|---|---|---|---|---|
| 1. | 29-30 | Buddha | Vajradhātu-mahā-m. | Vajra-tīkṣṇa, Vajra-kośa, Mañjughoṣa, Mañjuśrī, vajra-bodhi. |
| 2. | 103 | " | Vajra-guhya-vajra-m. | Vajra-kośa, Ādhāraṇī, Vajra-kośa-guhyā. |
| 3. | 120-1 | " | Vajra-jñāna-dharma-m. | Vajra-kośa, Prajñā-jñāna-mudrā. |
| 4. | 134 | " | Vajra-kārya-karma-m. | Mahāghoṣānugā |
| 6. | 192 | Vajra | Trilokavijaya-mahā-m. | Vajra-tīkṣṇa-krodha. |
| 7. | 215 | " | Krodha-guhya-mudrā-m. | Vajra-tīkṣṇa-krodhā. |
| 8. | 227 | " | Vajra-kula-dharma-jñāna-samaya-m. | Sūkṣma-vajra-krodha |
| 9. | 239 | " | Vajra-kula-karma-m. | Vajra-tīkṣṇa-rāgā. |
| 15 | 324 | Padma | Sakala-jagad-vinaya-mahā-m. | Padma-kumara |
| 16. | 344 | " | Padma-guhya-mudrā-m. | Dhī |
| 17. | 358 | " | Jñāna-m. | Jñāna-padma-kumāra |
| 18. | 367 | " | Karma-m. | Padma-karma-kumārī. |
| 19. | 391 | Ratna | Sarvārthasiddhi-mahā-m. | Ratna-kośāgrya |
| 20. | 408 | " | Ratna-guhya-mudrā-m. | Maṇi-samaya-kośā. |
| 21. | 418 | " | Jñāna-m. | Jñāna-maṇi-kośa. |
| 22. | 426 | " | Karma-maṇḍala | Maṇi-ratna-tīkṣṇa-samayā. |

## 16. VAJRAHETU
金剛因菩薩

Vairocana enters the samādhi named the religion consecration-vajra which has its origin in the samaya of Mahābodhisattva who turns the wheel of Law, who is Sahacittotpādita and utters the seed syllable which is called the the cakra samaya of All the Tathāgatas as *Vajra-hetu.* As it is uttered Vajradhara manifests himself as a host of Vajradhātu-maṇḍalas which coalesce into a vajra-wheel on Vairocana's hand After the usual special manifestations this becomes Bodhisattva Sahacittotpādita-dharmacakra-pravarti who says: "Oho I am vajra-made wheel of the followers of the supreme vajra-dharma, since just by producing the thought of Enlightenment one turns the dharma-wheel. Then this Mahā-bodhisattva emerges from the heart of Vairocana, stations himself in the left lunar disc of Stg. and pays his respects. Once again Vairocana enters the samādhi named cakra-vajra and gives cakra-vajra for attaining the supreme success in turning the wheel of law of Saddharma to the great Bodhisattva in his hands. Then he is consecrated by All the Tathāgatas. by the vajra name as Vajra-maṇḍa. Mahā-sattva Vajra-maṇḍa establishing All the Tathāgatas in the samādhi called *avaivartika* by vajra cakra says thus. "This purifier of All the dharmas of All the Buddhas being the wheel which never goes into reverse is thought of as the essence, *maṇḍa* of enlightenment.". (STTS 30-2).

Adhering the holder of vajra-wheel (Vajra-hetu) one turns the wheel of dharma. According to Tajima (p.181) Vajra-hetu occupies a seat in the north. Obstacles to the attainment I.1.16.

TZ.54.16

of Bodhi being destroyed and the true nature of our heart being well understood this Bodhisattva represents since then the cause, *hetu* that makes the wheel of law to go about for the beings. He is called

Sahacittotpāda-dharma-cakra-pravarti and Dharma-cakra-pravarti. He and Maitreya are identical. He is of flesh colour. His left hand is closed and right holds a cakra. It corresponds to the maṇḍala of Takao but Kongokai illustrates him as holding a lotus supporting the dharma-cakra by both of his hands

Vajra-hetu in the first maṇḍala of Gobu-shingan is named Vajra-hetu and Sahacittotpāda-dharma-cakra-pravarti. He is riding a peacock. His attribute dharma-cakra is placed upon the tip of his finger of the right hand. *tarjanī* and his left fist is resting on his thigh (TZ 54.16.).

First from the right is the mudrā of vajra-cakra, second is named as action mudrā and the last is his symbol, a cakra that is his cihna mudrā.

TZ.38.81.

Vajra-hetu in the mahā-maṇḍala of the graphic Vajradhātu holds the same attribute but here he differs in his hand posture. (TZ 38.19, Lokesh Chandra 424).

I.2.16. To depict the power, the śakti of Vajra-hetu he is personified as Sarva-cakra in the second maṇḍala of Gobu-shingan (TZ 54.54). Both of his hands in the dharma-cakra-mudrā are holding a lotus with six spoked dharma-cakra encircled by flames. Originally vajra-wheel is a transformation of a host of Vajradhātu-maṇḍalas thus here his feminine form is personified as vajra-guhya-maṇḍalā. Dhāraṇī under the illustration corres-

I.2.16.

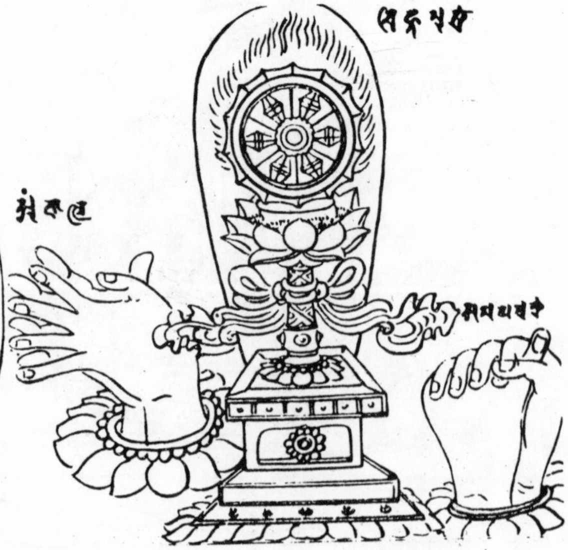

TZ.54.54

TZ.38.81

ponds to the STTS (p.103) as . *Om vajra-guhya-maṇḍale hum.* First from the right is samaya-mudrā, second is cihna-mudrā and the third is añjali.

Sarva-cakra in its symbolic form in the samaya-maṇḍala of graphic vajra-dhātu is depicted here as a wheel (TZ 38.81, Lokesh Chandra 486).

I.3.16. The third maṇḍala of Gobu-shingan illustrates Vajra-hetu as the mudrā of knowledge of entrance into cakra, that is maṇḍala: *Cakra-praveśa-jñāna-mudrā.* He is holding a cakra upon a lotus as in the preceded one. Dhāraṇī under

I.3.16.

TZ.54.87

the illustration is: Tiṣṭha vajra-cakra-*pravaeśa-jñāna-mudrā hṛdayam. But* STTS gives it as: *Tiṣṭha vajra-cakra hṛdayam praviśa* (STTS 121). His names in the Gobu-shingan and STTS are the same. Mudrās are not named but first and second from the right are samaya- and cihna-mudrās only the third differs from the second chapter. (TZ 54.87). He is the third dharma-samādhi of All the Tathāgatas according to STTS. praised as: *tiṣṭha vajra-cakra hṛdayam praviśa* (STTS 121). His names in Gobu-shingan and STTS are the same. Gobu-shingan differs slightly in its reading: *tiṣṭha vajra-cakra praveśa jñāna-mudra hṛdayam.*

Vajra-hetu in the dharma-maṇḍala is holding a cakra without spokes by both of his hands (TZ.38.154).

TZ.38.154

I.4.16

I.4.16. The fourth maṇḍala of Gobu-shingan and STTS name Vajra-hetu as Sarva-maṇḍala in his dhāraṇī but actually he is named as *Sarvammanu-praveśa* in Gobu-shingan and sarva-maṇḍala-praveśa in STTS. (p.134). Vajra hetu in its feminine form is holding a cakra in her right hand which is placed on a lotus and the left fist is placed on her thigh. The reading under the illustration is: *Om sarvatathāgata-maṇḍale hūm Sarvammanupraveśa* (TZ 54.120). Mudrās are the same as given before, STTS has a minor difference in reading: °*parivartādi,* °*nayaiḥ*. She is the third dharma-pūjā of All the Tathāgatas (STTS 134).

In the action maṇḍala of the graphic Vajradhātu vajra-hetu is holding a lotus. There is something round upon it which should be a cakra (TZ 38.227, Lokesh Chandra 632).

TZ.38.227

In the maṇḍalas of Trailokya-vijaya Vajra- hetu belongs to Vajrasena. II.1.16. In its mahā-maṇḍala his angry aspect is called Vajra-hetu-krodha: *Om vajra hetu-krodha praviśa praveśaya maṇḍale sarvam hūm phaṭ* (STTS 192). II.2.16. In the samaya-maṇḍala of the graphic Vajradhātu of Trailokya-vijaya Vajra-hetu is illustrated as an eight spoked cakra on a lotus just as it is in the samaya maṇḍala of the graphic Vajradhātu (TZ 37.408, Lokesh Chandra 807). In krodha-guhya mudrā-maṇḍala he is personified as great anger: *Om vajra-hetu mahā-krodhe praveśa cakra praveśaya sarvam diḥ* (STTS 215). II.3.16. Vajra hetu is the great cakra of subtle vajra-anger which has a power of destruction: *Om sūkṣma-vajra-krodha mahā-cakrà cchinda pātaya śiraḥ praviśya hṛdayam bhinda hūm phaṭ* (STTS 227), in the vajra-kula-dharma-jñāna-samaya-maṇḍala. II.4.16. In the action maṇḍala of Trailokya-vijaya he is sitting with his hands folded across his breast (TZ 38.331, Lokesh Chandra 738). He is Vajra-maṇḍala in the action maṇḍala of STTS. *Om vajra-maṇḍale rāge rāgaya hūm* (STTS 239).

III.1.16. In the maṇḍalas of Sakala-jagad-vinaya he attains a form of Harihara. Nīla-kaṇṭha, or blue neck is an attribute of Śiva, śaṅkha, cakra, gadā and padma belong to Viṣṇu, vyāghra-carma skin of an antilope is worn by Śiva, Śiva has a black snake as his yajño-pavīta. The divinity wears an upper garment covering his left shoulder. He is Nārāyaṇa with three eyes: *Om padma nīla-kaṇṭha-śaṅkha-cakra-gadā-padma-pāṇi-vyāghra-carma-nivasana kṛṣṇa-sarpa-yajñopavītājina-carma vāma-skandhottarīya nārāyaṇa rūpa-dhara trinetra mum-cāṭṭahāsam praveśaya samayān dehi me siddhim Avalokiteśvara hūm* (STTS 324). III.2.16. Vajra-hetu in padma-guhya-mudrā maṇḍala is Nīla-kaṇṭha. *Om padma-cakra-gadā-dhāriṇī nīla-kaṇṭhe siddhya siddhya hūm* (STTS 344). III.3.16. In its jñāna maṇḍala he is Nārāyaṇa. *Om jñāna-padma-nārāyaṇa hūm* (STTS 358). III.4.16. The same form is feminined in its action maṇḍala: *Om padma-karma nārāyaṇī hūm* (STTS 367).

IV.1.16. In mahā-maṇḍala of Sarvārthasiddhi Vajra-hetu is Ratna-cakra who turns the wheel: *Om maṇi-cakra-pravartaya hūm* (STTS 391). IV.2.16. His samaya form in the ratna guhya-mudrā maṇḍala is Maṇi samaya-cakra: *Om maṇi-samaya-cakra hūm* (STTS 408) IV.3.16. The gem wheel is the wheel of knowledge in knowledge maṇḍala: *Om jñāna-maṇi-cakra* (STTS 418). IV.4.16. In action maṇḍala he is saluted as: *Om maṇi-ratna-cakra-samaye hūm* (STTS 426).

Names of Vajrahetu in the sixteen maṇḍalas:

| Ch. | P. | Kula | Maṇḍala | Names |
|---|---|---|---|---|
| 1 | 30-32 | Buddhakula | Vajradhātu-mahāmaṇḍala | Vajrahetu, Sahacittotpāda-dharma-cakrapravartī, Vajra-cakra-Vajra-maṇḍa. |
| 2. | 103 | " | Vajraguhya-vajramaṇḍala | Sarvacakra, Vajra-guhya-maṇḍala. |
| 3. | 121 | " | Vajrajñāna-dharma-maṇḍala | Cakra-praveśa-jñāna-mudrā, Vajra-cakra. |
| 4. | 134 | " | Vajrakārya-karmamaṇḍala | Sarva-maṇḍala. |
| 6. | 192 | Vajrakula | Trilokavijaya-mahā-maṇḍala. | Vajra-hetu-krodha. |
| 7. | 215 | " | Krodhaguhya-mudrā-maṇḍala. | Vajra-hetu-mahā-krodhā. |
| 8. | 227 | " | Vajrakula-dharmajñāna-samayamaṇḍala. | Sūkṣma-vajra-Krodha mahā-cakra. |
| 9. | 239 | " | Vajrakula-karmamaṇḍala | Vajra-maṇḍala rāga. |
| 15. | 324 | Padmakula | Sakalajagadinaya-mahā-maṇḍala. | Nārāyaṇa, Avalokiteśvara. |
| 16. | 344 | " | Padmaguhya-mudrā-maṇḍala. | Nīla-kaṇṭha. |
| 17. | 358 | " | Jñānamaṇḍala | Jñāna-Padma-nārāyaṇa. |
| 18. | 367 | " | Karmamaṇḍala | Padma-karma-nārāyaṇī. |
| 19. | 391 | Ratnakula | Sarvārthasiddhi-mahā-maṇḍala. | Maṇi-cakra. |
| 20. | 408 | " | Ratnaguhya-mudrā-maṇḍala. | Maṇi-samaya-cakrā. |
| 21. | 418 | " | Jñānamaṇḍala | Jñāna-maṇi-cakra. |
| 22. | 426 | " | Karmamaṇḍala | Maṇi-ratna-cakra-samayā. |

## 17 VAJRABHĀṢA

金剛語菩薩

Bodhisattva Vajrabhāṣa sits in the western direction. He explains the law in an excellent way by means of secret utterance of Tathāgata, causes attest the Bodhi by all the kings. He has the tongue of Buddha. His colour is of flesh. In the maṇḍala of Takao he has the tongue of the Buddha which ends in a three pointed vajra but in Kongokai he has a three pointed vajra in a lotus (Tajima 181-182).

Vairocana enters the samādhi called Dharma-consecration-vajra which has its origin in the samaya of Mahābodhisattva Avāca and utters the jāpa-samaya of All the Tathāgatas that is Vajrabhāṣa. As soon as he utters this Vajrapāṇi manifests himself forthwith as Vajra-syllables which coalesce into the form of a Vajra-recitation. This turns into Bodhisattva Acāca, enters the heart of Vairocana and says : " I am the self-existant mystery which is concieved of as enigmas in that, they teach the Doctrine without a prolixity of words."

Then in the form of Avāca Mahābodhisattva he emerges from the heart of Bhagavān, stations himself in the back lunar disc of All the Tathāgatas and pays respects.

Then Bhagavān enters the samādhi called the concealed-word-vajra of All the Tathāgatas and gives vajra-jāpa to Mahābodhisattva Avāca which is the samaya of knowledge of words of All the Tathāgatas. Avāca Bodhisattva is consecrated with the name *Vajrāvāca*.. He utters this convessing with All the Tathāgatas by his Vajra-jāpa : 'This is Vajra-recitation of All the Boddhas which gives rapid success in mantras of All the Buddhas." (STTS 32-34).

I.1.17

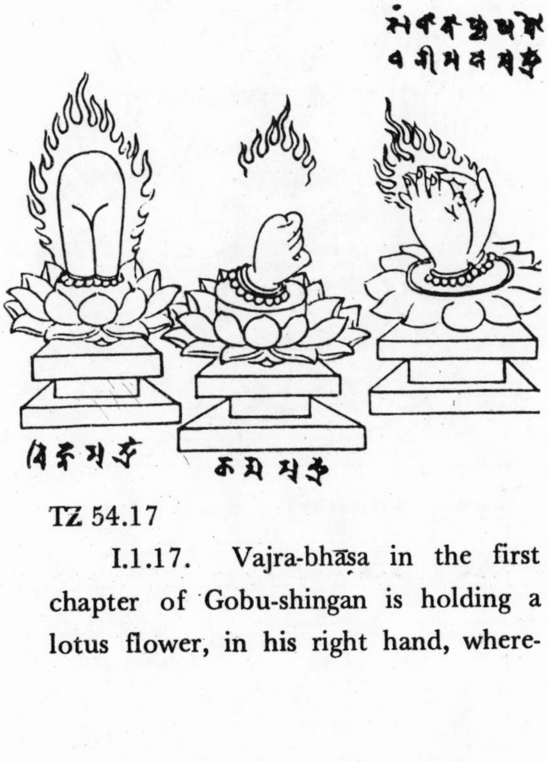

TZ 54.17

I.1.17. Vajra-bhāṣa in the first chapter of Gobu-shingan is holding a lotus flower, in his right hand, whereupon can be seen a tongue which signifies Vajra-jāpa, his attribute. (TZ 54.27). He is sitting on a lotus on a peacock. The script under the illustration is. *Om Vajra bhāṣa.* First mudrā from the right is mahāmudrā which apprehands the one who is conceived of a enigmas, second is action and third is symbolic mudrā. Actually the third is Vajrajāpa held by the divinity in the given illustration. (His attribute may not be named as Vajrajāpa here as no vajra is depicted with the tongue which shows jāpa, muttering of prayers.)

TZ 38.20

A tongue with a three pointed vajra atop is placed upon the palm of Vajra-bhāṣa inmahā-maṇḍala of Vajradhātu (TZ 38.20, Lokesh Chandra 425). Vajra-bhāṣa is sitting on a lotus . *Ram* is given as his seed syllable.

I.2.17. Vajrabhāṣa in the second chapter of Gobu-shingan is Sahasrāvartaja, one who is born by turning round a thousand times, but in STTS he is named Sahsrāvarta, means one who turns round a thousand times that is tongue. The same attribute is held by both of his hands. In its dhāraṇī he is

I.2.17.

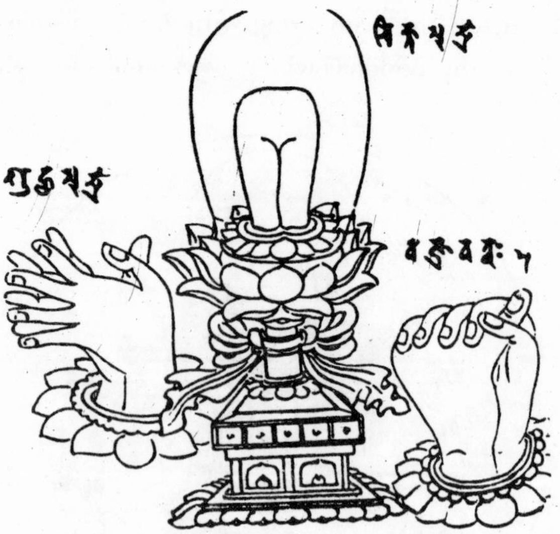

TZ.54.55

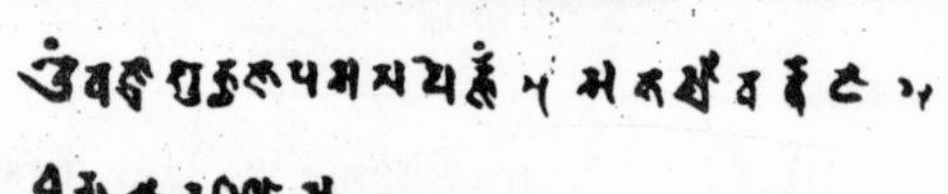

named as the samaya of the vairoconcealed prayers: *Om vajra-guhya-jāpa-samaya hūm. Vajra-bhāṣa.* She is the last dharma-dhāraṇī according to STTS. Her dhāraṇī is: *Om Vajra*

TZ. 38.82

*Om Vajra-guhya-jāpa-samaya hūm.* (103). The first mudrā from the right is Vajrabandha, second cihna-mudrā and third is guhyamudrā second mudrā is identical with the preceded third. (TZ 54.55)

Vajrabhāṣa in samaya-maṇḍala of the graphic Vajradhātu is depicted as a Vajra in a tongue (TZ 38.82, Lokesh Chandra 487) which is his essence that is Vajrabhāṣa.

I.3.17 Vajra-bhāṣa in the third chapter of Gobu-shingan is dharma-Vāgmudrā, without elucidations *Sarvatathāgata-niḥprapañca-dharma vāgmudrā.* of All the Tathāgatas. (TZ 54.88). He is holding the same attribute encircled by flames. In dhāraṇī he is named as Vajra-jihvāgra : *Om praviśa vajra-jihvāgra hṛdayam* . Here he is the last Dharma-samādhi. First and second mudrās from the right are identical with the given in the preceded group, those are Vajra-bandha and china-mudrā respectively. The third mudrā resembles the middle of the first chapter.

I.3.17.

Vajrabhāṣa in dharma maṇḍala of the grahpic Vajradhātu is sitting in Varada posture (TZ. 38.155, Lokesh Chandra 560). In STTS he is the knowledge-mudrā without elucidation of words of religion of All the Tathagatas : 'Sarvatathāgata-dharma-vāgniḥ-prapañca-jñāna mudrā , His Mantra is given as '*Vajra-jihvāgra hṛdaya :* In the preceded mantra for Vajraketu there are two verbs : tiṣṭha and praviśa, Here praviśa seems to be useless which in Gobu-shingan is added to Vajra-jihvāgra. Thus the dhāraṇī in STTS should be *praviśa vajra-jihvāgra hṛdaya.*

I.4.17. Vajrabhāṣa is Vajrāvāca in the fourth chapter of Gobu-shingan and STTS, O Vajrā vāca I pray by singing the Budha-songs together : *Om sarvatathāgata sandhā-bhāṣa- Buddhasangītibhir gāyan stunomi vajra-vāce vam* (STTS 134). As the last dharmapūjā she is called

I.4.17.

TZ.54.121

as Mantracaryā. But in Gobu-shingan she is named *Mantra ca pūjā* Dhāraṇī as the same Vajrā-vāca is holding the same attribute in her right hand and sitting on a lotus. Her attribute is a bit more stilized here which is distinct from the mudrā. There are three lotus flowers and there is a vajra under the two. Other mudras are the same as given before (TZ 54.19).

TZ 38.228.

This illustration of Vajrabhāṣa belongs to the action-maṇḍala of the Vajradhātu (38 228, Lokesh Chandra 633). The deity is holding a lotus stem by both of her hands and there is a three pointed vajra placed on the lotus. Tongue is missing here.

II.1.17. According to STTS he belongs to the circle of Vajrasena and named as Vajra-krodha-bhāṣa: *Om Vajra-krodha-bhāṣa a vada vada hūm phaṭ* (STTS 192). 2.2.17. Vajra-bhāṣa is Vajra-tongue, words of great anger in krodha-gahya-mudrā-maṇḍala: *Om Vajra-jihve mahā-krodha-bhāṣe vācam muñca dih* (STTS 215). In samaya-maṇḍala of Trailokaya-vijaya in the graphic Vajradhātu he is depicted in the same manner as in samaya maṇḍala of graphic vajradhātu (TZ.38.332, Lokesh Chandra 739) Vajra-bhāṣa sits besides samāpanna Mahāsattva in the maṇḍalas of Sakla-jagad-vinaya 3.1.17. In its Mahā-maṇḍala he is a lotus-born divinity named as Padma-bhāṣa: *Om dharma padma sambhava japa japa padma-bhāṣa hūm* (STTS 329). 3.2.17. In padma-guhya mudrā-maṇḍala he is said to reside in the blossom of jasmine. *Om pāṇḍara vāsini padma-sambhave vada vada hūm* (STTS 334). 3.3.17. He is personified as jñāna-padma-bhāṣa in knowlledge-maṇḍala and 3.4.17. Padma-karma-brāhmī in action-maṇḍala: *Om Jñāna-padma-bhāṣe hūm* (STTS 358); *Om Padma-karma-brāhmī hūm* (STTS 367).

In the maṇḍalas of Savārthasiddhi he belongs to the gem-family, 4.1.17 thus he is named Ratna-bhāṣa: *Om Ratna-bhāṣe hūm* (STTS 391). 4.2.17. He belongs to the maṇḍala of Ratnapadma. In Ratna-guhya-mudrā-maṇḍala he belongs to Maṇipadma as Maṇi-bhāṣāgri *Om Maṇi-bhāṣagri hūm* (STTS 408). 4.3.17. Knowledge-maṇḍala names him jñāna-maṇi-bhāṣa: *Om Jñāna-maṇi-bhāṣa* (STTS 418) 4.4.17. In Action-maṇḍala Maṇi ratna-bhāṣa is praised for speech. *Om Maṇi-ratna-bhāṣe-bhāṣa-vada vada hūm* (STTS 426).

Names of Vajra-bhāṣa in the sixteen maṇḍalas:

| Ch. | P. | Kula | Maṇḍala | Names. |
|---|---|---|---|---|
| 1. | 32-34 | Buddhakula | Vajradhātu-mahāmaṇḍala | Vajra-bhāṣa, Avāca-mahābodhi-sattva. |
| 2. | 103 | " | Vajraguhya-vajramaṇḍala | Vajra-guhya-jāpa-samayā, sahasrāvarta, sahasravartaja. |
| 3. | | " | Vajrajñāna-dharma-maṇḍala | Sarvatathāgata-dharma-vāgniḥ-prapañca-jñāna-mudrā. |
| 4. | 134 | " | Vajrakārya-karmamaṇḍala | Vajrā-vāca, Mantra-caryā, Mantra ca pūjā. |
| 6. | 192 | Vajrakula | Trilokavijaya-mahā-maṇḍala. | Vajra-krodha-Bhasa. |
| 7. | 215 | " | Krodhaguhya-mudrā-maṇḍala. | Vajra-jihvā mahā-krodha-bhāṣā. |
| 8. | 227 | " | Vajrakula-dharmajñāna-samayamaṇḍala. | Suksma-huṃkara-krodha. |
| 9. | 239 | " | Vajrakula-karmamaṇḍala | Vajra-vāg-rāgā. |
| 15. | 329 | Padmakula | Sakalajagadvinaya-mahā-maṇḍala | Padma-sambhava padma-bhāṣa. |
| 16. | 334 | " | Padmaguhya-mudrāmaṇḍala | Pāṇḍara-vāsinī padma-sambhavā. |
| 17. | 358 | " | Jñānamaṇḍala | Jñāna-padma-bhāṣa. |
| 18. | 367 | " | Karmamaṇḍala | Padma-karma-brāhmī. |
| 19. | 391 | Ratnakula | Sarvārthasiddhi-mahā-maṇḍala. | Ratna bhāṣa. |
| 20. | 408 | " | Ratnaguhya-mudrāmaṇḍala | Maṇi-bhāṣāgrī. |
| 21. | 418 | " | Jñānamaṇḍala | Jñāna-maṇi-bhāsa. |
| 22. | 426 | " | Karmamaṇḍala | Maṇi-ratna-bhāṣā. |

## 18. VAJRAKARMA

金剛業菩薩

Vajra-karma sits in the South. When Buddha enters nirvāṇa and destroys passions, this Bodhisattva signifies his algruistic action of conducting beings. He is of flesh colour, He raises his joint hands over his head. This gesture symbolises completion. (Tajima 183) Vairocana enters the samādhi named action-consecration-vajra which has its origin in the samaya *Sarvatathāgata-viśvakarma-mahābodhisattva-samayasambhava karmādhiṣṭāna-vajra* of Mahabodhi-sattva Sarvatathāgata Viśvatathāgata Viśvakarma and utters *Vajra-Karma*, which is the action-samaya of All the Tathāgatas.

As he utters this Vajrakarma manifests himself as a host of action-rays, *Karma-raśmayaḥ*. All the worlds are enlightened by these rays and filled with action. These rays coalesce into the form of an action-vajra on Vairocana's hand. After the regular special manifestations this turns into the form of Bodhisattva Vajra-karma, stations himself in the heart of Vairocana and says: "Oho I am the irresistible universal action of the Buddhas, in that the Vajra-action leads spontaneously to Buddhahood."

Mahābodhisattva Viśvakarmā emerges from the heart of Vairocana, stations himself in the back lunar disc of All the Tathāgatas and pays respects. Once more Vairocana enters the samadhi called the infallible Vajra of All the Tathāgatas: *Sarvathathāgatāmogha vajram* and gives action vajra which is the samaya of method of description of All actions which are boundless and infallible which engages in the worship of All the Tathāgatas to I.1.18.

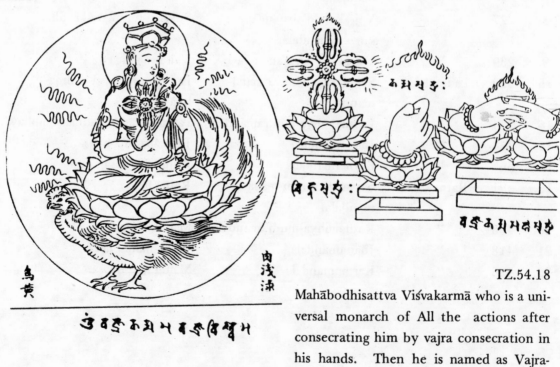

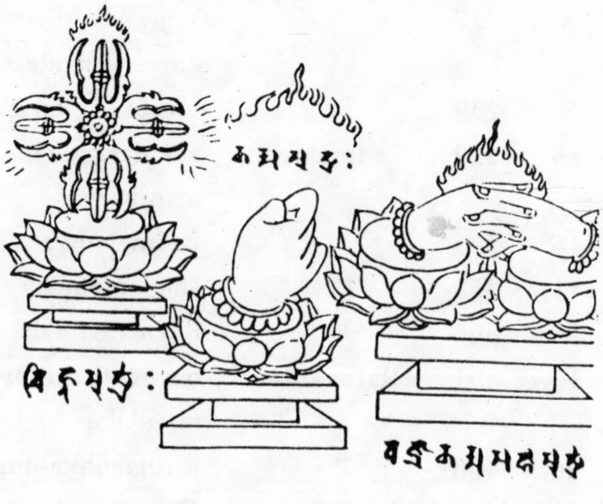

TZ.54.18

Mahābodhisattva Viśvakarmā who is a universal monarch of All the actions after consecrating him by vajra consecration in his hands. Then he is named as Vajraviśva by All the Tathāgatas. Vajraviśva establishes that Vajra in his heart, utters this verse employing in work. "This is the supreme enaction of universal action of All the Buddhas, I am given into my own hands, all is joined to All. (STTS 34-36).

1.1.18. Vajra-karma is also named as Vajraviśva in the first chapter of Gobu-shingan (TZ 54.18). There he is riding a hen and holding a viśvavajra in his right hand which shows his being Vajraviśva. First from the right in Vajrakarma-mahā-mudrā, second is karma- and the third is china-mudrā.

TZ.38.52

In mahāmaṇḍala of ghe graphic Vajradhātu he is sitting on a lotus and his hands are in a mudrā of completion (of action) (TZ 38.22, Lokesh Chandra 427) *Kam* is written as his bījākṣara.

I.2.18. Secret-action-samaya of Vajra-family is Siddhottarā: *Om Vajra-guhya-karma-samaya hūm. Siddhottarā.* She is the first karma-dhāraṇī (STTS 103). She is sitting on a lotus and holding the same Viśvavajra by both of her hands (TZ 54.56). Her

I.2.18.

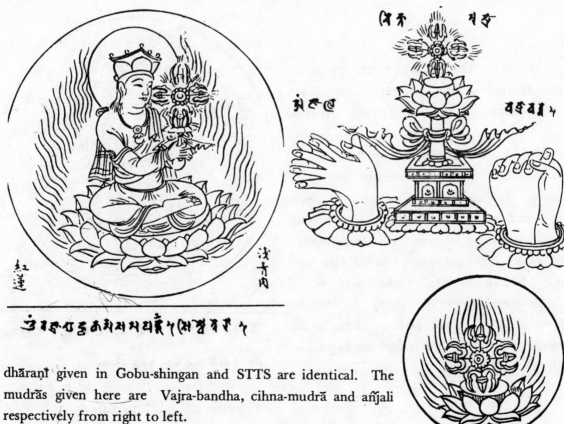

dhāraṇī given in Gobu-shingan and STTS are identical. The mudrās given here are Vajra-bandha, cihna-mudrā and añjali respectively from right to left.

A viśvavajara is the symbolic form of Vajra-karma in

samaya maṇḍala of graphic Vajradhātu (TZ 38.84, Lokesh Chandra 489).

I.3.18. The third chapter of Gobu-shingan personify him as mudrā of knowledge of all the actions of All the Tathāgatas: *Sarvatathāgata-viśva-karma-jñāna-mudrā.* (TZ 54.89). He has a vajra-nature *Vajrātmka* which emerges from subtle-vajra-reflection. *sūkṣma-vajra-bimbāt... Sarva-vajrātmaka* (STTS 121). Viśvavajra is placed upon the palms of both of his hands in his lap. STTS names him as he is named in Gobu-shingan. He is the first karma-samādhi. The first mudrā is Vajra-bandha, second is cihna-mudrā and the third is karama-mudrā as: given in the first

I.3.18.

TZ.54.89

chapter.

Hand-posture of vajra-karma in mahā- and dharma-maṇḍalas of graphic vajradhātu are identical. The only difference is that in the dharma-maṇḍala there is a vajra behind (TZ 38.157, Lokesh Chandra 562).

I.4.18. Satyavatī is another personification of Vajrakarma. The same attribute is placed on her right palm. Her dhāraṇī in Gobu-shingan is: *Om Sarvatathāgata-pūjā-ka (raṇa). (me) gha-spharṇa karma kara kara* (TZ 54.122). But *pūjā-megha* is replaced by *dhūpa-megha* in STTS (135). All the three mudrās are the same as given in the preceded chapter. She is first karma-pūjā of All the Tathāgatas.

I.4.18.

TZ.54.122

TZ.38.230

The drawing illustrated here is from the action-maṇḍala of graphic Vajradhātu (TZ.38.230, Lokesh Chandra 635). He is holding a lotus flower and viśvavajra is placed upon it, which is encircled by flames.

2.1.18. According to STTS he belongs to the family of Vajravesa. He is named Vajra-karma: *Om Vajra-karma* (STTS 193) in mahā-maṇḍala. 2.2.18. But in krodhagahya-mudrā maṇḍala he is the great anger of karma vajriṇī who has faces in all the directions: *Om sarva-mukha karma-vajriṇī mahā-krodha kuru sarvān hnīḥ* (STTS 215). In samaya-maṇḍala he should be a viśvavajra. The drawing given here looks like a disc which is expected to be a stylised form of viśavajra (TZ.38.411). 2.3.18. In samaya-maṇḍala of religious knowledge Vajra-karma is in the form of its subtle anger who can do all and accomplish all the actions: *Om sūkṣma-vajra-karma-krodha sarva-karma-karo bhava sarva-kāryāṇi sādhaya hūm phaṭ* (STTS 227).

TZ.38.411

2.4.18. The samaya form of karma is to wroship: *Om Vajra-karma-samaya pūjaya hūm* (STTS 239).

Vajrakarma is sitting with his folded hands as other deities of karma maṇḍala of Trailokaya-vijaya of the graphic vajradhātu (TZ.38.334, Lokesh Chandra 741).

Vajra-karma in the maṇḍala of Sakala-jagad-vinaya belongs to the one who has a lotus and a lance, 3.1.18. He is called Padma-naṭṭeśvara and Avalokiteśvara. This may be a changed form of Siva because he is called Naṭṭesvara but with a lotus. He worships All the Tathāgatas, attracts, makes others penetrate, confines, influences and gives accomplishment in all the actions: *Om Padma-naṭṭeśvara naṭṭa naṭṭa pūjaya sarva-tathāgatān vajra-karma-samayā-karṣaya praveśaya bandhayāveśaya sarva-karma-siddhim me prayacchā-valokiteśvara hūm* (STTS 325). 3.2.18. The same form is feminined in the Padma-guhya mudrā-maṇḍala: *Om padma-nṛtteśvara pūjaya sarva tathāgatān naṭṭa naṭṭa hūm* (STTS 344). 3.3.18. In knowledge maṇḍala he has a form of knowledge: *Om jñāna-padma-nṛtyeśvara hūm* (STTS 358) and 3.4.18. in action-maṇḍala he has an action form: *Om padma karma-nṛtyeśvarī hūm* (STTS 367).

4.1.18. Vajra-karma has the same form of Nṛtyeśvara in the maṇḍalas of Sarvārtha-siddhi. Only in mahā-maṇḍala he is named Maṇi-pūjā-samaya: *Om Maṇi-pūjā-samaya hūm* (STTS 392). 4.2.18. Dancing is also a characteristic of the samaya great worship: *Om Mahā pūjā-samaya nṛtya aḥ* (STTS 408). 4.3.18. He is named as the knowledge of dance of samaya form of worship of gem family: *Om Maṇi-jñāna-nṛtya-pūjā-samaya hūm* (STTS

418) in knowledge maṇḍala. 4.4.18. In action maṇḍala he has a feminine form of action of gem family: *Om Maṇi-ratna-karmaṇi hūm* (STTS 426).

Names of Vajra-karma in the sixteen maṇḍalas:

| Ch. | P. | Kula | Maṇḍala | Names. |
|---|---|---|---|---|
| 1. | 34-36 | Buddhakula | Vajradhātu-mahāmaṇḍala | Vajra-karma, Vajra-viśva, viśva-karma. |
| 2. | 103 | "" | Vajraguhya-vajramaṇḍala | Siddhottarā, Vajra-guhya-karma-samayā. |
| 3. | 121 | " | Vajrajñāna-dharma-maṇḍala. | Stg.-Viśva-karma-jñāna-mudrā. |
| 4. | 135 | " | Vajrakārya-karmamaṇḍala | Satyavatī. |
| 6. | 193 | Vajrakula | Trilokavijaya-mahā-maṇḍala, | Vajra-karma. |
| 7. | 215 | " | Krodhaguhya-mudrā-maṇḍala. | Sarva-mukha karma-vajriṇī-mahā krodhā. |
| 8. | 227. | " | Vajrakula-dharmajñāna-samayamaṇḍala. | Sūkṣma-vajra-karma-krodha. |
| 9. | 239 | " | Vajrakula-karmamaṇḍala | Vajra-karma-samayā. |
| 15. | 325 | Padmakula | Sakalajagadvinaya-mahā-maṇḍala. | Padma-naṭṭeśvara, Avalokiteś-vara. |
| 16. | 344 | " | Padmaguhya-mudrāmaṇḍala | Padma-nṛtteśvarā. |
| 17. | 358 | " | Jñānamaṇḍala | Jñāna-padma-nṛtyeśvara. |
| 18. | 367 | " | Karmamaṇḍala | Padma-karma-nṛtyeśvarī. |
| 19. | 392 | Ratnakula | Sarvārthasiddhi-mahā-maṇḍala. | Maṇi-pūjā-samayā. |
| 20. | 408 | " | Ratnaguhya-mudrā-m. | Mahā-pūjā-samayā. |
| 21. | 418 | " | Jñānamaṇḍala | Maṇi-jñāna-nṛtya-pūjā-samaya. |
| 22. | 426 | " | Karmamaṇḍala | Maṇi-ratna-karmaṇī. |

## 19. VAJRARAKṢA

金剛護菩薩

Mahābodhisattva Vajrakṣa sits in the Western side. When Vajrarakṣa conducts the beings he wears a halmet of great compassion and protects them against their enemies, the passions. He is of blue colour, Kongokai shows his fists pressing against the axils without streching the index fingers. But this gesture is deemed to be of tieing the ribbons of halmet. (Tajima 183). Vairocana enters the samādhi named action-consecration-vajra which has its origin in the samaya of Mahābodhisattva who is a heroic hard fighter and utters the seed syllable called protection-samaya of All the Tathāgatas. As he utters this, Vajradhara becomes a multiplicity of armour issuing from the hearts of All the Tathāgatas enters the heart of Vairocana, this coalesces into a single Vajra-armour on Vairocana's hand. From this Buddha forms stream out through space performing all those actions of protective ritual of All the Tathāgatas and then they become the Mahābodhisattva Duryōdhana-vīrya who recites this verse. "I am the armour which consists of bravery, the very firmest of the firm, because of my firmness I am the best maker of the Vajrabodies of those who are bodiless".

Duryodhanavīrya emerges from the heart of Bhagavān and stations himself in the right lunar disc of All the Tathāgatas and pays respects.

Now Bhagavān concentrates upon the samādhi called the strong vajra of All the Tathāgatas: *Sarva-tathāgatadṛḍhavajram* and gives the Vajra-armour which is Vīrya-pāramitā-3.1.19.

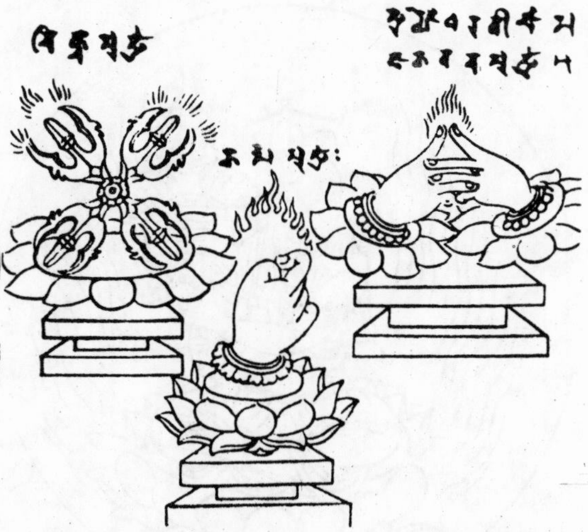

TZ.54.19

samaya to Mahābodhisattva Duryodhanavīrya in his hands. Then he is consecrated with the vajra-name-consecration by All the Tathāgatas as Vajramitra.

Mahāsattva Vajramitra envaloping All the Tathāgatas with his vajra armour utters this verse: "This is the supreme armour of friendship of All the Buddhas, the great protection of firmness and bravery named as the great friend". (STTS 37.38).

I.1.19. The first chapter of Gobu-shingan depicts Vajrarakṣa as a strong deity wearing an armour and all ornaments. He is holding a viśvavajra in his right hand and sitting on a lotus placed upon a hen (TZ.54.19). Because of his armour he is also named as Vajravarma. The first mudrā from the right is the great armour mudrā of the heroic hard fighter: *Ḍuryodhana-vīryamahā-kavacamudrā,* the second is karma-mudrā and the third is cihna-mudrā.

TZ.38.23

Vajra-rakṣa in the mahā-maṇḍala of the graphic Vajradhātu is sitting on a lotus with both of his fists put near his breast. He is looking towards his right in a serene pose. *Haṃ* is given as his seed syllable (TZ 38.23, Lokesh Chandra 428).

I.2.19. In the second chapter of Gobu-shing Vajra-rakṣa is expected to be protector of all and named as *sarvarakṣa.* Here she has a faminined form as a secred armour: *Om Vajra-guhya-kavace hūm. Sarvarakṣa.* She is holding a helmet and an armour on a Vajra that is Vajravarma. She is the second Sarvadhāraṇī according to 3.2.19.

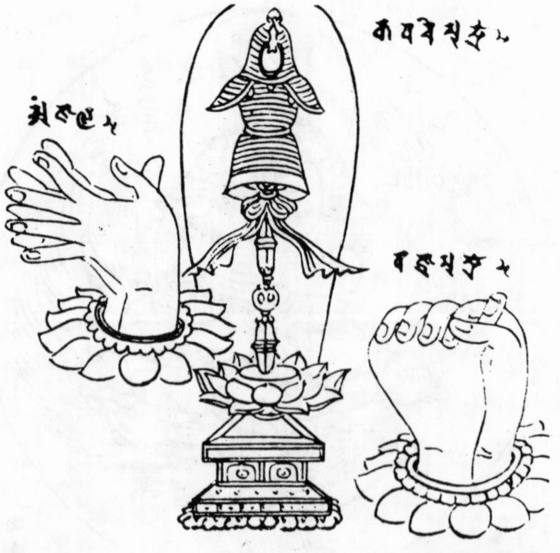

TZ.54.57

STTS (103). The three mudrās given here are vajra, kavaca and añjali respectively from right to left (TZ.54.57). Her dhāraṇī in STTS (p.103) is *Om guhya-vajra-kacace hūm.*

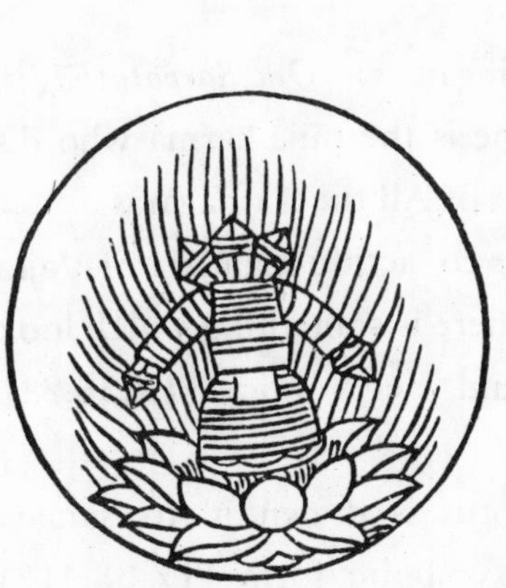

Vajrarakṣa in samaya-maṇḍala of graphic Vajradhātu is drawn as an armour placed on a lotus (TZ.38.85, Lokesh Chandra, 490).

I.3.19. Third chapter of Gobu-shingan illustrated Vajra-rakṣa in the form of a mudrā of knowledge of a heroic hard figheter: *Duryodhanavīryajñana mudrā.* He has a viśva-vajra placed on a lotus in his lap supported by both of his hands (TZ.54.90). He is the second karma-samādhi according to STTS (121). His dhāraṇī is: *Hṛd (hṛdaya) Vajra-kavaca.* The first is vajramudrā as given in the previous chapter, second shows his attribute, which can be named as his cihna-mudrā as it is in the first chapter, third is action mudrā which is also the same as given in the first chapter.

TZ.54.123

Vajra-rakṣa is holding a sword in his right hand and by his left hand he is doing a mudrā in dharma-maṇḍala of graphic Vajradhātu (TZ.38.158, Lokesh Chandra 563). Vvajra and lotus drawn here are general characteristics of this mandala.

TZ.38.158.

I.4.19. Mahābodhyaṅgavatī is vajra-rakṣa in the fourth chapter of Gobu-shingan. She is holding two one sided, three pointed vajras on her right palm Her dhāraṇī in STTS and Gobu-shingan is: *Om Sarvatathāgata puṣpa-prasara spharaṇa pūjā-karma kiri kiri* (STTS 135). She is the pūjā-karma who disperses flowers by quivering hands. She is the second karmapuja of All the Tathāgatas.

TZ.38.231

This drawing belongs to action-maṇḍala of Vajra-dhātu, upon the flower there is something which looks like a flower but it should be a vajra (TZ.38.231, Lokesh Chandra 636).

An armour on a lotus is drawn in its samaya maṇḍala to show his symbolic form (TZ.38.412). 2.3.19. He has a subtle form in samaya-maṇḍala of religious knoledge: *Om vajra-sūkṣma-kavaca-krodha-rakṣa rakṣa hūm phaṭ* (STTS 227). 2.4.19. He has a power of binding in the action maṇḍala: *Om vajra-karma rakṣaya hūm* (STTS 239).

Vajra-rakṣa in Trailokyavijaya-karma-maṇḍala has the same hand posture as given in the preceded chapters for other deities (TZ.38.335). 2.1.19. His angry form is praised for protection in mahā-maṇḍala of Trailokyavijaya in STTS (192-3). *Om vajra-kavaca-krodha rakṣa rakṣa hūm phaṭ*. 2.2.19. He belongs to circle of Vajrāveśa. The same obtains a feminined form in krodha-guhya-maṇḍala: *Om vajra-krodha rakṣa mām hnīḥ* (STTS 215-16)

In the maṇḍalas of Sakla-jagad-vinaya vajra-rakṣa is drawn besides the divinity who is four faced and has a lotus and lance in his hands. 3.1.19. In its mahā-maṇḍala he is named Avalokiteśvara who is the samaya form of armour of the lotus family. He protects the beings by his binding power and secures from fear: *Om abhayam dadātvavalokiteśvara rakṣa bandha padma-kavacam-samaya ham* (STTS 325). 3.2.19. Padma-guhya mudrā-maṇḍala has the same form as well: *Om abhya padma-kavaca-bandha rakṣa mām hūm ham* (STTS 344) 3.3.19. The chatarcteristic of protection prevails in the knoledge and action maṇḍalas. *Om jñāna-padma rakṣa hūm* (STTS 359) and 3.4.19. *Om padma-rakṣa-karma-samaya hūm* (STTS 367).

Armour and the power of protection is mentioned in the mandalas of Sarvārthasiddhi. 4.1.19. His dhāraṇī in mahā-maṇḍala is: *Om maṇi-bandha kavaca hūm*. There is a contratriety of words, it should be maṇi-kavaca bandha, that is the armour of gem family who binds (STTS 392). 4.2.19. He has a feminined form in the Ratna-guhya-mudrā maṇḍala: *Om Ratna-maṇi-samaya rakṣa ham* (STTS 408). 4.3.19. He is named as the knowledge of protection of gem family in jñāna-maṇḍala: *Om maṇi-jñāna-rakṣa* (STTS 418). 4.4.19. In action-maṇḍala he is personified as an armour: *Om maṇi-ratna-kavaca rakṣa hūm* (STTS 426).

Names o' 'ajra-rakṣa in the sixteen maṇḍalas.

| Ch. | P. | Kula | Maṇḍala | Names. |
|---|---|---|---|---|
| 1. | 37-38 | Buddhakula | Vajradhātu-mahāmaṇḍala | Vajra-rakṣa, vajra-varma, Duryodhanavīrya, Vajramitra. |
| 2. | 103 | " | Vajraguhya-vajramaṇḍala | Vajra-guhya-kavaca, sarvarakṣā. |
| 3. | 121 | " | Vajrajñāna-dharma-maṇḍala. | Duryodhanavīryajñānamudrā. |
| 4 | 135 | " | Vajrakārya-karma-maṇḍala | Sarvathāgata-puṣpa-prasara-spharaṇa pūjā-karma, mahā-bodhyaṅgavatī. |
| 6. | 192-3 | Vajrakula | Trilokavijaya-mahā-maṇḍala. | Vajra-kavaca-krodha |
| 7. | 215-16 | " | Krodhaguhya-mudrā-mandala. | Vajra-kavaca-krodhā. |
| 8. | 227 | " | Vajrakula-dharmajñāna-samayamaṇḍala. | Vajra-sūkṣma-kavaca-krodha. |
| 9. | 239 | " | Vajrakula-karmamaṇḍala | Vajra-bandha. |
| 15. | 325 | 'admakula | Sakalajagadvinaya-mahā-maṇḍala | Avalokitesvara, Padma-kavaca-samaya. |
| 16. | 344 | " | Padmaguhya-mudrā-maṇḍala. | Abhaya padma-kavaca-bandhā. |
| 17. | 359 | " | Jñānamaṇḍala | Jñāna-padma-rakṣa. |
| 18. | 367 | " | Karmamaṇḍala | Padma-rakṣa-karma-samayā. |
| 19. | 392 | Ratnakula | Sarvārthasiddhi-mahā-maṇḍala. | Maṇi-kavaca. |
| 20. | 408 | " | Ratnaguhya-mudrā-maṇḍala. | Ratna-maṇi-samaya-rakṣa. |
| 21. | 426 | " | Jñānamaṇḍala | Maṇi-jñāna-rakṣa. |
| 22. | 426 | " | Karmamaṇḍala | Maṇi-ratna-kavaca. |

## 20 VAJRAYAKṢA

金剛牙菩薩

Mahābodhisattva Vajrayakṣa resides in the eastern direction. Yakṣas are violent beings who have prominent canine teeth, hence their names are rendered in Chinese by teeth. This Bodhisattva inspires fear in sinners difficult to be converted. They devour their passions completely. He is of clear yallow colour. The two closed fists are pressed against the breast. In Kongokai the fists are a bit curved. Sometimes he forms the fist in vajra (Vajramuṣṭi). Small fingers are stretched in crochets and touch the mouth, index fingers are held upright in manner that they touch cheeks, they represent the teeth of yaksa (Tajima 183-184).

Bhagavān Vairocana enters the samādhi called the action-consecration-vajra which originates from the samaya of Mahābodhisattva who destroys all the passions and utters the seed syllable named upaya-samaya of All the Tathāgatas as Vajrayakṣa. After the utterence immediately Vajradhara manifests himself in a multiple form of weapons made of big teeth, enters the heart of Vairocana. These become a single vajra tooth and is stationed in his hands. After producing Buddha manifestations throughout space and performing magical rites for the subduing demons and so on, once more it obtains the form of the Bodhisattva Sarvamārapramardī and recites this verse . "Oho I am the great obedient of the compassionate Buddhas, in that while being gentle they act with fierceness for the benefit of living beings".

Now this Mahābodhisattva Sarvamārapramardī emerges from the heart of Bhagavān, stations himself in the left lunar disc of All the Tathagatas and pays respects. Now

I.1.20

TZ. 54.20

Bhagavān obtains the samādhi called pracaṇḍavajra and gives the weapon Vajradanṣṭra to sarva-mārapramardī in his hands. Then All the Tathāgatas oonsecrated him by the vajra-name-consecration as Vajracaṇḍa. Vajracaṇḍa places the weapon in his mouth and making All the Tathāgatas afraid speaks thus : "This is the means of subduing all the enemies of All the Budhas, a harsh vajra-armour with fangs an expedient of the compassionate ones". (STTS 39-40).

1.1.20. Vajra-yakṣa has a terrific appearence in the first chapter of Gobu-shingan. He holds a fanged Vajra-armour in his right hand. He is sitting on a lotus placed upon a hen. Big teeth are visible on both the sides. Mudrās given besides are named Vajrayakṣa-mahopāya-mudrā, (karma-mudrā) and Vajra-daṃṣṭra-mahā-cihna-mudrā. (TZ. 54.20).

TZ. 38.24

Vajra-yakṣa in mahā-maṇḍala of graphic Vajradhātu has the same hand posture as described by Tajima (TZ. 38.24, Lokesh Chandra 425). Both the fists are twisted and pressed towards his breast. *Hūm* is his seed syllable.

1.2.20. Vajrayakṣa has a serene mood in the second chapter of Gobu-shingan. He is holding a full blossomed lotus and upon the lotus are two fanged vajras (TZ. 54.58). As a guhya daṃṣṭra-dhāriṇī of vajra family Vajra-yakṣa is named *Tejaḥpratyāhāriṇī* (STTS 103). She is the third sarvadhāraṇī according to STTS. Vajrabandha, cihna-mudrā and the guhya-mudrā are the three mudrās given besides. Her dhāraṇī is: *Om guhya-vajra-danṣṭra-dhāriṇī hūm.*

1.2.20

TZ.54.58

TZ. 38.86

The drawing extracted here belongs to samaya-maṇḍala of Vajradhātu. Two vajras are placed upon a lotus. It may be a misunderstanding of the artist that fanged vajras are replaced by simple vajras. The only difference is that the middle-point is not bent (TZ. 38.86, Lokesh Chandra 491).

1.3.20. This portrait belongs to knowledge maṇḍala that is the third chapter of Gobu-shingan. Vajra-yakṣa is holding the same attribute, only his hand-posture is different as given in the previous drawing. This is the knowledge mudrā of destroying the maṇḍala of all evil beings : *sarva-māra-maṇḍala-vidhvansana-jñāna-mudrā* (TZ. 54.91 STTS 121). First and second mudrās are Vajra-bandha and cihna-mudrā as given in the previous chapter. Third does not occur in the preceded chapters so it can not be named. His dhāraṇī in STTS is : *Tiṣṭha vajra-yakṣa hṛdaya* (p. 121).

1.3.20

TZ. 38.159

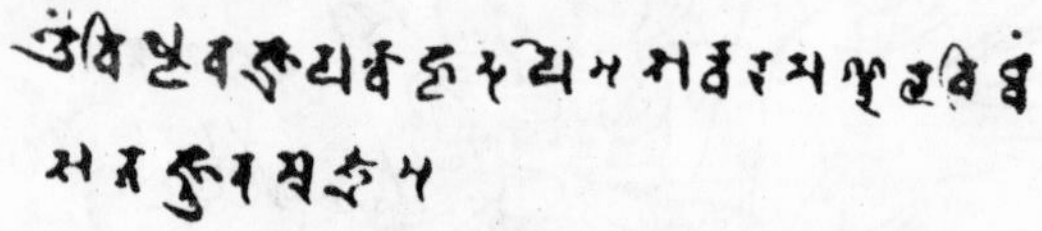

Tajima says that in Kongokai Vajra- yakṣa stretches his small fingers in crochats and touches the mouth, the index fingers are held upright in a manner that they touch cheeks, they represent teeth of yakṣa (p.183-184). In the given illustrations positions of fingers are the same but they are not touching his face. (TZ. 38.159, Lokesh Chandra 564). Position of thumbs is not described. It belongs to dharma-maṇḍala of graphic Vajradhātu. He is the third samādhi of All the Tathāgatas .

1.4.20. Vajra-yakṣa in the fourth chapter of Gobu-shingan has a fierce face expression. He holds a single Vajra-danṣṭra in his right hand. He is named cakṣuspati, may be because he has a third eye on his forehead. All the mudrās are identical with the he mudrās of the third chapter (TZ. 54.124). He is personified as the third karma-pūjā
1.4.20

TZ 54.124

who is related to the lamp which illuminates All the Tathāgatas : *om Sarvatathāgatālokajvālā-spharaṇa-pūjā-karme bhara bhara* (*STTS* 135). He is the third karma-pūjā. Because of his relation to lamp, he is named as cakṣuspati.

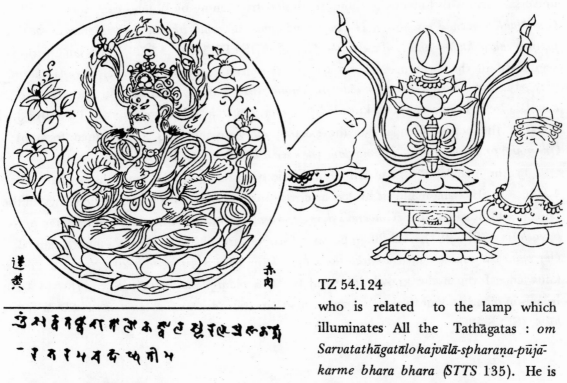

TZ. 38.232

In action-maṇḍala of graphic Vajradhātu Vajra-yakṣa holds a lotus flower. Two Vajras are placed upon a lotus (TZ.38.232, Lokesh Chandra 637).

In the maṇḍalas of Trailokyavijaya vajra-yakṣa belongs to the circle of Vajrāveśa. 2.1.20. In its samaya maṇḍala two Vajras are placed upon a lotus as they are in samaya-maṇḍala of Vajradhātu (TZ. 38.413). He has a devouring power according to the STTS (p.192-3) . *Om Vajra-yakṣa-krodha khāda khāda hūm phaṭ.* In Krodha-guhya-mudrā-maṇḍala he is called *Vajra-caṇḍa krodha, Mahā-yakṣiṇi, vajra-danṣṭra-karāla-bhīṣaṇī.* They are the distinguishing features of

Vajra-yakṣa. (STTS 216). 2.3.20. Vajra-yakṣa is called sūkṣma-vajra-yakṣa-krodha and Vajra-danṣṭra in vajrakula-dharma-jñāna-samaya-maṇḍala. He has a power of destroying and eating all the evil beings : *Om Sūkṣma-vajra-yakṣa-krodha hana bhakṣaya sarva-duṣṭān cintita-mātreṇa vajra-daṁṣ ṭra hūm phaṭ.* (*STTS227).*

2.4.20. In the fourth maṇḍala of Trailokyavijaya, the action-maṇḍala vajra-yakṣa is named vajra-yakṣiṇī : *Om vajra-yakṣiṇī maraya vajra-daṁṣṭrayabhinda hṛdayam amukasya hūm phaṭ* (STTS 239).

3.1.20. In mahā-maṇḍala of the Sakala-jagad-vinaya vajra has great violence, he has a universal form with hideous terifying teeth and frightening body who can horrify all : *Om Mahā-pracaṇḍa viśva-rūpa vikaṭa-padma-daṁṣṭra-karāla bhiṣaṇa-vaktra trāsaya sarvān padma-yakṣa khāda khāda dhik dhik dhik dhik* (STTS 325). 3.2.20. The same form is feminined in the next maṇḍala : *Om mahā-pracaṇḍi padma-yakṣiṇi viśva-rūpa-dhāriṇī bhiṣāpaya sarva-duṣṭān khāda khāda hūm phaṭ* (STTS 345). 3.3.20. In the knowledge-maṇḍala he is Padma-yakṣa of knowledge . *Om jñāna-padma-yakṣa hūm* (STTS 359). 3.4. 20. In the action maṇḍala of the sakala-jagad-vinaya he has a faminined form of a Om *mahā pracaṇḍi ghātanī padma-daṁṣṭra karma-kari hūm* (STTS 367).

In the maṇḍalas of Sarvārthasiddhi vajra-yakṣa belongs to maṇḍala of Ratnavṛṣṭi. 4.1.20. In its mahā-maṇḍala he has a terrific form because of his teeth,; he brings all the objects and horrifies all : *Om maṇi daṁṣṭra-karāla mahā-yakṣa hara hara sarvārthān bhīṣā-paya hūm* (STTS 392). 4.2.20. The same form occurs in the ratna-guhya-mudrā-maṇḍala : *Om vajra-maṇi-ratna-daṁṣṭra-karāle hara hara hūm* (STTS 408). 4.3.20. Yakṣa obtains a knowledge form in the knowledge-maṇḍala. *Om maṇi-jñāna-yakṣa* (STTS 418). 4.4.20. In action-maṇḍala Vajra-yakṣa is maṇi-ratnœ-daṁṣṭri : *Om mani-ratna daṁṣṭri khāda khāda hūm.* (STTS 426).

Names of Vajra-yakṣa in the sixteen maṇḍalas:

| Ch. | P. | Kula | Maṇḍala | Names. |
|---|---|---|---|---|
| 1. | 39-40 | Buddhakula | Vajradhātu-mahā-maṇḍala | Vajra-yakṣa, Sarvamāra-pramardī, Vajracaṇḍa. |
| 2. | 103 | " | Vajraguhya-vajramaṇḍala | Tejaḥ-pratyāhāriṇī. |
| 3. | 121 | " | Vajrajñāna-dharma-maṇḍala | Sarva-māra-maṇḍala-vidhvansana-mudrā. |
| 4. | 135 | " | Vajrakārya-karma-maṇḍala | Cakṣuṣpati, Sarvatathāgatā-loka-jvālā-spharaṇa-pūjā-karma. |
| 6. | 192-3 | Vajrakula | Trilokavijaya-mahā-maṇḍala. | Vajra-yakṣa-krodha. |
| 7. | 216 | " | Krodhaguhya-mudrā-maṇḍala | Vajra-caṇḍa-krodha, Mahā-yakṣiṇi, vajra-daṁṣṭra-karāla-bhīṣaṇī. |
| 8. | 227 | " | Vajrakula-dharmajñāna-samayamaṇḍala. | Sūkṣma-vajra-yakṣa-krodha. |
| 9. | 239 | " | Vajrakula-karmamaṇḍala | Vajra-yakṣiṇī. |
| 15. | 325 | Padmakula | Sakalajagadvinaya-mahā-maṇḍala | Mahā-pracaṇḍa, vikaṭa-padma-daṁṣṭra-karāla. |
| 16. | 345 | " | Padmaguhya-mudrā-maṇḍala. | Mahā-pracaṇḍi-padma-yakṣiṇī. |
| 17. | 359 | " | Jñānamaṇḍala | Jñāna-padma-yakṣa. |
| 18. | 367 | " | Karmamaṇḍala | Mahā-pracaṇḍi, Padma-daṁṣṭra. |
| 19. | 392 | Ratnakula | Sarvārthasiddhi-mahā-maṇḍala. | Maṇi-daṁṣṭra-karāla-mahā-Yakṣa. |
| 20. | 408 | " | Ratnaguhya-mudrāmaṇḍala | Vajra-maṇi-daṁṣṭra-karāla. |
| 21. | 418 | " | Jñānamaṇḍala | Maṇi-jñāna-yakṣa. |
| 22. | 426 | " | Karmamaṇḍala | Maṇi-ratna-daṁṣṭri. |

## 21. VAJRASANDHI
金剛拳菩薩

Mahābodhisattva Vajrasandhi has a seat in the northern direction. Sandhi signifies to close hands, to form a fist (muṣṭi). The heart of bodhi having been awakened, on account of Vajrasattva, the stages represented by the fifteen preceding bodhisattvas being crossed and the state of Buddha having been obtained. Vajrasandhi represents possession of all the virtues symbolysed by his hands that strike firmly. He is of blue colour. Both of his hands are closed and pressed against his breast, arms are bent a little and hand against trunk (Tajima 184).

Vairocana enters the samadhi called action-consecration-vajra which has its origin in samaya of Sarvatathāgata-muṣṭi-mahābodhisattva *Sarvatathāgata-muṣṭi-mahābodhisattva-samaya-sambhava-karmādhiṣṭhāna-vajram* and utters the seed syllable of All the Tathāgatas from his heart named Vajrabandha samaya of the body, mind and speech *Sarvatathāgatakāya-vāk-citta-vajra-bandha-samaya-vajra-samādhi.* As he utters this Vajradhara emerges as a multiplicity of hand gestures *mudrābandhaḥ*, enters the heart of Vairocana which coalesce into a single one on vairocana's hand. From this Buddha-forms stream forth into space and having performed magical acts associated with the knowledge of gestures of All the Tathāgatas they become one in the form of Bodhisattva Sarvatathāgatamuṣṭi, who recites this verse: 'O ho I am the very firm bond, the secramental pledge of firm minded ones, which consists in binding of those who are free with the purpose of I.1.21.

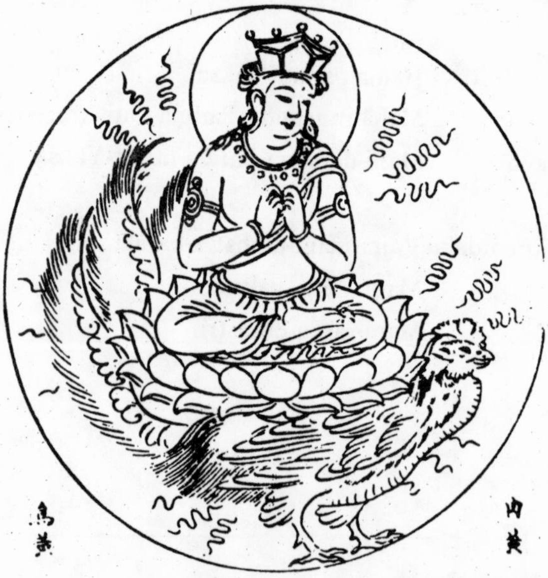

TZ.54.21

succeeding in all aspirations".

He is the form of Muṣṭi Mahābodhisattva emerges from the heart of Vairocana, stations himself in the back lunar disc of All the Tathāgatas and pays respects. Bhagavān once again enters the samādhi called the samaya-vajra and gives the vajra-bandha to Mahābodhisattva Muṣṭi in his hands for the knowledge of all the mudrās. Then he is consecrated with the vajra-name consecration as vajramuṣṭi. Mahāsattva vajramuṣṭi binding All the Tathāgatas by the help of vajramuṣṭi utters this verse: "This is the hand gesture exceedingly firm, of All the Buddhas, the secremental pledge for success in all Buddha aspirations which is so hard to transgress". (STTS 41-42). One becomes perfected in all symbolic gestures, thanks to the binding of vajramuṣṭi

I.1.21. Vajramuṣṭi in the first chapter of Gobu-shingan is riding a hen both of his fists are pressed against his breast (TZ 54.21). The first from of the right is vajra-muṣṭi-mahāsandhi-mudrā the second is action and the third is vajra-sandhi-mahācihna-mudrā.

I.2.21 TZ.38.25

Vajramuṣṭi in mahā-maṇḍala of graphic vajradhātu has the same hand gesture as described above (TZ.38.25, Lokesh Chandra 430).

I.2.21. Vajrasandhi is twice named as Dhāraṇī-mudrā and karma-dhāraṇī in the second chapter of Gohu-shingan (TZ.54.59). He is holding his attribute vajramuṣṭi which is placed on a lotus. Both of the fists are holding a two sided three pointed vajra, dhāraṇī is. *Om vajra-gahya-muṣṭi hūm* (STTS 103). This is feminined form of vajrasandhi

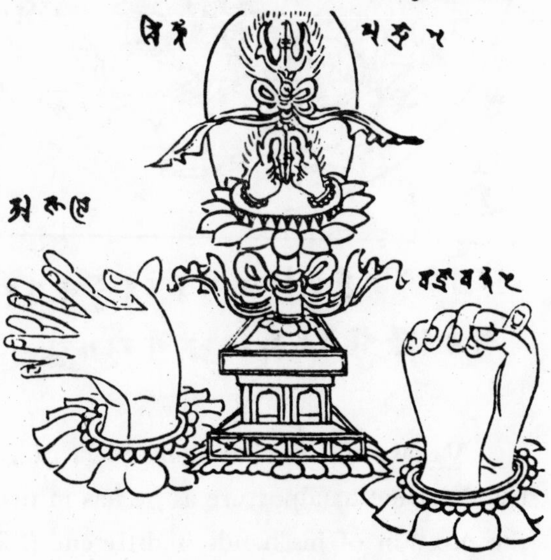

named dharani-mudra in STTS she is named as sarvadhāraṇī. Mudrās are Vajrabandha, cihna-mudrā and añjali respectively.

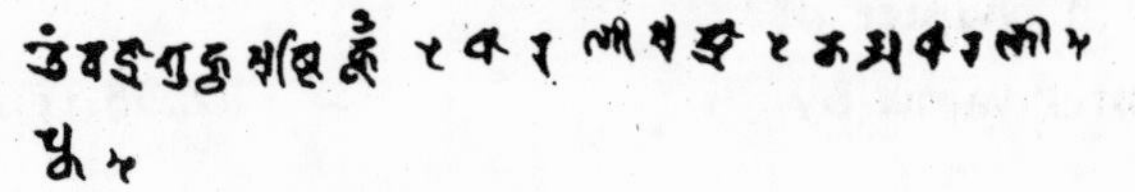

Dual fist is the symbol of Vajra-

TZ.38.87

muṣṭi. The drawing given here belongs to the samaya maṇḍala of Vajradhātu. (TZ.38.87, Lokesh Chandra 492)

I.3.12. As the last karmasamādhi of All the Tathāgatas vajra-muṣṭi called the mudrā of knowledge of binding All the Tathāgatas: *Sarvatathāgata-bandha-jñāna-mudrā* (SITS 121). He is praised as *vajra muṣṭi hṛdaya.* In the third chapter of Gobu-shingan he is holding a lotus whereupon a single pointed viśva-vajra is placed. The first mudrā is identical with the first mudrās in the first and second chapters, the second is cihna-mudrā and third is action mudrā as given in the first chapter (TZ.54.92).

I.3.12

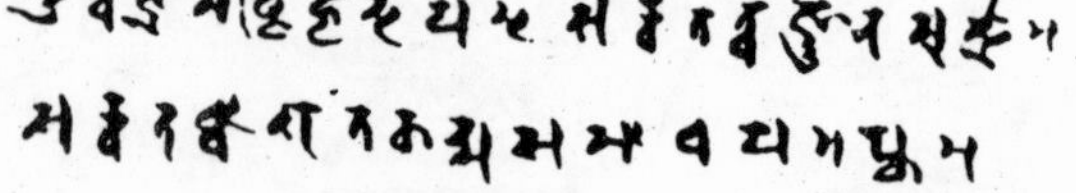

TZ.54.92

TZ.38.160

Vajrasandhi is dharma-maṇḍala of graphic vajradhātu has the same handposture as he has in mahā-maṇḍala, only the position of his hands is different (TZ.38.160, Lokesh Chandra 565).

I.4.21. As the last karmapūjā of All the Tathāgatas vajrasandhi is named Gandhavatī in the fourth chapter of the Gobu-shingan. He holds two single-pointed-vajras by

TZ.54.125

both of his fists (TZ.54.125). The script under the illustration runs as follows: *Om Sarvathāgata-gandha-samudra - spharaṇa - pūjā - karma kuru. Gandhavati Sarvatathāgata-karmapūjā.* It corresponds to STTS (135). Mudrās are the same as illustrated before except the middle one. They are vajrabandha, cihna-mudrā and karma-mudrā respectively.

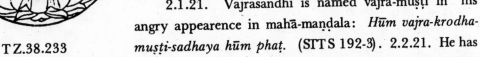

TZ.38.233

Two fists are drawn upon a lotus flower which is held by both of his hands. This is Vajrasandhi in action-maṇḍala of graphic vajradhātu (TZ.38.233, Lokesh Chandra 638).

In all the four maṇḍalas of Trailokya-vijaya he belongs to the cirlce of vajravesa.

2.1.21. Vajrasandhi is named vajra-muṣṭi in his angry appearence in mahā-maṇḍala: *Hūm vajra-krodha-muṣṭi-sadhaya hūm phaṭ.* (STTS 192-3). 2.2.21. He has a binding power according to krodha-guhya-mudrā-maṇḍala: *Om vajra-krodha-muṣṭi-bandha-hṇīḥ* (STTS 216). Two fists on a lotus are drawn in its samaya-maṇḍala as it is in samaya-maṇḍala of vajradhātu (TZ.38.414, Lokesh Chandra 813).

2.3.21. He has a subtle form in the Vajrakula-dharma-jñāna-samaya-maṇḍala: *Om sūkṣma-vajra muṣṭi-krodha bandha bandha hūm phaṭ.* (STTS 227). 2.4.21. According to action-maṇḍala of vajrakula he accomplishes: *Om vajra-karma-muṣṭi siddhaya siddhaya hūm phaṭ* (STTS 239). Vajrasandhi in karma maṇḍala of Trailokya-vijaya is sitting on a lotus with his hands crossed across his breast (TZ.38.337, Lokesh Chandra 744).

3.1.21. Vajra-muṣṭi of Trailokyavijaya-mahā-maṇḍala becomes Padma-muṣṭi in mahā-maṇḍala of sakalajagad-vinaya: *Om padma-muṣṭi-samayastvam bandha hūm phaṭ* (STTS 325). 3.2.21. In guhya-mudrā-maṇḍala of lotus family is a lotus-fist: *Om padma-muṣṭi-aḥ hūm.* The deity has a knowledge and action form in knowledge and action maṇḍalas respectively: *Om jñāna-padma-muṣṭi hūm* (STTS 359) 3.4.21. and *Om Padma-karma-muṣṭi ghātaya hūm* (STTS 367).

4.1.21. Binding is a characteristic of Vajra-sandhi, thus he is named ratna-bandha in mahā-maṇḍala of Sarvārthasiddhi: *Om maṇi-ratna-bandha-samaya hūm* (STTS 392). 4.2.21. In guhya-mudrā-maṇḍala of gem family he is called the subtle fist of gem family: *Om maṇi-samaya-muṣṭi hūm* (STTS 408). 4.3.21. Knowledge and 4.4.21. action are added to his names in the next two maṇḍalas: *Om Maṇi-jñāna-muṣṭi* (STTS 418) and *Om maṇi-ratna-karma-muṣṭi hūm* (STTS 426).

Names of Vajra-sandhi in the sixteen maṇḍalas:

| Ch. | P. | Kula | Maṇḍala | Names |
|---|---|---|---|---|
| 1. | 41-42 | Buddhakula | Vajradhātu-mahā-maṇḍala | Vajra-muṣṭi, Vajrasandhi, Muṣṭi. Mahābodhisattva. |
| 2. | 103 | " | Vajraguhya-vajramaṇḍala | Dhāraṇi-mudrā, Vajra-guhya-muṣṭi |
| 3. | 121 | " | Vajrajñāna-dharma-maṇḍala | Sarvatathāgata-bandha-jñāna-mudrā. |
| 4. | 135 | " | Vajrakārya-karma-maṇḍala | Sarvatathāgata-gandha-samudra-spharaṇa-pūjā-karmā. |
| 6. | 192-3 | Vajrakula | Trilokavijaya-mahā-maṇḍala. | Vajra-krodha-muṣṭi. |
| 7. | 216 | " | Krodhaguhya-mudrā-maṇḍala. | Vajra-krodha-muṣṭi. |
| 8. | 226 | " | Vajrakula-dharmajñāna-samayamaṇḍala. | Sūkṣma-vajra-muṣṭi-krodha. |
| 9. | 239 | " | Vajrakula-karmamaṇḍala | Vajra-karma-muṣṭi. |
| 15. | 325 | Padmakula | Sakalajagadvinaya-mahā-maṇḍala. | Padma-muṣṭi-samaya. |
| 16. | 345 | " | Padmaguhya-mudrā-maṇḍala. | Padma-muṣṭi. |
| 17. | 359 | " | Jñānamaṇḍala | Jñāna-padma-muṣṭi. |
| 18. | 367 | " | Karmamaṇḍala | Padma-karma-muṣṭi. |
| 19. | 392 | Ratnakula | Sarvārthasiddhi-mahā-maṇḍala. | Maṇi-ratna-bandha-samaya. |
| 20. | 408 | " | Ratnaguhya-mudrā-maṇḍala. | Maṇi-samaya-muṣṭi. |
| 21. | 418 | " | Jñānamaṇḍala | Maṇi-jñāna-muṣṭi. |
| 22. | 426 | " | Karmamaṇḍala | Maṇi-ratna-karma-muṣṭi. |

## 22. SATTVAVAJRI

金剛波羅蜜菩薩

Bodhisattvas that surround the great Buddhas symbolicse their dhyāna, they are also represented in the feminine form of asparas, wearing a superior garment with curbed, sleeves They are considered to be the matter of next great Buddha. The relationship is indicated by their names. Hizoki says vajrapārmitā is of blue black colour. With her right hand she carries a lotus on which there is one little trunk (with sūtras), her right hand makes the mudrā of Akṣobhya bhūmisparsá mudrā. As the sūtra held up by the left hand is Prajñāpāramitāsūtra she symbolises something like the genetic mother . she is the mother of Akṣobhya, who sits to the east of vairocana. Making the same as Akṣobhya does, she presonifies the corresponding dhyāna, of the sapience of the big round mirror ādarśasaṁjñāna (Tajima 173-174).

Tathāgata Akṣobhya produces the knowledge of Tathāgata vairocana, enters the samādhi called the vajra-consecration which has its origin in the samaya of vajra pāramitā for sealing the knowledge of All the Tathāgatas Sarvatathāgatajñāna mudraṇārtham and utters the mudrā of All the Tathāgatas named Vajra-pledge of All the Tathāgatas. As he utters this vajra-rays emerge from the hearts of All the Tathāgatas. And out of the rays come Bhagavān vajradhara in the form of Tathāgatas which coalesce into a single great vajra, stations itself in the back lunar disc of Vairocana and utters this verse: 'O ho I am the strong sattva vajra of All the Buddhas, which is formless because of its firmness, but it has a form of Vajra" (SITS 43).

I.1.22. Sattva-vajra is vajra-sattvi in the first chapter of Gobu-shingan. She is riding

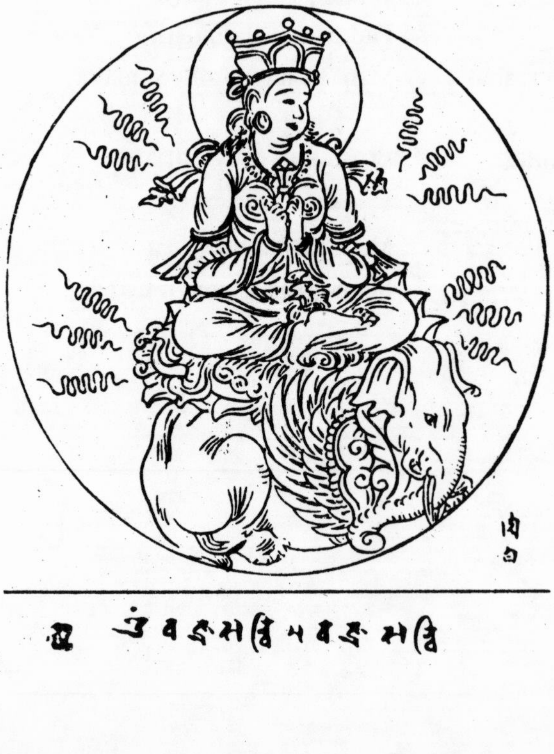

TZ.54.22

an elephant and holding a Vajra by both of her hands. Vajra is not distinct in the illustration but is distinct from cihna-

TZ.38.2

mudrā, the third among the mudrās given here. The first and the second are vajrasattvi-mahā-mudrā and karma-mudrā (TZ.54.22).

Vajrasattvī in mahā-maṇḍala of graphic vajra-dhātu is sitting on a lotus. She has her right hand in bhūmisparśa mudrā and her left fist is twisted and pressed against her breast as if it is to hold something (TZ.38.2).

I.2.22. Sattva-vajrī in the second chapter ot Gobu-shingan is vajrapāramitā. This is her esoteric from: *Om-guhya sattva-vajri hūm* (STTS 104, TZ.54.60). She is holding a viśva-vajra upon a lotus

I.2.22

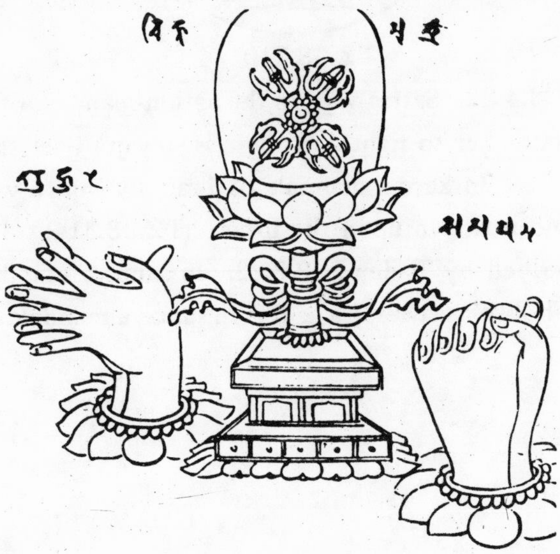

TZ.54.60

supported by both of her hands. The mudrās given here are samaya, cihna and guhya mudrās respectively from right to left.

Sattva-vajrī holds a vajra which shows her śakti. Thus vajra symbolises sattva-vajrī.

It is drawn in samaya maṇḍala of vajradhātu (TZ.38.64).

I.3.22. The second drawing given above of sattva-vajra belongs to knowledge maṇḍala of vajradhātu. She is holding a lotus with a vajra upon it in her left hand and the right is in bhūmisparśa mudrā (TZ.38.137).

TZ.38.210

TZ.38.314

I.4.22. Sattva-vajrī in the action-maṇḍala of vajradhātu holds a lotus stem, lotus is bent towards her to right and there is a vajra over there in the second illustration (TZ.38.210). 2.4.22. In karma maṇḍala of Trailokyavijaya vajra-sattvī is holding a lotus and something round is drawn upon the lotus. (TZ.38.314). It can be misdrawing of a trunk of sūtras as described by Tajima. 2.2.22. In samaya maṇḍala of Trailokyavijaya a vajra upon a lotus symbolises sattva-vajra as it is in samaya maṇḍala of the vajradhātu (TZ.38.391).

## 23. RATNAVAJRĪ

寶波羅蜜菩薩

Ratnavajrī is bodhisattva Ratnapāramitā. She is in the south of Vairocana. She holds a jem on a lotus by her left hand and by her right hand a cakra of gold in the shape of lozenge. She is of bright yellow colour. An image confirming to this description is found in the mandala of Takao. She makes varadamudrā like Ratnasambhava, the great Buddha who sits to the south of Vairocana and personifies to dhyana of sapience of quality of nature samatā-jñāna (Tajina 174).

Tathagata Ratnasambhava enters the samādhi called the vajra-consecration which has its origin in the samaya of Ratnapāramitā *Ratnapāramitāsamayasambhavajrādhiṣṭhāna* for stamping the knowledge of All the Tathāgatas *sarvathāgatajñānamudrāṇārtham* and utters his own mudrā which is the samaya of vajraratna *vajraratna-samayam Ratnavajrī.* As soon as he utters these words gem-rays emerge from the hearts of All the Tathāgatas. This is proceeded by obtaining the form of Tathāgatas by Vajradhara from the gem-rays, which coalesce into a single Vajra-gem, stations himself in the back lunar disc of Vairocana and utters this verse: 'O ho I am the pure dharma-vajra of All the Buddhas, even I am passionate still because of pure nature I am away from impurities". (SITS 544).

I.2.23. The first chapter of Gobu-shingan names her as Ratnavajram and Ratnasattvī: *Om ratnavajram. ratnasattvī.* She is riding a horse and holding a cintāmaṇī encircled I..1.23.

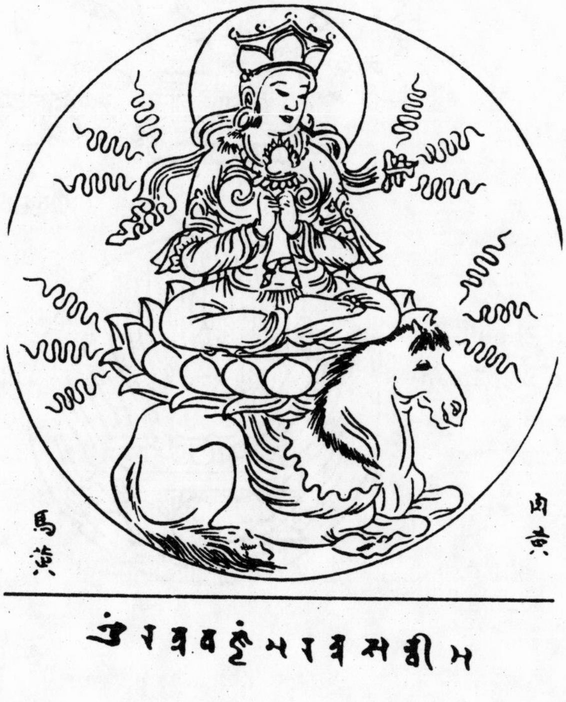

TZ.54.23

by flames placed upon a lotus (TZ.54.23). Mudrās are mahācintāmaṇi and cihna-mudrā.

Ratnavajrī in mahāmaṇḍala of vajra-

TZ.38.3

dhātu has a gem placed upon her right palm and in her left hand she has a gem on a lotus. She is sitting on a lotus (TZ.38.3).

I.2.23. The second chapter of Gobu-shingan personifies Ratnavajri as the estoric form of ratnavajra: *Om guhya ratna-vajra ratnavajra.* She is holding a garland made of vajras, placed upon a lotus, supported by both of her hands. Mudrās from the right are vajrabandha, vajramālācihna-mudrā and the guhya vajrāñjali (TZ.54.61).

A cintāmaṇi as a symbol of ratnavajra is placed upon a lotus in samaya maṇḍala of graphic vajradhātu

I.2.22.

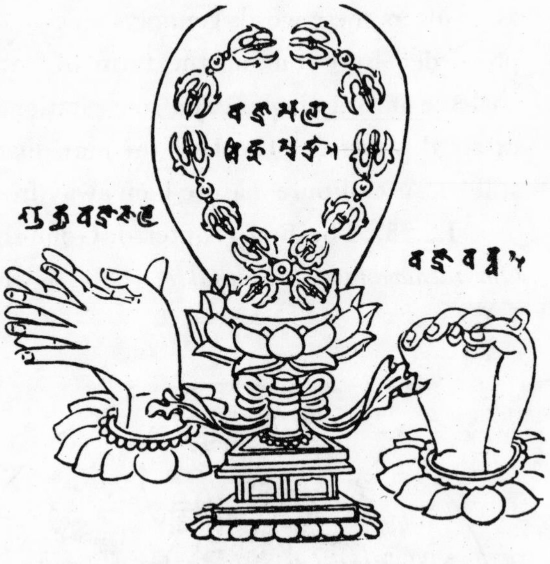

TZ.54.61

(TZ.38.65). According to SITS ratnavajrī should be placed in the lunar disc with flames in the mahāmaṇḍala of Vajradhātvīśvarī (SITS 104).

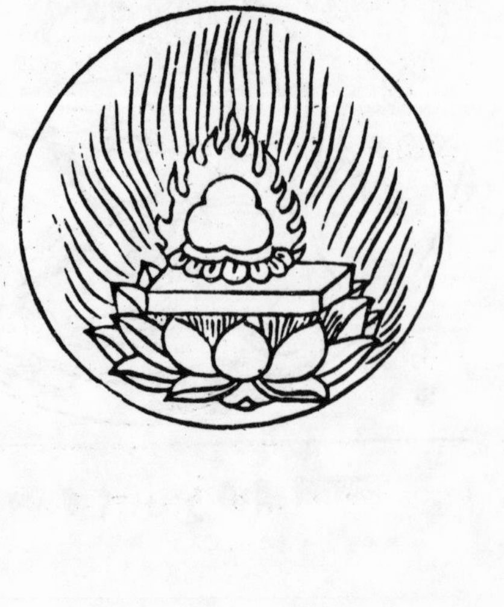

TZ.38.138

TZ.38.211

I.3.23. Here is a drawing of Ratnavajrī in knowledge-maṇḍala of graphic vajradhātu. She has a gem on a lotus which is held by her left hand and the right is in varada posture (TZ.38.138). I.4.23. Ratnavajrī in action maṇḍala of Vajradhātu is holding a lotus with cintāmaṇī by both of her hands (TZ.38.211).

2.2.23, 2.4.23. These are the illustrations of Ratnavajrī in karma and samaya maṇḍalas of the Trailokyavijaya. In the first she holds a gem on a lotus and her hand is open flat upwords (TZ.38. 315). The second shows a cakra which is drawn in samaya maṇḍala of Trailokyavijaya (TZ.38.392) Tajima mentions a wheel as one of her attributes as described before.

## 24. PADMAVAJRĪ

法波羅蜜菩薩

Bhagavan Lokeśvararāja enters the samādhi called the vajra-concentration which has its origin in the samaya of Dharmapāramitā and utters the Dharmasamaya mudrā from the heart: *Dharma-vajra..* As soon as he says thus, lotus rays emerge from the hearts of All the Tathāgatas, vajradhara attains the form of a great vajra-lotus from these lotus-rays. He stations himself in the back lunar disc of Lord Vairocana and speaks this verse: "O ho I am the pure religious vajra of all the Buddhas. Even it is passionate still because of its pure nature it is away from all impuriteis"

I.1.24.

TZ.54.24

I.1.24. Dharmavajrī in the first chapter of the Gobu-shingan is named as Dharmavajra and Padmasattvi under the illustration. She is holding a vajra-lotus by both of her hands and riding a peacock (TZ.54.24). The first from the right is the great hand-posture of vajra-lotus. Second is not named and the third is hys symbolic mudrā

Padmasattvī is the personification of Dharmavajrī in mahā-maṇḍala of Vajradhātu (TZ.38.4). She is holding a book on a lotus bent towards her left.

TZ.38.4

I.2.24.

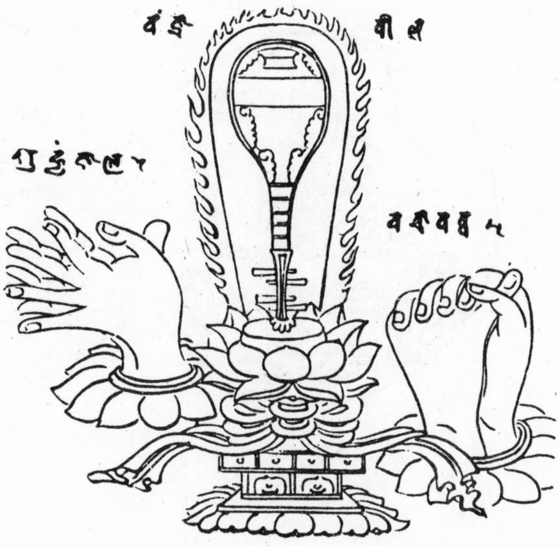

TZ.54.22

I.2.24. In the second chapter of Gobu-shingan Dharmavajrī is holding a musical instrument *Vīṇā* placed upon a lotus as it is with her verse under the illustration is: *Om guhya-dharma-vajra hūm.* But in STTS she is called as *Dharma-vajrī* (STTS 104).

A vajra with a lotus over head is placed upon a lotus in samaya-maṇḍala of Vajradhātu (TZ.38.66).

TZ.38.66

TZ.38.139

TZ.38.212

I.3.24, I.4.24, These are the two illustrations of Dharmravajrī as padmasattvī

TZ.38.316

in Lotus and action-maṇḍalas of Vajradhātu (TZ.38. 139, 212). In the first illustration she is holding a vajra in her lap and in the next she has a vajra-lotus upon a lotus.

2.4.24. The illustration extracted here belongs to the karma maṇḍala of Trailokya-vijaya. She has a lotus in her hands. (TZ.38.316).

## 25. KARMAVAJRĪ

羯磨波羅蜜菩

Karmavajrī or Karmapāramitā sits to the North of Vairocana. She is of blue colour and holds a trunk over a lotus by her left hand and by her right hand a four pointed vajra (karma-vajra). She personifies the dhyāna of the sapience *kṛtyanuṣṭāhajñāna*, as indicated by her attributes (Γ ajina 174).

Amoghasiddhi enters the samādhi named vajra-consecration which has its origin in the samaya of karmapāramitā and utters the action-pledge of All the Tathāgatas: *Karmavajrī.* Soon all the action rays emerge from the hearts of All the Tathāgatas and from these rays vajradhara becomes great action-vajra. He stations himself in the left lunar disc of Vairocana and utters this verse : "Oho I am the action-vajra of All the Buddhas who is one but skillful in action of all the sattva-dhātus". (SΓΓ S 46).

I.1.25. Karma-vajra in the first chapter of Gobu-shingan. She has a viśva-vajra supported by both of her hands. She is riding a hen, under the illustration she is named as I.1.25

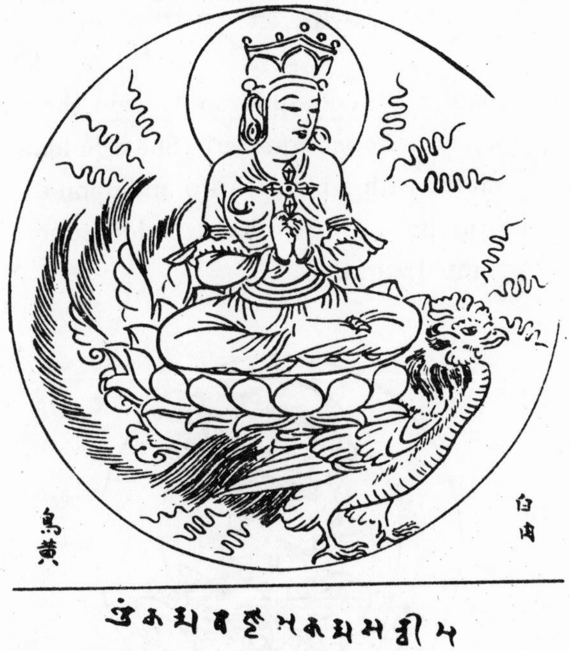

Γ Z.54.25

Karmasattvī.

The drawing belongs to mahāmaṇḍala of the graphic vajradhātu. A viśvavajra is placed upon her right palm and in her left she has a lotus flower (Γ Z.38.5). A rising moon with a disc is shown upon her forehead and upon the lotus held by her there is a figure which resembled it.

I.2.25. In vajra-guhya-vajra-maṇḍala of the STT S she is the esoteric form of karma-vajrī *Om Guhya-karma-vajrī hūm* (STT S 104). The same mantra is cited in the second I.2.25.

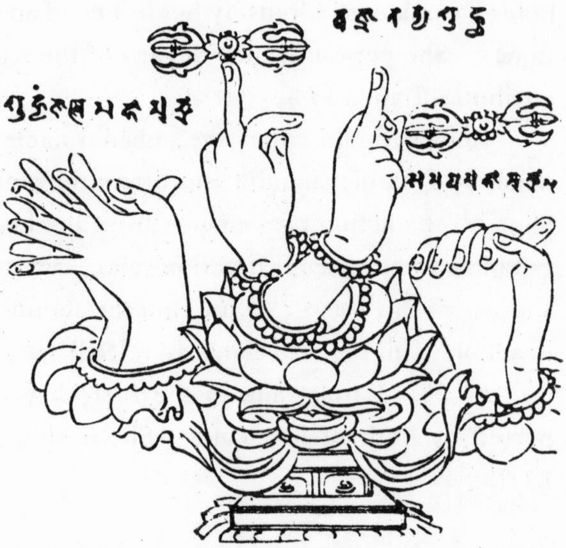

TZ.54.53

chapter of Gobu-shingan. Again she is named as *karmavajreśvarī.* She is holding a lotus with a big pericarp and upon the lotus there are two hands holding three pointed vajras.

T Z.38.67

T Z.38.140

A viśva-vajra placed upon a lotus is drawn in samaya maṇḍala of graphic vajra-dhātu (T Z.38.67).

I.3.25. In knowledge-maṇḍala of vajradhātu karmasattvī is doing a mudrā by her right hand and in her left hand she is holding a lotus with a viśvavajra. (T Z.38.140)

T Z.38.213

T Z.38.217

I.4.25. The drawing extracted here belongs to action-maṇḍala of vajradhātu. The divinity has the same attribute, a lotus with a viśvavajra (TZ 38.213).

2.4.25. In Trailokya-vijaya-karma-maṇḍala her attributes resemble that of knowledge-maṇḍala. Her right palm is opened flat upwards and in her left she has a lotus. (T Z.38.317).

2.2.25. This is again a viśvavajra in samaya-maṇḍala of Trailokya-vaijaya in the graphic vajradhātu but it is in a stylised form (T Z.38.394)

## 26 VAJRALĀSYĀ

金剛嬉菩薩

Bodhisattva Vajralāsyā sits in the southeast. It is consecrated by Vairocana to Akṣobhya . Buddha personifies the consolidation of bodhicitta and Vajralāsī, for praising the happiness of awakening the heart of bodhi, it is a bodhisattva of joyful appearence (T ajima 184-5 ) Vajralāsyā is the first interior pūjā-bodhisattva. Vairocana enters the samādhi called the vajra which has its origin in the samaya of Ratipūjā of All the Tathāgatas and utters Vajralāsyā, mahādevī of T athāgata-kula. Vajramudrās emerge from the hearts of All the T athāgatas as he says this .From these vajramudrās, Vajradhara becomes *Vajrasattvadayitā,* stations himself in the lunar disc towards the left of the maṇḍala of Akṣobhya and recites this verse: 'T here is no worship which can equal her, as all types of worship are initiated by the worship of Kāmarati. ( SΓΓ S 47) .

1.1.26.T he first chapter of Gobu-shingan says: Om vajramāle, vajramālā guhya-devī 1.1.26

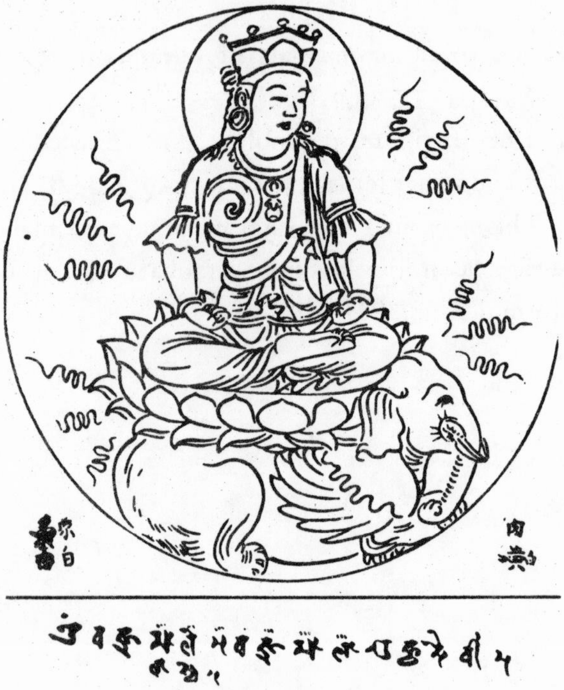

T Z.54.26

lasya. She has placed both of her twisted fists upon her thighs and is riding an elephant. (Γ Z.54.26) Γ he first mudrā is named as mahāmudrā of Vajralāsyā and Vajramālā. T he second and the third are action and symbolic mudrās. ( Vajramālā can be a wrong dhāraṇī here ) .T he hand posture described above is a bit different in this drawing extracted from mahā-maṇḍala of the graphic Vajradhātu. ( Γ Z.38,26, Lokesh Chandra 431) .

1.2.26. As mentioned in the first chapter of STT S she initiates all the worships.. In vajraguhya-vajra-maṇḍala she has an esoteric form as vajra-guhya-rati-pūjā-samaya : *Om vajra-guhya-rati-pūjā-samaya-sarva-pūjām pravartaya hūm*( SΓΓ S 104).

The picture given here belongs to samaya-maṇḍala of the graphic Vajradhātu. The vajra is a bit bent to have feel of dancing (Γ Z.38.88, Lokesh Chandra 493).

1.3.26. In the third chapter of the Gobu-shingan Lāsyā has a knowledge form, there she is named as Sarvatathāgatajñāna rati and Jañānalāsyā

1.3.26

Γ Z 54 97

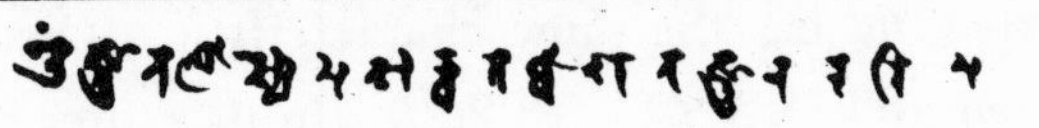

She has a vajra upon a Vajra supported by both of her hands in her lap (TZ54.97). Mudras are not named. The knowledge maṇḍala of the graphic Vajradhātu has Vajralāyā in the same posture as given before in its mahāmaṇḍala ( Γ Z.38.161, Lokesh Chandra 566).

1.4.2.6. Vajralāsyā in action-maṇḍala of the graphic Vajradhātu is holding a lotus with a vajra upon it (T Z.38.234, Lokesh Chandra 639).

1.4.26. The fourth chapter of Gobu-shingan personify Vajra-lāsyā as Sarvatathāgata-rati-ratā. She is not dealt with in the Vajra-kārya karma-maṇḍala of the STT S. Here she has single ponted vajras in both of her hands which is distinctly shown in the mudrā given in 1.4.26

TZ.54.126

middle. She is praised in the following words : *Om Sarvatathātata lāsya pūjā megha samanta spharaṇa samaya hūm sarvatathāgatarati-ratā.* ( T Z.554 126) .

The first and the third mudrās are the same as given in the third chapter.

The form of vajralāsyā in karma maṇḍala of Trailokya-vijaya ( T Z.38.338,Lokesh Chandra 745) resembles the first and the third chapters of Gobu-shingan and the samaya form is identical to the samaya maṇḍala of the graphic Vajradhātu. 2.1.26. Vajralāsyā has a power of impassionating according to mahā-maṇḍala of Trailokyavijaya : *Om vajra-lāsya samaya hūm phaṭ* (STTS 193).

3.1.26. In mahā-maṇḍala of sakala-jagad-vinaya she has the same characteristic : *Om Padma-lāsya samaya mahādevi rāga-pūjā-samaya hūm* (STTS 326) 3.2.26. In its esoteric mudrā maṇḍala worship of rati of the lotus families : *Om Padma-rati-pūjā hūm* (STT S 345) . 3.3.26. She has a knowledge form in knowledge maṇḍala: *Om jnana-padma-lasya hum.* (STT S 359 ) . 3.4.26. In action maṇḍala she is called Rati-pūjā : *Om Rati-pūjā hūm* (STT S 368) . Among the maṇḍalas of sarvārthasiddhi only mahā and action maṇḍala mention her as follows : *Om Maṇi-ratna-lāsya pūjaya hoḥ* ( STT S 426) .

## 27. VAJRAMĀLĀ

金剛鬘菩薩

Vajramālā has a seat in the south-west. He is offered by Vairocana to Ratnasambhava. This Buddha personifies the embelishment of the bliss of asceticism, Bodhisattva holds some garlands. He is of yellow colour. He decorates himself with precious garland of flowers. In kongokai he hangs up the garland by both of his hands (Tajima 185). Once again Vairocana enters the samādhi called the vajra which has its origin in the samaya of garland conscreation of All the Tathāgatas and utters Vajramālā as a mahādevī of the Tathāgatakula. As he says thus, mudrās of great gems emerge from the hearts of All the Tathāgatas and from these mudrās vajradhara obtains the form of mahādevī Vajramālā. He gets a seat in the full lunar disc towards the left of Ratnasambhava maṇḍala and recites this verse : 1.1.27.

TZ.54.27

Oho I am the incomparable who calls the gem-worship, who is worshipped in all the three worlds (SIT S 48).

1.1.27. She is mentioned as an estoeric goddess in first chapter of Gobu-shingan : Om *vajramālā, vajramāla-guhya-devī*. She is holding a garland by both of her hands and riding a horse. In her mudrās the first is mahā-mudrā of vajramālā (ha - is missing here), next two are action mudrās.

(T Z.54.27) . Vajramālā as extracted above from the mahā-maṇḍala of graphic vajradhātu (T Z.38.27, Lokesh Chandra 432) is holding a garland in the same manner as in the first chapter of Gobu-shingan.

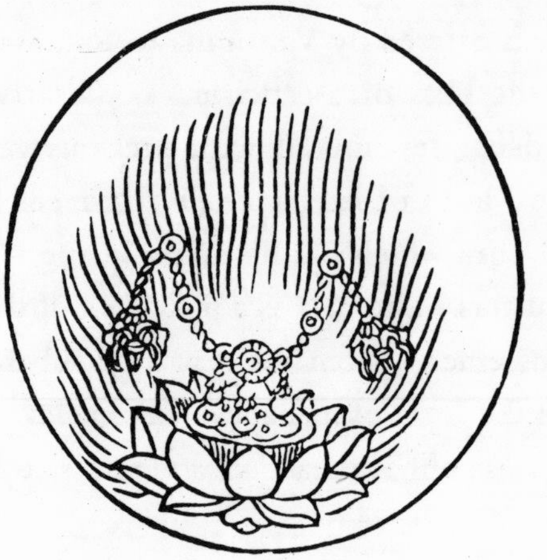

1.2.27. A garland placed upon a lotus is the samaya or symbolic form of Vajramālā in the samaya maṇḍala of graphic Vajradhātu (T Z.38.89, Lokesh Chandra 494). Vajra-guhya-vajra-maṇḍala of STTS calls her as the esoteric form of consecration worship of Vajraguhya : *Om vajra-guhyābhiṣeka-pūjā samaya sarva-pūjām pravartaya hūm*. (STTS 104).

← T Z.38.89

1.3.27.

T Z.54.98

1.3.27. The second chapter of Gobu-shingan does not mention Vajramālā. Its third chapter draws her as a divinity with a garland made of Viśva-vajras placed upon a lotus. She is named as knowledge-garland of All the Tathāgatas : *Om Sarvatathāgatajñānamālā. Sarvatathāgata-jñānamālā* (T Z.

54.98) . Mudrās are not named. The above-given drawing of Vajramālā belongs to knowledge-maṇḍala of graphic Vajradhātu (Γ Z.38.162 Lokesh Chandra 567) . The same attribute, a garland is held by both of her hands.

1.4.27.

T Z.54.127

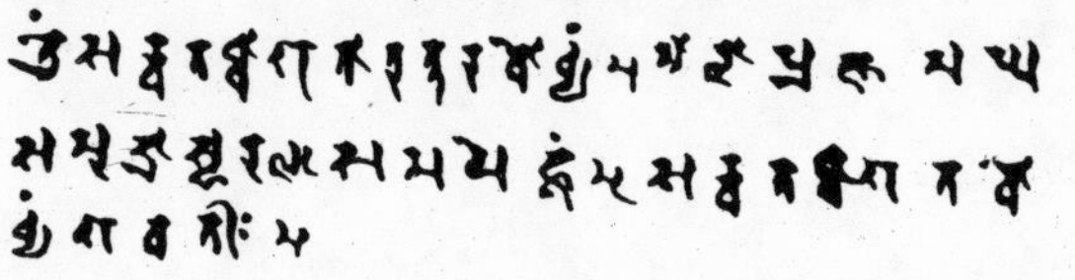

1.4.27. Last in Gobu-shingan is its fourth chapter. Again there is a garland in her hands in the form of Sarvatathāgata-bodhyaṅga-vatī : *Om Sarvatathāgatānuttarabodhyam. mālāpūjāmegha-samudra-spharaṇa samaya hūm sarvatathāgata-bodhyaṅgavatī* (Γ Z.54.127) . Mudrās are the same as given before but they are not named.

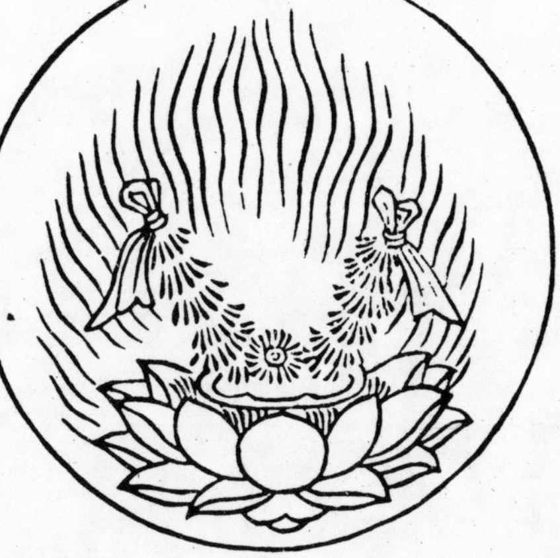

Γ Z.38.416

Vajramālā in karma maṇḍala of Trailokya-vijaya ( Γ Z.38.339,) has the same attributes her power of consecration : *Om Vajramālā 'bhiṣiñca hūm phaṭ* ( STTS 193). Krodha-guhya-mudrā-maṇḍala gives only her essence : *Vajra hūm ghum* ( STTS 216) . The illustration given here belongs to the samaya-maṇḍala of Trailokyavijaya (T Z.38. 416) .

In the maṇḍalas of sakala-jagad-vinaya she is called Lotus-garland who has a power of consecration. 3.1.27. Thus in mahā-maṇḍala she is called the samaya of consecration-worship : *Om padma-māle bhiṣiñcābhiṣeka pūjā samaya hūm* ( ( STTS 326) . 3.2.27. In guhya mudrā-maṇḍala of lotus family she is the consecration worship : *Om padmābhiṣeka pūjā raṭ* ( SΓΓ S 345) . 3.3.27. In knowledge maṇḍala she is the knowledge form of lotus-garland : *Om jāna-padma-māle hūm* ( SΓΓ S 359) . 3.4.27. Again she is consecration worship in the action maṇḍala : *Om abhiṣeka pūjā hūm* ( SΓΓ S 368) . 4.1.27. In mahā and 4.4.27. action maṇḍalas of Sarvārthasiddhi Vajra-mālā is Ratna-mālā : *Om ratna-māle hūm* ( SΓΓ S 392) and maṇiratna-mālābhiṣekā : *Om Maṇi-ratna-mālābhiṣeka pūjaya* ( 427).

## 28 VAJRAGĪTĀ
金剛歌菩薩

Vajragītā sits in the north west. She is consecrated over the virtues of predication, and the song of Bodhisattva, represents the excellent predication. She is of pale flesh colour. She holds a vīṇā against her right shoulder. In Kongokai she holds instrument by her left hand and by her right she makes its cords vibrate (Tajima 185-186).

Vairocana enters the samādhi called the vajra which has its origin in the samaya of music of All the Tathāgatas and utters from his heart vajra-gītā as a mahādevī of Tathāgatas. As soon as he speaks this religion mudrās emerge from the hearts of All the Tathāgatas, from these mudrās vajradhara obtains the form of vajragītā and takes a seat in the lunar disc towards the left of the maṇḍala of Lokeśvararāja. He utters this verse : Oho I am the worship composed of music of all the observers which satisfies by whorships. (STTS 49).

1.1.28.

T Z.54.28

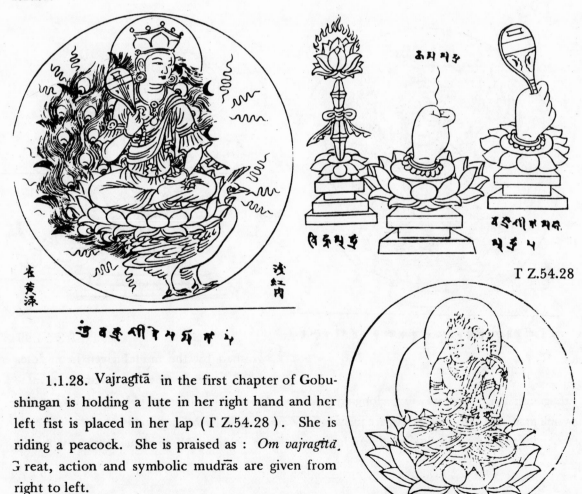

1.1.28. Vajragītā in the first chapter of Gobushingan is holding a lute in her right hand and her left fist is placed in her lap (TZ.54.28). She is riding a peacock. She is praised as : *Om vajragītā*. Great, action and symbolic mudrās are given from right to left.

As described by Tajima in mahā-maṇḍala of

graphic vajradhātu Vajragītā is holding a lute by left hand and by her right she is playing upon it ( T Z 38 28, Lokesh Chandra 433) .

1.2.28. The same lute with a three pointed vajra overhead is placed upon a lotus in the samaya-maṇḍala of Vajradhātu (T Z.38.90, Lokesh Chandra 495 ). STTS in its second chapter calls as the samaya of worship of the esoteric form of Vajra-gītā : *Om vajra-guhya gīta pūjā samaya sarva-pūjām pravartaya hūm* ( STTS 104) .

← T Z.38.90

1.3.28. In the third chapter of Gobu-shingan vajragītā has a different musical instruments which is placed upon a lotus by both of her hands. The attribute can be well distin-
1.3.28

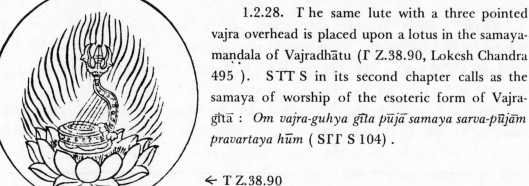

T Z.54.99

guished by the mudrā given in middle. ( T Z.54.99 ), She is named as sarvata-thāgata-jñāna. The drawing belonging to knowledge maṇḍala of graphic Vajradhātu has the same attribute only the strings are missing (T Z.38.163, Lokesh Chandra 568) .

1.4.28. Sarvatathāgata-gīta-sukhā or one who rejoices All the Tathāgatas by music

1.4.28

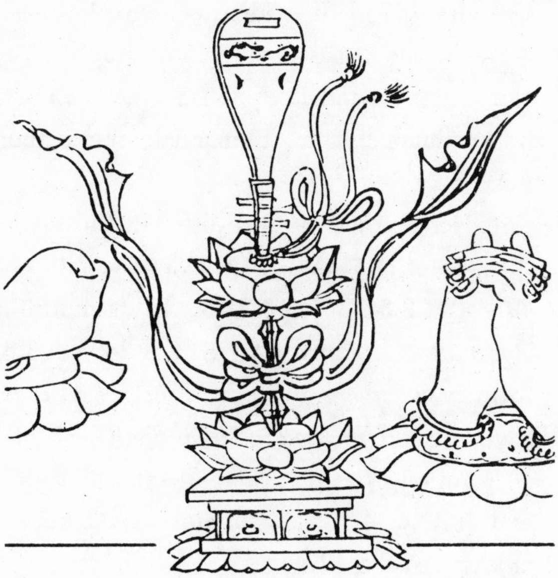

Γ Z.54.128

occurs in the fourth chapter of Gobu-shingan. ( Γ Z.54.128 ). She holds a small lute by her right hand as in the first chapter. Her mantra under the illustration can be read as follows : *Om sarvatathāgata-gīta-pūjā-megha-samudra-spharaṇa-samaya hūm. sarvatathāgata-gīta-sukhā.* T he middle one in the symbolic mudrā and others are identical with those of the third chapter.

T Z. 38.236

T Z. 38.340

In action-maṇḍala of graphic vajradhātu vajragītā is holding a lotus which is bent towards her right and a lute is placed upon it (Γ Z.38.236, Lokesh Chandra 641) . T he second illustration belongs to the karma maṇḍala of T railokya vijaya ( 38.340, Lokesh

Chandra 747) . . It is identical with knowledge maṇḍala and the samaya form is the same as given in the samaya-maṇḍala of graphic Vajradhātu. She is called for singing in Trailokya vijaya mahā-maṇḍala of STT S : *Om vajra-gītā gada gada hūm phaṭ* ( STT S 193) . 2.2.28. In its krodha-guhya-mudrā-maṇḍala she is mentioned only by her essence : *Vajra hūm tem* ( STT S 216) .

Her epithets do not differ in the maṇḍalas of Sakala-jagad : 3.1.28. In mahā-maṇḍala she is lotus gītā and the samaya of worship by music : *Om padma-gītā gada gīta-pūjā-samaya hūm* ( STT S 326) . 3.2.28. In its mudrā-maṇḍala she is again the worship of lotus gītā : *Om padma-gīta-pūjā giḥ* ( STT S 345) . 3.3.28. In knowledge maṇḍala she has a knowledge form : *Om jñāna-padma-gītā hūm* ( STT S 359) . 3.4.28. In action maṇḍala she is called as a worship : *Om gīta-pūjā hūm dhaḥ* ( STT S 368) .

Among the maṇḍalas of sarvārthasiddhi only mahā and action maṇḍalas mention her as follows : 4.1.28. *Om Ratna-gītā hūm* ( STT S 392) and 4.4.28. *Om maṇi-ratna-gītā pūjaya* ( STT S 427) .

Names of Vajragītā in the sixteen maṇḍalas

| Ch. | P. | Kula | Maṇḍala | Names |
|---|---|---|---|---|
| 1. | 49 | Buddhakula | Vajradhātu-mahāmaṇḍala | Vajragītā. |
| 2. | 104 | " | Vajraguhya-vajramaṇḍala | Vajra-guhya-gīta-pūjā-samayā. |
| 3. | - | " | Vajrajñāna-dharmamaṇḍala | Sarvatathāgatajñāna-gītā. |
| 4. | - | " | Vajrakārya-karmamaṇḍala | Sarvatathāgatagītasukhā. |
| 6. | 193 | Vajrakula | Γ rilokavijaya-mahāmaṇḍala | Vajragītā. |
| 7. | - | " | Krodhaguhya-mudrāmaṇḍala | |
| 8. | - | " | Vajrakula-dharmajñāna-samaya-maṇḍala. | |
| 9. | - | " | Vajrakula-karmamaṇḍala | |
| 15. | 326 | Padmakula | Sakalajagadvinaya-mahā-maṇḍala. | Padma-gītā, Gīta-pūja-samaya. |
| 16. | 345 | " | Padmaguhya-mudrāmaṇḍala | Padma-gīta-pūjā. |
| 17. | 359 | " | Jñānamaṇḍala | Jñāna-padma-gītā. |
| 18. | 368 | " | Karmamaṇḍala | Gīta-pūjā. |
| 19. | 392 | Ratnakula | Sarvārthasiddhi-mahāmaṇḍala | Ratna-gītā. |
| 20. | - | " | Ratnaguhya-mudrāmaṇḍala. | |
| 21. | - | " | Jñānamaṇḍala | |
| 22. | 427 | " | Karmamaṇḍala | Maṇi-ratna-gītā. |

## 29. VAJRANṚTYĀ

金剛舞菩薩

Vajranṛtyā is to sit in the North-eastern direction. She is consecrated to Amoghasiddhi. She is devoted to an animated dance. She is of blue colour. She has a mudrā called Vajramuṣṭi that is to press the fists in vajra. She moves her elbows while dancing. In the Kongokai she has her hands fully opened and makes them turn one over the other (Tajima 186).

Vairocana enters the samādhi called the vajra which has its origin in the samaya of worship by dancing of All the Tathagatas and utters the essence Vajranrtya as the last mahadevi of All the Tathāgatakula. As he says this multiplicity of methods of worships emerge from the hearts of All the Tathāgatas and from these pūjā-vidhivistaras Vajradhara obtains the form of Vajra-nṛttamahādevī and stations himself in the full lunar disc towards the left of the mandala of Tathāgata Amoghasiddhi and utters this verse: "Oho I am the exalted worship of all the worshippers, who performs Buddha worship by the way of dancing". (STTS 50)

1.1.29.

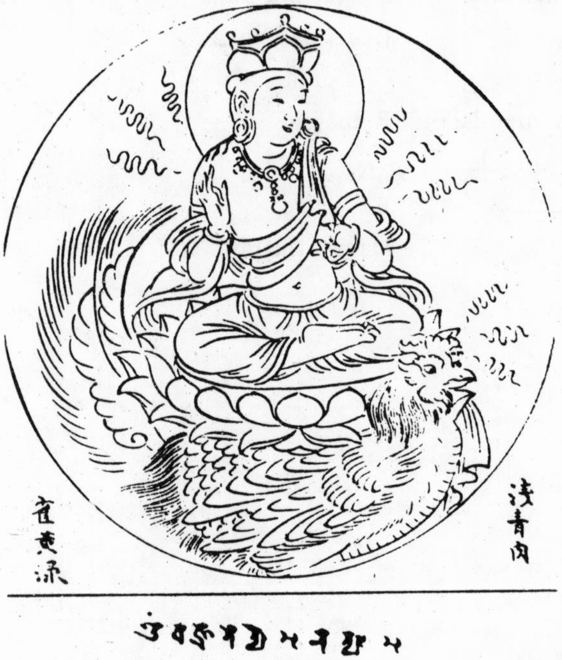

1.1.29. Vajranṛtyā in the first chapter of Gobu-shingan is sitting on a hen and doing mudrās by both of her hands. (Γ Z. 54.29). The first mudrā shows the posture of her left hand, second and third are action and symbolic mudrās. Vajra-nṛtyā in mahāmaṇḍala of graphic Vajradhātu has both of

her hands in a dancing posture. She is sitting on a a lotus (Γ Z.38.29, Lokesh Chandra 434).

1.2.29. Stylised viśvavajra is drawn to depict Vajranṛtyā in samaya-maṇḍala of graphic Vajradhātu (Γ Z.38.91, Lokesh Chandra 496). It is stylised in such a way that it gives a feeling of dance. In the second chapter of SΓΓ S she is the samaya form of esoteric worship by dance : *Om vajra-guhya nṛtya-pūjā-samaya sarva–pūjām pravartaya hūm* (SΓΓ S 104).

T Z.38.91

1.3.29

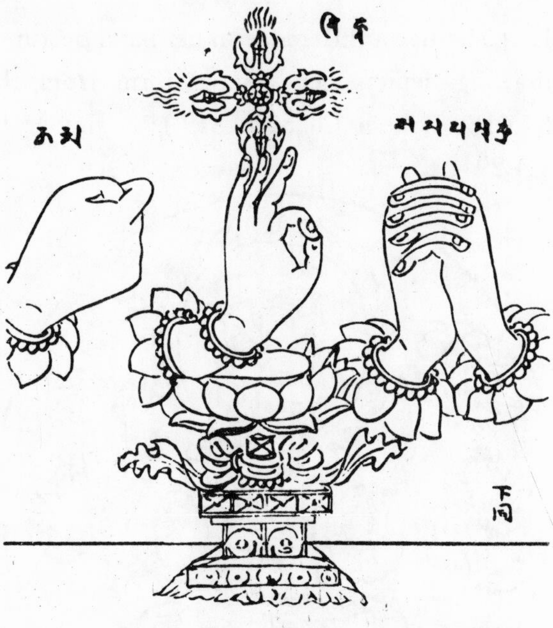

T Z.54.100

1.3.29. The knowledge form of dance belongs to the third chapter of Gobu-shingan. A lotus is placed on her joined hands and there-upon is a hand with a viśvavajra. She is sitting on a lotus. Under the illustration she is named as : *Sarvatathāgata jñānanṛtyā* and *sarvatathāgata jñāna-guhyaḥ*. Also samaya cihna-and karma-mudrās are given repectively from right to left. (Γ Z.54.100).

The first drawing given below belongs to the knowledge maṇḍala of graphic Vajrdhātu

T Z.38.164

T Z.38.341

Here she has a difference in her hand posture. (Γ Z.38.164, Lokesh Chandra) . Γ he second drawing depicts her samaya form from the samaya maṇḍala of Γ railokyavijaya ( T Z 37.418, Lokesh Chandra 817 ) is similar to the one in samaya mandala of Vajradhātu. 1.4.29

Γ Z.38.341

1.4.29. According to the fourth chapter of Gobu-shingan she pleases All the Γ athāgatas by performing dances : *Sarva-Ṭathāgata-nṛtya-sukhā.* She has two vajras placed upon the her palms opened flat upwards on both the sides (Γ Z.54.129) . Her samaya cihna-and action-mudrās are given with the illustration.

2.1.29. She is praised for her power of subduing in Γ railokyavijaya-mahā-maṇḍala : *Om vajra-nṛtyā vaśī-kuru hūm phaṭ* ( SΓΓ S 193) . 2.2.29. In Krodha-guhya-mudrā-maṇḍala only her essence is mentioned as : *Om vajra hūm stem* (STΓ S 210) .

In maṇḍalas of the sakala-jagad-vinaya she is related to lotus family. 3.1.29. In its mahā-maṇḍala she is the samaya of the one who performs all the worships by dance : *Om padma-nṛtyā nṛtya sarva-pūjā pravartana-samaya hūm* (SΓΓ S 326) . 3.2.29. Vajra-nṛtyā is worship by dance of the lotus family : *Om Padma nṛtyā-pūjā kṛṭ* ( SΓΓ S 345) . 3.3.29. She has a knowledge form in knowledge maṇḍala : *Om jñāna-padma-nṛtyā hūm* ( SΓΓ S 359) and 3.4.29. in action-maṇḍala she is nṛtya-pūjā : *Om nṛtya-pūjā hūm vaḥ* ( SΓΓ S 368) . 4.1.29. In mahā-maṇḍala of Sarvārthasiddhi she is Ratna-nṛtyā : *Om ratna-nṛtyā hūm* ( SΓΓ S 392) and 4.4.29. in karma-maṇḍala she is mentioned as : *Om ratna-nṛtyā pūjaya* ( STT S 427) .

Names of Vajranṛtyā in the sixteen maṇḍalas.

| Ch. | P. | Kula | Mandala | Names |
|---|---|---|---|---|
| 1. | 50 | Buddhakula | Vajradhātu-mahāmaṇḍala | Vajranṛtyā. |
| 2. | - | " | Vajraguhya-vajramaṇḍala | Vajraguhya-nrtya-puja-samayā. |
| 3. | - | " | Vajrajñāna-dharmamaṇḍala | Sarvatathāgatajñāna-nṛtyā, Sarvatathāgatajñānaguhyaḥ. |
| 4. | - | " | Vajrakārya-karmamaṇḍala | Sarvatathāgatanṛtyasukhā. |
| 6. | 104 | Vajrakula | Trilokavijaya-mahāmaṇḍala | Vajra-nṛtyā. |
| 7. | - | " | Krodhaguhya-mudrāmaṇḍala | |
| 8. | - | " | Vajrakula-dharmajñāna-samaya maṇḍala. | |
| 9. | - | " | Vajrakula-karmamaṇḍala | |
| 15. | - | Padmakula | Sakalajagadinaya-mahāmaṇḍala | Padma-nṛtyā. |
| 16. | - | " | Padmaguhya-mudrāmaṇḍala | Padma-nṛtya-pūjā. |
| 17. | - | " | Jñānamaṇḍala | Jñāna-padma-nṛtyā. |
| 18. | - | " | Karmamaṇḍala | Nṛtya-pūjā. |
| 19. | - | Ratnakula | Sarvārthasiddhi-mahāmaṇḍala | Ratna-nṛtyā. |
| 20. | - | " | Ratnaguhya-mudrāmaṇḍala | |
| 21. | - | " | Jñānamaṇḍala | |
| 22. | - | " | Karmamaṇḍala | Maṇi-ratna-nṛtyā. |

## 30. VAJRADHŪPĀ

金剛燒香菩薩

T he four exterior pūjā bodhisattvas are called the bearers of exterior offerings in opposition to the interior bearers of offerings to occupy the four angles of the second enclosure. T hey are pıoduced to offer to Vairocana, offering of the virtues of great Buddhas of the four cardinal points. T hey are all feminine bodhisattvas of the appearence of apsarās. Vajradhūpā is in the South-east. She corresponds to Akṣobhya. Dhūpā or incense symbolises virtues (*Śīla*) and removes impurities. Hence she offers incense and holds a burnt perfume by both of her hands. She is of black colour. (T ajima 186-187).

Bhagavān Akṣobhya T athāgata enters the samādhi called the vajra which has its origin in the pleasure of All the T athāgatas to worship T athāgata Vairocana and utters the essence, the courtisan of All the T athāgatas as Vajradhūpā. As he says this a multitude of clouds of perfume orginate trom the hearts of All the T athāgatas, it is followed by the transformation of these clouds into the form of divinity, that is Vajradhūpā. She stations herself in the left lunar disc of kūṭāgāra which has a top of vajra-gems and recites this verse: "Oho I am an auspicious great worship full of pleasure, which obtains enlightenment because of its true influence. ( STTS 51).

I.1.30.

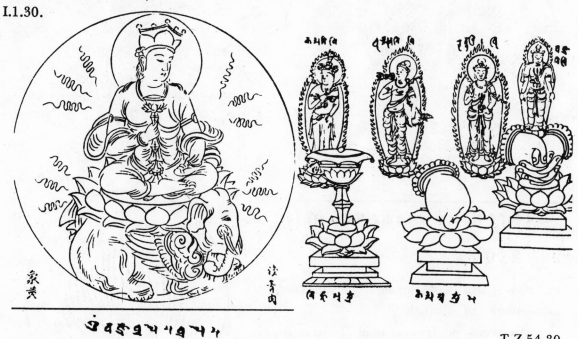

T Z.54.30

I.1.30. In the first chapter of Gobu-shingan vajradhūpā is holding a vajra with an incense pot placed upon a lotus in her right hand and her left fist is placed upon an elephat. ( T Z.54.30 ). Down below are action and symbolic mudrās.

I.2.30.

As described by Tajima vajradhūpā in mahā-maṇḍala of vajradhātu is holding an incense-pot by both of her hands. (Γ Z.38.30, Lokesh Chandra 435).

I.2.30. Guhya-dhūpeśvarī is the form of vajra-dhūpā in the second chapter of Gobushingan. Again she is holding a vajra with a pot by both of her hands but in a different posture (Γ Z.54.64). The script under the illustration can be read as: *Om vajra-guhya-rati-samaya sarva-pūjā pravartaya hūm.* Guhyadhūpeśvarī ('pe' is missing). Mudrās are named as: *Samayamudrā, guhyadhūpeśvarī-cihnamudrā and vajrāñjali.*

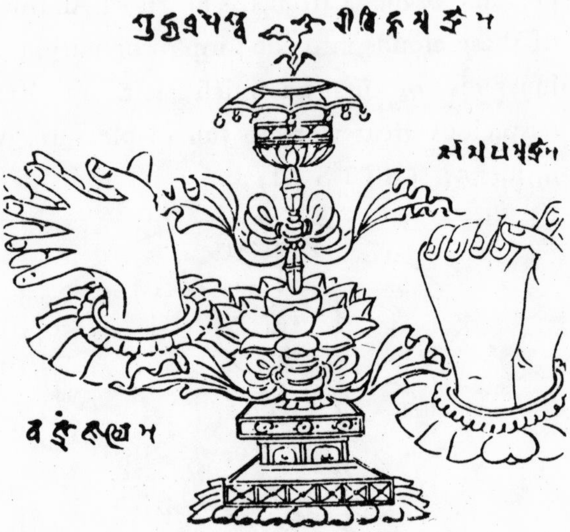

Γ Z.54.64

An incense pot is her symbol. Thus in samaya maṇḍala of graphic vajradhātu it is placed upon a lotus. (Γ Z.38.92, Lokesh Chandra 497).

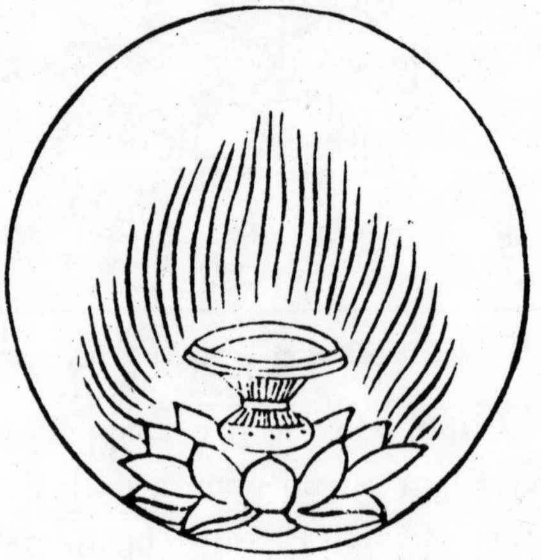

I.3.30. Vajradhūpā has an appearence in the third chapter of Gobu-shingan as Jñāna-dhūpā: *Om Jñānadhūpa Jñānadhūpā* (T Z.54.101) . Mudrās are named but they should be

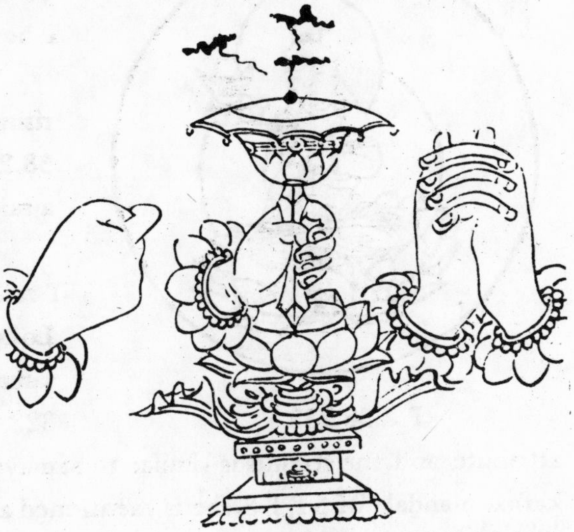

T Z.54.101

samaya, cihna and karma-mudrās respectively.

In knowledge mandala of graphic vajra-

dhātu instead of an incense pot lotus with its leaf is drawn ( T Z.38.165, Lokesh Chandra 574) . ( T his might be because of same misunderstanding of artist) .

I.4.30. Gobu-shingan in its fourth chapter draws vajradhūpā as worship by incense of All theT athāgatas: *Om Sarva-tathāgata - dhūpa-pūjā-megha - samudra-*

Γ Z.38.238

*spharaṇa-samaya hūm. Sarvatathāgata-dhūpa-pūjā.* (T Z.54.130). She has a pot in her right hand. T he mudras are identical with the previous drawing.

T he pot in the given drawing seems to be a rising moon with a star placed upon a lotus (Γ Z. 38.238, Lokesh Chandra 647). ( T his can be a misunderstanding of an incense pot).

2.4.30, 2.2.30. T he first drawing belongs to T railokyavijaya-karma-maṇḍala (Γ Z.38.342, Lokesh Chandra 758). and the second to its samaya-maṇḍala ( T Z.37.238, Lokesh Chandra 822 ). In the first vajradhūpā has the same attribute and the second is similar to samaya maṇḍala of vajradhūpā. In T railokya-vijaya-karma-maṇḍala of S Γ Γ S she is mentioned as samaya form: *Om vajradhūpa-pūjā-spharaṇa-samaya-hūm phaṭ* (ST T S 193).

3.1.30. In mahā-maṇḍala of sakala-jagad-vinaya she is praised as the samaya-form of incense-worship of lotus family, a beloved woman (dayitā, Yamada has separated it as dayi te), great courtizam (mahā-gaṇikā, may be 'ka' is missing here), and lotus rati : *Om padma-dhūpa-pūjā-samaya prahlādaya padma-kula dayite mahā-gaṇi-( kā ) padma-rati hūm* ( ST T S 326). 3.2.30. In padma-guhya-mudrā-maṇḍala she is dhūpa-radminī : *Om dhūpa-radminī hūm* ( STT S 345). 3.3.30. In its knowledge maṇḍala she is Padma-jñāna-dhūpā: *Om padma-jñāna-dhūpā hūm* ( ST T S 359) and 3.4.30. in action maṇḍala she is named dhūpa-pūjā *Om dhūpa-pūjā aḥ.* ( S T T S 368).

4.1.30. Last of all vajra-dhūpā comes in mahā-and 4.4.30. action-maṇḍalas of Sarvārthasiddhi: *Om dhūpa-ratna* ( SΓT S 392) and *Om Maṇi-ratna dhūpā pujaya* (SΓ Γ S 427).

Names of Vajra-dhūpā in the sixteen maṇḍalas

| Ch. | P. | Kula | Maṇḍala | Names |
|---|---|---|---|---|
| 1. | 51 | Buddhakula | Vajradhātu-mahāmaṇḍala | Vajra-dhūpā. |
| 2. | - | " | Vajraguhya-vajramaṇḍala | Guhya-dhūpeśvarī, vajra-guhya-ratipūjā-samayā. |
| 3. | - | " | Vajrajñāna-dharmaṇḍala | Jñānadhūpā. |
| 4. | - | " | Vajrakārya-karmamaṇḍala | Sarvatathāgatadhūpa-pūjā. |
| 6. | - | " | Γ rilokavijaya-mahāmaṇḍala | Vajra-dhūpa-pūjā-spharaṇa-samaya. |
| 7. | - | " | Krodhaguhya-mudrāmaṇḍala | - |
| 8. | - | " | Vajrakula-dharmajñāna samayamaṇḍala. | - |
| 9. | - | " | Vajrakula-karmamaṇḍala | - |
| 15. | 326 | Padmakula | Sakalajagadvinaya-mahāmaṇḍala | Padma-dhūpa-pūjā-samaya |
| 16. | 345 | " | Padmaguhya-mudrāmaṇḍala | Dhūpa-radiminī. |
| 17. | 359 | " | Jñānamaṇḍala | Padma-jñāna-dhūpa. |
| 18. | 368 | " | Karmamaṇḍala | Dhūpa-pūjā. |
| 19. | 392 | Ratnakula | Sarvārthasiddhi-mahāmaṇḍala | Dhūpa-ratna. |
| 20. | - | " | Ratnaguhya-mudrāmaṇḍala | – |
| 21. | - | " | Jñānamaṇḍala. | – |
| 22. | 427 | " | Karmamaṇḍala | Maṇi-ratna-dhūpā. |

## 31 VAJRAPUṢPĀ
金剛華菩薩

Vajrapuṣpā occupies the South-western angle. She corresponds to Buddha Ratnasambhava. Puṣpa or flower symbolises the decoration of perfection. Ratnasambhava is the divinity embelished with beautitude through perfection of asceticism; hence she offers a flower. In addition the Mahākaruṇā-garbhamaṇḍala. Ratnasambhava is named Saṁkusumitarāja. It is not without reason that flower is the attribute of this Bodhisattva. She is of light bluish-green colour and carries some fresh flowers. (T ajima 187) .

Bhagavān Ratnasambhava enters the samādhi named the vajra which has its origin in the samaya of worship by gem ornaments for worshipping T athāgata Vairocana and utters the seed syllable Vajra-puṣpa, a door keeper ( *pratihāri* ) of All the T athāgatas.

As soon as he utters this, Vajradhara obtains a multiple form of flowers of worship. Afterwards he becomes the divinity Vajrapuṣpā from these flowers. She takes a seat towards the left of the kūṭāgāra and recites this verse : "Oho I am the flower-worship who decorates everything which soon gains Tathāgata-gems after worshipping." (STTS 52). I.1.31

I.1.31. Vajrapuṣpā in the first chapter of G obu-shingan is holding a lotus flower in her right hand and the left is resting on her thigh. She is riding a horse. Mudrās are vajra-puṣpa-mudrā, karma-mudrā and cihna-mudrā. ( T Z. 54.31 ) . In vajradhātu-mahā-maṇḍala vajrapuṣpā has a lotus flower on its leaf in her right hand supporting it by the left (T Z.38.31, Lokesh Chandra 436). She is sitting in the pericarp of a lotus.

I.2.31. The esoteric form of vajrapuṣpā is guhya. She is called the samaya of esoteric consecration :*Omvajra-guhyābhiṣekapūjāsamaya hūm. Sarva-pūjām prvartaya Guhyapuṣpā.* I.2.31.

Guhyapuṣpeśvarī and guhyañjali. (T Z.54.65).

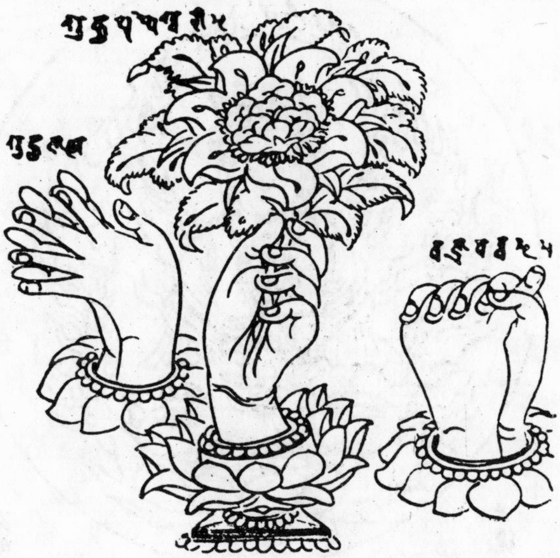

T Z.54.65

In both of her hands she has a flower with its stem and leaves. The mudrās from right to left are vajrabandha,

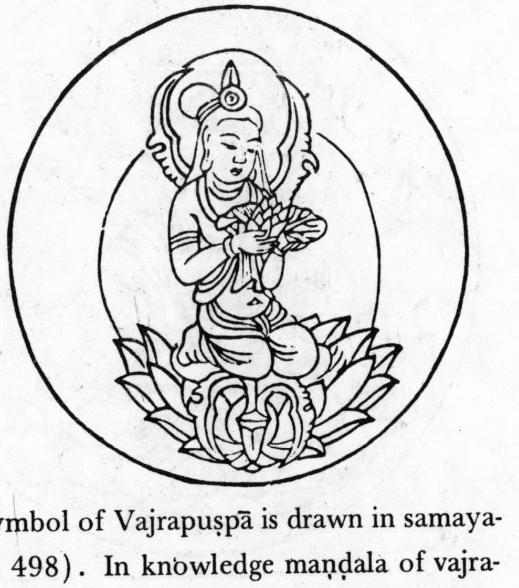

A lotus flower placed upon its leaf being the symbol of Vajrapuṣpā is drawn in samaya-maṇḍala of vajradhātu (T Z.38.93, Lokesh Chandra 498). In knowledge maṇḍala of vajra-dhātu vajrapuṣpā with flowers in her hands is sitting in such a posture as if she is offering

flowers (Γ Z.38.166, Lokesh Chandra 575).

I.3.31. Vajrapuṣpā becomes knowledge flower in the third chapter of Gobu-shingan: *Om sarvatathāgata-jñāna-puṣpa, jñāna-puṣpa.* She has a lotus in her lap supported by both

I.3.31.

Γ Z.54.102

of her hands. A hand is drawn in its pericarp which is holding a garland of flower (Γ Z.54.102). Mudras are vajrabandha, cihnamudrā and karma-mudrā.

I.4.31.

I.4.31. Sarvatathāgatapuṣpā is the form of vajrapuṣpā in the fourth chapter of Gobu-shingan she is holding a flower in her right hand. The script under the illustration reads as follows :*Om sarvatathāgata-puṣpa-pūjā-samudra-spharaṇa-samaya hūm.* *Sarvatathāgatapuṣpa* (TZ.54.151). Mudrās are the same as in the preceded illustration of Gobu-shingan.

In action maṇḍala of vajradhātu also vajrapuṣpā is holding a flower in her hands (TZ.38.23, Lokesh Chandra 648).

Vajrapuṣpā in the action-mandala of vajra-dhātu and Trailokyavijaya-karma-maṇḍala is the same (TZ.38,343, Lokesh Chandra 754). Her samaya form is identical with samaya maṇḍala of vajradhātu.

2.1.31 STTS mentions her as the samaya form of Vajra-puṣpā in Trailokyavijayamahā-maṇḍala: *Om vajra-puṣpa-pūjā-spharaṇa-samaya hūm phaṭ.* (STTS 193). 3.1.31. Vajra-puṣpā in lotus family, that is sakalajagadvinaya-mahā-maṇḍala is considered to reside in a lotus. As a doorkeeper, pratihāra of lotus family she accomplishes thing: *Om padma-puṣpa-pūjā-samaya padma-vāsinī mahāśrīye padmakula pratihan sarvār-thān śadbaya hūm.* (STTS 326). 3.2.31. In mudrā-maṇḍala of lotus family she is padma-puṣpā: *Om padma-puṣpa hūm* (STTS 345). 3.3.31. In knowledge maṇḍala she is know-ledge-flower: *Om padma-jñāna-puṣpa hūm* (STTS 359), 3.4.31. in action maṇḍala she is flower-worship: *Om puṣpa pūjā hūm traḥ* (STTS 368). Puṣpa-maṇi comes in mahā-maṇḍala of sarvārthasiddhi (STTS 393), and maṇi-ratna-puṣpā in its action maṇḍala: *Om maṇi-ratna-puṣpa pūjaya* (STTS 427).

Names of Vajra-puṣpā in the sixteen maṇḍalas:

| Ch. | P. | Kula | Maṇḍala | Names |
|---|---|---|---|---|
| 1. | 52 | Buddhakula | Vajradhātu-mahāmaṇḍala | Vajra-puṣpā. |
| 2. | - | ,, | Vajrajñāna-vajra-mandala | Vajra-guhyābhiṣeka pūjā-samayā. |
| 3. | - | ,, | Vajrajñāna-dharmamaṇḍala | Sarvatathāgata-jñāna-puṣpā. |
| 4. | - | ,, | Vajrakārya-karmamaṇḍala | Sarvatathāgata-puṣpā. |
| 6. | 193 | Vajrakula | T rilokavijaya-mahāmaṇḍala | Vajra-puṣpa-spharaṇa-samaya. |
| 7. | - | ,, | Krodhaguhya-mudrāmaṇḍala. | |
| 8. | - | ,, | Vajrakula-dharmajñāna-samaya-maṇḍala. | |
| 9. | - | ,, | Vajrakula-karmamaṇḍala. | |
| 15. | 326 | Padmakula | Sakalajagadvinaya-mahā-maṇḍala. | Padma-puṣpa-pūjā-samaya |
| 16. | 345 | ,, | Padmaguhya-mudrāmaṇḍala | Padma-puṣpī. |
| 17. | 359 | ,, | Jñānamaṇḍala | Padma-jñāna-puṣpā. |
| 18. | 368 | ,, | Karmamaṇḍala | Puṣpa-pūjā. |
| 19. | 393 | Ratnakula | Sarvārthasiddhi-mahāmaṇḍala | Puṣpa-maṇi. |
| 20. | - | ,, | Ratnaguhya-mudrāmaṇḍala. | — |
| 21. | - | ,, | Jñānamaṇḍala | — |
| 22. | 427 | ,, | Karmamaṇḍala | Maṇi-ratna-puṣpā. |

## 32. VAJRĀLOKĀ

金剛燈菩薩

Vajradīpā or vajrālokā has a seat in the North-western angle. She corresponds to Amitāyu. Ālokā makes to see the view, the aspect, the blaze. Ālokā symbolizes the light of knowledge, illuminating the darkness of ignorance. Amitāyu is the divinity of descipline of knowledge and presides over the comprehension of bodhi, of lamp brought by vajrālokā, she is of white colour. She rests her closed left hand in her bosom and in her right hand she holds a lotus with a candlewick or a lamp upon it (Γ ajima 187) .

Lokeśvararāja enters the vajra-samādhi which has its origin in the samaya of lamp worship of All theT athāgatas and utters the seed syllable of the female messenger as vajrālokā. As he utters this vajradhara emerge from the hearts of All theΓ athāgatas in a multiplicity of All lamp worships. Γ hese lamp worships coalesce into a single divinity vajraloka. She stations herself in the lunar disc in left corner of the kūṭāgāra and recites this verse: "Oho I am the auspicious lamp-worship full of great generocity. All the buddhas are soon visible because of her light". ( SΓΓ S 53) .

I.1.32.

I.1.32. Vajrālokā is named vajradīpā in the first chapter of Gobu-shingan. (T Z.54.32) She is holding a lamp with a vajra in her right hand and riding a peacock. T hree mudrās given above are Vajrāloka-mahāmudrā, karma-mudrā and cihanmudrā, and the divinities drawn below are vajradhara, Ratnadhara, Padmadhara and karmadhara.

Vajrālokā is vajradīpa in mahā-maṇḍala of vajra-dhātu 'Dīḥ' is given as her seed syllable with the preceded illustration. She holds a lamp by both of her hands which is bent towards her right (T Z.38.32, Lokesh Chandra 437).

I.2.32. Esoteric form of Vajraloka is guhyadipa in the second chapter of Gobu-shingan **Om** sarva-*guhyā-loka-pūjā-pravarttana-samaya sarva-pūjām pravarttaya, Guhyadīpā. She has*

I.2.32.

T Z.54.66

ā lotus flower in her hands whereupon is the lamp. T he mudrās are samayamudrā, guhyadīpa and guhyāñjali. (T Z.54.66)

A candle wick in a pot upon a lotus is drawn to show the esoteric form of vajrālokā in samaya maṇḍala of vajradhātu (T Z.38.94, Lokesh Chandra 499).

I.3.32. T he divinity is named twice in the third chapter of Gobu-shingan as: *Om sarva-tathāgatagatajñānālokā. Sarva-tathāgata-jñānadipā.* A lotus is placed in her lap, which is supported by both of her hands, therefore a hand holding a lamp upon a lotus. (T Z.54.103). Mudrās are not named

T Z.38.94

I.3.32.

T Z.54.103

but they must be samaya, cihna and karma-mudrās.

T Z.38.167

T Z.38.240

In knowledge maṇḍala of vajradhātu vajrālokā is worshipping by a lamp which is held by both of her hands (T Z.38.167, Lokesh Chandra 567) .T he second drawing extracted above belongs to the action maṇḍala of the Vajradhātu. Vajrālokā is holding a lotus with a candle by both of her hands (T Z.38.240, Lokesh Chandra 649) .

I.4.32. Vajrālokā in the fourth chapter ofG obushingan holds a lamp in her right hand It seems to be a pot with gems and not with a wick. She is called sarvatathāgatadīpā : *Om*

1.4.32.

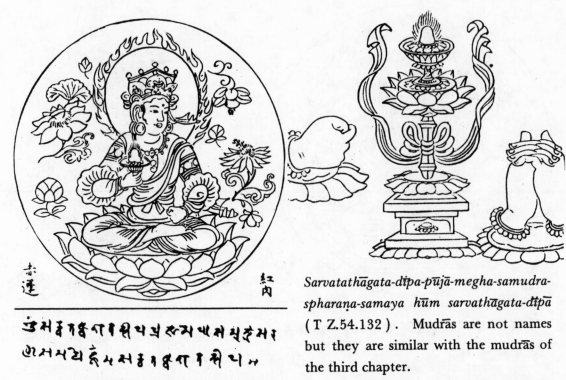

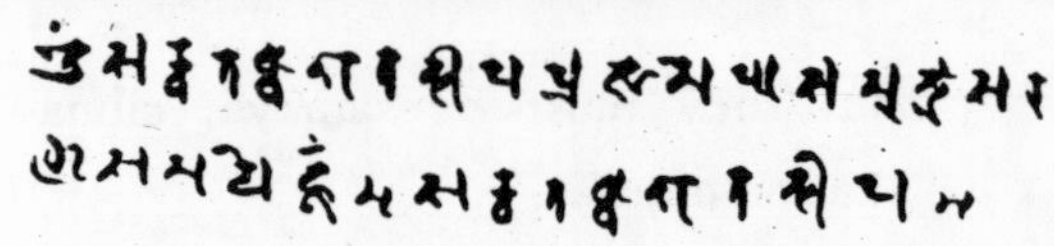

*Sarvatathāgata-dīpa-pūjā-megha-samudra-spharaṇa-samaya hūm sarvathāgata-dīpā* ( T Z.54.132 ). Mudrās are not names but they are similar with the mudrās of the third chapter.

Vajraloka in the T railokya-vijaya-karma-maṇḍala is identical with the preceded; the only difference is that here the flower is bent towards her left ( Γ Z.38.344, Lokesh Chandra 755). Her samaya form ( Γ Z.38.421, Lokesh Chandra 824) is the same as it is in the samaya maṇḍala of the vajradhātu. 2.1.32. T he T railokya-vijaya-mahāmaṇḍala of the SΓΓ S names her to be the samaya form of lamp worship : *Om Vajrāloka-pūjā-spharaṇa-samaya-hūm phaṭ* ( SΓΓ S 193-4).

3.1.32. Vajrālokā has a power of producing light, she is the beautiful great massenger of the lotus family and the samaya form of lamp worship : *Om padma-dīpa-pūjā-samaya-padma-kula sundari mahādūtyāloka sañjanaya padma-sarasvati hūm* ( SΓΓ S 326-7). 3.2.32. In the mudrā-maṇḍala of the lotus family Vajrālokā is Dharmālokā : *Om padma-kula sundari dharmālokā pūjaya hūm* ( S TT S 345). 3.3.32 Padma-jñāna belongs to knowledge maṇḍala : *Om padma-jñāna dīpā hūm* ( STT S 359) and 3.4.32 Āloka-pūjā in the action maṇḍala : *Om Āloka-pūjā hūm dhīḥ* ( SΓΓ S 368). 4.1.32. In the mahā-maṇḍala of sarvārthasiddhi Vajrālokā is Ratnālokā : *Om ratnālokā* ( SΓΓ S 393). 4.4.32. Last of all is the action maṇḍala wherein Vajrālokā is mentioned as Maṇi-ratna-dīpā : *Om maṇi-ratna dīpe pūjaya ( S TTS 427 ).*

## 33. VAJRAGANDHĀ

金剛塗香菩薩

Vajragandhā occupies the north-eastern angle. She corresponds to Amonghasiddhi. G andhā, that is to say the sandal powder serves to clean impurities of the body and symbolise the purification of heart. Amoghasiddhi who is identical with Śakyamuni purifies all the aberations of the beings born from this deity earth and makes them enter the nirvāṇa. Hence Vajragandhā represents the sandal. She is of blue colour. Her closed left hand rests on her thigh and the other holds a sandal grater. In the maṇḍala of T akao she holds in her left hand an elongated sandal grater and by her right hand she makes the gesture of taking powder with the tip of her small finger drawings of sūkṣma-maṇḍala, the complementary third maṇḍala of the Vajradhātu and of the pūjā-maṇḍala, fourth maṇḍala are in addition concerned in the same fashion. T he first two exterior Bodhisattvas are kneeling but in the maṇḍala of T akao all the four Bodhisattvas are represented cross-legged (T ajima 187-8). Bhagavān Amoghasiddhi enters the Vajrasamādhi which has its origin in the samaya of incense worship of All the T athāgatas and utters the essence of female servant as Vajragandhā. As he utters these words Vajradhara manifests himself in a multiple form of all the incense worships which at last coalesce into a single deity called Vajragandhā. Vajragandhā recites this verse : "Oho I am the divine pleasing worship of incense which gives T athāgata incense to all the bodies ( STT S 54) .

1.1.33.

T Z.54.33

1.1.33. In the first chapter of Gobu-shingan Vajragandhā has a pot of incense in her right hand and her left fist is resting upon her thigh. Mudrās are Vajragandha-mahā-mudrā, Karma-mudrā and Cihna mudrā. In the cihna-mudrā sandal powder is distnct.

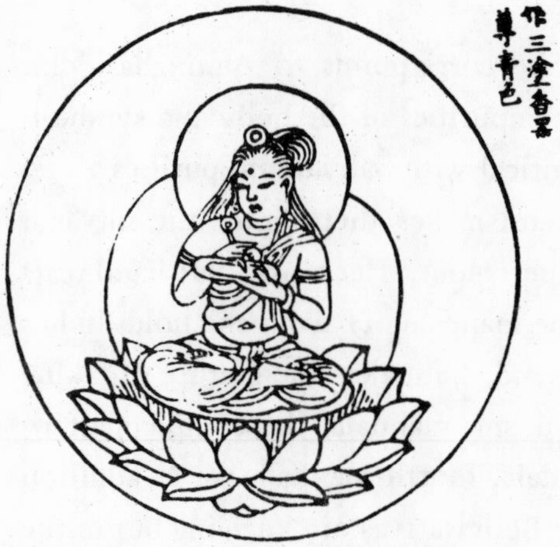


In Vajradhātu-mahā-maṇḍala Vajragandhā has an incense pot in her left hand and by her right she is making of a gesture of throwing incense powder (T Z.38.33, Lokesh Chandra 438) . . 'Gaḥ' is her seed syllable.

1.2.33. Vajragandhā is guhyagandhā in the second chapter of Gobu-shingan : *Om Sarva-guhya-gandha-pūjā-samaya sarva-pūjām pravarttaya hūm, Guhyagandhā.* She has a lotus flower in her hands and upon the lotus is placed an incense pot. She is sitting on a lotus pericarp.

1.2.33

T Z.54.67

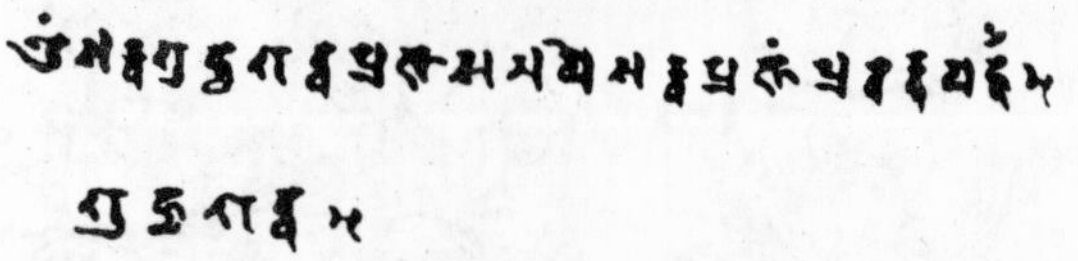

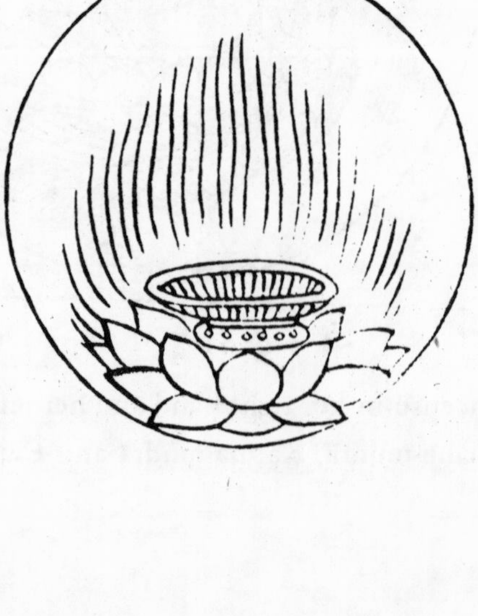

Vajragandhā in samaya maṇḍala of Vajradhātu is depicted as an incense pot placed on a lotus (T Z.38.95, Lokesh Chandra 500) .

1.3.33. Vajragandhā is named as Sarvatathāgata-dhātupūjā in the third chapter of Gobu-shingan. She holds a lotus and upon the lotus can be seen a hand

1.3.33.

T Z.54.104

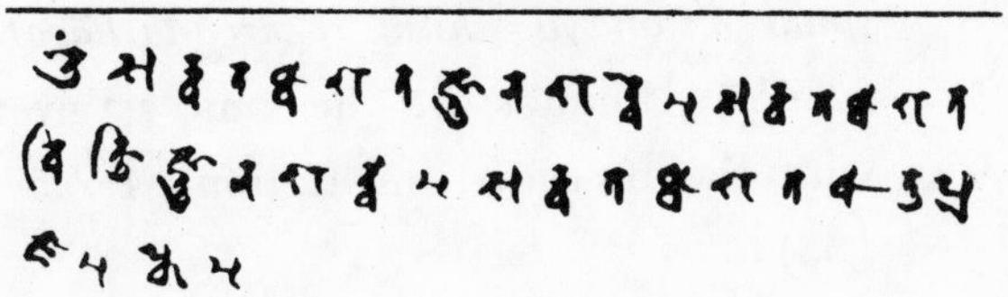

upon which there is a pot full of incense. The script under the illustration is *Om sarvatathāgata-jñāna-gandhā sarvatathāgata-vimukti-jñāna-gandha sarvatathāgata dhātu-pūjā. (TZ.*54.104). Mudrās are not named but they should be samaya-, cihna- and karma-mudrās.

T Z.38.168

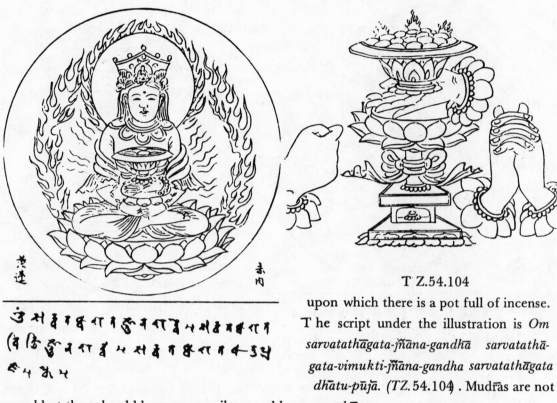

T Z.38.241

Vajragandhā in sūkṣma or knowledge maṇḍala of graphic vajradhātu is kneeling with a pot in her hands (T Z .38.168). In pūjā or action maṇḍala she is holding a lotus in her hands and incense pot is placed upon it which is bent towards her right. (T Z.38.241, Lokesh Chandra).

1.4.33. Sarvatathāgata-gandhā in the fourth chapter of Gobu-shingan holds a pot in her right hand and the left fist is resting on her thigh. The script can be read as : *Om Sarva-*

1.4.33

Γ Z.54.133

*tathāgata-gandha-pūjā-megha-samudra-spharṇa-samaya hūm. sarva-tathāgata gandhā.* Mudrās are the same as given with the preceded illustration ( Γ Z.54. 133) .

T he illustration of Vajragandhā in karma-maṇḍala of Γ rilokyavijaya ( Γ Z.38.395, Lokesh Chandra 756 ) is similar to pūjā-maṇḍala of Vajradhātu. ( Γ Z.38.422,Lokesh Chandra 825) . Her samaya form (Γ Z.38.422, Lokesh Chandra 825) is similar to samaya- of Vajradhātu. 2.1.33. In SΓΓ S in Γ railokyavijaya-mahā-maṇḍala she has a samaya form : *Om Vajra-gandha-pūjā-spharaṇa-samaya hūm phaṭ* (SΓΓ S 194) . 3.1.33. In Sakalajagad-vinaya mahā maṇḍala she is revered in this mantra : *Om padma-gandha-pūjā-padma siddhi hūm* ( SΓΓ S 326-7) . 3.2.33. In its mudrā-maṇḍala she is padma-gandhā : *Om Padma-gandhā hūm* (SΓΓ S 345) . 3.3.33 She is named as knowledge incense of lotus family in its knowledge maṇḍala : *Om jñāna padma-gandhā hūm* ( SΓΓ S 359) 3.4.33 and she is incense worship in the action maṇḍala : *Om gandha-pūje hūm vam* (SΓΓ S 368) . 4.1.33. Incense of gem family is mentioned in mahā and 4.4.33 action maṇḍalas of sarvārthasiddhi : *Om maṇi gandhā* ( SΓΓ S 394) and *Om maṇi-ratna-gandhe pūjaya* ( SΓΓ S 427) .

Names of Vajragandhā in the Sixteen Maṇḍalas:

| Ch. | P. | Kula | Maṇḍala | Names. |
|---|---|---|---|---|
| 1. | 54 | Buddhakula | Vajradhātu-mahāmaṇḍala | Vajra-gandhā. |
| 2. | - | ” | Vajraguhya-vajramaṇḍala | guhya-gandhā. |
| 3. | - | ” | Vajrajñāna-dharmamaṇḍala | Sarvatathāgata-dhātu-pūjā. |
| 4. | - | ” | Vajrakārya-karmamaṇḍala | Sarvatathāgata-gandhā. |
| 6. | 194 | Vajrakula | T rilokavijaya-mahā-maṇḍala | Vajra-gandha-pūjā-spharaṇa-samayā. |
| 7. | - | ” | Kordhaguhya-mudrā-maṇḍala. | — |
| 8. | - | ” | Vajrakula-dharmajñāna-samayamaṇḍala. | — |
| 9. | - | ” | Vajrakula-karmamaṇḍala | — |
| 15. | 326-7 | Padmakula | Sakalajagadvinaya-mahā-maṇḍala. | Padma-gandha-pūjā-samaya. |
| 16. | 345 | ” | Padmaguhya-mudrāmaṇḍala | Padma-gandhā. |
| 17. | 359 | ” | Jñānamaṇḍala | Jñāna-padma-gandhā. |
| 18. | 368 | ” | Karmamaṇḍala | Gandha-pūjā. |
| 19. | 394 | Ratnakula | Sarvārthasiddhi-mahā-maṇḍala. | Maṇi-gandhā. |
| 20. | - | ” | Ratnaguhya-mudrāmaṇḍala | — |
| 21. | - | ” | Jñānamaṇḍala | — |
| 22. | 927 | ” | Karmamaṇḍala | Maṇi-ratna-gandhā. |

## 34. VAJRĀṄKUŚA.

金剛鉤菩薩

T he four saṅgraha bodhisattvas represent the means of salvation by which Vairocana dresses the beings in the Buddhakṣetra. Hençe they are posted at the four gates of the second enclosure. T hey correspond to the four attractive forces *catavāri-saṅgrahavastūnī* of popular Buddhism respectively are : dāna : alms, priyavāditā: affectionate talk, Samanā-rthatā : mutual assistance, arthaçaryā : actions beneficial to others. Γ hey are represented in feminine forms. Sits in the east with the hook of solid bodhicitta, she detracts the being of the evil gates. Her left hand is closed and the right holds an aṅkuśa in Kongokai. She is of black colour. (T ajima 188-189) .

Vairocana enters the Vajra-samādhi which originates from the samaya of mahāsattva Aṅkuśa and utters Gaṇapati of all the mudrās as vajrāṅkuśa. As soon as he says this vajra-dhara becomes a mustiplicity of mudrās. T hese mudrās are transformed into vajrāṅkuśa who stations himself in the lunar disc placed in vajradvāra of kūṭāgāra. He recites this verse while attracting the samaya of All the Γ athagatas : " Oho I am the strong attration of All the Buddhas as all the maṇḍalas are attracted by me". ( SΓΓ S 55) .

1.1.34

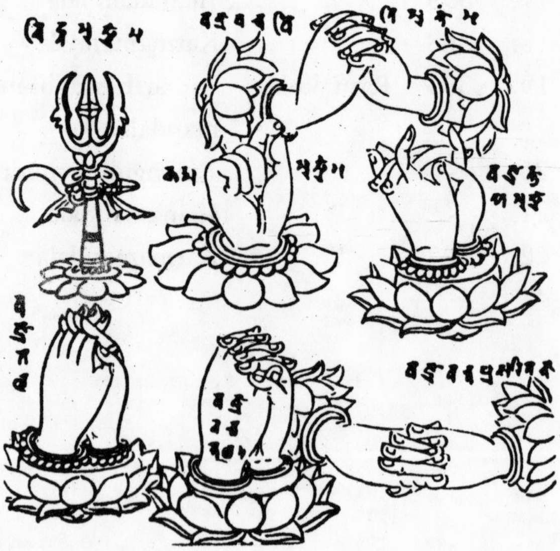

T Z.54.34

1.1.34. In the first chapter of G obu-shingan Vajrāṅkuśa is sitting in a lotus on an elephant. She has a hook, aṅkuśa in her right hand. (Γ Z.54.34) . Mudrās given above are : *Vajrabandha vinimuktam, vajrāṅkuśa-mahā-mudrā, karma-mudrā and cihna-mudrā.*

Vajrāṅkśa has the same attribute in the graphic Vajradhātu-mahā-maṇḍala ( T Z.38.34, Lokesh Chandra 439) . She is sitting on a lotus flower.

1.2.34. Vajrāṅkuśa is represented as Guhyāṅkuśī in the second chapter of Gobu-shin-gan ( ΓZ.54.67) . She has a hook with a three pointed Vajra in both of her hands and sitting

1.2.34.

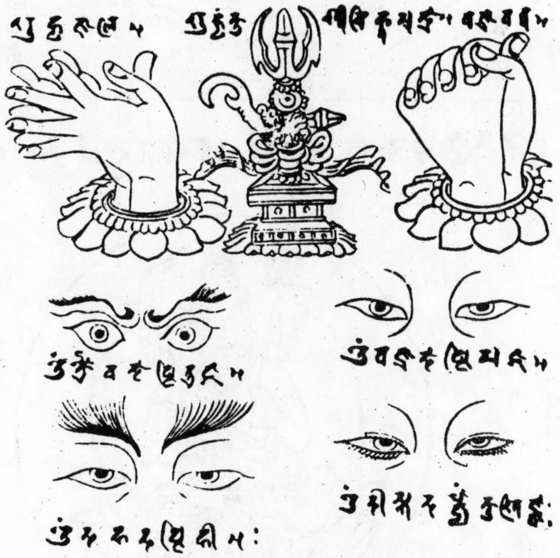

ΓZ.54.67

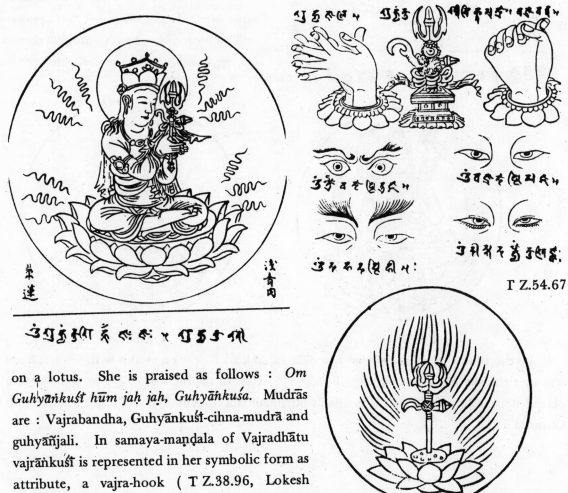

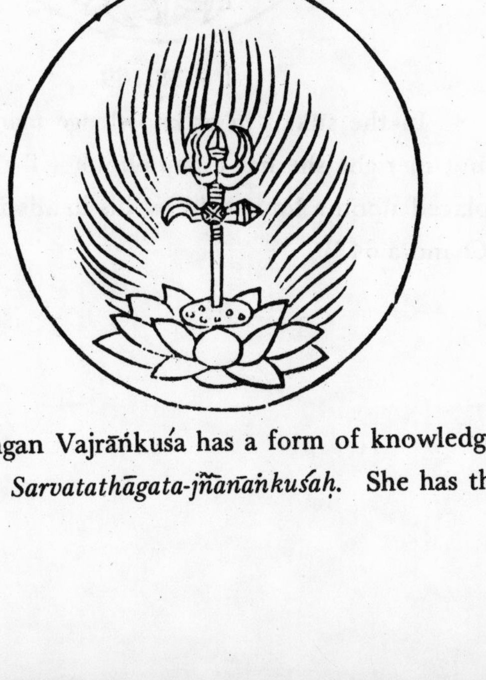

on a lotus. She is praised as follows : *Om Guhyāṅkuśī hūm jaḥ jaḥ, Guhyāṅkuśa.* Mudrās are : Vajrabandha, Guhyāṅkuśī-cihna-mudrā and guhyāñjali. In samaya-maṇḍala of Vajradhātu vajrāṅkuśī is represented in her symbolic form as attribute, a vajra-hook ( T Z.38.96, Lokesh Chandra 501) .

1.3.34. In the third maṇḍala of G obu-shingan Vajrāṅkuśa has a form of knowledge hook of All the T athāgatas : *Om jñānaṅkuśaḥ Sarvatathāgata-jñānaṅkuśaḥ.* She has the

1.3.34

T Z.54.93

same attribute placed in her lap supported by both of her hands. Mudrās should be vajrabandha, cihna and karma-mudrā (T Z.54.93).

T Z.38.169

T Z.38.346

In the sūkma m or knowledge maṇḍala vajrāṅkuśa is doing a mudrā with her left hand and in right she has a vajra-hook (T Z.38.169, Lokesh Chandra 570). T he vajra-hook is placed upon a lotus held by his hands in pūjā-maṇḍala of vajradhātu (T Z.38.346, Lokesh Chandra 643).

T Z.54.134

1.4.34. Because of her power of attraction vajrāṅkuśa is named as Vajrākarṣā in the fourth chapter of Gobushingan. T he attribute and the posture is identical with the third chapter. ( Γ Z.54.134 ) . T he script given under the illustration is : *Om Sarvatathāgata-karma-pūjā-samudra-spharaṇa samaya hūm. Sarvatathāgatakarṣe.* Mudrās are the same as they are in the third chapter.

In karma-maṇḍala of T railokya-vijaya the illustration ( Γ Z.38.346, Lokesh Chandra 749 ) . is the same as it is in the pūjā-maṇḍala of the vajradhātu. T he symbolic form (T Z.38.423, Lokesh Chandra 818 ) resembles the drawing given in samaya-maṇḍala of Vajra-dhātu. 2.1.34. Vajrāṅkuśa is praised for his power of attraction in T railokya-vijaya-maha-mandala of STT S : *Om vajrāṅ-kuśa mahā-krodhā-karṣaya sarva-samayān hūm jjaḥ* ( SΓΓ S 194) .

Vajrāṅkuśa is personified as Hayagrīva in the maṇḍalas of sakala-jagad-vinaya. 3.1.34. In mahā-maṇḍala she is named Hayagrīva with a great lotus hook : *Om Hayagrīva mahā-padmāṅkuśā-karṣaya śīghram sarva-padma-kula-samayān padmāṅkuśa-dhara hūm jjaḥ.* ( STT S 327) 3.2.34. T he same form is mentioned in its mudrā-maṇḍala : *Om padmāṅ-kuśākarṣaya mahā-padma-kulān hayagrīva-samaya hūm* ( SΓΓ S 346) . 3.3.34. Knowledge-hook of the lotus family is praised as : *Om padma-jñānaṅkuśa hūm* ( SΓΓ S 359) . 3.4.34. Again in the action-maṇḍala he is called Hayagrīva : *Om Hayagrīve ānaya hūm jaḥ* ( SΓΓ S 368) .

4.1.34. In mahā-maṇḍala of Sarvārthasiddhi vajrāṅkuśa incites and attracts Ākāśa-garbha : *Om sarvaratnākarṣa āryāruṇa mahā-sattva bhagavantam ākāśagarbham codayākar-ṣaya śīghram hoḥ jaḥ* ( STT S 393) . 4.4.34. In its action maṇḍala he is called the attraction of gem-hooks : *Om Ratnāṅkuśyākarṣa jjaḥ* ( SΓΓ S 427) .

Names of Vajrāṅkuśa in the 16 maṇḍalas:

| Ch. | P. | Kula | Maṇḍala | Names |
|---|---|---|---|---|
| 1. | 55 | Buddhakula | Vajradhātu-mahā-m. | Vajrāṅkuśa. |
| 2. | - | ” | Vajraguhya-vajra-m. | G uhyāṅkuśa |
| 3. | - | ” | Vajrajñāna-dharma-m. | Sarvatathāgatajñānāṅkuśa. |
| 4. | - | ” | Vajrakārya-karma-m. | Sarvatathāgatākarṣā. |
| 6. | 194 | Vajrakula | Γ rilokavijaya-mahā-m. | Vajrāṅkuśa-mahā-krodha. |
| 7. | - | Vajrakula | Krodhaguhya-mudrā maṇḍala | Vajrāṅkuśa-mahā-krodhā. |
| 8. | - | ” | Vajrakula-dharmajñāna-ṣamayamaṇḍala. | — |
| 9. | - | ” | Vajrakula-karmamaṇḍala | — |
| 15. | 327 | Padmakula | Sakalajagadvinaya-mahā-maṇḍala. | Hayagrīva. |
| 16. | 346 | ” | Padmaguhya-mudrā-maṇḍala | Padmāṅkuśa, Hayagrīva-samayā. |
| 17. | 359 | ” | Jñānamaṇḍala | Padma-jñānāṅkuśa. |
| 18. | 368 | ” | Karmamaṇḍala | Hayagrīva. |
| 19. | 393 | Ratnakula | Sarvārthasiddhi-mahā-maṇḍala. | Sarva-ratnākarṣa. |
| 20. | - | ” | Ratnaguhya-mudrā-maṇḍala. | — |
| 21. | - | ” | Jñānamaṇḍala | — |
| 22. | 427 | ” | Karmamaṇḍala | Ratnāṅkuśyākarṣā. |

## 35. VAJRAPĀŚA

金剛索菩薩

Bodhisattva Vajrapāśa sits in the South. He has beings of asceticism of beautitude which attracts the beings the state of Buddha. His right hand draws a pasa and his left fist is kept on his thigh. He is of yellow colour. (Γ ajima 189). Bhagavān enters the sattva-vajra samādhi which originates from the samaya of praveśa- mahā-sattva and utters the seed syllable Vajrapāśa. As soon as he utters these words Vajradhara emerges from the hearts of All the Γ athāgatas in the form of groups of mudras of the samaya praveśa of all the Γ athāgatas. Mahābodhi-sattva vajrapāśa is formed from these mudrās who sits in the lunar disc in gem door and recites these verse while making All the T athāgatas enters: "Oho I am the strong vajrapāśa of All the Buddhas as all those who are entered into every particle are entered by me again." ( SΓΓ S 56 ) .

I.1.35

Γ Z.54.35

I.1.35. Vajrapāśa in the first chapter of Gobu-shingan has a noose in his right hand and the left fist in resting upon his thigh as usual. He is riding a horse (Γ Z.54.35) . Among the mudrās the first is Vajrabandha-mahā-mudrā the second in between is action-mudrā and the the third showing his attribute is the cihna mudrā.

In vajradhātu-mahā-maṇḍala vajrapāśa has the same attribute as mentioned above but the noose is looking like a snake-noose (nāga-pāśa) . he is sitting on a lotus ( T Z.38.35, Lokesh Chandra).

I.2.35. Vajrapāśa in his esoteric form in the

T Z.54.69

second chapter of Gobu-shingan is holding a lotus flower by both of his hands and upon the lotus there is a noose with three pointed vajras on both the edges. He is praised as: *Om guhya-pāśa hūm hūm hūm hūm, guhya-pāśa.* (T Z. 54.69). Here are five mudrās of vajra-pāśa : *vajra-bandha, cihnamudrā, vajrāñjali-guhya-mahā-mudrā and vajrabandhaguhyamahā-mudrā.*

Vajrapāśa in samaya-maṇḍala of vajradhātu is depicted by his attribute a noose on a lotus flower (T Z.38.97, Lokesh Chandra 502).

In sūkṣma-maṇḍala of Vajradhātu the attribute of vajrapāśa is indistinct. He is sitting on a lotus (T Z. 38.170, Lokesh Chandra 571). He is doing mudrās by both of his hands.

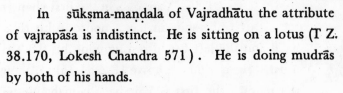

I.3.35.

T Z.54.94

I.3.35. Sarvatathāgata-jñāna-pāśa is the form of vajra-pāśa in the third chapter of Gobu-shingan. He has the same attribute a vajra-noose placed on a lotus (TZ.54.94).

I.4.35.

I.4.35. As vajrapāśa enters the beings with the help of his noose, he is named sarvatathāgata-praveśa in the fourth chapter of Gobu-shingan: *Om sarvathāgata-praveśa-pūjā-spharaṇa-megha-samudra-samaya hūm. Sarvatathāgata-praveśa.* He holds a noose kept straight in his lap by both of his hands (T Z.54.135) His vajrabandha, cihna and action mudrās are given besides.

T Z.54.135

Noose has a different shape in action-maṇḍala of vajradhātu, held by vajra-pāśa by both of his hands. (T Z. 38.243, Lokesh Chandra 644).

In Γ railokaya-vijaya-karma-maṇḍala vajrapāśa ( T Z.38.347, Lokesh Chandra 750). has the same attribute with the same posture as given in the preceeded drawing and his samaya form. (T Z.38.427, Lokesh Chandra 819) is identical with the samaya-maṇḍala of the vajradhātu. 2.1.35. In T railokya-vijaya-mahā-maṇḍala in STT S vajrapāśa is applauded for his power of entering in the angry representation *Om vajra-pāśa mahā krodha praveśaya sarva-samayān hūm phaṭ* (STT S 194). 3.1.35. Γ he unfailing lotus noose in its angry appearance attracts maha pasupati, Vama, Varuna, Kubera, Brahmā and Veśadhara: *Om Amogha-padma-pāśa-krodhākarṣaya pravesaya mahā-paśupati Yama varuṇa Kubera-Brahmā Veśa-dhara padma-kula, samayān-hūm hūm* (STTS 346). 3.3.35. Amoghapāśa in knowledge-maṇḍala is mentioned in this dhāraṇī *Om padma jñānāmoghapāśa hūm* ( STTS 359) and 3.4.35. in action-maṇḍala: *Om Amoghapāśa-krodha pīḍaya hūm phaṭ* (STTS 368).

4.1.35. In mahā-maṇḍala of sarvārthasiddhi he is named as sarva-ratna-praveśa-samaya and ratnapāśa: *Om sarva-ratna-praveśa-samaya praveśaya samayān mahā-maṇi rājakulam ratna-pāśa hūm* (STTS 393). 4.4.35. Gem-noose belongs to its action-maṇḍala: *Om maṇi-ratna-paśe hūm* ( S TTS 427).

Names of Vajrapāśa in the 16 maṇḍalas:

| Ch. | P. | Kula | Maṇḍala | Names. |
|---|---|---|---|---|
| 1. | 56 | Buddhakula | Vajradhātu-mahā-m. | Vajrapāśa. |
| 2. | - | " | Vajraguhya-vajra-m. | Guhya-pāśa. |
| 3. | - | " | Vajrajñāna-dharma-m. | Sarvatathāgata-jñāna-pāśa. |
| 4. | - | " | Vajrakārya-karma-m. | Sarvatathāgata-praveśa. |
| 6. | 194 | Vajrakula | Trilokavijaya-mahā-m. | Vajra-pāśa-mahā-krodha |
| 7. | - | " | Krodhaguhya-mudrā-m. | — |
| 8. | - | " | Vajrakula-dharmajñāna samayamaṇḍala. | — |
| 9. | - | " | Vajrakula-karmamaṇḍala | — |
| 15. | 327 | Padmakula | Sakalajagadvinaya-mahā maṇḍala | Amogha-padma-pāśa-krodha. |
| 16. | 346 | " | Padmaguhya-mudrā-maṇḍala. | Amoghapāśa-krodha-samaya. |
| 17. | 359 | " | Jñānamaṇḍala | Padma-jñānāmogha-pāśa. |
| 18. | 368 | " | Karmamaṇḍala | Amoghapāśa-krodha. |
| 19. | 393 | Ratnakula | Sarvārthasiddhi-m. | Ratna pāśa. |
| 20. | - | " | Ratnaguhya-mudrā-m. | — |
| 21. | - | " | Jñānamaṇḍala | — |
| 22. | 427 | " | Karmamaṇḍala | Maṇi-ratna-pāśa. |

## 36. VAJRASPHOṬA

金剛鏁菩薩

Vajra-sphoṭa occupies the Western direction. Sphoṭa properly signifies blaze, it is the blossoming of the bodhicitta. The Chinese word souo signifies chain or chain terminated by a grapnel, that is held by the bodhisattva in kongokai. This chain serves her in well-fixing the beings in the bodhi. His left hand is closed and the right hand carries the chain. He is of flesh colour (Γajima 189).

Bhagavān enters the samādhi sattva-vajra which originates from the samaya of mahā-sattva-sphoṭa and utters the samaya seed-syllable of All the Tathāgatas as vajra-sphoṭa. As he utters this vajradhara emerges from the hearts of All the Tathāgatas in the form of group of mudrās of samaya-bandha of All the Tathāgatas which coalese into the form of Mahā-bodhisattva-vajrasphoṭa who stations himself in the religion door in a lunar disc. Binding All the Tathāgatas he recites this verse : "Oho I am the strong vajra-chain of All the Tathā-gatas, because he wants to bind all those who are free from all bondages (STTS 57).
I.1.36.

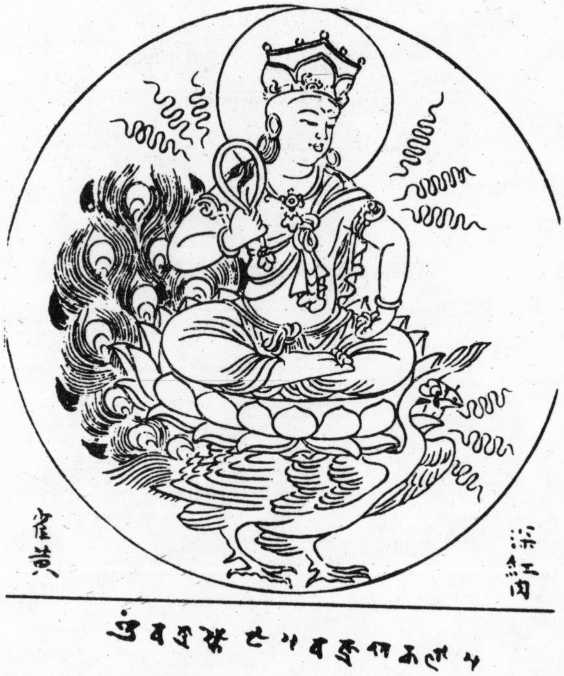

Γ Z.54.36

I.1.36. In the first chapter of Gobu-shingan vajra-sphoṭa is called vajra-sphoṭa and vajra sakala: Om vajra-sphota, vajra-sakala. He is called vajra-sakala because of his attributes, a chain in his right hand he is riding a peacock (T Z.54.36). The mudrās are named as vajra-sphoṭa-mahā-mudrā, karma-mudrā and cihna-mudrā.

Vajra-sphoṭa in vajradhātu-mahā-maṇḍala holds a chain with vajras on both of its edges in his right hand with his palm opened upwards. He is sitting on a lotus (T Z.38.36, Lokesh Chandra 444).

I.2.36. Vajra-sphoṭa in his esoteric appearence appears in the second chapter of Gobu-shingan as Guhya-sphoṭa: *Om Guhya-sphoṭa vam vam vam vam. Guhya-sphoṭa.* She has a vajra in her hands and is sitting on a lotus. (T Z.54.70). Mudras are

T Z.38.36

I.2.36.;

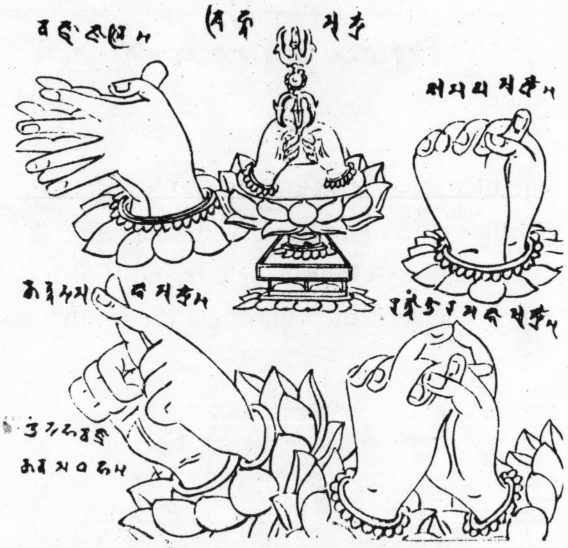

samaya, cihna, vajrājñali, ratnāṅkuśa and ?

Vajrasphoṭa in vajradhātu-samaya-maṇḍala is depicted as a vajra placed in a lotus (T Z.38.98, Lokesh Chandra 503).

I.3.36. The same attribute appears in the third chapter of Gobu-shingan under the name: *Sarva-tathāgatasphoṭa Om jñāna-sphoṭa, Sarvatathāgata-sphoṭa.* He is holding a lotus. Upon the lotus can be seen a pair of hands holding a vajra

I.3.36.

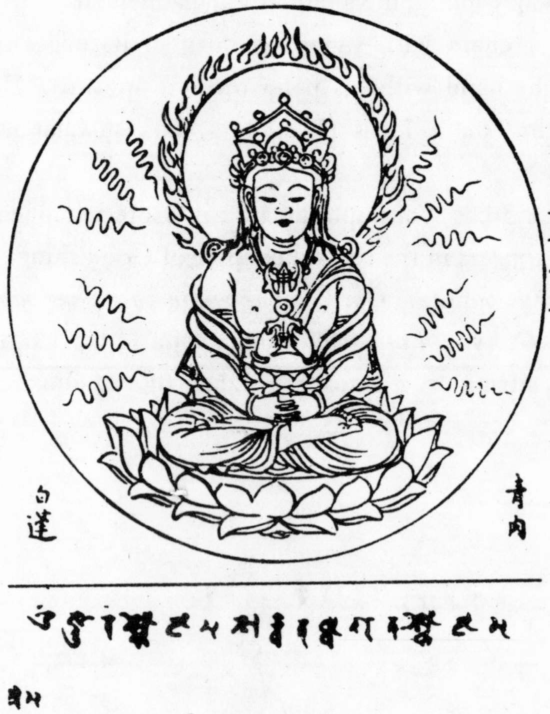

Γ Z.54.95

(Γ Z.54.95) . His samaya-bandha, cihna and action-mudrās are given with the illustration.

Vajrasphoṭa in sūkṣma-maṇḍala of vajradhātu has a vajra chain in his right hand like the preceded drawing. Vajra on his hand is visible (Γ Z.38.171, Lokesh Chandra 572) .

I.4.36. A lotus is held by both of his hand straight in the lap of vajra-sphota upon which is placed the vajra-chain the script under the illustration is as follows : *Om sarvata-*

Γ Z.54.136

*thāgata - pūjā - spharaṇa - megha-samudra -bandha-samaya hūm. Sarvatathāgata bandha-samaya.* (Γ Z.54.136) . Again the same mudrās are given with the illustration.

三

A chain on a lotus is held by Vajrasphota in his hands. He is sitting on a lotus (T Z.38.244, Lokesh Chandra 645) .

The same illustration is given in Trailokya-vijayakarma maṇḍala (T Z.38.348, Lokesh Chandra 751) . The illustration of vajrashoṭa in its samaya maṇḍala (T Z.38.425, Lokesh Chandra 820) is the same as it is given in vajradhātu-samayamaṇḍala. 2.1.36. In Trailokyavijaya-mahā-maṇḍala of STTS he has a terrific appearence: *Om vajra-sphoṭa-mahā-krodha bandha bandha sarva-samayan hūm phaṭ* (STTS 194) . 3.1.36. In mahā-maṇḍala of sakala-jagad-vinaya vajra-shopṭa is named as padma-sphoṭa because of his family: *Om padma-sphoṭa bandha sarva-padma-kula-samaya śīghram hūm vam* (STTS 327) . 3.2.36. In the next three maṇḍalas he is named as saṅkala of the lotus family, knowledge and action; in its mudrā maṇḍala he is mentioned as: *Om padma-saṅkala vam* (STTS 346) , 3.3.36. in the knowledge-maṇḍala: *Om padma jñāna-sphoṭa hūm* (STTS 359) ; and 3.4.36, action mandala : *Om padma-saṅkala-bandha hūm phat* (STTS 368).

4.1.36. In sarvārthasiddhi-mahā-maṇḍala he is called for his binding power: *Om maṇi-bandha hūm vam* (STTS 393) and 4.4.36, in its action maṇḍala: *Om maṇi-ratna-sphoṭa vam* (STTS 427) .

Names of Vajrasphoṭa in the sixteen maṇḍalas

| Ch. | P | Kula | Maṇḍala | Names. |
|---|---|---|---|---|
| 1. | 57 | Buddhakula | Vajradhātu-mahā-m. | Vajra-sphoṭa-vajra-saṅkala |
| 2. | - | " | Vajraguhya-vajra-m. | Guhya-sphoṭa. |
| 3. | - | " | Vajrajñāna-dharma-m. | Sarvatathāgata-sphoṭa. |
| 4. | - | " | Vajrakārya-karma-m. | Sarvatathāgatabandha-samaya |
| 6. | 194 | Vajrakula | T rilokavijaya-mahā-maṇḍala. | Vajra-sphoṭa-mahā-kraodha. |
| 7. | - | " | Krodhaguhya-mudrā-m. | — |
| 8. | - | " | Vajrakula-dharmajñāna-samayamaṇḍala. | — |
| 9. | - | " | Vajrakula-karma-m. | — |
| 15. | 327 | Padmakula | Sakalajagadvinaya-mahāmaṇḍala. | Padma-sphoṭa |
| 16. | 346 | " | Padmaguhya-mudrā-m. | Padma-saṅkala. |
| 17. | 359 | " | Jñānamaṇḍala | Padma-jñāna-sphoṭa |
| 18. | 368 | " | Karmamaṇḍala | Padma-saṅkala-bandha |
| 19. | 394 | Ratnakula | Sarvārthasiddhi-mahā-maṇḍala | Maṇi-bandha |
| 20. | - | " | Ratnaguhya-mudrā-m | — |
| 21. | - | " | Jñānamaṇḍala. | — |
| 22. | 427 | " | Karmamaṇḍala | Maṇi-ratna-sphoṭa. |

## 37. VAJRAGHAṆṬA.

金剛鈴菩薩

Vajraghaṇṭa or Vajrāveśa occupies the North. Āveśana signifies entry, introduction, as the Chinese translators have interpreted this name. The word is also taken in the meaning of reuniting and making penetrate and to cause to penetrate together, the sound of the sonnet pentrates on all sides. The bodhisattva causes all the beings to enter the nirvana and causes them to obtain deliverance and the felicity. The sound of the sonnet pleases the men, and the sonnet is the emblem of felicity. The mantra of Vajrāveśa contains the word ghaṇṭaḥ. His left haṇd remains closed on the thigh and the right holds the sonnet and supports it against the breast. (Tajima 189-190).

Bhagavān Vajradhara enter the sattva-vajra-samādhi which has its origin in the samaya mahāsattva Āveśa and utters the mudrā-ceṭa as Vajrāveśa. As soon as he utters this, vajradhara himself becomes groups of mudrās which is further transforemed into the body of mahābodhisattve vajrāveśa. He has a seat in the action door and recites this verse while making All the Tathagatas entered: "Oho I am the strong entrance of all the Buddhas who becomes servants after becoming kings" (STTS 58) .

I.1.37.

T Z.54.37

I.1.37. Vajraghaṇṭa in the first chapter of Gobu-shingan is riding a hen, and holding a vajra-bell by his right hand and the left fist is placed upon his thigh. *Om vajraghaṇṭa, Ghaṇṭa* is written under the illustration (TZ.54.37) . The mudrās given in the illustration are vajraghaṇṭa-mahā-mudrā, karma-mudrā and cihna-mudrā. Here ends the first chapter of vajradhātumahāmaṇḍala.

TZ.38.37

Vajraghaṇṭa in graphic vajra-dhātu-mahā-maṇḍala is doing a mudrā of holding a vajraghaṇṭa by his right hand and the left is in the same pose. (TZ.38.37, Lokesh Chandra 442).

I.2.37. A vajraghaṇṭa placed on a lotus is held by vajragahaṇṭa by both of his hands towards his left. He is named as guhya-ghaṇṭa and vajra-ghaṇṭa: *Om Guhya-ghanṭa aḥ aḥ aḥ aḥ vajra-ghantaḥ vajra-dhātu-guhyadhāraṇī (smap) natam.* The five mudrās given with the illustration are: *Vajrabandha, cihna mudrā, guhyāñjali, Om guhya-tāla-samaya and vajra mu(drā) (TZ.54.71 ).*

I.2.37.

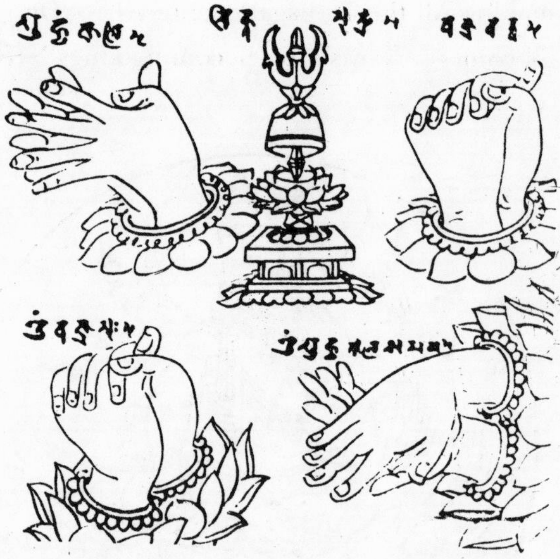

T Z.54.71

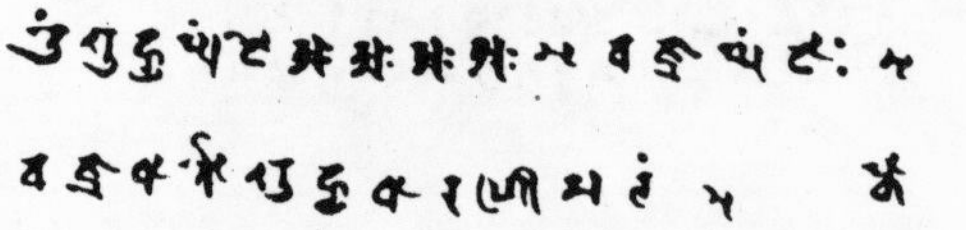

Vajraghaṇṭa in his samaya-form appears as a vajra-ghaṇṭa placed on a lotus in the vajradhātu samaya maṇḍala (TZ.39.99, Lokesh Chandra 504).

I.3.37. The third chapter of Gobu-shingan belongs to knowledge, thus the knowledge bell appears in this chapter: *Om jñāna-ghaṇṭa, sarvatathāgata-*

I.3.37.

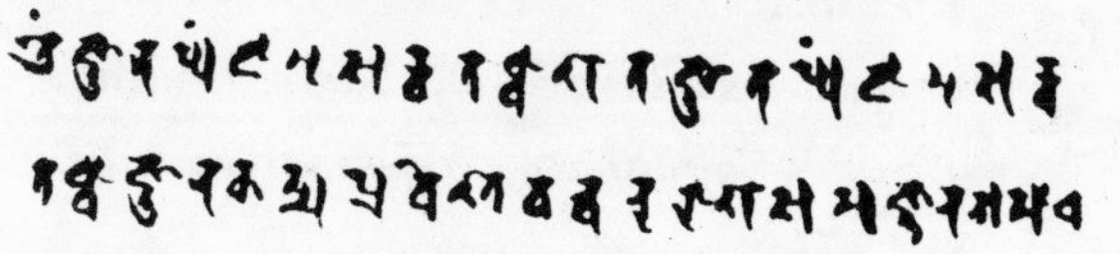

T Z.54.71

*jñāna-ghaṇṭa-, sarvatathāgata jñāna-karma-praveśa-bandhā-nurāga-samayajñāna-samādha(yaḥ).* He has the same attribute,a vajra-bell (TZ.54.71) .

TZ.38.172

TZ.38.245

Again in the sūkṣma maṇḍala of vajradhātu he is holding a bell with a three pointed vajra in his right hand as if he is ringing the bell (TZ.38.172, Lokesh Chandra 573) . In action-maṇḍala of Vajradhātu vajraghaṇṭa is holding lotus in his hands and his attribute is placed over there (TZ.38.245, Lokesh Chandra 646)

1.4.37. Sarvatathāgata-ghaṇṭa belongs to the fourth chapter of Gobu-shingan. A vajra-ghaṇṭa or a lotus is placed in his lap and his hands are in such a posture as if they are supporting his attribute. With this illustration ends pūjā : *Om Sarvatathāgatāveśa-pūjā-*

I.4.37

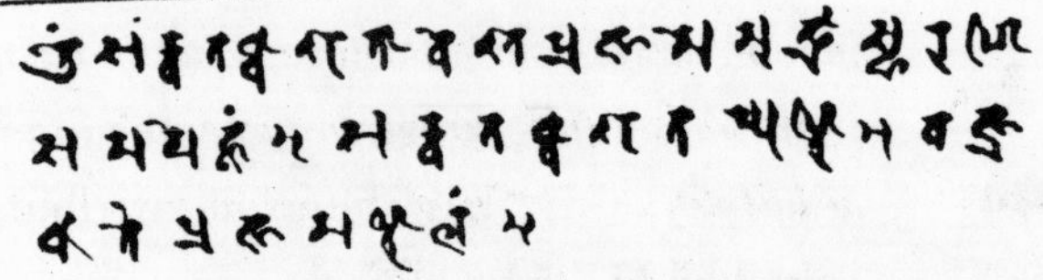

Γ Z.38.137

*samundra-samaya hūm. Sarvatathāgata-ghaṇṭa. Vajradhātu-pūjā-maṇḍala ( TZ. 54.137).*

2.4.31. Γhe same form is illustrated in the puja maṇḍala of graphic Vajradhātu and Trailokyavijaya-karma maṇḍala (T Z.38.349, Lokesh Chandra 752) 2.2.37. In its samaya maṇḍala the given illustration ( TZ.38.426) is identical with Vajradhātu-samaya-maṇḍala. 2.1.37. In Trailokyavijaya-karma-maṇḍala of S TTS Vajraghaṇṭa has a terrific appearance. *Om vajrāveśa-mahā-krodhāveśaya sarva-samayān hūm aḥ* ( SΓΓ S 194). 3.1.37. Vajra-ghaṇṭa in the sakalajagad-vinaya-mahā-maṇḍala is named as Sanatkumāra and padmāveśa with six heads, who rings the lotusbell, makes all the samayas of lotus family utters, performs all the genstures and offers accomplishments : *Om Ṣaṇmukha santakumāra veśa-dhara padma-ghaṇṭayā-veśaya sarva-mudrām bandhaya sarva-siddhayu me prayaccha padmāveśa aḥ ah ah ah ah* ( SΓΓ S 327). 3.2.37. The six headed divinity has a feminine form in the next maṇḍala : *Om padma-ghaṇṭa–dhāri śīghram āveśaya samayān ṣaṇmukhi aḥ* 3.3.37. In its knowledge maṇḍala he is referred as jñānaveśa : *Om padma-jñānāveśa hūm* ( SΓΓ S 359) 3.4.37. Vajra-ghaṇṭa is lotus-bell in action-maṇḍala : *Om padma-ghaṇṭāveśaya hūm phaṭ* ( STT S 368).

4.1.37, 4.4.37. In the mahā- and action maṇḍalas of Sarvārtha-siddhi he is named maṇi-ratnāveśa and maṇi-ratnāveśa : *Om maṇi-ratnāveśa aḥ* ( SΓΓ S 393) and *Om maṇi-ratnāveśa aḥ* ( SΓΓ S 427).

Names of the vajra-ghaṇṭa in the sixteen maṇḍalas:

| Ch. | P. | Kula | Maṇḍala | Names |
|---|---|---|---|---|
| 1. | 58 | Buddhakula | Vajradhātu-mahā-m. | Vajra-ghaṇṭa. |
| 2. | - | ” | Vajraguhya-vajra-m. | Guhya-ghaṇṭa, vajraghaṇṭa. |
| 3. | - | ” | Vajrajñāna-dharma-m. | Sarvatathāgata-jñāna-ghaṇṭa. |
| 4. | - | ” | Vajrakārya-karma-m. | Sarvatathāgata-ghaṇṭa. |
| 6. | 194 | Vajrakula | Trilokavijaya-mahā-maṇḍala. | Vajrāveśa-mahā-krodha |
| 7. | - | ” | Krodhaguhya-mudrā-m. | — |
| 8. | - | ” | Vajrakula-dharma-jñāna-samayamaṇḍala. | — |
| 9. | - | ” | Vajrakula-karma-m. | — |
| 15. | 32 | Padmakula | Sakaljagadvinaya-mahā-maṇḍala | Sanatkumāra padmāveśa. |
| 16. | 346 | ” | Padmaguhya-mudrā-m. | Padma-ghaṇṭa-dhārī. |
| 17. | 359 | ” | Jñānamaṇḍala | Padma-jñānāveśa. |
| 18. | 368 | ” | Karmamaṇḍala | Padma-ghaṇṭa. |
| 19. | 393 | Ratnakula | Sarvārthasiddhi-mahā-Maṇḍala. | Maṇi-ratnāveśa. |
| 20. | - | ” | Ratnaguhya-mudrā-m. | — |
| 21. | - | ” | Ratnaguhya-mudrā-m. | — |
| 22. | 427 | ” | Karmamaṇḍala | Maṇi -ratnāveśa. |

## TWENTY DEITIES OF OUTER CIRCLE

### 1. MĀYĀVAJRA-VIDYĀRĀJA (Nārāyaṇa)

那羅延天

Māyāvajra-vidyārāja as the first among the twenty deities of the outer circle has a cakra as his attribute. According to Tajima (191) he is of flesh colour.

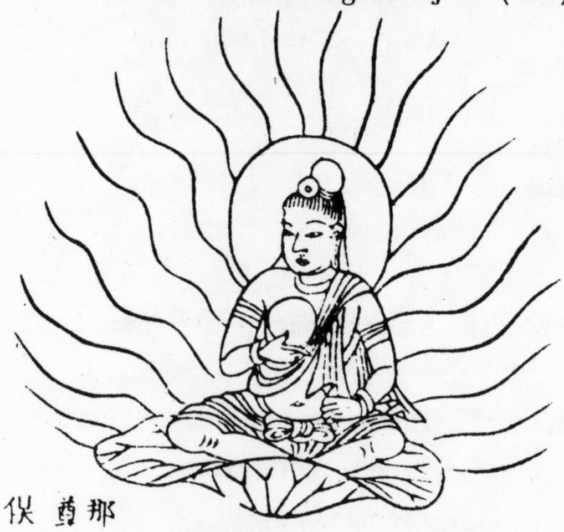


*TZ. 38.39*

In Trilokacakra-mahā-maṇḍala of STTS he has a power of tearing through : *Om Vajra-māya vidarśaya sarvam hūm phaṭ* (STTS 261).

The given illustration belongs to the mahā-maṇḍala of graphic Vajradhātu. The deity is sitting on a lotus leaf and holding a disc in his right hand which should be a wheel (TZ. 38.39). In STTS while explaining the delineation of this mandala he is mentioned as Vajra-cakra : *Om Vajra-cakra hūm* (STTS. 270).

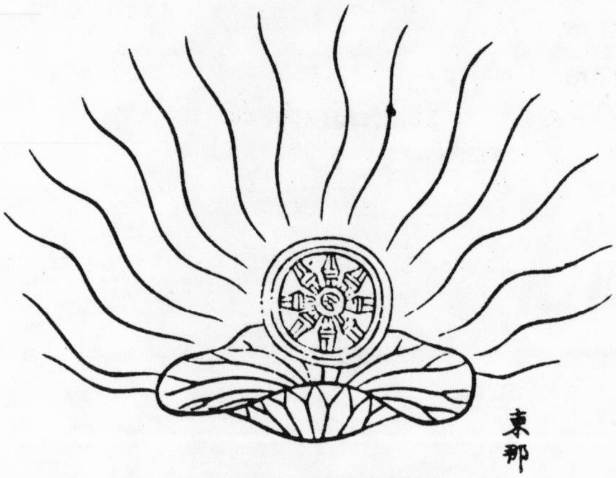


TZ.38.116

TZ.38.189

In vajra maṇḍala of STTS he is mentioned as vajra-cakra, as the mudrā of Vajramāya-vidyārāja : *Om vajra-cakra hūm* (STTS 282). In the samaya-maṇḍala of Vajradhātu he is depicted as a wheel (TZ. 38.116).

In sarva-vajra-kula-dharma-samaya-maṇḍala of STTS Māyā-vajra is praised for his power of tearing. *Om cchinda cchinda hūm phaṭ.* (STTS 293). In the second illustration given above belongs to dharma-maṇḍala of Vajradhātu. He holds a wheel in his right hand

(TZ. 38.189). In action mandala of sarva-Vajra-kula ofSTT S. he is called Vajra-hemā who can cut through with her wheel : *Om vajra heme cihinda cakreṇa vajriṇī hūm phaṭ* (STT S 301). In action maṇḍala of Vajradhātu he holds a six-spoked wheel which is placed upon his right hand (TZ. 38.262). He has the same form in Trailokyavijaya-karma-maṇḍala (TZ. 38.366). His symbolic form is the same in the samaya mandalas of Vajradhātu and Trailokyavijaya (TZ. 38.443)..

## 2.VAJRA-GHAṆṬA VIDYĀRĀJA (Kumāra)

拘摩羅天

Vajraghaṇṭa or Kumāra has the aspect of a young boy. He is of clear pale colour. He has three tufts in his hair. His left hand is closed and his right hand holds a small bell (Tajima 191-2). In Triloka-vijaya-mahā-maṇḍala he is named as Sanatkumāra and his attribute is a vajra-ghaṇṭa . *Sanatkumārāya vajraghaṇṭaḥ (STTS172).*

TZ. 38.40

His devī is Ṣaṣṭhī and her sattvārthatā is Vajrakaumārī : Ṣaṣthyai Vajrakaumārī (STT S 173).

The drawing of Vajraghaṇṭa extracted here belongs mahā-maṇḍala of graphic Vajradhātu (TZ.38.40). The deity is there sitting on a lotus leaf with a vajra bell in his right hand. Three tufts of hair as explained by Tajima are distincitly visible. The left fist is resting upon his thigh. He is the third vidyārāja who is praised for ringing the bell : *Om vajra-ghaṇṭa raṇa raṇa hūm phaṭ* (STT S)

Sūkṣma or samaya-maṇḍala of graphic Vajradhātu portrays him as a vajra-bell placed on a lotus leaf (TZ. 38.117). In vajra-kula-vajra maṇḍala vajra-ghaṇṭa utters his mudrā as vajra-ghaṇṭikā : *Om Vajra-ghaṇṭikā hūm* (STT S 283). The third and the fourth dharma-and karma-maṇḍalas of graphic Vajradhātu (TZ. 38.190, 963) and mahā-maṇḍala of Trailokyavijaya (TZ. 38.367) have the same forms of Vajraghaṇṭa. There is a slight change in his hair dressing in the first two drawings of these

TZ.38.117

three. In sarva-vajra-kula-dharma-samaya-maṇḍala in SITS he is praised for his power of overpowering : *Om āviśāviśa hūm phaṭ* (SITS 293). In action-maṇḍala of sarva-vajra-kula of in SITS he is named as Vajra-kaumārī. Her karma-samaya : *Om vajra-kaumārī śīghram āveśaya ghaṇṭā-śabdena vajra-pāṇi-pūjā vajra-samayam-anusmara raṇa raṇa hūm phaṭ* (SITS 301).

The samaya form of Vajra-ghaṇṭa in samaya-maṇḍala of Trailokyavijaya (TZ. 444) is the same as it is in samaya-maṇḍala of graphic Vajradhātu.

## MAUNAVAJRA (Brahmā)

梵天

Lotus is an attribute of Brahmā. According to Tajima he is of flesh colour and carries a blossomed flower (Tajima 194). Maunavajra is said to be his attribute in Trilokavijaya-jaya-mahā-maṇḍala . *Brahmaṇe maunavajraḥ.* (SITS 172) Brahmāṇī is his devī and her sattvarthata is Vajraśānti . *Brahmaṇyai Vajraśāntiḥ* (SITS 173).

The drawing given here belongs to Vajradhātu-mahā-maṇḍala (TZ. 38.42). Brahmā is holding a lotus flower in his right hand and the left is resting upon his thigh. He is sitting on a lotus leaf.

Maunavajra as the fourth vidyā-rāja gives his essence as follows : *Om vajra-mauna mahā-vrata hūm phaṭ* (SITS 261). While delineating this maṇḍala SITS (270) mentions him with a wooden stick : *Om vajra daṇḍa kāṣṭha hūm* (SITS 270).

TZ.38.42

In samaya-maṇḍala of graphic Vajra-dhātuBrahmā obtains a symbolic form as a flower placed in a lotus-leaf (TZ.38.119). Brahmā as Maunavajra in sarva-vajra-kula-vajra-maṇḍala is mentioned as daṇḍa-kāṣṭha : *Om Vajra-daṇḍa-kāṣṭha hūm* (SITS 283).

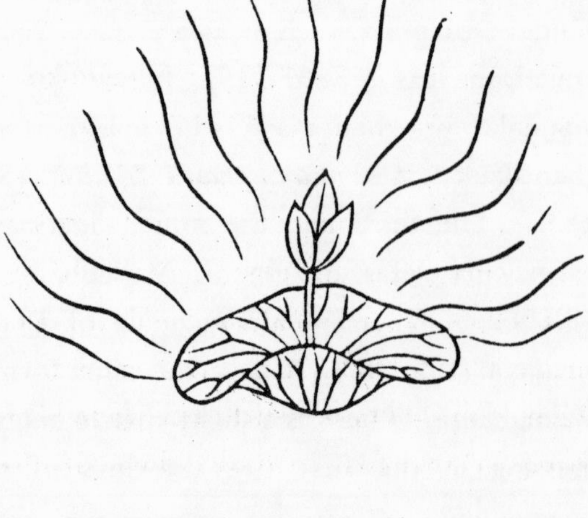

In dharma-maṇḍala of graphic Vajra-dhātu he has the same form as given in mahā-maṇḍala (TZ. 38.192). Dharma-samaya-maṇḍala of Vajra-kula applauds Brahmā in the following mantra . *Om bhūr bhuvaḥ sva hūm phaṭ* (STTS 293).

TZ. 38.265

Action-maṇḍala of graphic Vajradhātu portrays Brahmā holding a staff with a lotus. Something in the form of an umbrella is drawn upon a triśūla placed over the lotus. A type of banner is also added. All these come as attributes of Brahmā seperately but here they are combined (TZ.38.265).

The action-maṇḍala of STTS Brahmā has his feminined form as Vajraśānti Mahādevī who tells beads and kills the evil being only by his grave vision : *Om Vajraśānta jāpa japākṣa-mālayā sarvān māraya śānta-dṛṣṭayā hūm phaṭ* (STTS 301).

Brahmā in Trilokya-vijaya-karma maṇḍala has the same form as he has in the Vajra-dhātu-mahā-maṇḍala (TZ.38.369) and his form in samaya-maṇḍala of Trailokya-vijaya is identical with Vajra-dhātu-samaya-maṇḍala (TZ.38.446).

## 4. VAJRĀYUDHA (Indra)

帝釋天

TZ.38.43

Indra is of flesh colour. He holds a vajra by one hand according to Tajima (Tajima 194). In Trailokyavijaya-mahā-maṇḍalahe is named Indra and his attribute is vajrāyudha, Indrāṇī is his devī and her sattvārthatā is Vajramuṣṭi (STTS 172-3).

Mahāmaṇḍala of graphic Vajradhātu depicts Indra doing a mudrā with his right hand and his left fist rests upon his thigh (TZ.38.43). STTS in its Trilokacakra-mahā-maṇḍala depicts him as a subduer with the help of his attribute, vajra. Thus he is called vajrāyudha in this maṇḍala and its delineation : *Om vajrāyudha dāmaka hūm phaṭ*. Om vajrāyudha hūm (STTS 261, 270).

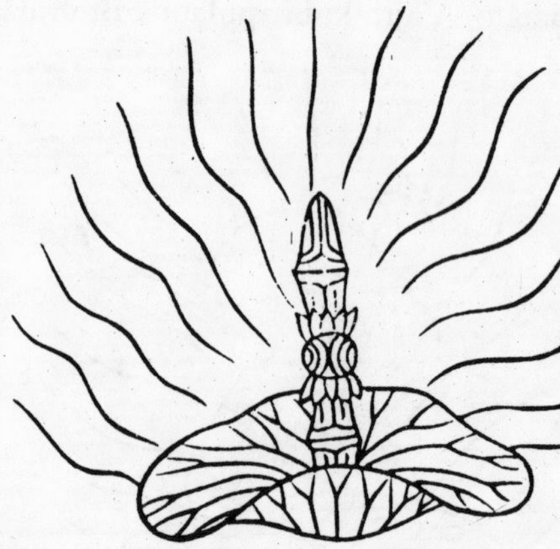

In vajra-kula-vajra-maṇḍala of trilokacakra in STTS his śakti is called vajra : *Om vajre hūm* (STTS 283). In samaya-maṇḍala of graphic Vajradhātu he is portrayed as a vajra also (TZ.38.120). Indra in dharma maṇḍala of graphic Vajradhātu has the same form as extracted above from mahā-maṇḍala. (TZ.38.193). In Dharma-maṇḍala of Trilokacakra he is said to have a power of splitting *Om bhinda bhinda hūm phaṭ* (STTS 293). There is a difference only in his head dress in action-maṇḍala of graphic maṇḍala (TZ.38.266). Indra is named Vajramuṣṭi who can destroy, split and torment all the evil beings by his vajra : *Om Vajramuṣṭi hana hana vajreṇa bhinda bhinda pīḍaya sarva-duṣṭa-hṛdyāni om śumbha niśumbha hūm phaṭ* (STTS 301). The drawings of Indra in karma and samaya-maṇḍalas of Trailokya-vijaya are identical with the depictions given above from mahā-and samaya-maṇḍalas of graphic vajradhātu (TZ.38.370,447).

## 5. VAJRAKUṆḌALĪ (Āditya)

日天

Tajima says that Āditya is of flesh colour and holds a sun disc (Tajima 194). In Trilokavijaya-mahā-maṇḍala he is called Vajrakuṇḍali in the name of his attribute : *vajrakundle Vajra-kuṇḍali. His devi is Amṛtā and her sattvārthatā* is Vajrāmṛtā : *Amṛtāyai Vajrāmṛtā* (STTS 172, 173).

Āditya in graphic Vajradhātu-mahā-maṇḍala holds a sun disc by his right hand and sits on a lotus leaf (TZ.38.44). Vajrakuṇḍali is described as the first vajrakrodha in Triloka-cakra-mahā-maṇḍala. He is mahā-vajra-krodha who can seize or tame, slay, burn, devour, destroy by his vajra, quiver heads and split hearts : *Om Vajrakuṇḍali mahā-vajra-krodha grhna hana daha paca vidhvansa vajrena murdhanam sphalaya bhinda hrdayam vajra krodha hum phat*(STTS 262).

He is related to flames while he is mentioned in the delineation of maṇḍala : *Om pra-*

T Z. 38.44

*jvalita pradīpta vajra hūm* (STTS 271).

He has a feminined form of a vajra with flames in vajra-maṇḍala of Triloka-cakra : *Om vajra-jvāle hūm* (STTS 283). But samaya-maṇḍala of graphic vajradhātu depicts him as a sun disc placed on a lotus leaf (TZ. 38.121).

Dharma and action maṇḍalas of graphic Vajradhātu depict the same forms of Āditya as it is in mahā-maṇḍala (TZ.38.194, 267). He is praised for his characterestic of taming the evil beings in dharma-maṇḍala : *Om dama dama hūm phaṭ* (STTS 294). He has a feminined form as Vajrāmṛtā in action-maṇḍala who has the same qualities as in mahā-maṇḍala. She can subdue, bind, kill, devour, destroy, split, cut, burn all the evil beings : *Om vajrāmṛte sarva-duṣṭān gṛhṇa bandha hana paca vidhvansaya vināśaya bhinda cchinda bhasmīkuru mūrdhān tanuya vajreṇa ye ketu mām amukasya vighna-vināyaka tam dāmaya dīpta-krodha-vajriṇi hūm phaṭ.*

Trailokyavijaya-karma and samaya-maṇḍalas have the same forms of Āditya as they are in graphic mahā and samaya-maṇḍalas of Vajradhātu (TZ.38.371, 448).

## 6. VAJRAPRABHA (Candra)

月天

Candra is of flesh colour, his left hand is closed, his right hand carries a crescent of moon (Tajima 194). He is personified as Indu in Triloka-vijaya-mahā-maṇḍala, vajraprabha is his attribute, his devī is Rohiṇī and her sattvārthatā is vajrakānti : *Rohiṇyai Vajrakāntiḥ* (STTS 172-173).

TZ.38.45

Candra holds a crescent of moon by his right hand and sits on a lotus leaf in graphic Vajradhātu-maṇḍala (TZ.38.45). He attains an angry form in Trilokacakramahā-maṇḍala but that anger is tranquil : *Om vajra-saumya hūm* (STTS 271). His śakti is Vajra-samaya in Vajra-maṇḍala : *Om vajra-samaya hūm* (STTS 284).

But in samaya-maṇḍala of graphic Vajradhātu he

TZ.38.122

is depicted as a crescent of moon placed on a lotus leaf (TZ.38.122).

In dharma and action maṇḍalas he has the same forms as given above in mahā-maṇḍala (TZ.38.195, 268). In dharma-maṇḍala of Trilokacakra he is praised for his power of slaying : *Om māraya māraya hūm phaṭ* (STTS 294).

In action-maṇḍala of Trilokacakra he is called Vajrakānti who kills with her tranquil appearence and burning passions, she is Vajradharā who splits the hearts by satya, she is a great flame, terrific and white rays : *Om vajrakānti māraya saumya-rūpe pradīpta-rāgeṇa śighram hṛdayam vajra-dhara satyena mahā-jyotsnā karāle sita-raśmi vajriṇi hūm phaṭ* (STTS 302).

Candra obtains the same forms in Trailokgavijaya-karma and samaya-maṇḍalas and the Vajradhātu-mahā and samaya-maṇḍalas (TZ.38.372, 449).

## 7. VAJRADAṆḌA (Ketu)

彗星天

41

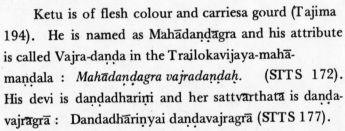

TZ.38.47

Ketu is of flesh colour and carriesa gourd (Tajima 194). He is named as Mahādaṇḍāgra and his attribute is called Vajra-daṇḍa in the Trailokavijaya-mahā-maṇḍala : *Mahādaṇḍagra vajradaṇḍaḥ.* (STTS 172). His devi is daṇḍadhariṇī and her sattvārthatā is daṇḍa-vajrāgrā : Dandadhāriṇyai daṇḍavajragrā (STTS 177).

Ketu holds a gourd by his right hand and his left hand is placed upon his left thigh (TZ.38.47) in mahā-maṇḍala of graphic Vajradhātu. He is called Vajra-daṇḍa in Trilokacakra-mahā-maṇḍala : *Om Vajra-daṇḍa tanuya sarva-duṣṭān-mahā-krodha hūm phaṭ* (STTS *Om Vajra-daṇḍa hūm* (STTS 271).

A gourd with a flower overhead placed in a lotus

TZ.38.124

TZ.38.197

leaf is the symbolic form of ketu in samaya-maṇḍala of graphic Vajradhātu (TZ.38.124). This form is named as vajra-daṇḍa in vajra-maṇḍala of Trilokacakra : *Om Vajra-daṇḍe hūm* (STTS 284). The gourd which is held by ketu by his right hand in the dharma-maṇḍala shows a crescent of moon with a spot (TZ.38.197). Otherwise the illustration is the same as given above. He has a power of striking down according to dharma-maṇḍala of Trilokackra : *Om ghātaya ghātaya hūm phaṭ* (STTS 294). Action-maṇḍala of Vajradhātu also depicts Ketu in the same manner. It can be a triratna or a cintāmaṇī shown over his gourd (TZ.38.270). Action maṇḍala of Trilokacakra calls him Vajra-daṇḍāgra : *Om Vajra-daṇḍāgre ghātaya hūm phaṭ* (STTS 302). Trailokyavijaya-karma and samaya-maṇḍalas form ketu in the same manner as mahā-and samaya-maṇḍalas of graphic Vajradhātu (TZ. 38.374. 451).

## 8. VAJRAPIṄGALA (piṅgala)

熒惑天

Fire is an attribute of Piṅgala and he is of flesh colour (Tajima 194). Trilokavijaya-mahā-maṇḍala in STTS names him as Piṅgala and his attribute as Vajrapiṅgala : *Piṅgalāya vajra-piṅgalaḥ* (STTS 172). His devī is called Jātahāriṇī and her tattvārthatā is Vajramekhalā (STTS 173).

The drawing given below belongs to graphic Vajradhātu-maṇḍala. A fire disc is placed upon his right palm opened flat near his chest (TZ.38.48). According to STTS in Trilokcakra-mahā-maṇḍala he is vajra-piṅgala and fearful anger who can horrify evil beings : *Om Vajra-piṅgala bhiṣaya sarva-duṣṭān bhīma-krodha hūm phaṭ* (STTS 262). But while

TZ.38.48

TZ.38.125

delineating the maṇḍala he is named as Vajra-vikṛta : *Om Vajra-vikṛta hūm* (STTS 271). Fire being an attribute of ketu is placed on a lotus leaf as his symbol in graphic Vajradhātu-samaya-maṇḍala (TZ.38.125). But in vajra-maṇḍala of Trilokacakra his terrific appearence is identified : *Om Vajra-bhīṣane hūm* (STTS 284).

In graphic Vajradhātu-dharma-maṇḍala ketu iṣ doing a mudrā by his right hand and sitting on a lotus leaf (TZ.38.198). His terrific appearence terrifies the beings, thus in dharma-maṇḍala of Trilokacakra he is praised in these words : *Om bhaya bhaya hūm phaṭ* . (STTS 294).

Action-maṇḍala forms him like mahā-maṇḍala in the drawing extracted before (TZ.38.271). Action maṇḍala of Trilokacakra has a total different appearence in the name of Vajramekhalā : *Om vajra-mekhala khana khana śabdena vaśīkuru dṛṣṭya māraya bhīṣaṇi hūm phaṭ* (STTS 303). Trailokyavijaya in its karma and samaya-maṇḍalas portray ketu like the maṇḍalas of graphic Vajradhātu (TZ.375,452).

TZ.38.271

## 9. VAJRASAUNDA (Vajracchinna)

金剛摧天

There are four Vināyakas, each occupying the middle of a side of the enclosure and the fifth that is Gaṇeśa. According to Tajima he holds a white parasol (Tajima 192-193). In mahā-maṇḍala of Trailokyavijaya he is named as Madhumatta and his attribute is Vajra-śauṇḍa : *Madhumattāya Vajraśauṇḍaḥ* (STTS 172). Māraṇī is his devī and her sattvārthatā is Vajravijayā : *Māraṇyai Vajravijayā* (*STTS 173*).

TZ.38.41

The given drawing belongs to mahā-maṇḍala of graphic Vajradhātu (TZ.38.41). Here Vajra-śauṇḍa is sitting on a lotus leaf and holding a parasol by both of his hands. Vajra-śauṇḍa as the first Gaṇapati utters his essence for bhagavān Vajrapāṇi : *Om vajra-śauṇḍa-mahā-gaṇapati rakṣa sarva duṣṭebhyo Vajra-dharājñām pālaya hūm phaṭ* (*STTS 263*). *He is* to rescue from all the evil beings and obey the orders of Vajradhara. In the delineation of the maṇḍala he is called Vajra-mahā : *Om Vajra-mahā hūm* (STTS 271).

The symbolic form of Vajra-śauṇḍa as a parasol is given in samaya-maṇḍala of graphic Vajradhātu (TZ.38.118). His symbolic form is named Vajra-mada in sarva-vajra-kula-vajra-maṇḍala in STTS : *Om Vajra-made hūm* (STTS 284). In dharma (TZ.38.191) and action-maṇḍala a (TZ.38.264) of graphic vajradhātu-maṇḍala he holds his parasol by his right hand and the left rests upon his mahā-maṇḍala of Trailokyavijaya has the same form as extracted above (TZ.38.368). Dharma-samaya-maṇḍala of vajrakula praises him for his power of intoxication: *Om mada mada hūm phaṭ* (STTS 294). Vajra-śauṇḍa is vajravilaya in action-maṇḍala who has a power of cutting, peercing, splitting, intoxication, extravagence and drinking : *Om Vajra-vilaye cchinda sina bhinda vajriṇi mādayonmādaya piva piva hūm phaṭ* (STTS 303).

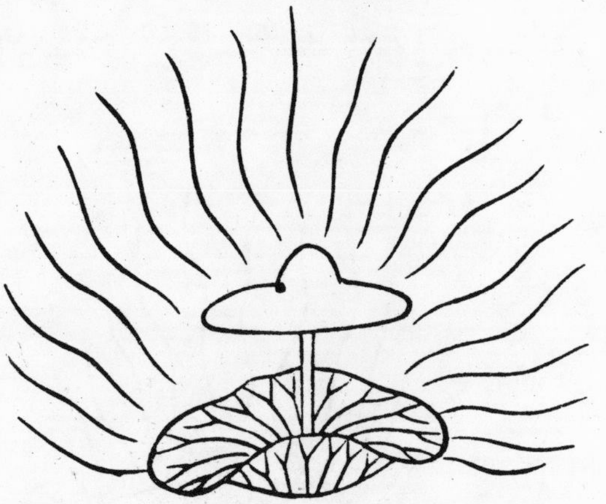

TZ.38.118

Trailokyavijaya-samaya-maṇḍala (TZ.38.445) has the same form of Vajraśauṇḍa as given above from samaya-maṇḍala of graphic Vajradhātu.

## 10. VAJRAMĀLA (Vajrabhakṣaṇa)

華縵毘那夜迦

Hizoki calls him Vināyaka carrying a garland, mālya Vināyaka. He holds a garland of flowers (Tajima 194). He is Madhukara and holds a vajramālā in the Trailokyavijaya-mahā-maṇḍala: *madhukarāya vajramālā* (STTS 172). Aśanā is his devī and her sattvārthatā is vajrāśanā: *aśanāyai vajrāśanā* (STTS 173).

TZ.38.46

Vajrabhakṣaṇa carries a garland of flowers in right hand and sits on a lotus leaf (TZ.38.46). in mahā-maṇḍala of graphic Vajradhātu. In mahā-maṇḍala of Trilokacakra he is defined as a deity who garlands and attracts and then ties and controls : *Om Vajra-māla-gaṇapataye mālayākarṣaya praveśayāveśaya bandhaya vaśīkuru māraya hūm phaṭ* (STTS 263). In its delineation he is called Vajra-mālā : Om Vajra-mālā hūm (STTS 271).

In the illustration given below there is a garland placed on a lotus leaf in samaya maṇḍala of graphic Vajradhātu (TZ.38.123). This symbolic form of Vajra-mālā is named as Vajra-māla in Vajra-maṇḍala of Triloka cakra : *Om Vajra-māla hūm* (STTS 284).

Vajramāla in dharma-maṇḍala of graphic Vajra-

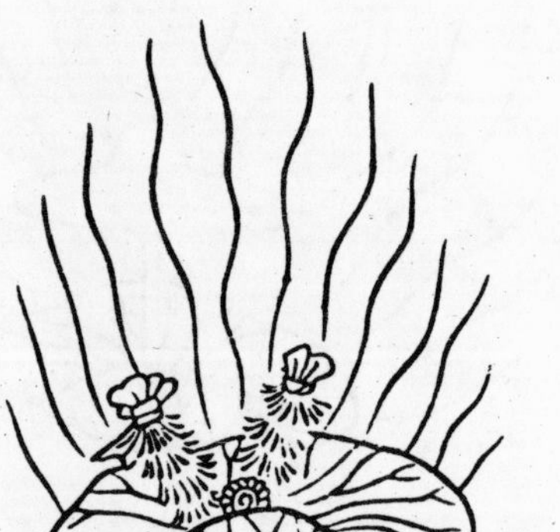

TZ.38.123

TZ.38.196

dhātu-maṇḍala holds a garland by his right hand and a sword by the left (TZ.38.196). In dharmā-maṇḍala of Trilokacakra he is praised for his quality of tying : *Om bandha bandha hūm phaṭ* (STTS 294).

In action maṇḍala Vajramāla holds a garland by both of his hands (TZ.38.269). He is

TZ38.269

feminined in the name of Vajrāśana who has a power of devouring all the evil beings. She has vajra like teeth she is full of strength, she eats human flesh, but she brings all the riches: *Om Vajrāśane bhakṣaya sarva-duṣṭān vajra-daśani śakti-dhāriṇī manuṣa-mānshāre nara-rucira śubha-priye majja vasānulepana vilipta-gātre ānaya sarva-dhana-dhānya-hiraṇya-suvarṇādīni saṁkrāmaya bala-deva-rakṣiṇī hūm phaṭ* (STTS 303).

Vajramāla attains the same form in Trailokya-vijaya-karma-maṇḍala (TZ.38.373) as in action maṇḍala and his symbolic form in Trailokya-vijaya (TZ.38.450) is identical with samaya-maṇḍala of graphic Vajradhātu.

## 11. VAJRAVAŚĪ
金剛衣天

Vajravaśī is called Vināyaka by Hizoki carrying a bow and arrows (Tajima 195). STTS in its Trilọkavijaya-maha-mandala names as jaya, his attribute is Vajravaśī, his devī is Vaśanā, her sattvārthatā is Vajravaśanā : *Vaśanāyai vajra-vasānā (STTS 172-173).*

TZ.38.51

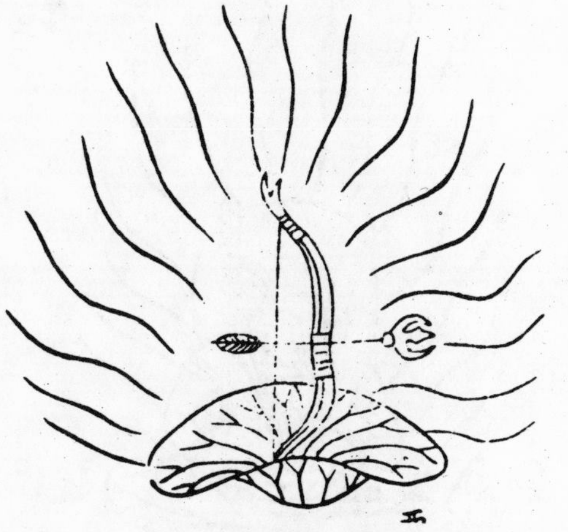

TZ.38.128

The drawing given above belongs to graphic Vajradhātu-mahā-maṇḍala. Jaya or Vajra-vaśī is carrying a bow and an arrow by his hands (TZ.38.51). He has a power of subduing the beings, thus he is praised for his Vaśīkaraṇa : *Om Vajravaśī mahā-gaṇapati vaśī-kuru. hūm phaṭ* (STTS 263). But while delineating the maṇḍala he is called Vajrārtha : *Om hūm phaṭ* (STTS 263). But while delineating the maṇḍala he is called Vajrārtha: *Om Vajrārtha hūm* (STTS 271).

A bow with an arrow symbolize Vajravaśī in samaya-maṇḍala of graphic Vajradhātu (TZ.38.128). In vajra-maṇḍala of Trilokacakra he is praised as: *Om Vajravaśe hūm* (STTS 285).

Dharma and karma-maṇḍalas of graphic Vajradhātu and Trailokya-vijaya-mahā-maṇḍala also have the same forms of Vajravaśī (TZ.38.201,279,378). In dharma-maṇḍala of cakra he is praised for being subdued: *Om Vaśī bhava hūm* (STTS 294). He is personified as Vajra-vaśī in action-maṇḍala of Trilokacakra who can subdue all the men and women and enslave them, whe rejoices those who are angry, she brings victory: *Om Vajra-vaśī ānaya vaśī-kuru sarva-puruṣān dāsī-kuru krudham prasādaya vyavahārebhyo'pyuttarāya vijayam karī vajra-patākā-dhāriṇī hūm phaṭ* (STTS 304).

Trilokya-samaya-maṇḍala personifies him in the form of a bow and an arrow like the graphic Vajradhātu-samaya-maṇḍala (TZ.38.455).

## 12 VINĀYAKA (Jaya)

毘那夜迦天

Vinayakawith a sword is called Jaya, he is of pale flesh colour (Tajima 195). Triloka-vijaya-mahā-maṇḍala in STTS names him Jayāvaha amd his attribute is named as Vijaya-vajra *Jayāvahāya vijayavajraḥ* (STTS 172). Rati is his devī and vajravaśā is her tattvārthatā. *Ratyai Vajravaśā* (STTS 173).

Jaya is shown with a vajra-sword in his left hand in the graphic Vajradhātu-mahā-maṇḍala (TZ.38.56). His attribute Vijaya-vajra brings victory according to the Trilokacakra-mahā-maṇḍala in STTS: *Om Vajra-vijaya vijayam kuru mahāgaṇapati hūm phaṭ* (STTS 263).

Jaya in the graphic Vajradhātu-samaya-maṇḍala is illustrated as a vajra-sword placed on a lotus leaf (TZ. 133). In Trilokacakravajra-maṇḍala he is personified as Vajrāparājitā: *Om vajrāparājite hūm* (STTS 285). In dharma and action maṇḍalas of graphic Vajradhātu (TZ. 38.206,279) and the trilokavijaya-mahā-maṇḍala (TZ. 38.383) Jaya holds his attribute in his right hand. Otherwise the illustrations are identical with mahā-maṇḍala. His symbolic form in Trailokyavijaya-samaya-maṇḍala is identical with the one given above (TZ.38. 460). He is called Jaya in dharma-maṇḍala: *Om Jaya Jaya hūm phaṭ* (STTS 294). He is personified as Vajra-vaśanā in action-maṇḍala of Trilokacakra. She brings garments and all sorts of food and drinks, she bears a Vajra-sword : *Om Vajra-vaśane ānaya sarva-vastrānna-pānādyupakaraṇāmi śīghram vaśī-kuru enan me prayacchaviśāviśa satyam kathaya Vajra-koṣa-dhāriṇī hūm phaṭ* ( STTS 304).

## 13. VAJRA-MUSALA (Rākṣasa)

羅刹天

西二羅刹天そ
三梏尊赤
肉色

A club is an attribute of Rākṣasa (Tajima 194). He carries club in his right hand. In Trilokavijayamahā-maṇḍala of STTS he is named as Koṣapāla and his attribute is vajra-musala : *Koṣapālāya Vajramusalaḥ.* His devī is Śivā and her tattvārthathā is Vajradūti : *Śivāyai Vajradūti* ( STTS 172,173).

In graphic Vajradhātu-maṇḍala Rākṣasa or Nirṛti holds a club in his right hand and his left hand is placed upon his thigh (TZ.38.49). He is praised for estroying all the evil beings : *Om Vajra-musala kṛṭṭa kuṭṭa sarva-duṣṭān dūta hūm phaṭ* ( STTS 264).

A club surrounded by flames is placed on

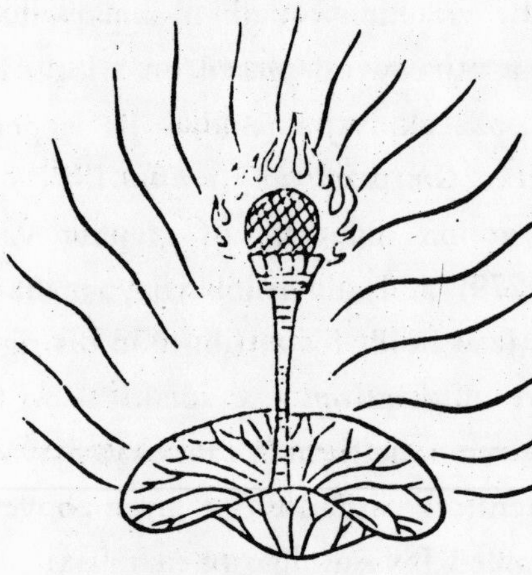

T Z.38.126

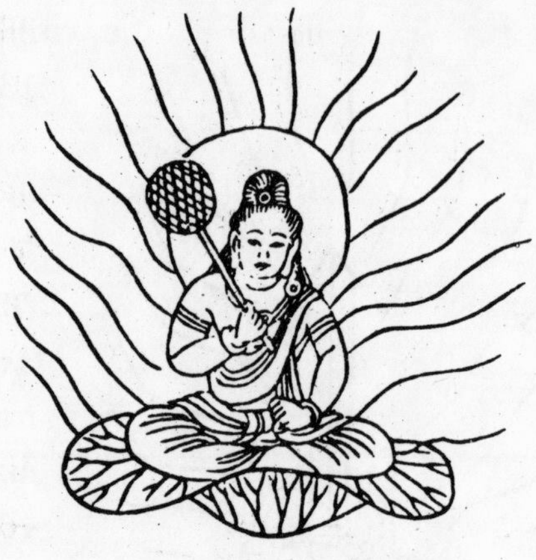

T Z.38.272

a lotus leaf to symbolize Rākṣasa in samaya maṇḍala of graphic Vajradhātu (T Z.38.126). He is personified as Vajra-musala-graha in vajra-maṇḍala of Trilokacakra : *Om Vajra-musala-grahe hūm* ( STT S 285). There is a slight difference in the formation of club of Rākṣasa in dharma-maṇḍala of graphic Vajradhātu (T Z.38.199).

In dharma-maṇḍala of Trilokacakra he is praised as : *Om bhyo bhyo hūm phaṭ* ( STT S 294). The drawing given here belongs to action-maṇḍala of graphic vajradhātu. The club held by Rākṣasa is the same as it is given in samaya-maṇḍala ( T Z.38.272 ). In action-maṇḍala he is personified as Vajradūtī : *Om Vajra-dūti- ānaya sarvān maṇḍalān praveśayā-veśaya bandhaya sarva-karmāṇi me kuru śīghram vajra-khaḍga-dhāriṇi hūm phaṭ* ( STT S 305).

Triratna encircled by flames is shown on club held by Rākṣasa by his right hand (T Z. 38.376) in Trailokyavijaya-karma maṇḍala. In its samaya-maṇḍala the symbolic form is identical with the preceded one (T Z.38.453).

## 14. VAJRĀNILA ( Vāyu )

風天

According to Tajima (195) Vāyu is of red-flesh colour. He carries a flying banner : Vajrānila is the name of his attribute given in Trilokavijaya-maṇḍala of STT S ( STT S 172) Vāyavī is his devī and Vegavajriṇī is her tattvārthatā : *Vāyavyai Vegavajriṇī* ( STT S 173).

Vāyu holds a banner by his right hand. A crescent of moon with a star is drawn over the banner in Trailokyavijaya-maha-mandala (T Z. 38.50). Vajrānila in theT rilokacakra-mahā-maṇḍala of STT S is also named as mahāvega : *Om Vajrānila mahāvegānaya sarva-duṣṭān hūm phaṭ* ( STT S 264 ). While delineating the maṇḍala he is called Vajra-paṭa because of his banner: *Om Vajra-paṭa hūm* ( STT S 272).

Γ Z.38.50

T Z.38.127

His attribute is placed on a lotus leaf in graphic Vajradhātu-samaya-maṇḍala ( T Z. 38.127). This form in the Vajra-maṇḍala of Trilokacakra is named as Vajrapaṭa : *Om Vajra-paṭa hūm* ( STT S 285 ). Dharma-maṇḍala of Vajradhātu portrays the same form as mahā-maṇḍala (T Z.38.200). While the banner flies with great speed it makes a sound of ghū-ghū. Dharma-maṇḍala ofT rilokacakra says : *Om Ghū ghū hūm phaṭ* ( SΓΓ S 294).

T Z .38.273

T Z.38.377

Vāyu obtains the form of an old man in action-maṇḍala of graphic Vajradhātu. No flag is attached to the stick held by both of his hands (Γ Z.38.273) in the action-maṇḍala of Vajradhātu. Vegavajriṇī in the action-maṇḍala ofΓ rilocakra can destroy the evil beings just by its sound : *Om Vegavajriṇi ghū ghū ghū ghū śabdena māraya vikira Vidhvansaya Vajra-*

*paṭa-dhāriṇī hūm phaṭ* ( STT S 305) .

T he symbolic form of Vāyu in Γ rilokyavijaya-samaya-maṇḍala is again a banner but there is a group of stars or gems placed on the crescent of moon (Γ Z.38.454) . T railokya-vijaya-karma-maṇḍala illustrates Vāyu with a banner with a triśūla in his right hand ( Γ Z. 38.377) .

## 15. VAJ RĀNALA (Agni)
火天

Agni is of red flesh colour, his left hand holds a rod of rsi and the right hand holds the emblem of knowledge as fire. T he emblem is a triangular, it represents according to tne Mahāvairocana-sūtra and its commentary the three marks of ashes of the Brāhmins in the cult of fire (T ajima 195) . According to the T rilokavijaya-mahā-maṇḍala Vajrānala is the attribute of Agni : *Agnaye vajrānalaḥ.* Agnedhrya is his devī and her ṭattvārthatā is Vajra-jvāḷā : *Agnedryāyai vajrajvālā* ( STT S 172, 173) .

Γ Z.38.52

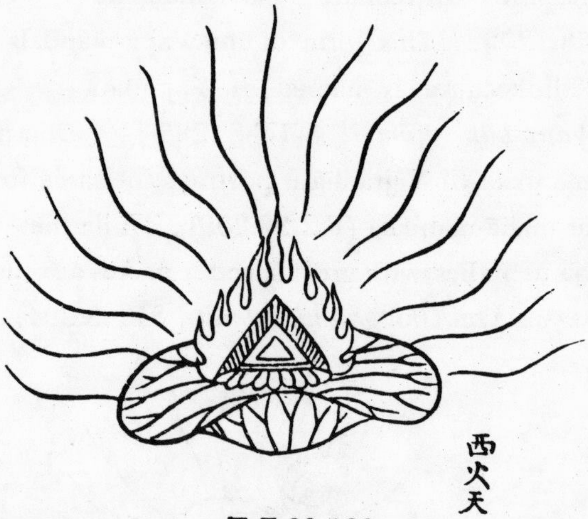


T Z.38.129

T he drawing extracted here belongs to graphic Vajradhātu-mahā-maṇḍala. He holds a triangular by his right hand and by his left hand he does a mudra (T Z.38.52) . He has a power of destroying the evil beings by reducing them to ashes : *Om Vajrakāla mahādūta jvālaya sarvam bhasmīkuru sarva duṣṭān hūm phaṭ* ( STT S 264) . He is called Vajra-jvālā while delineating the maṇḍala : *Om Vajra-vajra-jvāla hūm* ( SΓT S 272) .

Again his form of flames is mentioned in Vajra-maṇḍala of his symbolic form : *Om vajra-jvāle hūm* ( STT S 285) . In samaya-maṇḍala of Vajradhātu he is portrayed as triangular encircled by flames (Γ Z.38.129) .

TZ.38.202

TZ.38.275

Agni in the dharma-maṇḍala of graphic Vajradhātu holds a triangular by the right hand and a rod by the left (TZ.38.202). Dharma-maṇḍala of Trilokacakra praises him for his power of burning : *Om jvala jvala hūm phaṭ* ( STTS 294) .

Agni in action-maṇḍala of graphic Vajradhātu is represented as an old man. He holds something round by his right hand which can be a fruit and in his left he has a sword (TZ. 38.275) . The same characterstic of Agni is mentioned in action-maṇḍala of Trilokacakra as given in its dharma-maṇḍala : *Om Vajra-jvāla jvālaya sarvam vajra jvālaya dha dha bhasmīkuru hūm phaṭ* ( STTS 305) .

The attribute of Agni in his right hand looks like a stupa in the given picture. He holds a sword with vajra in his left hand (TZ.38.379). The samaya form of Agni in the Trailokyavijaya is the same as given before from graphic Vajra-dhātu-samaya-maṇḍala (TZ.38.456) .

## 16. VAJRA-BHAIRAVA ( *Vaiśravaṇa* )

毘沙門天

Vaiśravaṇa is of yellow colour, he carries a stūpa by his left hand and a club by the right ( Tajima calls red, 195) . In Trilokavijaya-mahā-maṇḍala in STTS Vaiśravaṇa is called Kubera, his attribute is Vajrabhairava : *Kuberāya vajrabhairavaḥ* ( STTS 172). His devī is named as Kuberā and her tattvārthatā is Vajravikaṭā : *Kuberyai vajravikaṭā ( STTS 173 ).*

Γ Z.38.53

T he drawing is an extract from graphic Vajradhātu-mahā-maṇḍala. He is wearing an armour and a crown. He is holding a club by the right hand and a stūpa is placed upon his left palm opened flat upwords ( Γ Z. 38.53 ) . He is personified as Vajra-bhairava, Vajra-dūta and mahā-yakṣa in Trilokacakra-mahā-maṇḍala of S TTS : *Om Vajra-bhairava vajra-dūta bhakṣaya sarva-duṣṭān mahā-yakṣa hūm phaṭ* ( S ΓΓ S 264 ) . In its delineation he is called vajra-graha : *Om vajra-graha hūm* ( STT S 272) .

Vaiśravaṇa is symbolised as a club in graphic Vajradhātu-samaya-maṇḍala (T Z.38. 130 ) . This form in Trilokacakra-Vajra-maṇḍala in STT S is called Vajragraha : *Om vajra-graha hūm* ( S ΓΓ S 286 ) . Vaiśravaṇa obtains the same forms in dharma-and action-maṇḍalas of graphic Vajradhātu ( Γ Z.38.203, 276 ) and Γ railokyavijaya-mahā-maṇḍala 38.380) . He has a form of Yakṣa also thus in dharma-maṇḍala of Trilokacakra he is praised for devouring: *Om khāda khāda hūm phaṭ* ( SΓΓ S 294 ) . Vaiśravaṇa is personified as vajravikaṭā in the action-maṇḍala : *Om Vajra-vikaṭe pravikaṭa damṣṭra- karāla-bhīṣaṇa-vaktre śīghram bhakṣaya rudhiram mahā-yakṣiṇi vajra-pāśa-dhāriṇi hūm phaṭ* ( SΓΓ S 306) . T he samaya form in Γ railokyavijaya is identical with the preceded one ( SΓΓ S 38.457) .

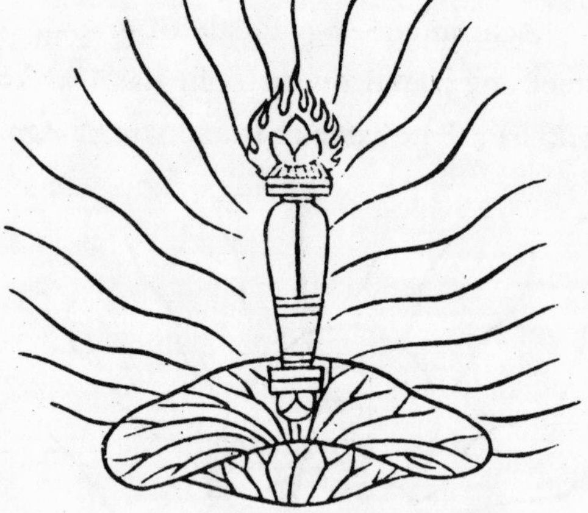

## 17. VAJRĀṄKUŚA (Vajra-mukha)

金剛面天

Vajramukha is also called varāha-mukha, a deity with the head of a wild boar. He is of blackish red colour. He has a human body and holds an ankusa ( Γ ajima 195) . He is

named as Varaha inT rilokavijaya-mahā-maṇḍala in STT S , his attribute is Vajrāṅkuśa : *Varāhāya vajrāṅkuśaḥ* ( SΓΓ S 172) . His devī is Vārāhī and her tattvārthatā is Vajramukhī : *Vārāhyai Vajramukhi* ( SΓT S 173) .

As explained by T ajima in the preceded para he has a face of a boar and holds an aṅkuśa by his right hand (Γ Z.36.54 ) . Aṅkuśa is an attribute which has a power of attraction : *Om Vajrāṅkuśākarṣaya sarvam mahā-ceṭa hūm phaṭ* ( STT S 265) . Because of his strong teeth he is called Vajra-daṁṣṭra in Γ rilokacakra-mahā maṇḍala : *Om Vajra-hūm* ( SΓΓ S 272) .

Vajradhātu-samaya-maṇḍala delineates Vajramukha in the form of a vajrāṅkuśa placed on a lotus leaf ( Γ Z.38.131) . But samaya-maṇḍala of Γ rilokacakra names him as Vajra-danṣṭra : *Om Vajra-daṁṣṭre hūm* ( SΓΓ S 286) . Vajra-mukha in the dharma and karma-maṇḍalas of graphic Vajradhātu ( T Z.38.204, 277 ) and T railokyavijaya-karma-maṇḍala has the same forms as given in Vajradhātu-mahā-maṇḍala. His Vajra-teeth are quite distinct in the illustration given in T railokyavijaya-mahā-maṇḍala. Its samaya-maṇḍala illustrates him in the way as of graphic Vajradhātu ( T Z.38.458 ) . Dharma maṇḍala of Trilokacakra praises him for his quality of excavation : *Om khana hūm phaṭ* ( SΓΓ S 295) . His feminined form in action maṇḍala is called Vajramukhī vajraceṭī. She has vajra-like teeth, terrific appearence, abode in the netherlands, she has a power of digging and devouring; she is praised for entering into the mouth and break the vital parts of the bodies of all the evil beings : *Om Vajramukhi ānaya vajrdaṁṣṭra bhayānike pātāla-nivāsini khana khana khāhi khāhi sarvam mukhe praveśaya sphoṭaya marmāṇi sarva-duṣṭānām vajra-niśitāsi dhāriṇi hūm phaṭ* (SΓΓ S 306) .

Γ Z.38.131

## 18. VAJRAKĀLA (Yama)

琰魔天

Yama is of flesh colour, he holds a stick with a human head, this is the emblem of knowledge of Yama ( Tajima 195 ). According to Trilokavijaya-mahā-maṇḍala of SΓΓ S Yama's attribute is called as Vajrakāla : *Yamāya vajrakālaḥ* ( SΓΓ S 172 ). His devī is Cāmuṇḍa and her tattvārthatā is vajrakālī : *Cāmuṇḍāyai vajrakālī* ( SΓΓ S 173 ).

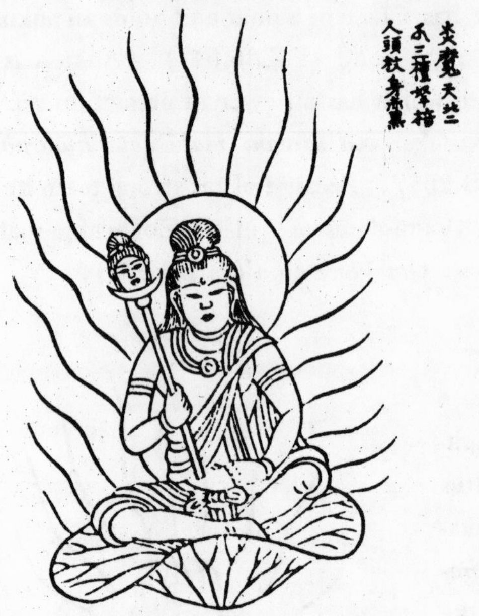

Graphic Vajradhātu-mahā-maṇḍala illustrates Yama as he is described above by Tajima (195) . He has a stick with a human head in his right hand (Γ Z.38.55) . He is related to death, thus Trilokacakra-mahā-maṇḍala calls him as the bearer of great death : *Om Vajra-kāla mahā-mṛtyum utpādaya hūm phaṭ* ( STT S 265 ). Again because of his relation to death he is called Vajra-māraṇa in delineation of maṇḍala : *Om vajra-māraṇa hūm* ( SΓΓ S 272 ).

Stick with a human head is the attribute of Yama illustrated in the samaya-maṇḍala of graphic Vajradhātu (Γ Z.38.132). But in Trilockra-samaya-maṇḍala this form is names as Vajra-māraṇī : *Om Vajra-māraṇī* ( SΓΓ S 286 ). Yama has the same forms in dharma and action-maṇḍalas of graphic Vajradhātu (T Z.38. 205, 278) and Trailokya-vijaya-karma-maṇḍala (T Z. 38.382 ) as depicted above from Vajradhātu-mahā-maṇḍala. His symbolic form in vajra- ṣamaya-maṇḍala is identical with the above also ( Γ Z.38.459 ). Yama in action-maṇḍala ofT rilokacakra is described as a horrific deity. His feminined form is called Vajrakālī she has the form of a great preta, she relishes human flesh and blood, she is vajra-ḍākinī, Vajra-śaṅkalā, she takes away lives, adorned with a garland of skulls, she has a vajra-khaṭvāṅga, she enters the bodies of dead ones, she subdues all the evil beings and kills them : *Om Vajra-kāli-mahā-preta-rūpiṇi mānuṣa-mānsa-rudhira-priye ehy ehi gṛhṇa gṛhṇa bhakṣaya vajra-ḍākini vajra-saṅkale sarva-deva-gaṇa-mātṛbhūte hara hara prāṇān amukasya kapāla-mālālaṅkṛta sarva-kāye kiñci rayasi vajra-khaṭvāṅga-dhāriṇi preta-mānuṣa-śarīre śīghram āveśaya praveśaya bandhaya vaśīkuru māraya vajra-rākṣasi hūm hūm hūm hūm phaṭ* ( SΓΓ S 307).

## 19. VAJRA-VINĀYAKA (Vināyaka)

調伏天

Vināyaka is called the god of good luck. He holds a turnip in his left hand and in his right hand a modaka (Γ ajima 195-196). The Trilokavijaya-mahā-maṇḍala in SΓΓ S personifies Vināyaka as Pṛthivīcūlikā, his attribute is Vajravināyaka : *Pṛthivī-cūlikāyai vajravināyakaḥ* (SΓΓ S 172-3). His devī is named as Chinnanāsā and her tattvārthatā is vajraputana : *Chinnanāsāyai vajrapūtanā* (SΓΓ S 173).

Vināyaka in the graphic Vajradhātu-mahā-maṇḍala bears a modaka in his right hand, the attribute of the left hand is not distinct (Γ Z.38.57). He is a god of good luck, he removes all the obstacles : *Oṃ Vajra-vināyakasyā-vinghnam kuru hūm phaṭ* (SΓΓ S 265). In its delineation he is called vajra-vighna : *Oṃ Vajra-vighna hūm* (SΓΓ S 272).

Γ he same form is denoted in next maṇḍala that is the Vajra maṇḍala of Γ rilokcakra : *Oṃ Vajrā-vighne hūm* (S ΓΓ S 286). In samaya-maṇḍala of graphic Vajradhātu he is symbolised as a modaka placed on a lotus leaf (Γ Z.38.134).

In dharma and action-maṇḍalas of graphic Vajradhātu Vināyaka holds a turnip in his right hand and a modaka in the left (T Z.38.207, 280). In T rilokyavijaya-karma maṇḍala he bears nothing in his left hand (Γ Z.38.384). Its samaya form (Γ Z. 38.461) is the same as extracted before from Vajra-dhātu-samaya-maṇḍala.

In dharma-maṇḍala of Trilokacakra in STT S he is praised as : *Oṃ gṛhṇa gṛhṇa hūm phaṭ* (S ΓΓ S 295). In its action-maṇḍala he is personified as Vajra-pūtanā : *Oṃ Vajra-pūtanā mānuṣa-mānsa vasā rudhira mūtra puriṣa śleṣma siṅghānaka reto grarbha kariṇya ya-hi śīghram idam asya kuru Vajra-śodhanikā-dhāriṇi sarva-karmāṇi me kuru hūm phaṭ* (SΓΓ S 307).

*TZ.38.134*

## 20. NĀGAVAJRA (Varuṇa)

水天

Varuṇa is of blue colour, his left hand is closed and the right has a cord ( Γ ajima 196 ). His attribute is called nāgavajra in Trilokavijaya-mahā-maṇḍala in SΓΓ S *Varuṇāya nāgvaraḥ* ( SΓΓ S 173) his devī is Vāruṇī and her tattvārthatā is Vajramakarī : *Vāruṇyai vajra-makarī* ( SΓΓ S 173) .

Γ Z.38.54

Varuṇa in graphic Vajradhātu-mahā-maṇḍala holds a nāgapāśa in his right hand as described by Tajima ( Γ Z.38.58) . He is the last ceṭa given in Trilokacakra-mahā-maṇḍala. He brings all the riches : *Om nāga- vajrānaya sạrva-dhana-dhānya-hiraṇya-su varṇa-maṇi-muktālaṅkārādīni sarvopaka raṇāni vajra-dhara-samayam anusmara kāddha gṛhṇa bandha hara hara prāṇān mahā-ceṭa hūm phaṭ* ( SΓΓ S 266) . In its delineation he is called Vajra-haraṇa : *Om Vajra-haraṇa hūm* ( SΓΓ S 272) .

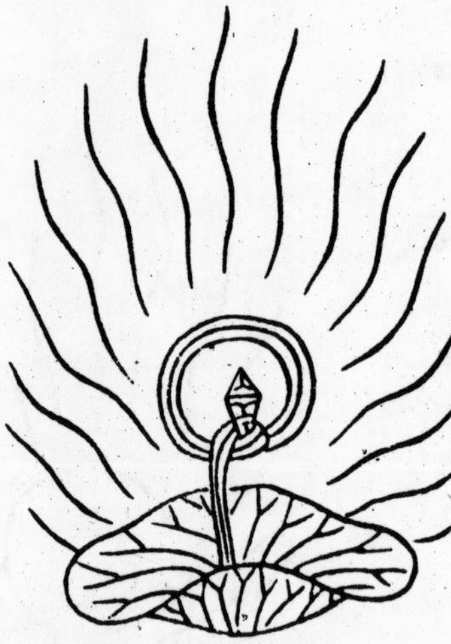

Γ Z.38.135

Γ Z.38.385

In the samaya-maṇḍala of graphic Vajradhātu nāgapāśa symbolise him placed in a lotus leaf ( Γ Z.38.135 ) Vajra-maṇḍala of Trilokavijaya names this form as vajra hāriṇī : *Om vajra-hāriṇī hūm* ( SΓΓ S 286) . Varuṇa bears the same attributes in the dharma and action maṇḍalas of the Vajradhātu (Γ Z.38.208, 281 ) and the Trailokyavijaya-karma-maṇḍala.

But in the drawing extracted here and the action maṇḍala he wears a crown of snakes. (ābhoga). The symbolic form in the Trailokyavijaya is the same as extracted before (TZ. 38.462). The Dharma-maṇḍala of Trilokacakra praises him as : *Om vibha vibha hūm phaṭ* (STTS 295). In its action-maṇḍala he is personified as Vajra-makarī : *Om vajra-makarī grasa grasa śīghraṁ praveśaya pātālān bhakṣaya vajra-makara-dhāriṇī hūm phaṭ* (STTS 307).

## LITERATURE CITED


Bakshi, D.N. , Hindu Divinities in Japanese Buddhist Pantheon, Benten publication, Calcutta, 1979

Bhattacharyya, Benoytosh, An Introduction to Buddhist Esoterism, Motilal Banarsidas, Delhi, 1980

Bhattacharyya, Dipak Chandra, Studies in Buddhist Iconography, Manohar Book Service, New Delhi, 1978

Tāntric Buddhist Iconographic Sources, Munshiram Manoharlal, New Delhi, 1974

Edgerton, Franklin, Buddhist Hybrid Sanskrit Grammar and Dictionary, Motilal Banarsidas, Delhi, 1977

Hakeda, Yoshito S. , Kukai, Major Works, Columbia University Press, New York and London, 1972

Japanese English Buddhist Dictionary, Tokyo, 1965

Kiyota, Minoru, Shingon Buddhism: Theory and practice, Buddhist Books International, Los Angeles and Tokyo

Lessing Wayman Mkhas grub rje's Fundamentals of Buddhist Tantras, The Hague Mouton

Lokesh Chandra, Esoteric Iconography of Japanese Maṇḍalas, International Academy of Indian Culture, New Delhi

Manabe, Maṇḍala, Seibu Musem of Art.

Matsunga, Daigan and Alicia, Foundation of Japanese Buddhism, Buddhist Books International, Los Angeles and Tokyo, 1978

Mizuno, Kogen, Buddhist Sutras, Kosei Publishing Co, Tokyo, 1982.

Nj. Bunyiu Nanjio, A Catalogue of the Chinese translation of the Buddhist Tripiṭaka, Oxford Clarendon press, 1883

S TTS, TS, Sarvatathāgata-tattva-saṅgraha-nāma-mahāyāna-sūtra, Isshi Yamada, New Delhi, 1981

T, Taisho Edition of ChineseT ripitaka,T aisho Issaikyo ed.T akakusu Junjoro and Watanabe Kaigyoku, Tokyo, 1924-29

Tajima, Ryuzun, Lex Deux Grands Mandalas et la Doctrine de 1 'Esoterisme Shingon, Maison Franco-Japanaise,T okyo and presses Universitaires de France, Paris, 1959

Toh, Hakuju, Ui et al, A Complete Catalogue of Tibetan Buddhist Canons, Sendai Tohoku Imperial University, 1934

TZ, Taisho Shinshu Daizokyo Zuzo, The Tripiṭaka in Chinese ( picture section) , ed, J. Takakusu and G. Ono, Tokyo, the Daizo Shupan Kabushiki, Kwaisha.

Wayman, Alex, The Buddhist Tantras, Samuel Weiser New York 1973

Yoga of the Guhyasamāja-tantra, Motilal Banarsidas, Delhi, 1977

Yamada, Isshi, S TTS

Yamamoto, Chikyo, Cultural Treasures of Koyasan, Koyasan, 1965

Introduction to the Maṇḍala, Dohosha, 1980